# AHEAD OF

# ALL PARTING

# Ahead of All Parting

## The Selected Poetry and Prose of Rainer Maria Rilke

Edited and Translated by
Stephen Mitchell

THE MODERN LIBRARY
NEW YORK

1995 Modern Library Edition

Translation copyright © 1995 by Stephen Mitchell

Many of these translations were first published in *The Selected Poetry of Rainer Maria Rilke*, Random House, 1982; *The Notebooks of Malte Laurids Brigge*, Random House, 1983; and *The Sonnets to Orpheus*, Simon & Schuster, 1985.

Other translations first appeared in the following periodicals: *American Poetry Review, 89¢, Grand Street, Ironwood, Kenyon Review, New York Review of Books, Occident, Paris Review, Talisman, The Ten Directions, The Threepenny Review*, and *Zero*.

Twenty-seven translations were published in *Rainer Maria Rilke/Last Poems*, Okeanos Press, 1989, in an edition of 200 copies.

Grateful acknowledgment is made to the following for permission to reprint previously published material: Bechtle Verlag (Munich): Excerpts from Rainer Maria Rilke's *Briefwechsel mit Benvenuta*, edited by Magda von Hattingberg.

Jacket photograph courtesy of The Bettmann Archive

Printed on recycled, acid-free paper

Library of Congress Cataloging-in-Publication Data

Rilke, Rainer Maria, 1875–1926.
[Selections. English & German. 1995]
Ahead of all parting: the selected poetry and prose of Rainer
Maria Rilke/edited and translated by Stephen Mitchell.
p.  cm.
English and German.
ISBN 0-679-60161-9 (alk. paper)
1. Rilke, Rainer Maria, 1875–1926—Translations into English.
I. Mitchell, Stephen, 1943–  .  II. Title.
PT2635.I65A2525   1995
831'.912—dc20      94-43917

Manufactured in the United States of America

2 4 6 8 9 7 5 3 1

To
Robert Aitken, Rōshi

This symbol, ✳, indicates a space between sections of a poem whenever such spaces are lost in pagination.

# Contents

## PART 1 / *Selected Poems*

### FROM THE BOOK OF HOURS (1905)

[I live my life in widening rings]                                    5
[I am, O Anxious One. Don't you hear my voice]                        7
[I find you, Lord, in all Things and in all]                          9

### FROM THE BOOK OF PICTURES (1902, 1906)

Lament                                                               13
Autumn Day                                                           15
Evening                                                              17
The Blindman's Song                                                  19
The Drunkard's Song                                                  21
The Idiot's Song                                                     23
The Dwarf's Song                                                     25

### FROM NEW POEMS (1907, 1908)

Love Song                                                            29
The Panther                                                          31
The Gazelle                                                          33
The Swan                                                             35
The Grown-up                                                         37
Going Blind                                                          39
Before Summer Rain                                                   41
The Last Evening                                                     43
Portrait of My Father as a Young Man                                 45
Self-Portrait, 1906                                                  47
Spanish Dancer                                                       49
Tombs of the Hetaerae                                                51

Orpheus. Eurydice. Hermes 55
Alcestis 61
Archaic Torso of Apollo 67
Washing the Corpse 69
Black Cat 71
The Flamingos 73
Buddha in Glory 75

FROM REQUIEM (1909)

Requiem for a Friend 79

UNCOLLECTED POEMS, 1911–1920

[To Lou Andreas-Salomé] 97
[The Almond Trees in Blossom] 101
The Spanish Trilogy 103
Ariel 109
[Straining so hard against the strength of night] 113
[Ignorant before the heavens of my life] 115
[Overflowing heavens of lavished stars] 117
[Startle me, Music, with rhythmical fury!] 119
[Behind the innocent trees] 121
The Vast Night 123
[You who never arrived] 125
Turning-point 127
Lament 131
'We Must Die Because We Have Known Them' 133
To Hölderlin 135
[Exposed on the cliffs of the heart] 137
[Again and again, however we know the landscape of love] 139
Death 141
To Music 143
[You, you only, exist] 145
Haiku 147

UNCOLLECTED POEMS, 1922–1926

| | |
|---|---|
| [We, in the struggling nights] | 151 |
| Odette R . . . . | 153 |
| [We say release, and radiance, and roses] | 155 |
| Imaginary Career | 157 |
| Little Tear-Vase | 159 |
| Dedication to M . . . . | 161 |
| For Max Picard | 163 |
| For Hans Carossa | 165 |
| The Magician | 167 |
| [As once the wingèd energy of delight] | 169 |
| [Along the sun-drenched roadside, from the great] | 171 |
| [What birds plunge through is not the intimate space] | 173 |
| Duration of Childhood | 175 |
| [World was in the face of the beloved] | 179 |
| Palm | 181 |
| Gravity | 183 |
| Mausoleum | 185 |
| O Lacrimosa | 187 |
| [Ah, not to be cut off] | 191 |
| [Now it is time that gods came walking out] | 193 |
| [Rose, oh pure contradiction] | 195 |
| Idol | 197 |
| Gong | 199 |
| [Four Sketches] | 201 |
| For Veronika Erdmann | 205 |
| Elegy | 207 |
| [Dove that ventured outside] | 211 |
| NOTES | 213 |

PART 2 / *Selected Prose*

FROM THE NOTEBOOKS OF MALTE LAURIDS BRIGGE

[Faces]                                      245
[The Death of Chamberlain Brigge]            246
[For the Sake of a Single Poem]              250
[Fears]                                      251
[The Man with St. Vitus' Dance]              252
[The Bird-feeders]                           256
[Ibsen]                                      258
[Costumes]                                   261
[Neighbors]                                  266
[The Temptation of the Saint]                271
[The Prodigal Son]                           272

UNCOLLECTED PROSE, 1902–1922

The Lion Cage                                281
A Meeting                                    283
The Fishmonger's Stall                       286
Acrobats                                     288
An Experience                                290
On the Young Poet                            293
Primal Sound                                 299
Mitsou                                       304
The Young Workman's Letter                   308

NOTES                                        319

## Lucy Robbins Welles Library
09/15/2020 12:15 PM

**Ahead of all parting : the selected**
32512061943904
**DUE DATE: 10-07-20**

Number of items checked out: 1

**By using Lucy Robbins Welles
Library today, you saved $18.00.**

**To Renew Items:**
860-665-8700
www.newingtonct.gov/library

Thank you for using
Lucy Robbins Welles Library.

# PART 3 / *Duino Elegies and The Sonnets to Orpheus*

## DUINO ELEGIES (1923)

The First Elegy 331
The Second Elegy 339
The Third Elegy 345
The Fourth Elegy 351
The Fifth Elegy 357
The Sixth Elegy 365
The Seventh Elegy 369
The Eighth Elegy 377
The Ninth Elegy 383
The Tenth Elegy 389

## APPENDIX TO DUINO ELEGIES

[Fragment of an Elegy] 399
[Original Version of the Tenth Elegy] 401
Antistrophes 405

## THE SONNETS TO ORPHEUS (1923)

### FIRST PART

I 411
II 413
III 415
IV 417
V 419
VI 421
VII 423
VIII 425
IX 427
X 429
XI 431

| | |
|---|---|
| XII | 433 |
| XIII | 435 |
| XIV | 437 |
| XV | 439 |
| XVI | 441 |
| XVII | 443 |
| XVIII | 445 |
| XIX | 447 |
| XX | 449 |
| XXI | 451 |
| XXII | 453 |
| XXIII | 455 |
| XXIV | 457 |
| XXV | 459 |
| XXVI | 461 |

## SECOND PART

| | |
|---|---|
| I | 463 |
| II | 465 |
| III | 467 |
| IV | 469 |
| V | 471 |
| VI | 473 |
| VII | 475 |
| VIII | 477 |
| IX | 479 |
| X | 481 |
| XI | 483 |
| XII | 485 |
| XIII | 487 |
| XIV | 489 |
| XV | 491 |
| XVI | 493 |
| XVII | 495 |
| XVIII | 497 |
| XIX | 499 |
| XX | 501 |
| XXI | 503 |

XXII                                                      505
XXIII                                                     507
XXIV                                                      509
XXV                                                       511
XXVI                                                      513
XXVII                                                     515
XXVIII                                                    517
XXIX                                                      519

APPENDIX TO THE SONNETS TO ORPHEUS

[I]                                                       523
[II]                                                      525
[III]                                                     527
[IV]                                                      529
[V]                                                       531
[VI]                                                      533
[VII]                                                     535
[VIII]                                                    537
[IX]                                                      539
[Fragments]                                               541


NOTES                                                     547

ACKNOWLEDGMENTS                                           599

INDEX OF TITLES AND FIRST LINES (GERMAN)                  601
INDEX OF TITLES AND FIRST LINES (ENGLISH)                 609

# PART 1

# *Selected Poems*

FROM

*The Book of Hours*

*(1905)*

Ich lebe mein Leben in wachsenden Ringen,
die sich über die Dinge ziehn.
Ich werde den letzten vielleicht nicht vollbringen,
aber versuchen will ich ihn.

Ich kreise um Gott, um den uralten Turm,
und ich kreise jahrtausendelang;
und ich weiß noch nicht: bin ich ein Falke, ein Sturm
oder ein großer Gesang.

# [I live my life in widening rings]

I live my life in widening rings
which spread over earth and sky.
I may not ever complete the last one,
but that is what I will try.

I circle around God, the primordial tower,
and I circle ten thousand years long;
and I still don't know if I'm a falcon, a storm,
or an unfinished song.

Ich bin, du Ängstlicher. Hörst du mich nicht
mit allen meinen Sinnen an dir branden?
Meine Gefühle, welche Flügel fanden,
umkreisen weiß dein Angesicht.
Siehst du nicht meine Seele, wie sie dicht
vor dir in einem Kleid aus Stille steht?
Reift nicht mein mailiches Gebet
an deinem Blicke wie an einem Baum?

Wenn du der Träumer bist, bin ich dein Traum.
Doch wenn du wachen willst, bin ich dein Wille
und werde mächtig aller Herrlichkeit
und ründe mich wie eine Sternenstille
über der wunderlichen Stadt der Zeit.

## [I am, O Anxious One. Don't you hear my voice]

I am, O Anxious One. Don't you hear my voice
surging forth with all my earthly feelings?
They yearn so high that they have sprouted wings
and whitely fly in circles around your face.
My soul, dressed in silence, rises up
and stands alone before you: can't you see?
Don't you know that my prayer is growing ripe
upon your vision, as upon a tree?

If you are the dreamer, I am what you dream.
But when you want to wake, I am your wish,
and I grow strong with all magnificence
and turn myself into a star's vast silence
above the strange and distant city, Time.

Ich finde dich in allen diesen Dingen,
denen ich gut und wie ein Bruder bin;
als Samen sonnst du dich in den geringen
und in den großen giebst du groß dich hin.

Das ist das wundersame Spiel der Kräfte,
daß sie so dienend durch die Dinge gehn:
in Wurzeln wachsend, schwindend in die Schäfte
und in den Wipfeln wie ein Auferstehn.

## [I find you, Lord, in all Things and in all]

I find you, Lord, in all Things and in all
my fellow creatures, pulsing with your life;
as a tiny seed you sleep in what is small
and in the vast you vastly yield yourself.

The wondrous game that power plays with Things
is to move in such submission through the world:
groping in roots and growing thick in trunks
and in treetops like a rising from the dead.

FROM

## *The Book of Pictures*

*(1902, 1906)*

## KLAGE

O wie ist alles fern
und lange vergangen.
Ich glaube, der Stern,
von welchem ich Glanz empfange,
ist seit Jahrtausenden tot.
Ich glaube, im Boot,
das vorüberfuhr,
hörte ich etwas Banges sagen.
Im Hause hat eine Uhr
geschlagen . . .
In welchem Haus? . . .
Ich möchte aus meinem Herzen hinaus
unter den großen Himmel treten.
Ich möchte beten.
Und einer von allen Sternen
müßte wirklich noch sein.
Ich glaube, ich wüßte,
welcher allein
gedauert hat,—
welcher wie eine weiße Stadt
am Ende des Strahls in den Himmeln steht . . .

# LAMENT

Everything is far
and long gone by.
I think that the star
glittering above me
has been dead for a million years.
I think there were tears
in the car I heard pass
and something terrible was said.
A clock has stopped striking in the house
across the road . . .
When did it start? . . .
I would like to step out of my heart
and go walking beneath the enormous sky.
I would like to pray.
And surely of all the stars that perished
long ago,
one still exists.
I think that I know
which one it is—
which one, at the end of its beam in the sky,
stands like a white city . . .

## HERBSTTAG

Herr: es ist Zeit. Der Sommer war sehr groß.
Leg deinen Schatten auf die Sonnenuhren,
und auf den Fluren laß die Winde los.

Befiehl den letzten Früchten voll zu sein;
gieb ihnen noch zwei südlichere Tage,
dränge sie zur Vollendung hin und jage
die letzte Süße in den schweren Wein.

Wer jetzt kein Haus hat, baut sich keines mehr.
Wer jetzt allein ist, wird es lange bleiben,
wird wachen, lesen, lange Briefe schreiben
und wird in den Alleen hin und her
unruhig wandern, wenn die Blätter treiben.

# AUTUMN DAY

Lord: it is time. The huge summer has gone by.
Now overlap the sundials with your shadows,
and on the meadows let the wind go free.

Command the fruits to swell on tree and vine;
grant them a few more warm transparent days,
urge them on to fulfillment then, and press
the final sweetness into the heavy wine.

Whoever has no house now, will never have one.
Whoever is alone will stay alone,
will sit, read, write long letters through the evening,
and wander on the boulevards, up and down,
restlessly, while the dry leaves are blowing.

## ABEND

Der Abend wechselt langsam die Gewänder,
die ihm ein Rand von alten Bäumen hält;
du schaust: und von dir scheiden sich die Länder,
ein himmelfahrendes und eins, das fällt;

und lassen dich, zu keinem ganz gehörend,
nicht ganz so dunkel wie das Haus, das schweigt,
nicht ganz so sicher Ewiges beschwörend
wie das, was Stern wird jede Nacht und steigt—

und lassen dir (unsäglich zu entwirrn)
dein Leben bang und riesenhaft und reifend,
so daß es, bald begrenzt und bald begreifend,
abwechselnd Stein in dir wird und Gestirn.

# EVENING

The sky puts on the darkening blue coat
held for it by a row of ancient trees;
you watch: and the lands grow distant in your sight,
one journeying to heaven, one that falls;

and leave you, not at home in either one,
not quite so still and dark as the darkened houses,
not calling to eternity with the passion
of what becomes a star each night, and rises;

and leave you (inexpressibly to unravel)
your life, with its immensity and fear,
so that, now bounded, now immeasurable,
it is alternately stone in you and star.

## DAS LIED DES BLINDEN

Ich bin blind, ihr draußen, das ist ein Fluch,
ein Widerwillen, ein Widerspruch,
etwas täglich Schweres.
Ich leg meine Hand auf den Arm der Frau,
meine graue Hand auf ihr graues Grau,
und sie führt mich durch lauter Leeres.

Ihr rührt euch und rückt und bildet euch ein
anders zu klingen als Stein auf Stein,
aber ihr irrt euch: ich allein
lebe und leide und lärme.
In mir ist ein endloses Schrein
und ich weiß nicht, schreit mir mein
Herz oder meine Gedärme.

Erkennt ihr die Lieder? Ihr sanget sie nicht
nicht ganz in dieser Betonung.
Euch kommt jeden Morgen das neue Licht
warm in die offene Wohnung.
Und ihr habt ein Gefühl von Gesicht zu Gesicht
und das verleitet zur Schonung.

# THE BLINDMAN'S SONG

I am blind, you outsiders. It is a curse,
a contradiction, a tiresome farce,
and every day I despair.
I put my hand on the arm of my wife
(colorless hand on colorless sleeve)
and she walks me through empty air.

You push and shove and think that you've been
sounding different from stone against stone,
but you are mistaken: I alone
live and suffer and howl.
In me there is an endless outcry
and I can't tell what's crying, whether it's my
broken heart or my bowels.

Are the tunes familiar? You don't sing them like this:
how could you understand?
Each morning the sunlight comes into your house,
and you welcome it as a friend.
And you know what it's like to see face-to-face;
and that tempts you to be kind.

## DAS LIED DES TRINKERS

Es war nicht in mir. Es ging aus und ein.
Da wollt ich es halten. Da hielt es der Wein.
(Ich weiß nicht mehr was es war.)
Dann hielt er mir jenes und hielt mir dies
bis ich mich ganz auf ihn verließ.
Ich Narr.

Jetzt bin ich in seinem Spiel und er streut
mich verächtlich herum und verliert mich noch heut
an dieses Vieh, an den Tod.
Wenn der mich, schmutzige Karte, gewinnt,
so kratzt er mit mir seinen grauen Grind
und wirft mich fort in den Kot.

# THE DRUNKARD'S SONG

It wasn't in me. It went out and in.
I wanted to hold it. It held, with Wine.
(I no longer know what it was.)
Then Wine held this and held that for me
till I came to depend on him totally.
Like an ass.

Now I'm playing his game and he deals me out
with a sneer on his lips, and maybe tonight
he will lose me to Death, that boor.
When *he* wins me, filthiest card in the deck,
he'll take me and scratch the scabs on his neck,
then toss me into the mire.

## DAS LIED DES IDIOTEN

Sie hindern mich nicht. Sie lassen mich gehn.
Sie sagen es könne nichts geschehn.
Wie gut.
Es kann nichts geschehn. Alles kommt und kreist
immerfort um den heiligen Geist,
um den gewissen Geist (du weißt)—,
wie gut.

Nein man muß wirklich nicht meinen es sei
irgend eine Gefahr dabei.
Da ist freilich das Blut.
Das Blut ist das Schwerste. Das Blut ist schwer.
Manchmal glaub ich, ich kann nicht mehr—.
(Wie gut.)

Ah was ist das für ein schöner Ball;
rot und rund wie ein Überall.
Gut, daß ihr ihn erschuft.
Ob der wohl kommt wenn man ruft?

Wie sich das alles seltsam benimmt,
ineinandertreibt, auseinanderschwimmt:
freundlich, ein wenig unbestimmt.
Wie gut.

# THE IDIOT'S SONG

They're not in my way. They let me be.
They say that nothing can happen to me.
How good.
Nothing can happen. All things flow
from the Holy Ghost, and they come and go
around that particular Ghost (you know)—,
how good.

No we really mustn't imagine there is
any danger in any of this.
Of course, there's blood.
Blood is the hardest. Hard as stone.
Sometimes I think that I can't go on—.
(How good.)

Oh look at that beautiful ball over there:
red and round as an Everywhere.
Good that you made it be.
If I call, will it come to me?

How very strange the world can appear,
blending and breaking, far and near:
friendly, a little bit unclear.
How good.

## DAS LIED DES ZWERGES

Meine Seele ist vielleicht grad und gut;
aber mein Herz, mein verbogenes Blut,
alles das, was mir wehe tut,
kann sie nicht aufrecht tragen.
Sie hat keinen Garten, sie hat kein Bett,
sie hängt an meinem scharfen Skelett
mit entsetztem Flügelschlagen.

Aus meinen Händen wird auch nichts mehr.
Wie verkümmert sie sind: sieh her:
zähe hüpfen sie, feucht und schwer,
wie kleine Kröten nach Regen.
Und das Andre an mir ist
abgetragen und alt und trist;
warum zögert Gott, auf den Mist
alles das hinzulegen.

Ob er mir zürnt für mein Gesicht
mit dem mürrischen Munde?
Es war ja so oft bereit, ganz licht
und klar zu werden im Grunde;
aber nichts kam ihm je so dicht
wie die großen Hunde.
Und die Hunde haben das nicht.

# THE DWARF'S SONG

My soul itself may be straight and good;
ah, but my heart, my bent-over blood,
all the distortions that hurt me inside—
it buckles under these things.
It has no garden, it has no sun,
it hangs on my twisted skeleton
and, terrified, flaps its wings.

Nor are my hands of much use. Look here:
see how shrunken and shapeless they are:
clumsily hopping, clammy and fat,
like toads after the rain.
And everything else about me is torn,
sad and weather-beaten and worn;
why did God ever hesitate
to flush it all down the drain?

Is it because he's angry at me
for my face with its moping lips?
It was so often ready to be
light and clear in its depths;
but nothing came so close to it
as big dogs did.
And dogs don't have what I need.

F R O M

*New Poems*

*(1907, 1908)*

## LIEBES-LIED

Wie soll ich meine Seele halten, daß
sie nicht an deine rührt? Wie soll ich sie
hinheben über dich zu andern Dingen?
Ach gerne möcht ich sie bei irgendwas
Verlorenem im Dunkel unterbringen
an einer fremden stillen Stelle, die
nicht weiterschwingt, wenn deine Tiefen schwingen.
Doch alles, was uns anrührt, dich und mich,
nimmt uns zusammen wie ein Bogenstrich,
der aus zwei Saiten *eine* Stimme zieht.
Auf welches Instrument sind wir gespannt?
Und welcher Geiger hat uns in der Hand?
O süßes Lied.

## LOVE SONG

How can I keep my soul in me, so that
it doesn't touch your soul? How can I raise
it high enough, past you, to other things?
I would like to shelter it, among remote
lost objects, in some dark and silent place
that doesn't resonate when your depths resound.
Yet everything that touches us, me and you,
takes us together like a violin's bow,
which draws *one* voice out of two separate strings.
Upon what instrument are we two spanned?
And what musician holds us in his hand?
Oh sweetest song.

## DER PANTHER

*Im Jardin des Plantes, Paris*

Sein Blick ist vom Vorübergehn der Stäbe
so müd geworden, daß er nichts mehr hält.
Ihm ist, als ob es tausend Stäbe gäbe
und hinter tausend Stäben keine Welt.

Der weiche Gang geschmeidig starker Schritte,
der sich im allerkleinsten Kreise dreht,
ist wie ein Tanz von Kraft um eine Mitte,
in der betäubt ein großer Wille steht.

Nur manchmal schiebt der Vorhang der Pupille
sich lautlos auf—. Dann geht ein Bild hinein,
geht durch der Glieder angespannte Stille—
und hört im Herzen auf zu sein.

# THE PANTHER

*In the Jardin des Plantes, Paris*

His vision, from the constantly passing bars,
has grown so weary that it cannot hold
anything else. It seems to him there are
a thousand bars; and behind the bars, no world.

As he paces in cramped circles, over and over,
the movement of his powerful soft strides
is like a ritual dance around a center
in which a mighty will stands paralyzed.

Only at times, the curtain of the pupils
lifts, quietly—. An image enters in,
rushes down through the tensed, arrested muscles,
plunges into the heart and is gone.

## DIE GAZELLE

*Gazella Dorcas*

Verzauberte: wie kann der Einklang zweier
erwählter Worte je den Reim erreichen,
der in dir kommt und geht, wie auf ein Zeichen.
Aus deiner Stirne steigen Laub und Leier,

und alles Deine geht schon im Vergleich
durch Liebeslieder, deren Worte, weich
wie Rosenblätter, dem, der nicht mehr liest,
sich auf die Augen legen, die er schließt:

um dich zu sehen: hingetragen, als
wäre mit Sprüngen jeder Lauf geladen
und schösse nur nicht ab, solang der Hals

das Haupt ins Horchen hält: wie wenn beim Baden
im Wald die Badende sich unterbricht:
den Waldsee im gewendeten Gesicht.

# THE GAZELLE
*Gazella Dorcas*

Enchanted thing: how can two chosen words
ever attain the harmony of pure rhyme
that pulses through you as your body stirs?
Out of your forehead branch and lyre climb,

and all your features pass in simile, through
the songs of love whose words, as light as rose-
petals, rest on the face of someone who
has put his book away and shut his eyes:

to see you: tensed, as if each leg were a gun
loaded with leaps, but not fired while your neck
holds your head still, listening: as when,

while swimming in some isolated place,
a girl hears leaves rustle, and turns to look:
the forest pool reflected in her face.

## DER SCHWAN

Diese Mühsal, durch noch Ungetanes
schwer und wie gebunden hinzugehn,
gleicht dem ungeschaffnen Gang des Schwanes.

Und das Sterben, dieses Nichtmehrfassen
jenes Grunds, auf dem wir täglich stehn,
seinem ängstlichen Sich-Niederlassen—:

in die Wasser, die ihn sanft empfangen
und die sich, wie glücklich und vergangen,
unter ihm zurückziehn, Flut um Flut;
während er unendlich still und sicher
immer mündiger und königlicher
und gelassener zu ziehn geruht.

# THE SWAN

This laboring through what is still undone,
as though, legs bound, we hobbled along the way,
is like the awkward walking of the swan.

And dying—to let go, no longer feel
the solid ground we stand on every day—
is like his anxious letting himself fall

into the waters, which receive him gently
and which, as though with reverence and joy,
draw back past him in streams on either side;
while, infinitely silent and aware,
in his full majesty and ever more
indifferent, he condescends to glide.

## DIE ERWACHSENE

Das alles stand auf ihr und war die Welt
und stand auf ihr mit allem, Angst und Gnade,
wie Bäume stehen, wachsend und gerade,
ganz Bild und bildlos wie die Bundeslade
und feierlich, wie auf ein Volk gestellt.

Und sie ertrug es; trug bis obenhin
das Fliegende, Entfliehende, Entfernte,
das Ungeheuere, noch Unerlernte
gelassen wie die Wasserträgerin
den vollen Krug. Bis mitten unterm Spiel,
verwandelnd und auf andres vorbereitend,
der erste weiße Schleier, leise gleitend,
über das aufgetane Antlitz fiel

fast undurchsichtig und sich nie mehr hebend
und irgendwie auf alle Fragen ihr
nur eine Antwort vage wiedergebend:
In dir, du Kindgewesene, in dir.

# THE GROWN-UP

All this stood upon her and was the world
and stood upon her with all its fear and grace
as trees stand, growing straight up, imageless
yet wholly image, like the Ark of God,
and solemn, as if imposed upon a race.

And she endured it all: bore up under
the swift-as-flight, the fleeting, the far-gone,
the inconceivably vast, the still-to-learn,
serenely as a woman carrying water
moves with a full jug. Till in the midst of play,
transfiguring and preparing for the future,
the first white veil descended, gliding softly

over her opened face, almost opaque there,
never to be lifted off again, and somehow
giving to all her questions just one answer:
In you, who were a child once—in you.

## DIE ERBLINDENDE

Sie saß so wie die anderen beim Tee.
Mir war zuerst, als ob sie ihre Tasse
ein wenig anders als die andern fasse.
Sie lächelte einmal. Es tat fast weh.

Und als man schließlich sich erhob und sprach
und langsam und wie es der Zufall brachte
durch viele Zimmer ging (man sprach und lachte),
da sah ich sie. Sie ging den andern nach,

verhalten, so wie eine, welche gleich
wird singen müssen und vor vielen Leuten;
auf ihren hellen Augen die sich freuten
war Licht von außen wie auf einem Teich.

Sie folgte langsam und sie brauchte lang
als wäre etwas noch nicht überstiegen;
und doch: als ob, nach einem Übergang,
sie nicht mehr gehen würde, sondern fliegen.

## GOING BLIND

She sat just like the others at the table.
But on second glance, she seemed to hold her cup
a little differently as she picked it up.
She smiled once. It was almost painful.

And when they finished and it was time to stand
and slowly, as chance selected them, they left
and moved through many rooms (they talked and laughed),
I saw her. She was moving far behind

the others, absorbed, like someone who will soon
have to sing before a large assembly;
upon her eyes, which were radiant with joy,
light played as on the surface of a pool.

She followed slowly, taking a long time,
as though there were some obstacle in the way;
and yet: as though, once it was overcome,
she would be beyond all walking, and would fly.

## VOR DEM SOMMERREGEN

Auf einmal ist aus allem Grün im Park
man weiß nicht was, ein Etwas, fortgenommen;
man fühlt ihn näher an die Fenster kommen
und schweigsam sein. Inständig nur und stark

ertönt aus dem Gehölz der Regenpfeifer,
man denkt an einen Hieronymus:
so sehr steigt irgend Einsamkeit und Eifer
aus dieser einen Stimme, die der Guß

erhören wird. Des Saales Wände sind
mit ihren Bildern von uns fortgetreten,
als dürften sie nicht hören was wir sagen.

Es spiegeln die verblichenen Tapeten
das ungewisse Licht von Nachmittagen,
in denen man sich fürchtete als Kind.

# BEFORE SUMMER RAIN

Suddenly, from all the green around you,
something—you don't know what—has disappeared;
you feel it creeping closer to the window,
in total silence. From the nearby wood

you hear the urgent whistling of a plover,
reminding you of someone's *Saint Jerome:*
so much solitude and passion come
from that one voice, whose fierce request the downpour

will grant. The walls, with their ancient portraits, glide
away from us, cautiously, as though
they weren't supposed to hear what we are saying.

And reflected on the faded tapestries now:
the chill, uncertain sunlight of those long
childhood hours when you were so afraid.

## LETZTER ABEND

*(Aus dem Besitze Frau Nonnas)*

Und Nacht und fernes Fahren; denn der Train
des ganzen Heeres zog am Park vorüber.
Er aber hob den Blick vom Clavecin
und spielte noch und sah zu ihr hinüber

beinah wie man in einen Spiegel schaut:
so sehr erfüllt von seinen jungen Zügen
und wissend, wie sie seine Trauer trügen,
schön und verführender bei jedem Laut.

Doch plötzlich wars, als ob sich das verwische:
sie stand wie mühsam in der Fensternische
und hielt des Herzens drängendes Geklopf.

Sein Spiel gab nach. Von draußen wehte Frische.
Und seltsam fremd stand auf dem Spiegeltische
der schwarze Tschako mit dem Totenkopf.

# THE LAST EVENING

*(By permission of Frau Nonna)*

And night and distant rumbling; now the army's
carrier-train was moving out, to war.
He looked up from the harpsichord, and as
he went on playing, he looked across at her

almost as one might gaze into a mirror:
so deeply was her every feature filled
with his young features, which bore his pain and were
more beautiful and seductive with each sound.

Then, suddenly, the image broke apart.
She stood, as though distracted, near the window
and felt the violent drum-beats of her heart.

His playing stopped. From outside, a fresh wind blew.
And strangely alien on the mirror-table
stood the black shako with its ivory skull.

## JUGEND-BILDNIS MEINES VATERS

Im Auge Traum. Die Stirn wie in Berührung
mit etwas Fernem. Um den Mund enorm
viel Jugend, ungelächelte Verführung,
und vor der vollen schmückenden Verschnürung
der schlanken adeligen Uniform
der Säbelkorb und beide Hände—, die
abwarten, ruhig, zu nichts hingedrängt.
Und nun fast nicht mehr sichtbar: als ob sie
zuerst, die Fernes greifenden, verschwänden.
Und alles andre mit sich selbst verhängt
und ausgelöscht als ob wirs nicht verständen
und tief aus seiner eignen Tiefe trüb—.

Du schnell vergehendes Daguerreotyp
in meinen langsamer vergehenden Händen.

# PORTRAIT OF MY FATHER AS A YOUNG MAN

In the eyes: dream. The brow as if it could feel
something far off. Around the lips, a great
freshness—seductive, though there is no smile.
Under the rows of ornamental braid
on the slim Imperial officer's uniform:
the saber's basket-hilt. Both hands stay
folded upon it, going nowhere, calm
and now almost invisible, as if they
were the first to grasp the distance and dissolve.
And all the rest so curtained with itself,
so cloudy, that I cannot understand
this figure as it fades into the background—.

Oh quickly disappearing photograph
in my more slowly disappearing hand.

## SELBSTBILDNIS AUS DEM JAHRE 1906

Des alten lange adligen Geschlechtes
Feststehendes im Augenbogenbau.
Im Blicke noch der Kindheit Angst und Blau
und Demut da und dort, nicht eines Knechtes
doch eines Dienenden und einer Frau.
Der Mund als Mund gemacht, groß und genau,
nicht überredend, aber ein Gerechtes
Aussagendes. Die Stirne ohne Schlechtes
und gern im Schatten stiller Niederschau.

Das, als Zusammenhang, erst nur geahnt;
noch nie im Leiden oder im Gelingen
zusammgefaßt zu dauerndem Durchdringen,
doch so, als wäre mit zerstreuten Dingen
von fern ein Ernstes, Wirkliches geplant.

## SELF-PORTRAIT, 1906

The stamina of an old, long-noble race
in the eyebrows' heavy arches. In the mild
blue eyes, the solemn anguish of a child
and, here and there, humility—not a fool's,
but feminine: the look of one who serves.
The mouth quite ordinary, large and straight,
composed, yet not unwilling to speak out
when necessary. The forehead still naive,
most comfortable in shadows, looking down.

This, as a whole, just hazily foreseen—
never, in any joy or suffering,
collected for a firm accomplishment;
and yet, as though, from far off, with scattered Things,
a serious, true work were being planned.

## SPANISCHE TÄNZERIN

Wie in der Hand ein Schwefelzündholz, weiß,
eh es zur Flamme kommt, nach allen Seiten
zuckende Zungen streckt—: beginnt im Kreis
naher Beschauer hastig, hell und heiß
ihr runder Tanz sich zuckend auszubreiten.

Und plötzlich ist er Flamme, ganz und gar.

Mit einem Blick entzündet sie ihr Haar
und dreht auf einmal mit gewagter Kunst
ihr ganzes Kleid in diese Feuersbrunst,
aus welcher sich, wie Schlangen die erschrecken,
die nackten Arme wach und klappernd strecken.

Und dann: als würde ihr das Feuer knapp,
nimmt sie es ganz zusamm und wirft es ab
sehr herrisch, mit hochmütiger Gebärde
und schaut: da liegt es rasend auf der Erde
und flammt noch immer und ergiebt sich nicht—.
Doch sieghaft, sicher und mit einem süßen
grüßenden Lächeln hebt sie ihr Gesicht
und stampft es aus mit kleinen festen Füßen.

## SPANISH DANCER

As on all its sides a kitchen-match darts white
flickering tongues before it bursts into flame:
with the audience around her, quickened, hot,
her dance begins to flicker in the dark room.

And all at once it is completely fire.

One upward glance and she ignites her hair
and, whirling faster and faster, fans her dress
to passionate flames, till it becomes a furnace
from which, like startled rattlesnakes, the long
naked arms uncoil, aroused and clicking.

And then: as if the fire were too tight
around her body, she takes and flings it out
haughtily, with an imperious gesture,
and watches: it lies raging on the floor,
still blazing up, and the flames refuse to die—.
Till, moving with total confidence and a sweet
exultant smile, she looks up finally
and stamps it out with powerful small feet.

## HETÄREN-GRÄBER

In ihren langen Haaren liegen sie
mit braunen, tief in sich gegangenen Gesichtern.
Die Augen zu wie vor zu vieler Ferne.
Skelette, Munde, Blumen. In den Munden
die glatten Zähne wie ein Reise-Schachspiel
aus Elfenbein in Reihen aufgestellt.
Und Blumen, gelbe Perlen, schlanke Knochen,
Hände und Hemden, welkende Gewebe
über dem eingestürzten Herzen. Aber
dort unter jenen Ringen, Talismanen
und augenblauen Steinen (Lieblings-Angedenken)
steht noch die stille Krypta des Geschlechtes,
bis an die Wölbung voll mit Blumenblättern.
Und wieder gelbe Perlen, weitverrollte,—
Schalen gebrannten Tones, deren Bug
ihr eignes Bild geziert hat, grüne Scherben
von Salben-Vasen, die wie Blumen duften,
und Formen kleiner Götter: Hausaltäre,
Hetärenhimmel mit entzückten Göttern.
Gesprengte Gürtel, flache Skarabäen,
kleine Figuren riesigen Geschlechtes,
ein Mund der lacht und Tanzende und Läufer,
goldene Fibeln, kleinen Bogen ähnlich
zur Jagd auf Tier- und Vogelamulette,
und lange Nadeln, zieres Hausgeräte
und eine runde Scherbe roten Grundes,
darauf, wie eines Eingangs schwarze Aufschrift,
die straffen Beine eines Viergespannes.
Und wieder Blumen, Perlen, die verrollt sind,
die hellen Lenden einer kleinen Leier,
und zwischen Schleiern, die gleich Nebeln fallen,
wie ausgekrochen aus des Schuhes Puppe:
des Fußgelenkes leichter Schmetterling.

So liegen sie mit Dingen angefüllt,
kostbaren Dingen, Steinen, Spielzeug, Hausrat,

# TOMBS OF THE HETAERAE

They lie in their long hair, and the brown faces
have long ago withdrawn into themselves.
Eyes shut, as though before too great a distance.
Skeletons, mouths, flowers. Inside the mouths,
the shiny teeth like rows of pocket chessmen.
And flowers, yellow pearls, slender bones,
hands and tunics, woven cloth decaying
over the shriveled heart. But there, beneath
those rings, beneath the talismans and gems
and precious stones like blue eyes (lovers' keepsakes),
there still remains the silent crypt of sex,
filled to its vaulted roof with flower-petals.
And yellow pearls again, unstrung and scattered,
vessels of fired clay on which their own
portraits once were painted, the green fragments
of perfume jars that smelled like flowers, and images
of little household gods upon their altars:
courtesan-heavens with enraptured gods.
Broken waistbands, scarabs carved in jade,
small statues with enormous genitals,
a laughing mouth, dancing-girls, runners,
golden clasps that look like tiny bows
for shooting bird- and beast-shaped amulets,
ornamented knives and spoons, long needles,
a roundish light-red potsherd upon which
the stiff legs of a team of horses stand
like the dark inscription above an entryway.
And flowers again, pearls that have rolled apart,
the shining flanks of a little gilded lyre;
and in between the veils that fall like mist,
as though crept out from the sandal's chrysalis:
the delicate pale butterfly of the ankle.

And so they lie, filled to the brim with Things,
expensive Things, jewels, toys, utensils,

zerschlagnem Tand (was alles in sie abfiel),
und dunkeln wie der Grund von einem Fluß.

Flußbetten waren sie,
darüber hin in kurzen schnellen Wellen
(die weiter wollten zu dem nächsten Leben)
die Leiber vieler Jünglinge sich stürzten
und in denen der Männer Ströme rauschten.
Und manchmal brachen Knaben aus den Bergen
der Kindheit, kamen zagen Falles nieder
und spielten mit den Dingen auf dem Grunde,
bis das Gefälle ihr Gefühl ergriff:

Dann füllten sie mit flachem klaren Wasser
die ganze Breite dieses breiten Weges
und trieben Wirbel an den tiefen Stellen;
und spiegelten zum ersten Mal die Ufer
und ferne Vogelrufe—, während hoch
die Sternennächte eines süßen Landes
in Himmel wuchsen, die sich nirgends schlossen.

broken trinkets (how much fell into them!)
and they darken as a river's bottom darkens.

For they *were* riverbeds once,
and over them in brief, impetuous waves
(each wanting to prolong itself, forever)
the bodies of countless adolescents surged;
and in them roared the currents of grown men.
And sometimes boys would burst forth from the mountains
of childhood, would descend in timid streams
and play with what they found on the river's bottom,
until the steep slope gripped their consciousness:

Then they filled, with clear, shallow water,
the whole breadth of this broad canal, and set
little whirlpools turning in the depths,
and for the first time mirrored the green banks
and distant calls of birds—, while in the sky
the starry nights of another, sweeter country
blossomed above them and would never close.

## ORPHEUS. EURYDIKE. HERMES

Das war der Seelen wunderliches Bergwerk.
Wie stille Silbererze gingen sie
als Adern durch sein Dunkel. Zwischen Wurzeln
entsprang das Blut, das fortgeht zu den Menschen,
und schwer wie Porphyr sah es aus im Dunkel.
Sonst war nichts Rotes.

Felsen waren da
und wesenlose Wälder. Brücken über Leeres
und jener große graue blinde Teich,
der über seinem fernen Grunde hing
wie Regenhimmel über einer Landschaft.
Und zwischen Wiesen, sanft und voller Langmut,
erschien des einen Weges blasser Streifen,
wie eine lange Bleiche hingelegt.

Und dieses einen Weges kamen sie.

Voran der schlanke Mann im blauen Mantel,
der stumm und ungeduldig vor sich aussah.
Ohne zu kauen fraß sein Schritt den Weg
in großen Bissen; seine Hände hingen
schwer und verschlossen aus dem Fall der Falten
und wußten nicht mehr von der leichten Leier,
die in die Linke eingewachsen war
wie Rosenranken in den Ast des Ölbaums.
Und seine Sinne waren wie entzweit:
indes der Blick ihm wie ein Hund vorauslief,
umkehrte, kam und immer wieder weit
und wartend an der nächsten Wendung stand,—
blieb sein Gehör wie ein Geruch zurück.
Manchmal erschien es ihm als reichte es
bis an das Gehen jener beiden andern,
die folgen sollten diesen ganzen Aufstieg.
Dann wieder wars nur seines Steigens Nachklang

## ORPHEUS. EURYDICE. HERMES

That was the deep uncanny mine of souls.
Like veins of silver ore, they silently
moved through its massive darkness. Blood welled up
among the roots, on its way to the world of men,
and in the dark it looked as hard as stone.
Nothing else was red.

There were cliffs there,
and forests made of mist. There were bridges
spanning the void, and that great gray blind lake
which hung above its distant bottom
like the sky on a rainy day above a landscape.
And through the gentle, unresisting meadows
one pale path unrolled like a strip of cotton.

Down this path they were coming.

In front, the slender man in the blue cloak—
mute, impatient, looking straight ahead.
In large, greedy, unchewed bites his walk
devoured the path; his hands hung at his sides,
tight and heavy, out of the falling folds,
no longer conscious of the delicate lyre
which had grown into his left arm, like a slip
of roses grafted onto an olive tree.
His senses felt as though they were split in two:
his sight would race ahead of him like a dog,
stop, come back, then rushing off again
would stand, impatient, at the path's next turn,—
but his hearing, like an odor, stayed behind.
Sometimes it seemed to him as though it reached
back to the footsteps of those other two
who were to follow him, up the long path home.
But then, once more, it was just his own steps' echo,

und seines Mantels Wind was hinter ihm war.
Er aber sagte sich, sie kämen doch;
sagte es laut und hörte sich verhallen.
Sie kämen doch, nur wärens zwei
die furchtbar leise gingen. Dürfte er
sich einmal wenden (wäre das Zurückschaun
nicht die Zersetzung dieses ganzen Werkes,
das erst vollbracht wird), müßte er sie sehen,
die beiden Leisen, die ihm schweigend nachgehn:

Den Gott des Ganges und der weiten Botschaft,
die Reisehaube über hellen Augen,
den schlanken Stab hertragend vor dem Leibe
und flügelschlagend an den Fußgelenken;
und seiner linken Hand gegeben: *sie*.

Die So-geliebte, daß aus einer Leier
mehr Klage kam als je aus Klagefrauen;
daß eine Welt aus Klage ward, in der
alles noch einmal da war: Wald und Tal
und Weg und Ortschaft, Feld und Fluß und Tier;
und daß um diese Klage-Welt, ganz so
wie um die andre Erde, eine Sonne
und ein gestirnter stiller Himmel ging,
ein Klage-Himmel mit entstellten Sternen—:
Diese So-geliebte.

Sie aber ging an jenes Gottes Hand,
den Schritt beschränkt von langen Leichenbändern,
unsicher, sanft und ohne Ungeduld.
Sie war in sich, wie Eine hoher Hoffnung,
und dachte nicht des Mannes, der voranging,
und nicht des Weges, der ins Leben aufstieg.
Sie war in sich. Und ihr Gestorbensein
erfüllte sie wie Fülle.
Wie eine Frucht von Süßigkeit und Dunkel,
so war sie voll von ihrem großen Tode,
der also neu war, daß sie nichts begriff.

\*

or the wind inside his cloak, that made the sound.
He said to himself, they had to be behind him;
said it aloud and heard it fade away.
They had to be behind him, but their steps
were ominously soft. If only he could
turn around, just once (but looking back
would ruin this entire work, so near
completion), then he could not fail to see them,
those other two, who followed him so softly:

The god of speed and distant messages,
a traveler's hood above his shining eyes,
his slender staff held out in front of him,
and little wings fluttering at his ankles;
and on his left arm, barely touching it: *she.*

A woman so loved that from one lyre there came
more lament than from all lamenting women;
that a whole world of lament arose, in which
all nature reappeared: forest and valley,
road and village, field and stream and animal;
and that around this lament-world, even as
around the other earth, a sun revolved
and a silent star-filled heaven, a lament-
heaven, with its own, disfigured stars—:
So greatly was she loved.

But now she walked beside the graceful god,
her steps constricted by the trailing graveclothes,
uncertain, gentle, and without impatience.
She was deep within herself, like a woman heavy
with child, and did not see the man in front
or the path ascending steeply into life.
Deep within herself. Being dead
filled her beyond fulfillment. Like a fruit
suffused with its own mystery and sweetness,
she was filled with her vast death, which was so new,
she could not understand that it had happened.

\*

Sie war in einem neuen Mädchentum
und unberührbar; ihr Geschlecht war zu
wie eine junge Blume gegen Abend,
und ihre Hände waren der Vermählung
so sehr entwöhnt, daß selbst des leichten Gottes
unendlich leise, leitende Berührung
sie kränkte wie zu sehr Vertraulichkeit.

Sie war schon nicht mehr diese blonde Frau,
die in des Dichters Liedern manchmal anklang,
nicht mehr des breiten Bettes Duft und Eiland
und jenes Mannes Eigentum nicht mehr.

Sie war schon aufgelöst wie langes Haar
und hingegeben wie gefallner Regen
und ausgeteilt wie hundertfacher Vorrat.

Sie war schon Wurzel.

Und als plötzlich jäh
der Gott sie anhielt und mit Schmerz im Ausruf
die Worte sprach: Er hat sich umgewendet—,
begriff sie nichts und sagte leise: Wer?

Fern aber, dunkel vor dem klaren Ausgang,
stand irgend jemand, dessen Angesicht
nicht zu erkennen war. Er stand und sah,
wie auf dem Streifen eines Wiesenpfades
mit trauervollem Blick der Gott der Botschaft
sich schweigend wandte, der Gestalt zu folgen,
die schon zurückging dieses selben Weges,
den Schritt beschränkt von langen Leichenbändern,
unsicher, sanft und ohne Ungeduld.

She had come into a new virginity
and was untouchable; her sex had closed
like a young flower at nightfall, and her hands
had grown so unused to marriage that the god's
infinitely gentle touch of guidance
hurt her, like an undesired kiss.

She was no longer that woman with blue eyes
who once had echoed through the poet's songs,
no longer the wide couch's scent and island,
and that man's property no longer.

She was already loosened like long hair,
poured out like fallen rain,
shared like a limitless supply.

She was already root.

And when, abruptly,
the god put out his hand to stop her, saying,
with sorrow in his voice: He has turned around—,
she could not understand, and softly answered
Who?

                                 Far away,
dark before the shining exit-gates,
someone or other stood, whose features were
unrecognizable. He stood and saw
how, on the strip of road among the meadows,
with a mournful look, the god of messages
silently turned to follow the small figure
already walking back along the path,
her steps constricted by the trailing graveclothes,
uncertain, gentle, and without impatience.

## ALKESTIS

Da plötzlich war der Bote unter ihnen,
hineingeworfen in das Überkochen
des Hochzeitsmahles wie ein neuer Zusatz.
Sie fühlten nicht, die Trinkenden, des Gottes
heimlichen Eintritt, welcher seine Gottheit
so an sich hielt wie einen nassen Mantel
und ihrer einer schien, der oder jener,
wie er so durchging. Aber plötzlich sah
mitten im Sprechen einer von den Gästen
den jungen Hausherrn oben an dem Tische
wie in die Höh gerissen, nicht mehr liegend,
und überall und mit dem ganzen Wesen
ein Fremdes spiegelnd, das ihn furchtbar ansprach.
Und gleich darauf, als klärte sich die Mischung,
war Stille; nur mit einem Satz am Boden
von trübem Lärm und einem Niederschlag
fallenden Lallens, schon verdorben riechend
nach dumpfem umgestandenen Gelächter.
Und da erkannten sie den schlanken Gott,
und wie er dastand, innerlich voll Sendung
und unerbittlich,—wußten sie es beinah.
Und doch, als es gesagt war, war es mehr
als alles Wissen, gar nicht zu begreifen.
Admet muß sterben. Wann? In dieser Stunde.

Der aber brach die Schale seines Schreckens
in Stücken ab und streckte seine Hände
heraus aus ihr, um mit dem Gott zu handeln.
Um Jahre, um ein einzig Jahr noch Jugend,
um Monate, um Wochen, um paar Tage,
ach, Tage nicht, um Nächte, nur um Eine,
um Eine Nacht, um diese nur: um die.
Der Gott verneinte, und da schrie er auf
und schrie's hinaus und hielt es nicht und schrie
wie seine Mutter aufschrie beim Gebären.

\*

## ALCESTIS

Then all at once the messenger was there,
amid the simmer of wedding guests: dropped in
like the last ingredient into a bubbling pot.
They kept on drinking and did not feel the stealthy
entrance of the god, who held his aura
as tight against his body as a wet cloak,
and seemed to be like any one of them
as he walked on. But abruptly, halfway through
a sentence, one guest saw how the young master
was startled from his couch at the table's head,
as though he had been snatched up into the air
and mirroring, all over, with all his being,
a strangeness that addressed him, horribly.
And then, as though the mixture cleared, there was
silence; on the bottom, just the dregs
of muddy noise and a precipitate
of falling babble, already giving off
the rancid smell of laughter that has turned.
For now they recognized the slender god,
and, as he stood before them, filled with his message
and unentreatable,—they almost knew.
And yet, when it was uttered, it was beyond
all understanding; none of them could grasp it.
Admetus must die. When? Within the hour.

But by this time he had broken through the shell
of his terror; and he thrust out both his hands
from the jagged holes, to bargain with the god.
For years, for only one more year of youth,
for months, for weeks, for just a few more days,
oh not for days: for nights, for just a night,
for one more night, for just this one: for this.
The god refused; and then *he* started screaming,
and screamed it out, held nothing back, screamed
as his own mother once had screamed in childbirth.

\*

Und die trat zu ihm, eine alte Frau,
und auch der Vater kam, der alte Vater,
und beide standen, alt, veraltet, ratlos,
beim Schreienden, der plötzlich, wie noch nie
so nah, sie ansah, abbrach, schluckte, sagte:
Vater,
liegt dir denn viel daran an diesem Rest,
an diesem Satz, der dich beim Schlingen hindert?
Geh, gieß ihn weg. Und du, du alte Frau,
Matrone,
was tust du denn noch hier: du hast geboren.
Und beide hielt er sie wie Opfertiere
in Einem Griff. Auf einmal ließ er los
und stieß die Alten fort, voll Einfall, strahlend
und atemholend, rufend: Kreon, Kreon!
Und nichts als das; und nichts als diesen Namen.
Aber in seinem Antlitz stand das Andere,
das er nicht sagte, namenlos erwartend,
wie ers dem jungen Freunde, dem Geliebten,
erglühend hinhielt übern wirren Tisch.
Die Alten (stand da), siehst du, sind kein Loskauf,
sie sind verbraucht und schlecht und beinah wertlos,
du aber, du, in deiner ganzen Schönheit—

Da aber sah er seinen Freund nicht mehr.
Er blieb zurück, und das, was kam, war *sie*,
ein wenig kleiner fast als er sie kannte
und leicht und traurig in dem bleichen Brautkleid.
Die andern alle sind nur ihre Gasse,
durch die sie kommt und kommt—: (gleich wird sie da sein
in seinen Armen, die sich schmerzhaft auftun).

Doch wie er wartet, spricht sie; nicht zu ihm.
Sie spricht zum Gotte, und der Gott vernimmt sie,
und alle hörens gleichsam erst im Gotte:

Ersatz kann keiner für ihn sein. Ich *bins*.
Ich bin Ersatz. Denn keiner ist zu Ende

And she came up beside him, an old woman,
and his father came up also, his old father,
and both stood waiting—old, decrepit, helpless—
beside the screaming man, who, as never before
so closely, saw them, stopped, swallowed, said:
Father,
do you care about the wretched scrap of life
still left you, that will just stick in your throat?
Go spit it out. And you, old woman, old
Mother,
why should you stay here? you have given birth.
And grabbed them both, like sacrificial beasts,
in his harsh grip. Then suddenly let them go,
pushed the old couple off, inspired, beaming,
breathing hard and calling: Creon! Creon!
And nothing else; and nothing but that name.
Yet in his features stood the other name
he could not utter, namelessly expectant
as, glowing, he held it out to the young guest,
his dearest friend, across the bewildered table.
These two old people (it stood there) are no ransom,
they are used up, exhausted, nearly worthless,
but you, Creon, you, in all your beauty—

But now he could no longer see his friend,
who stayed behind; and what came forth was *she*,
almost a little smaller than as he knew her,
slight and sad in her pale wedding dress.
All the others are just her narrow path,
down which she comes and comes—: (soon she will be
there, in his arms, which painfully have opened).

But while he waits, she speaks; though not to him.
She is speaking to the god, and the god listens,
and all can hear, as though within the god:

No one can be his ransom: only I can.
I *am* his ransom. For no one else has finished

wie ich es bin. Was bleibt mir denn von dem
was ich hier war? Das *ists* ja, daß ich sterbe.
Hat sie dirs nicht gesagt, da sie dirs auftrug,
daß jenes Lager, das da drinnen wartet,
zur Unterwelt gehört? Ich nahm ja Abschied.
Abschied über Abschied.
Kein Sterbender nimmt mehr davon. Ich ging ja,
damit das Alles, unter Dem begraben
der jetzt mein Gatte ist, zergeht, sich auflöst—.
So führ mich hin: ich sterbe ja für ihn.

Und wie der Wind auf hoher See, der umspringt,
so trat der Gott fast wie zu einer Toten
und war auf einmal weit von ihrem Gatten,
dem er, versteckt in einem kleinen Zeichen,
die hundert Leben dieser Erde zuwarf.
Der stürzte taumelnd zu den beiden hin
und griff nach ihnen wie im Traum. Sie gingen
schon auf den Eingang zu, in dem die Frauen
verweint sich drängten. Aber einmal sah
er noch des Mädchens Antlitz, das sich wandte
mit einem Lächeln, hell wie eine Hoffnung,
die beinah ein Versprechen war: erwachsen
zurückzukommen aus dem tiefen Tode
zu ihm, dem Lebenden—

Da schlug er jäh
die Hände vors Gesicht, wie er so kniete,
um nichts zu sehen mehr nach diesem Lächeln.

with life as I have. What is left for me
of everything I once was? Just my dying.
Didn't she tell you when she sent you down here
that the bed waiting inside belongs to death?
For I have taken leave. No one dying
takes more than that. I left so that all this,
buried beneath the man who is now my husband,
might fade and vanish——. Come: lead me away:
already I have begun to die, for him.

And veering like a wind on the high seas,
the god approached as though she were already
dead, and instantly was there beside her,
far from her husband, to whom, with an abrupt
nod, he tossed the hundred lives of earth.
The young man hurried, staggering, toward the two
and grasped at them as in a dream. But now
they had nearly reached the entrance, which was crowded
with sobbing women. One more time he saw
the girl's face, for just a moment, turning toward him
with a smile that was as radiant as a hope
and almost was a promise: to return
from out of the abyss of death, grown fully,
to him, who was still alive——

At that, he flung
his hands before his own face, as he knelt there,
in order to see nothing but that smile.

## ARCHAÏSCHER TORSO APOLLOS

Wir kannten nicht sein unerhörtes Haupt,
darin die Augenäpfel reiften. Aber
sein Torso glüht noch wie ein Kandelaber,
in dem sein Schauen, nur zurückgeschraubt,

sich hält und glänzt. Sonst könnte nicht der Bug
der Brust dich blenden, und im leisen Drehen
der Lenden könnte nicht ein Lächeln gehen
zu jener Mitte, die die Zeugung trug.

Sonst stünde dieser Stein entstellt und kurz
unter der Schultern durchsichtigem Sturz
und flimmerte nicht so wie Raubtierfelle;

und bräche nicht aus allen seinen Rändern
aus wie ein Stern: denn da ist keine Stelle,
die dich nicht sieht. Du mußt dein Leben ändern.

# ARCHAIC TORSO OF APOLLO

We cannot know his legendary head
with eyes like ripening fruit. And yet his torso
is still suffused with brilliance from inside,
like a lamp, in which his gaze, now turned to low,

gleams in all its power. Otherwise
the curved breast could not dazzle you so, nor could
a smile run through the placid hips and thighs
to that dark center where procreation flared.

Otherwise this stone would seem defaced
beneath the translucent cascade of the shoulders
and would not glisten like a wild beast's fur:

would not, from all the borders of itself,
burst like a star: for here there is no place
that does not see you. You must change your life.

## LEICHEN-WÄSCHE

Sie hatten sich an ihn gewöhnt. Doch als
die Küchenlampe kam und unruhig brannte
im dunkeln Luftzug, war der Unbekannte
ganz unbekannt. Sie wuschen seinen Hals,

und da sie nichts von seinem Schicksal wußten,
so logen sie ein anderes zusamm,
fortwährend waschend. Eine mußte husten
und ließ solang den schweren Essigschwamm

auf dem Gesicht. Da gab es eine Pause
auch für die zweite. Aus der harten Bürste
klopften die Tropfen; während seine grause
gekrampfte Hand dem ganzen Hause
beweisen wollte, daß ihn nicht mehr dürste.

Und er bewies. Sie nahmen wie betreten
eiliger jetzt mit einem kurzen Huster
die Arbeit auf, so daß an den Tapeten
ihr krummer Schatten in dem stummen Muster

sich wand und wälzte wie in einem Netze,
bis daß die Waschenden zu Ende kamen.
Die Nacht im vorhanglosen Fensterrahmen
war rücksichtslos. Und einer ohne Namen
lag bar und reinlich da und gab Gesetze.

# WASHING THE CORPSE

They had, for a while, grown used to him. But after
they lit the kitchen lamp and in the dark
it began to burn, restlessly, the stranger
was altogether strange. They washed his neck,

and since they knew nothing about his life
they lied till they produced another one,
as they kept washing. One of them had to cough,
and while she coughed she left the vinegar sponge,

dripping, upon his face. The other stood
and rested for a minute. A few drops fell
from the stiff scrub-brush, as his horrible
contorted hand was trying to make the whole
room aware that he no longer thirsted.

And he did let them know. With a short cough,
as if embarrassed, they both began to work
more hurriedly now, so that across
the mute, patterned wallpaper their thick

shadows reeled and staggered as if bound
in a net; till they had finished washing him.
The night, in the uncurtained window-frame,
was pitiless. And one without a name
lay clean and naked there, and gave commands.

## SCHWARZE KATZE

Ein Gespenst ist noch wie eine Stelle,
dran dein Blick mit einem Klange stößt;
aber da, an diesem schwarzen Felle
wird dein stärkstes Schauen aufgelöst:

wie ein Tobender, wenn er in vollster
Raserei ins Schwarze stampft,
jählings am benehmenden Gepolster
einer Zelle aufhört und verdampft.

Alle Blicke, die sie jemals trafen,
scheint sie also an sich zu verhehlen,
um darüber drohend und verdrossen
zuzuschauern und damit zu schlafen.
Doch auf einmal kehrt sie, wie geweckt,
ihr Gesicht und mitten in das deine:
und da triffst du deinen Blick im geelen
Amber ihrer runden Augensteine
unerwartet wieder: eingeschlossen
wie ein ausgestorbenes Insekt.

# BLACK CAT

A ghost, though invisible, still is like a place
your sight can knock on, echoing; but here
within this thick black pelt, your strongest gaze
will be absorbed and utterly disappear:

just as a raving madman, when nothing else
can ease him, charges into his dark night
howling, pounds on the padded wall, and feels
the rage being taken in and pacified.

She seems to hide all looks that have ever fallen
into her, so that, like an audience,
she can look them over, menacing and sullen,
and curl to sleep with them. But all at once

as if awakened, she turns her face to yours;
and with a shock, you see yourself, tiny,
inside the golden amber of her eyeballs
suspended, like a prehistoric fly.

## DIE FLAMINGOS

*Jardin des Plantes, Paris*

In Spiegelbildern wie von Fragonard
ist doch von ihrem Weiß und ihrer Röte
nicht mehr gegeben, als dir einer böte,
wenn er von seiner Freundin sagt: sie war

noch sanft von Schlaf. Denn steigen sie ins Grüne
und stehn, auf rosa Stielen leicht gedreht,
beisammen, blühend, wie in einem Beet,
verführen sie verführender als Phryne

sich selber; bis sie ihres Auges Bleiche
hinhalsend bergen in der eignen Weiche,
in welcher Schwarz und Fruchtrot sich versteckt.

Auf einmal kreischt ein Neid durch die Volière;
sie aber haben sich erstaunt gestreckt
und schreiten einzeln ins Imaginäre.

# THE FLAMINGOS

*Jardin des Plantes, Paris*

With all the subtle paints of Fragonard
no more of their red and white could be expressed
than someone would convey about his mistress
by telling you, "She was lovely, lying there

still soft with sleep." They rise above the green
grass and lightly sway on their long pink stems,
side by side, like enormous feathery blossoms,
seducing (more seductively than Phryne)

themselves; till, necks curling, they sink their large
pale eyes into the softness of their down,
where apple-red and jet-black lie concealed.

A shriek of envy shakes the parrot cage;
but *they* stretch out, astonished, and one by one
stride into their imaginary world.

## BUDDHA IN DER GLORIE

Mitte aller Mitten, Kern der Kerne,
Mandel, die sich einschließt und versüßt,—
dieses Alles bis an alle Sterne
ist dein Fruchtfleisch: Sei gegrüßt.

Sieh, du fühlst, wie nichts mehr an dir hängt;
im Unendlichen ist deine Schale,
und dort steht der starke Saft und drängt.
Und von außen hilft ihm ein Gestrahle,

denn ganz oben werden deine Sonnen
voll und glühend umgedreht.
Doch in dir ist schon begonnen,
was die Sonnen übersteht.

# BUDDHA IN GLORY

Center of all centers, core of cores,
almond self-enclosed and growing sweet—
all this universe, to the furthest stars
and beyond them, is your flesh, your fruit.

Now you feel how nothing clings to you;
your vast shell reaches into endless space,
and there the rich, thick fluids rise and flow.
Illuminated in your infinite peace,

a billion stars go spinning through the night,
blazing high above your head.
But *in* you is the presence that
will be, when all the stars are dead.

F R O M

*Requiem*

*(1909)*

## REQUIEM FÜR EINE FREUNDIN

Ich habe Tote, und ich ließ sie hin
und war erstaunt, sie so getrost zu sehn,
so rasch zuhaus im Totsein, so gerecht,
so anders als ihr Ruf. Nur du, du kehrst
zurück; du streifst mich, du gehst um, du willst
an etwas stoßen, daß es klingt von dir
und dich verrät. O nimm mir nicht, was ich
langsam erlern. Ich habe recht; du irrst
wenn du gerührt zu irgend einem Ding
ein Heimweh hast. Wir wandeln dieses um;
es ist nicht hier, wir spiegeln es herein
aus unserm Sein, sobald wir es erkennen.
    Ich glaubte dich viel weiter. Mich verwirrts,
daß *du* gerade irrst und kommst, die mehr
verwandelt hat als irgend eine Frau.
Daß wir erschraken, da du starbst, nein, daß
dein starker Tod uns dunkel unterbrach,
das Bisdahin abreißend vom Seither:
das geht uns an; das einzuordnen wird
die Arbeit sein, die wir mit allem tun.
Doch daß du selbst erschrakst und auch noch jetzt
den Schrecken hast, wo Schrecken nicht mehr gilt;
daß du von deiner Ewigkeit ein Stück
verlierst und hier hereintrittst, Freundin, hier,
wo alles noch nicht *ist;* daß du zerstreut,
zum ersten Mal im All zerstreut und halb,
den Aufgang der unendlichen Naturen
nicht so ergriffst wie hier ein jedes Ding;
daß aus dem Kreislauf, der dich schon empfing,
die stumme Schwerkraft irgend einer Unruh
dich niederzieht zur abgezählten Zeit—:
dies weckt mich nachts oft wie ein Dieb, der einbricht.
Und dürft ich sagen, daß du nur geruhst,
daß du aus Großmut kommst, aus Überfülle,
weil du so sicher bist, so in dir selbst,

# REQUIEM FOR A FRIEND

I have my dead, and I have let them go,
and was amazed to see them so contented,
so soon at home in being dead, so cheerful,
so unlike their reputation. Only you
return; brush past me, loiter, try to knock
against something, so that the sound reveals
your presence. Oh don't take from me what I
am slowly learning. I'm sure you have gone astray
if you are moved to homesickness for anything
in this dimension. We transform these Things;
they aren't real, they are only the reflections
upon the polished surface of our being.

    I thought you were much further on. It troubles me
that *you* should stray back, you, who have achieved
more transformation than any other woman.
That we were frightened when you died . . . no; rather:
that your stern death broke in upon us, darkly,
wrenching the till-then from the ever-since—
this concerns *us:* setting it all in order
is the task we have continually before us.
But that you too were frightened, and even now
pulse with your fear, where fear can have no meaning;
that you have lost even the smallest fragment
of your eternity, Paula, and have entered
here, where nothing yet exists; that out there,
bewildered for the first time, inattentive,
you didn't grasp the splendor of the infinite
forces, as on earth you grasped each Thing;
that, from the realm which already had received you,
the gravity of some old discontent
has dragged you back to measurable time—:
this often startles me out of dreamless sleep
at night, like a thief climbing in my window.
If I could say it is only out of kindness,
out of your great abundance, that you have come,
because you are so secure, so self-contained,

daß du herumgehst wie ein Kind, nicht bange
vor Örtern, wo man einem etwas tut—:
doch nein: du bittest. Dieses geht mir so
bis ins Gebein und querrt wie eine Säge.
Ein Vorwurf, den du trügest als Gespenst,
nachtrügest mir, wenn ich mich nachts zurückzieh
in meine Lunge, in die Eingeweide,
in meines Herzens letzte ärmste Kammer,—
ein solcher Vorwurf wäre nicht so grausam,
wie dieses Bitten ist. Was bittest du?
    Sag, soll ich reisen? Hast du irgendwo
ein Ding zurückgelassen, das sich quält
und das dir nachwill? Soll ich in ein Land,
das du nicht sahst, obwohl es dir verwandt
war wie die andre Hälfte deiner Sinne?
    Ich will auf seinen Flüssen fahren, will
an Land gehn und nach alten Sitten fragen,
will mit den Frauen in den Türen sprechen
und zusehn, wenn sie ihre Kinder rufen.
Ich will mir merken, wie sie dort die Landschaft
umnehmen draußen bei der alten Arbeit
der Wiesen und der Felder; will begehren,
vor ihren König hingeführt zu sein,
und will die Priester durch Bestechung reizen,
daß sie mich legen vor das stärkste Standbild
und fortgehn und die Tempeltore schließen.
Dann aber will ich, wenn ich vieles weiß,
einfach die Tiere anschaun, daß ein Etwas
von ihrer Wendung mir in die Gelenke
herübergleitet; will ein kurzes Dasein
in ihren Augen haben, die mich halten
und langsam lassen, ruhig, ohne Urteil.
Ich will mir von den Gärtnern viele Blumen
hersagen lassen, daß ich in den Scherben
der schönen Eigennamen einen Rest
herüberbringe von den hundert Düften.
Und Früchte will ich kaufen, Früchte, drin
das Land noch einmal ist, bis an den Himmel.

that you can wander anywhere, like a child,
not frightened of any harm that might await you . . .
But no: you're pleading. This penetrates me, to
my very bones, and cuts at me like a saw.
The bitterest rebuke your ghost could bring me,
could scream to me, at night, when I withdraw
into my lungs, into my intestines,
into the last bare chamber of my heart,—
such bitterness would not chill me half so much
as this mute pleading. What is it that you want?

　　Tell me, must I travel? Did you leave
some Thing behind, some place, that cannot bear
your absence? Must I set out for a country
you never saw, although it was as vividly
near to you as your own senses were?

　　I will sail its rivers, search its valleys, inquire
about its oldest customs; I will stand
for hours, talking with women in their doorways
and watching, while they call their children home.
I will see the way they wrap the land around them
in their ancient work in field and meadow; will ask
to be led before their king; will bribe the priests
to take me to their temple, before the most
powerful of the statues in their keeping,
and to leave me there, shutting the gates behind them.
And only then, when I have learned enough,
I will go to watch the animals, and let
something of their composure slowly glide
into my limbs; will see my own existence
deep in their eyes, which hold me for a while
and let me go, serenely, without judgment.
I will have the gardeners come to me and recite
many flowers, and in the small clay pots
of their melodious names I will bring back
some remnant of the hundred fragrances.
And fruits: I will buy fruits, and in their sweetness
that country's earth and sky will live again.

Denn Das verstandest du: die vollen Früchte.
Die legtest du auf Schalen vor dich hin
und wogst mit Farben ihre Schwere auf.
Und so wie Früchte sahst du auch die Fraun
und sahst die Kinder so, von innen her
getrieben in die Formen ihres Daseins.
Und sahst dich selbst zuletzt wie eine Frucht,
nahmst dich heraus aus deinen Kleidern, trugst
dich vor den Spiegel, ließest dich hinein
bis auf dein Schauen; das blieb groß davor
und sagte nicht: das bin ich; nein: dies ist.
So ohne Neugier war zuletzt dein Schaun
und so besitzlos, von so wahrer Armut,
daß es dich selbst nicht mehr begehrte: heilig.

So will ich dich behalten, wie du dich
hinstelltest in den Spiegel, tief hinein
und fort von allem. Warum kommst du anders?
Was widerrufst du dich? Was willst du mir
einreden, daß in jenen Bernsteinkugeln
um deinen Hals noch etwas Schwere war
von jener Schwere, wie sie nie im Jenseits
beruhigter Bilder ist; was zeigst du mir
in deiner Haltung eine böse Ahnung;
was heißt dich die Konturen deines Leibes
auslegen wie die Linien einer Hand,
daß ich sie nicht mehr sehn kann ohne Schicksal?

Komm her ins Kerzenlicht. Ich bin nicht bang,
die Toten anzuschauen. Wenn sie kommen,
so haben sie ein Recht, in unserm Blick
sich aufzuhalten, wie die andern Dinge.

Komm her; wir wollen eine Weile still sein.
Sieh diese Rose an auf meinem Schreibtisch;
ist nicht das Licht um sie genau so zaghaft
wie über dir: sie dürfte auch nicht hier sein.
Im Garten draußen, unvermischt mit mir,
hätte sie bleiben müssen oder hingehn,—
nun währt sie so: was ist ihr mein Bewußtsein?

＊

For that is what you understood: ripe fruits.
You set them before the canvas, in white bowls,
and weighed out each one's heaviness with your colors.
Women too, you saw, were fruits; and children, molded
from inside, into the shapes of their existence.
And at last, you saw yourself as a fruit, you stepped
out of your clothes and brought your naked body
before the mirror, you let yourself inside
down to your gaze; which stayed in front, immense,
and didn't say: I am that; no: this is.
So free of curiosity your gaze
had become, so unpossessive, of such true
poverty, it had no desire even
for you yourself; it wanted nothing: holy.

    And that is how I have cherished you—deep inside
the mirror, where you put yourself, far away
from all the world. Why have you come like this
and so denied yourself? Why do you want
to make me think that in the amber beads
you wore in your self-portrait, there was still
a kind of heaviness that can't exist
in the serene heaven of paintings? Why do you show me
an evil omen in the way you stand?
What makes you read the contours of your body
like the lines engraved inside a palm, so that
I cannot see them now except as fate?

    Come into the candlelight. I'm not afraid
to look the dead in the face. When they return,
they have a right, as much as other Things do,
to pause and refresh themselves within our vision.

    Come; and we will be silent for a while.
Look at this rose on the corner of my desk:
isn't the light around it just as timid
as the light on you? It too should not be here,
it should have bloomed or faded in the garden,
outside, never involved with me. But now
it lives on in its small porcelain vase:
what meaning does it find in my awareness?

*

Erschrick nicht, wenn ich jetzt begreife, ach,
da steigt es in mir auf: ich kann nicht anders,
ich muß begreifen, und wenn ich dran stürbe.
Begreifen, daß du hier bist. Ich begreife.
Ganz wie ein Blinder rings ein Ding begreift,
fühl ich dein Los und weiß ihm keinen Namen.
Laß uns zusammen klagen, daß dich einer
aus deinem Spiegel nahm. Kannst du noch weinen?
Du kannst nicht. Deiner Tränen Kraft und Andrang
hast du verwandelt in dein reifes Anschaun
und warst dabei, jeglichen Saft in dir
so umzusetzen in ein starkes Dasein,
das steigt und kreist, im Gleichgewicht und blindlings.
Da riß ein Zufall dich, dein letzter Zufall
riß dich zurück aus deinem fernsten Fortschritt
in eine Welt zurück, wo Säfte *wollen*.
Riß dich nicht ganz; riß nur ein Stück zuerst,
doch als um dieses Stück von Tag zu Tag
die Wirklichkeit so zunahm, daß es schwer ward,
da brauchtest du dich ganz: da gingst du hin
und brachst in Brocken dich aus dem Gesetz
mühsam heraus, weil du dich brauchtest. Da
trugst du dich ab und grubst aus deines Herzens
nachtwarmem Erdreich die noch grünen Samen,
daraus dein Tod aufkeimen sollte: deiner,
dein eigner Tod zu deinem eignen Leben.
Und aßest sie, die Körner deines Todes,
wie alle andern, aßest seine Körner,
und hattest Nachgeschmack in dir von Süße,
die du nicht meintest, hattest süße Lippen,
du: die schon innen in den Sinnen süß war.

O laß uns klagen. Weißt du, wie dein Blut
aus einem Kreisen ohnegleichen zögernd
und ungern wiederkam, da du es abriefst?
Wie es verwirrt des Leibes kleinen Kreislauf
noch einmal aufnahm; wie es voller Mißtraun
und Staunen eintrat in den Mutterkuchen
und von dem weiten Rückweg plötzlich müd war.

Don't be frightened if I understand it now;
it's rising in me, ah, I'm trying to grasp it,
*must* grasp it, even if I die of it. Must grasp
that you are here. As a blind man grasps an object,
I feel your fate, although I cannot name it.
Let us lament together that someone pulled you
out of your mirror's depths. Can you still cry?
No: I see you can't. You turned your tears'
strength and pressure into your ripe gaze,
and were transforming every fluid inside you
into a strong reality, which would rise
and circulate, in equilibrium, blindly.
Then, for the last time, chance came in and tore you
back, from the last step forward on your path,
into a world where bodies have their will.
Not all at once: tore just a shred at first;
but when, around this shred, day after day,
the objective world expanded, swelled, grew heavy—
you needed your whole self; and so you went
and broke yourself, out of its grip, in pieces,
painfully, because your need was great.
Then from the night-warm soilbed of your heart
you dug the seeds, still green, from which your death
would sprout: your own, your perfect death, the one
that was your whole life's perfect consummation.
And swallowed down the kernels of your death,
like all the other ones, swallowed them, and were
startled to find an aftertaste of sweetness
you hadn't planned on, a sweetness on your lips, you
who inside your senses were so sweet already.

Ah let us lament. Do you know how hesitantly,
how reluctantly your blood, when you called it back,
returned from its incomparable circuit?
How confused it was to take up once again
the body's narrow circulation; how,
full of mistrust and astonishment, it came
flowing into the placenta and suddenly
was exhausted by the long journey home.

Du triebst es an, du stießest es nach vorn,
du zerrtest es zur Feuerstelle, wie
man eine Herde Tiere zerrt zum Opfer;
und wolltest noch, es sollte dabei froh sein.
Und du erzwangst es schließlich: es war froh
und lief herbei und gab sich hin. Dir schien,
weil du gewohnt warst an die andern Maße,
es wäre nur für eine Weile; aber
nun warst du in der Zeit, und Zeit ist lang.
Und Zeit geht hin, und Zeit nimmt zu, and Zeit
ist wie ein Rückfall einer langen Krankheit.

   Wie war dein Leben kurz, wenn du's vergleichst
mit jenen Stunden, da du saßest und
die vielen Kräfte deiner vielen Zukunft
schweigend herabbogst zu dem neuen Kindkeim,
der wieder Schicksal war. O wehe Arbeit.
O Arbeit über alle Kraft. Du tatest
sie Tag für Tag, du schlepptest dich zu ihr
und zogst den schönen Einschlag aus dem Webstuhl
und brauchtest alle deine Fäden anders.
Und endlich hattest du noch Mut zum Fest.

   Denn da's getan war, wolltest du belohnt sein,
wie Kinder, wenn sie bittersüßen Tee
getrunken haben, der vielleicht gesund macht.
So lohntest du dich: denn von jedem andern
warst du zu weit, auch jetzt noch; keiner hätte
ausdenken können, welcher Lohn dir wohltut.
Du wußtest es. Du saßest auf im Kindbett,
und vor dir stand ein Spiegel, der dir alles
ganz wiedergab. Nun war das alles *Du*
und ganz *davor*, und drinnen war nur Täuschung,
die schöne Täuschung jeder Frau, die gern
Schmuck umnimmt und das Haar kämmt und verändert.

   So starbst du, wie die Frauen früher starben,
altmodisch starbst du in dem warmen Hause
den Tod der Wöchnerinnen, welche wieder
sich schließen wollen und es nicht mehr können,
weil jenes Dunkel, das sie mitgebaren,
noch einmal wiederkommt und drängt und eintritt.

*

You drove it on, you pushed it forward, you dragged it
up to the hearth, as one would drag a terrified
animal to the sacrificial altar;
and wanted it, after all that, to be happy.
Finally, you forced it: it was happy,
it ran up and surrendered. And you thought,
because you had grown used to other measures,
that this would be for just a little while.
But now you were in time, and time is long.
And time goes on, and time grows large, and time
is like a relapse after a long illness.

How short your life seems, if you now compare it
with those empty hours you passed in silence, bending
the abundant strengths of your abundant future
out of their course, into the new child-seed
that once again was fate. A painful task:
a task beyond all strength. But you performed it
day after day, you dragged yourself in front of it;
you pulled the lovely weft out of the loom
and wove your threads into a different pattern.
And still had courage enough for celebration.

When it was done, you wished to be rewarded,
like children when they have swallowed down the draught
of bittersweet tea that perhaps will make them well.
So you chose your own reward, being still so far
removed from people, even then, that no one
could have imagined what reward would please you.
But you yourself knew. You sat up in your childbed
and in front of you was a mirror, which gave back
everything. And this everything was you,
and right in front; inside was mere deception,
the sweet deception of every woman who smiles
as she puts her jewelry on and combs her hair.

And so you died as women used to die,
at home, in your own warm bedroom, the old-fashioned
death of women in labor, who try to close
themselves again but can't, because that ancient
darkness which they have also given birth to
returns for them, thrusts its way in, and enters.

\*

Ob man nicht dennoch hätte Klagefrauen
auftreiben müssen? Weiber, welche weinen
für Geld, und die man so bezahlen kann,
daß sie die Nacht durch heulen, wenn es still wird.
Gebräuche her! wir haben nicht genug
Gebräuche. Alles geht und wird verredet.
So mußt du kommen, tot, und hier mit mir
Klagen nachholen. Hörst du, daß ich klage?
Ich möchte meine Stimme wie ein Tuch
hinwerfen über deines Todes Scherben
und zerrn an ihr, bis sie in Fetzen geht,
und alles, was ich sage, müßte so
zerlumpt in dieser Stimme gehn und frieren;
blieb es beim Klagen. Doch jetzt klag ich an:
den Einen nicht, der dich aus dir zurückzog,
(ich find ihn nicht heraus, er ist wie alle)
doch alle klag ich in ihm an: den Mann.

Wenn irgendwo ein Kindgewesensein
tief in mir aufsteigt, das ich noch nicht kenne,
vielleicht das reinste Kindsein meiner Kindheit:
ich wills nicht wissen. Einen Engel will
ich daraus bilden ohne hinzusehn
und will ihn werfen in die erste Reihe
schreiender Engel, welche Gott erinnern.

Denn dieses Leiden dauert schon zu lang,
und keiner kanns; es ist zu schwer für uns,
das wirre Leiden von der falschen Liebe,
die, bauend auf Verjährung wie Gewohnheit,
ein Recht sich nennt und wuchert aus dem Unrecht.
Wo ist ein Mann, der Recht hat auf Besitz?
Wer kann besitzen, was sich selbst nicht hält,
was sich von Zeit zu Zeit nur selig auffängt
und wieder hinwirft wie ein Kind den Ball.
Sowenig wie der Feldherr eine Nike
festhalten kann am Vorderbug des Schiffes,
wenn das geheime Leichtsein ihrer Gottheit
sie plötzlich weghebt in den hellen Meerwind:
so wenig kann einer von uns die Frau

Once, ritual lament would have been chanted;
women would have been paid to beat their breasts
and howl for you all night, when all is silent.
Where can we find such customs now? So many
have long since disappeared or been disowned.
That's what you had to come for: to retrieve
the lament that we omitted. Can you hear me?
I would like to fling my voice out like a cloth
over the fragments of your death, and keep
pulling at it until it is torn to pieces,
and all my words would have to walk around
shivering, in the tatters of that voice;
if lament were enough. But now I must accuse:
not the man who withdrew you from yourself
(I cannot find him; he looks like everyone),
but in this one man, I accuse: all men.

When somewhere, from deep within me, there arises
the vivid sense of having been a child,
the purity and essence of that childhood
where I once lived: then I don't want to know it.
I want to form an angel from that sense
and hurl him upward, into the front row
of angels who scream out, reminding God.

For this suffering has lasted far too long;
none of us can bear it; it is too heavy—
this tangled suffering of spurious love
which, building on convention like a habit,
calls itself just, and fattens on injustice.
Show me a man with the right to his possession.
Who can possess what cannot hold its own self,
but only, now and then, will blissfully
catch itself, then quickly throw itself
away, like a child playing with a ball.
As little as a captain can hold the carved
Nikē facing outward from his ship's prow
when the lightness of her godhead suddenly
lifts her up, into the bright sea-wind:
so little can one of us call back the woman

anrufen, die uns nicht mehr sieht und die
auf einem schmalen Streifen ihres Daseins
wie durch ein Wunder fortgeht, ohne Unfall:
er hätte denn Beruf und Lust zur Schuld.
　　Denn *das* ist Schuld, wenn irgendeines Schuld ist:
die Freiheit eines Lieben nicht vermehren
um alle Freiheit, die man in sich aufbringt.
Wir haben, wo wir lieben, ja nur dies:
einander lassen; denn daß wir uns halten,
das fällt uns leicht und ist nicht erst zu lernen.

　　Bist du noch da? In welcher Ecke bist du?—
Du hast so viel gewußt von alledem
und hast so viel gekonnt, da du so hingingst
für alles offen, wie ein Tag, der anbricht.
Die Frauen leiden: lieben heißt allein sein,
und Künstler ahnen manchmal in der Arbeit,
daß sie verwandeln müssen, wo sie lieben.
Beides begannst du; beides ist in Dem,
was jetzt ein Ruhm entstellt, der es dir fortnimmt.
Ach du warst weit von jedem Ruhm. Du warst
unscheinbar; hattest leise deine Schönheit
hineingenommen, wie man eine Fahne
einzieht am grauen Morgen eines Werktags,
und wolltest nichts, als eine lange Arbeit,—
die nicht getan ist: dennoch nicht getan.
　　Wenn du noch da bist, wenn in diesem Dunkel
noch eine Stelle ist, an der dein Geist
empfindlich mitschwingt auf den flachen Schallwelln,
die eine Stimme, einsam in der Nacht,
aufregt in eines hohen Zimmers Strömung:
So hör mich: Hilf mir. Sieh, wir gleiten so,
nicht wissend wann, zurück aus unserm Fortschritt
in irgendwas, was wir nicht meinen; drin
wir uns verfangen wie in einem Traum
und drin wir sterben, ohne zu erwachen.
Keiner ist weiter. Jedem, der sein Blut
hinaufhob in ein Werk, das lange wird,

who, now no longer seeing us, walks on
along the narrow strip of her existence
as though by miracle, in perfect safety—
unless, that is, he wishes to do wrong.
    For *this* is wrong, if anything is wrong:
not to enlarge the freedom of a love
with all the inner freedom one can summon.
We need, in love, to practice only this:
letting each other go. For holding on
comes easily; we do not need to learn it.

    Are you still here? Are you standing in some corner?—
You knew so much of all this, you were able
to do so much; you passed through life so open
to all things, like an early morning. I know:
women suffer; for love means being alone;
and artists in their work sometimes intuit
that they must keep transforming, where they love.
You began both; both exist in that
which any fame takes from you and disfigures.
Oh you were far beyond all fame; were almost
invisible; had withdrawn your beauty, softly,
as one would lower a brightly-colored flag
on the gray morning after a holiday.
You had just one desire: a years-long work—
which was not finished; was somehow never finished.
    If you are still here with me, if in this darkness
there is still some place where your spirit resonates
on the shallow soundwaves stirred up by my voice:
hear me; help me. We can so easily
slip back from what we have struggled to attain,
abruptly, into a life we never wanted;
can find that we are trapped, as in a dream,
and die there, without ever waking up.
This can occur. Anyone who has lifted
his blood into a years-long work may find

kann es geschehen, daß ers nicht mehr hochhält
und daß es geht nach seiner Schwere, wertlos.
Denn irgendwo ist eine alte Feindschaft
zwischen dem Leben und der großen Arbeit.
Daß ich sie einseh und sie sage: hilf mir.
    Komm nicht zurück. Wenn du's erträgst, so sei
tot bei den Toten. Tote sind beschäftigt.
Doch hilf mir so, daß es dich nicht zerstreut,
wie mir das Fernste manchmal hilft: in mir.

that he can't sustain it, the force of gravity
is irresistible, and it falls back, worthless.
For somewhere there is an ancient enmity
between our daily life and the great work.
Help me, in saying it, to understand it.

    Do not return. If you can bear to, stay
dead with the dead. The dead have their own tasks.
But help me, if you can without distraction,
as what is farthest sometimes helps: in me.

# Uncollected Poems

## 1911–1920

## [AN LOU ANDREAS-SALOMÉ]

### I

Ich hielt mich überoffen, ich vergaß,
daß draußen nicht nur Dinge sind und voll
in sich gewohnte Tiere, deren Aug
aus ihres Lebens Rundung anders nicht
hinausreicht als ein eingerahmtes Bild;
daß ich in mich mit allem immerfort
Blicke hineinriß: Blicke, Meinung, Neugier.
   Wer weiß, es bilden Augen sich im Raum
und wohnen bei. Ach nur zu dir gestürzt,
ist mein Gesicht nicht ausgestellt, verwächst
in dich und setzt sich dunkel
unendlich fort in dein geschütztes Herz.

### II

Wie man ein Tuch vor angehäuften Atem,
nein: wie man es an eine Wunde preßt,
aus der das Leben ganz, in einem Zug,
hinauswill, hielt ich dich an mich: ich sah,
du wurdest rot von mir. Wer spricht es aus,
was uns geschah? Wir holten jedes nach,
wozu die Zeit nie war. Ich reifte seltsam
in jedem Antrieb übersprungner Jugend,
und du, Geliebte, hattest irgendeine
wildeste Kindheit über meinem Herzen.

### III

Entsinnen ist da nicht genug, es muß
von jenen Augenblicken pures Dasein
auf meinem Grunde sein, ein Niederschlag
der unermeßlich überfüllten Lösung.
Denn ich *gedenke* nicht, das, was ich *bin*
rührt mich um deinetwillen. Ich erfinde
dich nicht an traurig ausgekühlten Stellen,

# [TO LOU ANDREAS-SALOMÉ]

## I

I kept myself too open, I forgot
that outside there are not just Things, not just
animals at home within themselves,
whose eyes do not reach out from their life's roundness
differently than a picture from its frame;
that all along I snatched into myself
glances, opinion, curiosity.
    For all we know, eyes may appear in space,
staring down. Only when hurled in you
is my face not imperiled, as it grows
into you, as it continues darkly
forever onward within your sheltered heart.

## II

As one would hold a handkerchief in front of
one's piled-up breath . . . no: as one would press it
against a wound from which life, all in one spurt,
is trying to escape—I held you close
till you were red with me. Who can describe
what happened to us? We made up for all
that there had been no time for. I ripened strangely
in every impulse of my unlived youth,
and you, Beloved, found yourself beginning
a kind of savage childhood in my heart.

## III

Remembering them will not suffice: there must,
from all those moments, still remain a pure
existence in my depths, the sediment
from a measurelessly overfilled solution.
For I am not recalling: what I *am*
moves me because of you. It's not that I
discover you at the sad, cooled-off places

von wo du wegkamst; selbst, daß du nicht da bist,
ist warm von dir und wirklicher und mehr
als ein Entbehren. Sehnsucht geht zu oft
ins Ungenaue. Warum soll ich mich
auswerfen, während mir vielleicht dein Einfluß
leicht ist, wie Mondschein einem Platz am Fenster.

you left; the very fact that you're not there
is warm with you and realer and is more
than a privation. Yearning ends so often
in vagueness. Why should I be desperate while
your presence still can fall upon me, gently
as moonlight on a seat beside the window.

*Die Mandelbäume in Blüte: alles, was wir*
*hier leisten können, ist, sich ohne Rest erkennen*
*in der irdischen Erscheinung.*

Unendlich staun ich euch an, ihr Seligen, euer Benehmen,
wie ihr die schwindliche Zier traget in ewigem Sinn.
Ach wers verstünde zu blühn: dem wär das Herz über alle
schwachen Gefahren hinaus und in der großen getrost.

# [THE ALMOND TREES IN BLOSSOM]

*The almond trees in blossom: all we can
achieve here is the traceless recognition of
ourselves in earthly appearance.*


Endlessly I gaze at you in wonder, blessed ones, at your
    composure,
at how in eternal delight you bear your vanishing beauty.
Ah, if only we knew how to blossom: our heart would pass
    beyond every
small danger, and would find peace in the greatest danger of
    all.

## DIE SPANISCHE TRILOGIE

### [I]

Aus dieser Wolke, siehe: die den Stern
so wild verdeckt, der eben war—(und mir),
aus diesem Bergland drüben, das jetzt Nacht,
Nachtwinde hat für eine Zeit—(und mir),
aus diesem Fluß im Talgrund, der den Schein
zerrissner Himmels-Lichtung fängt—(und mir);
aus mir und alledem ein einzig Ding
zu machen, Herr: aus mir und dem Gefühl,
mit dem die Herde, eingekehrt im Pferch,
das große dunkle Nichtmehrsein der Welt
ausatmend hinnimmt—, mir und jedem Licht
im Finstersein der vielen Häuser, Herr:
ein Ding zu machen; aus den Fremden, denn
nicht Einen kenn ich, Herr, und mir und mir
*ein* Ding zu machen; aus den Schlafenden,
den fremden alten Männern im Hospiz,
die wichtig in den Betten husten, aus
schlaftrunknen Kindern an so fremder Brust,
aus vielen Ungenaun und immer mir,
aus nichts als mir und dem, was ich nicht kenn,
das Ding zu machen, Herr Herr Herr, das Ding,
das welthaft-irdisch wie ein Meteor
in seiner Schwere nur die Summe Flugs
zusammennimmt: nichts wiegend als die Ankunft.

### [II]

Warum muß einer gehn und fremde Dinge
so auf sich nehmen, wie vielleicht der Träger
den fremdlings mehr und mehr gefüllten Marktkorb
von Stand zu Stand hebt und beladen nachgeht
und kann nicht sagen: Herr, wozu das Gastmahl?

*

# THE SPANISH TRILOGY

## I

From this cloud, look!, which has so wildly covered
the star that just now shone there—(and from me),
from these dark clustered hills which hold the night,
the night-winds, for a while—(and from me),
from this stream in the valley which has caught
the jagged glow of the night sky—(and from me);
from me, Lord, and from all of this, to make
one single Thing; from me and the slow breathing
with which the flock, penned in the fold at dusk,
endures the great dark absence of the world—,
from me and every candle flickering
in the dimness of the many houses, Lord:
to make one Thing; from strangers, for I know
no one here, Lord, and from me, from me,
to make *one* Thing; from sleepers in these houses,
from old men left alone at the asylum
who cough in bed, importantly, from children
drunk with sleep upon the breasts of strangers,
from so much that is uncertain and from me,
from me alone and from what I do not know,
to make the Thing, Lord Lord Lord, the Thing
which, earthly and cosmic, like a meteor
gathers within its heaviness no more than
the sum of flight: and weighs nothing but arrival.

## II

Why must a man be always taking on
Things not his own, as if he were a servant
whose marketing-bag grows heavier and heavier
from stall to stall and, loaded down, he follows
and doesn't dare ask: Master, why this banquet?

✳

Warum muß einer dastehn wie ein Hirt,
so ausgesetzt dem Übermaß von Einfluß,
beteiligt so an diesem Raum voll Vorgang,
daß er gelehnt an einen Baum der Landschaft
sein Schicksal hätte, ohne mehr zu handeln.
Und hat doch nicht im viel zu großen Blick
die stille Milderung der Herde. Hat
nichts als Welt, hat Welt in jedem Aufschaun,
in jeder Neigung Welt. Ihm dringt, was andern
gerne gehört, unwirtlich wie Musik
und blind ins Blut und wandelt sich vorüber.

Da steht er nächtens auf und hat den Ruf
des Vogels draußen schon in seinem Dasein
und fühlt sich kühn, weil er die ganzen Sterne
in sein Gesicht nimmt, schwer—, o nicht wie einer,
der der Geliebten diese Nacht bereitet
und sie verwöhnt mit den gefühlten Himmeln.

[III]

Daß mir doch, wenn ich wieder der Städte Gedräng
und verwickelten Lärmknäul und die
Wirrsal des Fahrzeugs um mich habe, einzeln,
daß mir doch über das dichte Getrieb
Himmel erinnerte und der erdige Bergrand,
den von drüben heimwärts die Herde betrat.
Steinig sei mir zu Mut
und das Tagwerk des Hirten scheine mir möglich,
wie er einhergeht und bräunt und mit messendem Steinwurf
seine Herde besäumt, wo sie sich ausfranst.
Langsamen Schrittes, nicht leicht, nachdenklichen Körpers,
aber im Stehn ist er herrlich. Noch immer dürfte ein Gott
heimlich in diese Gestalt und würde nicht minder.
Abwechselnd weilt er und zieht, wie selber der Tag,
und Schatten der Wolken
durchgehn ihn, als dächte der Raum
langsam Gedanken für ihn.

\*

Why must a man keep standing like a shepherd,
exposed, in such an overflow of power,
so much a part of this event-filled landscape,
that if he were to lean back against a tree trunk
he would complete his destiny, forever.
Yet does not have, in his too open gaze,
the silent comfort of the flock: has nothing
but world; has world each time he lifts his head;
each time he looks down—world. What gladly yields
to others, pierces him like music, blindly
enters his blood, changes, disappears.

At night he stands up, the distant call of birds
already deep inside him; and feels bold
because he has taken all the galaxies
into his face, not lightly—, oh not like someone
who prepares a night like this for his beloved
and treats her to the skies that he has known.

## III

Let me, though, when again I have all around me
the chaos of cities, the tangled
skein of commotion, the blare of the traffic, alone,
let me, above the most dense confusion,
remember this sky and the darkening rim of the valley
where the flock appeared, echoing, on its way home.
Let my courage be like a rock,
let the daily task of the shepherd seem possible to me,
as he moves about and, throwing a stone to measure it,
fixes the hem of his flock where it has grown ragged.
His solemn, unhurried steps, his contemplative body,
his majesty when he stands: even today a god
could secretly enter this form and not be diminished.
He alternately lingers and moves, like the day itself,
and shadows of clouds
pass through him, like thoughts which space
is thinking, slowly, for him.

\*

Sei er wer immer für euch. Wie das wehende Nachtlicht
in den Mantel der Lampe stell ich mich innen in ihn.
Ein Schein wird ruhig. Der Tod
fände sich reiner zurecht.

Let him be whomever you wish. Like a fluttering candle
into a stormlamp, I place myself there inside him.
A glow becomes peaceful. May death
more easily find its way.

## DER GEIST ARIEL
*(Nach der Lesung von Shakespeares Sturm)*

Man hat ihn einmal irgendwo befreit
mit jenem Ruck, mit dem man sich als Jüngling
ans Große hinriß, weg von jeder Rücksicht.
Da ward er willens, sieh: und seither dient er,
nach jeder Tat gefaßt auf seine Freiheit.
Und halb sehr herrisch, halb beinah verschämt,
bringt mans ihm vor, daß man für dies und dies
ihn weiter brauche, ach, und muß es sagen,
*was* man ihm half. Und dennoch fühlt man selbst,
wie alles das, was man mit ihm zurückhält,
fehlt in der Luft. Verführend fast und süß:
ihn hinzulassen—, um dann, nicht mehr zaubernd,
ins Schicksal eingelassen wie die andern,
zu wissen, daß sich seine leichte Freundschaft,
jetzt ohne Spannung, nirgends mehr verpflichtet,
ein Überschuß zu dieses Atmens Raum,
gedankenlos im Element beschäftigt.
Abhängig fürder, länger nicht begabt,
den dumpfen Mund zu jenem Ruf zu formen,
auf den er stürzte. Machtlos, alternd, arm
und doch *ihn* atmend wie unfaßlich weit
verteilten Duft, der erst das Unsichtbare
vollzählig macht. Auflächelnd, daß man dem
so winken durfte, in so großen Umgang
so leicht gewöhnt. Aufweinend vielleicht auch,
wenn man bedenkt, wie's einen liebte und
fortwollte, beides, immer ganz in Einem.

(Ließ ich es schon? Nun schreckt mich dieser Mann,
der wieder Herzog wird. Wie er sich sanft
den Draht ins Haupt zieht und sich zu den andern
Figuren hängt und künftighin das Spiel

## ARIEL

*(After reading Shakespeare's* Tempest)

Once, somewhere, somehow, you had set him free
with that sharp jolt which as a young man tore you
out of your life and vaulted you to greatness.
Then he grew willing; and, since then, he serves,
after each task impatient for his freedom.
And half imperious, half almost ashamed,
you make excuses, say that you still need him
for this and that, and, ah, you must describe
*how* you helped him. Yet you feel, yourself,
that everything held back by his detention
is missing from the air. How sweet, how tempting:
to let him go—to give up all your magic,
submit yourself to destiny like the others,
and know that his light friendship, without strain now,
with no more obligations, anywhere,
an intensifying of this space you breathe,
is working in the element, thoughtlessly.
Henceforth dependent, never again empowered
to shape the torpid mouth into that call
at which he dived. Defenseless, aging, poor,
and yet still breathing *him* in, like a fragrance
spread endlessly, which makes the invisible
complete for the first time. Smiling that you ever
could summon him and feel so much at home
in that vast intimacy. Weeping too, perhaps,
when you remember how he loved and yet
wished to leave you: always both, at once.

(Have I let go already? I look on,
terrified by this man who has become
a duke again. How easily he draws
the wire through his head and hangs himself
up with the other puppets; then steps forward
to ask the audience for their applause

um Milde bittet. . . . Welcher Epilog
vollbrachter Herrschaft. Abtun, bloßes Dastehn
mit nichts als eigner Kraft: "und das ist wenig.")

and their indulgence. . . . What consummate power:
to lay aside, to stand there nakedly
with no strength but one's own, "which is most faint.")

So angestrengt wider die starke Nacht
werfen sie ihre Stimmen ins Gelächter,
das schlecht verbrennt. O aufgelehnte Welt
voll Weigerung. Und atmet doch den Raum,
in dem die Sterne gehen. Siehe, dies
bedürfte nicht und könnte, der Entfernung
fremd hingegeben, in dem Übermaß
von Fernen sich ergehen, fort von uns.
Und nun geruhts und reicht uns ans Gesicht
wie der Geliebten Aufblick; schlägt sich auf
uns gegenüber und zerstreut vielleicht
an uns sein Dasein. Und wir sinds nicht wert.
Vielleicht entziehts den Engeln etwas Kraft,
daß nach uns her der Sternenhimmel nachgiebt
und uns hereinhängt ins getrübte Schicksal.
Umsonst. Denn wer gewahrts? Und wo es einer
gewärtig wird: wer darf noch an den Nacht-Raum
die Stirne lehnen wie ans eigne Fenster?
Wer hat dies nicht verleugnet? Wer hat nicht
in dieses eingeborne Element
gefälschte, schlechte, nachgemachte Nächte
hereingeschleppt und sich daran begnügt?
Wir lassen Götter stehn um gohren Abfall,
denn Götter locken nicht. Sie haben Dasein
und nichts als Dasein, Überfluß von Dasein,
doch nicht Geruch, nicht Wink. Nichts ist so stumm
wie eines Gottes Mund. Schön wie ein Schwan
auf seiner Ewigkeit grundlosen Fläche:
so zieht der Gott und taucht und schont sein Weiß.

Alles verführt. Der kleine Vogel selbst
tut Zwang an uns aus seinem reinen Laubwerk,
die Blume hat nicht Raum und drängt herüber;
was will der Wind nicht alles? Nur der Gott,
wie eine Säule, läßt vorbei, verteilend
hoch oben, wo er trägt, nach beiden Seiten
die leichte Wölbung seines Gleichmuts.

## [Straining so hard against the strength of night]

Straining so hard against the strength of night,
they fling their tiny voices on the laughter
that will not burn. Oh disobedient world,
full of refusal. And yet it breathes the space
in which the stars revolve. It doesn't need us,
and, at any time, abandoned to the distance,
could spin off in remoteness, far from us.
And now it deigns to touch our faces, softly,
like a loved woman's glance; it opens up
in front of us, and may be spilling out
its essence on us. And we are not worth it.
Perhaps the angels' power is slightly lessened
when the sky with all its stars bends down to us
and hangs us here, into our cloudy fate.
In vain. For who has noticed it? And even
if someone has: who dares to lean his forehead
against the night as on a bedroom window?
Who has not disavowed it? Who has not
dragged into this pure inborn element
nights shammed and counterfeited, tinsel-nights,
and been content (how easily) with those?
We ignore the gods and fill our minds with trash.
For gods do not entice. They have their being,
and nothing else: an overflow of being.
Not scent or gesture. Nothing is so mute
as a god's mouth. As lovely as a swan
on its eternity of unfathomed surface,
the god glides by, plunges, and spares his whiteness.

Everything tempts. Even the little bird,
unseen among the pure leaves, can compel us;
the flower needs space and forces its way over;
what doesn't the wind lay claim to? Only the god,
like a pillar, lets us pass, distributing
high up, where he supports, to either side
the light arch of his equanimity.

Unwissend vor dem Himmel meines Lebens,
anstaunend steh ich. O die großen Sterne.
Aufgehendes und Niederstieg. Wie still.
Als wär ich nicht. Nehm ich denn Teil? Entriet ich
dem reinen Einfluß? Wechselt Flut und Ebbe
in meinem Blut nach dieser Ordnung? Abtun
will ich die Wünsche, jeden andern Anschluß,
mein Herz gewöhnen an sein Fernstes. Besser
es lebt im Schrecken seiner Sterne, als
zum Schein beschützt, von einer Näh beschwichtigt.

## [Ignorant before the heavens of my life]

Ignorant before the heavens of my life,
I stand and gaze in wonder. Oh the vastness
of the stars. Their rising and descent. How still.
As if I didn't exist. Do I have any
share in this? Have I somehow dispensed with
their pure effect? Does my blood's ebb and flow
change with their changes? Let me put aside
every desire, every relationship
except this one, so that my heart grows used to
its farthest spaces. Better that it live
fully aware, in the terror of its stars, than
as if protected, soothed by what is near.

Überfließende Himmel verschwendeter Sterne
prachten über der Kümmernis. Statt in die Kissen,
weine hinauf. Hier, an dem weinenden schon,
an dem endenden Antlitz,
um sich greifend, beginnt der hin-
reißende Weltraum. Wer unterbricht,
wenn du dort hin drängst,
die Strömung? Keiner. Es sei denn,
daß du plötzlich ringst mit der gewaltigen Richtung
jener Gestirne nach dir. Atme.
Atme das Dunkel der Erde und wieder
aufschau! Wieder. Leicht und gesichtlos
lehnt sich von oben Tiefe dir an. Das gelöste
nachtenthaltne Gesicht giebt dem deinigen Raum.

## [Overflowing heavens of lavished stars]

Overflowing heavens of lavished stars
glory above your grief. Not into your pillow:
weep upward. Here, close to your weeping face,
close to your face that is ending,
begins the expansive, ravishing, trans-
figuring world-space. Who would interrupt,
once you appear there,
that current? No one. Only yourself,
if you suddenly struggled out of the powerful impulse
of those stars streaming toward you. Breathe.
Breathe-in the darkness of earth and again
look up! Again. Airy and faceless,
from above, the depths bend toward you. The face that is
    dissolved
and contained in the night will give more space to your own.

Bestürz mich, Musik, mit rhythmischen Zürnen!
Hoher Vorwurf, dicht vor dem Herzen erhoben,
das nicht so wogend empfand, das sich schonte. Mein Herz:
    *da*:
sieh deine Herrlichkeit. Hast du fast immer Genüge,
minder zu schwingen? Aber die Wölbungen warten,
die obersten, daß du sie füllst mit orgelndem Andrang.
Was ersehnst du der fremden Geliebten verhaltenes
    Antlitz?—
Hat deine Sehnsucht nicht Atem, aus der Posaune des
    Engels,
der das Weltgericht anbricht, tönende Stürme zu stoßen:
oh, so *ist* sie auch nicht, nirgends, wird nicht geboren,
die du verdorrend entbehrst . . .

## [Startle me, Music, with rhythmical fury!]

Startle me, Music, with rhythmical fury!
Lofty reproach, lifted before the heart
that never could feel with such surges, that spared itself. My
    heart: *there:*
behold your magnificence. Are you almost always contented
with lesser vibrations? But the uppermost arches wait
for you to fill them with organ-resounding impulse.
Why do you long for the hidden face of the distant
    beloved?—
If your yearning lacks enough breath to compel
    ear-shattering storms
out of the angel's trumpet that will sound on the world's last
    day:
oh, then she too doesn't exist, anywhere, will never be born,
she in whose absence you are withering . . .

Hinter den schuld-losen Bäumen
langsam bildet die alte Verhängnis
ihr stummes Gesicht aus.
Falten ziehen dorthin . . .
Was ein Vogel hier aufkreischt,
springt dort als Weh-Zug
ab an dem harten Wahrsagermund.

O und die bald Liebenden
lächeln sich an, noch abschiedslos,
unter und auf über ihnen geht
sternbildhaft ihr Schicksal,
nächtig begeistert.
Noch zu erleben nicht reicht es sich ihnen,
noch wohnt es
schwebend im himmlischen Gang,
eine leichte Figur.

## [Behind the innocent trees]

Behind the innocent trees
old Destiny is slowly forming her mute
expressionless face.
Wrinkles are moving onto it . . .
What a bird screeches, here,
springs up there as a furrow of pain
on the harsh prophetic mouth.

Oh and the soon-to-be lovers
smile and are still departureless;
above them their fate sets and rises
like a constellation,
enraptured by night.
Not yet does it offer itself to them;
it remains
hovering in the paths of the sky,
an ethereal form.

## DIE GROSSE NACHT

Oft anstaunt ich dich, stand an gestern begonnenem Fenster,
stand und staunte dich an. Noch war mir die neue
Stadt wie verwehrt, und die unüberredete Landschaft
finsterte hin, als wäre ich nicht. Nicht gaben die nächsten
Dinge sich Müh, mir verständlich zu sein. An der Laterne
drängte die Gasse herauf: ich sah, daß sie fremd war.
Drüben—ein Zimmer, mitfühlbar, geklärt in der Lampe—,
schon nahm ich teil; sie empfandens, schlossen die Läden.
Stand. Und dann weinte ein Kind. Ich wußte die Mütter
rings in den Häusern, was sie vermögen—, und wußte
alles Weinens zugleich die untröstlichen Gründe.
Oder es sang eine Stimme und reichte ein Stück weit
aus der Erwartung heraus, oder es hustete unten
voller Vorwurf ein Alter, als ob sein Körper im Recht sei
wider die mildere Welt. Dann schlug eine Stunde—,
aber ich zählte zu spät, sie fiel mir vorüber.—
Wie ein Knabe, ein fremder, wenn man endlich ihn zuläßt,
doch den Ball nicht fängt und keines der Spiele
kann, die die andern so leicht an einander betreiben,
dasteht und wegschaut,—wohin—?: stand ich und plötzlich,
daß *du* umgehst mit mir, spielest, begriff ich, erwachsene
Nacht, und staunte dich an. Wo die Türme
zürnten, wo abgewendeten Schicksals
eine Stadt mich umstand und nicht zu erratende Berge
wider mich lagen, und im genäherten Umkreis
hungernde Fremdheit umzog das zufällige Flackern
meiner Gefühle—: da war es, du Hohe,
keine Schande für dich, daß du mich kanntest. Dein Atem
ging über mich. Dein auf weite Ernste verteiltes
Lächeln trat in mich ein.

# THE VAST NIGHT

Often I gazed at you in wonder: stood at the window begun
the day before, stood and gazed at you in wonder. As yet
the new city seemed forbidden to me, and the strange
unpersuadable landscape darkened as though
I didn't exist. Even the nearest Things
didn't care whether I understood them. The street
thrust itself up to the lamppost: I saw it was foreign.
Over there—a room, feelable, clear in the lamplight—,
I already took part; they noticed, and closed the shutters.
Stood. Then a child began crying. I knew what the mothers
all around, in the houses, were capable of—, and knew
the inconsolable origins of all tears.
Or a woman's voice sang and reached a little beyond
expectation, or downstairs an old man let out
a cough that was full of reproach, as though his body were
    right
and the gentler world mistaken. And then the hour
struck—, but I counted too late, it tumbled on past me.—
Like a new boy at school, who is finally allowed to join in,
but he can't catch the ball, is helpless at all the games
the others pursue with such ease, and he stands there staring
into the distance,—where—?: I stood there and suddenly
grasped that it was you: *you* were playing with me, grown-up
Night, and I gazed at you in wonder. Where the towers
were raging, where with averted fate
a city surrounded me, and indecipherable mountains
camped against me, and strangeness, in narrowing circles,
prowled around my randomly flickering emotions—:
it was then that in all your magnificence
you were not ashamed to know me. Your breath moved
    tenderly
over my face. And, spread across solemn distances,
your smile entered my heart.

Du im Voraus
verlorne Geliebte, Nimmergekommene,
nicht weiß ich, welche Töne dir lieb sind.
Nicht mehr versuch ich, dich, wenn das Kommende wogt,
zu erkennen. Alle die großen
Bilder in mir, im Fernen erfahrene Landschaft,
Städte und Türme und Brücken und un-
vermutete Wendung der Wege
und das Gewaltige jener von Göttern
einst durchwachsenen Länder:
steigt zur Bedeutung in mir
deiner, Entgehende, an.

Ach, die Gärten bist du,
ach, ich sah sie mit solcher
Hoffnung. Ein offenes Fenster
im Landhaus—, und du tratest beinahe
mir nachdenklich heran. Gassen fand ich,—
du warst sie gerade gegangen,
und die Spiegel manchmal der Läden der Händler
waren noch schwindlich von dir und gaben erschrocken
mein zu plötzliches Bild.—Wer weiß, ob derselbe
Vogel nicht hinklang durch uns
gestern, einzeln, im Abend?

## [You who never arrived]

You who never arrived
in my arms, Beloved, who were lost
from the start,
I don't even know what songs
would please you. I have given up trying
to recognize you in the surging wave of the next
moment. All the immense
images in me—the far-off, deeply-felt landscape,
cities, towers, and bridges, and un-
suspected turns in the path,
and those powerful lands that were once
pulsing with the life of the gods—
all rise within me to mean
you, who forever elude me.

You, Beloved, who are all
the gardens I have ever gazed at,
longing. An open window
in a country house—, and you almost
stepped out, pensive, to meet me. Streets that I chanced
    upon,—
you had just walked down them and vanished.
And sometimes, in a shop, the mirrors
were still dizzy with your presence and, startled, gave back
my too-sudden image. Who knows? perhaps the same
bird echoed through both of us
yesterday, separate, in the evening . . .

# WENDUNG

*Der Weg von der Innigkeit zur Größe*
*geht durch das Opfer.* —Kassner

Lange errang ers im Anschaun.
Sterne brachen ins Knie
unter dem ringenden Aufblick.
Oder er anschaute knieend,
und seines Instands Duft
machte ein Göttliches müd,
daß es ihm lächelte schlafend.

Türme schaute er so,
daß sie erschraken:
wieder sie bauend, hinan, plötzlich, in Einem!
Aber wie oft, die vom Tag
überladene Landschaft
ruhete hin in sein stilles Gewahren, abends.

Tiere traten getrost
in den offenen Blick, weidende,
und die gefangenen Löwen
starrten hinein wie in unbegreifliche Freiheit;
Vögel durchflogen ihn grad,
den gemütigen; Blumen
wiederschauten in ihn
groß wie in Kinder.

Und das Gerücht, daß ein Schauender sei,
rührte die minder,
fraglicher Sichtbaren,
rührte die Frauen.

Schauend wie lang?
Seit wie lange schon innig entbehrend,
flehend im Grunde des Blicks?

\*

## TURNING-POINT

*The road from intensity to greatness
passes through sacrifice.* —Kassner

For a long time he attained it in looking.
Stars would fall to their knees
beneath his compelling vision.
Or as he looked on, kneeling,
his urgency's fragrance
tired out a god until
it smiled at him in its sleep.

Towers he would gaze at so
that they were terrified:
building them up again, suddenly, in an instant!
But how often the landscape,
overburdened by day,
came to rest in his silent awareness, at nightfall.

Animals trusted him, stepped
into his open look, grazing,
and the imprisoned lions
stared in as if into an incomprehensible freedom;
birds, as it felt them, flew headlong
through it; and flowers, as enormous
as they are to children, gazed back
into it, on and on.

And the rumor that there was someone
who knew how to look,
stirred those less
visible creatures:
stirred the women.

Looking how long?
For how long now, deeply deprived,
beseeching in the depths of his glance?

\*

Wenn er, ein Wartender, saß in der Fremde; des Gasthofs
zerstreutes, abgewendetes Zimmer
mürrisch um sich, und im vermiedenen Spiegel
wieder das Zimmer
und später vom quälenden Bett aus
wieder:
da beriets in der Luft,
unfaßbar beriet es
über sein fühlbares Herz,
über sein durch den schmerzhaft verschütteten Körper
dennoch fühlbares Herz
beriet es und richtete:
daß es der Liebe nicht habe.

(Und verwehrte ihm weitere Weihen.)

Denn des Anschauns, siehe, ist eine Grenze.
Und die geschautere Welt
will in der Liebe gedeihn.

Werk des Gesichts ist getan,
tue nun Herz-Werk
an den Bildern in dir, jenen gefangenen; denn du
überwältigtest sie: aber nun kennst du sie nicht.
Siehe, innerer Mann, dein inneres Mädchen,
dieses errungene aus
tausend Naturen, dieses
erst nur errungene, nie
noch geliebte Geschöpf.

When he, whose vocation was Waiting, sat far from home—
the hotel's distracted unnoticing bedroom
moody around him, and in the avoided mirror
once more the room, and later
from the tormenting bed
once more:
then in the air the voices
discussed, beyond comprehension,
his heart, which could still be felt;
debated what through the painfully buried body
could somehow be felt—his heart;
debated and passed their judgment:
that it did not have love.

(And denied him further communions.)

For there is a boundary to looking.
And the world that is looked at so deeply
wants to flourish in love.

Work of the eyes is done, now
go and do heart-work
on all the images imprisoned within you; for you
overpowered them: but even now you don't know them.
Learn, inner man, to look on your inner woman,
the one attained from a thousand
natures, the merely attained but
not yet beloved form.

## KLAGE

Wem willst du klagen, Herz? Immer gemiedener
ringt sich dein Weg durch die unbegreiflichen
Menschen. Mehr noch vergebens vielleicht,
da er die Richtung behält,
Richtung zur Zukunft behält,
zu der verlorenen.

Früher. Klagtest? Was wars? Eine gefallene
Beere des Jubels, unreife.
Jetzt aber bricht mir mein Jubel-Baum,
bricht mir im Sturme mein langsamer
Jubel-Baum.
Schönster in meiner unsichtbaren
Landschaft, der du mich kenntlicher
machtest Engeln, unsichtbaren.

## LAMENT

Whom will you cry to, heart? More and more lonely,
your path struggles on through incomprehensible
mankind. All the more futile perhaps
for keeping to its direction,
keeping on toward the future,
toward what has been lost.

Once. You lamented? What was it? A fallen berry
of jubilation, unripe.
But now the whole tree of my jubilation
is breaking, in the storm it is breaking, my slow
tree of joy.
Loveliest in my invisible
landscape, you that made me more known
to the invisible angels.

## 'MAN MUSS STERBEN WEIL MAN SIE KENNT'

*('Papyrus Prisse'. Aus den Sprüchen des Ptah-hotep,*
*Handschrift um 2000 v. Ch.)*

'Man muß sterben weil man sie kennt.' Sterben
an der unsäglichen Blüte des Lächelns. Sterben
an ihren leichten Händen. Sterben
an Frauen.

Singe der Jüngling die tödlichen,
wenn sie ihm hoch durch den Herzraum
wandeln. Aus seiner blühenden Brust
sing er sie an:
unerreichbare! Ach, wie sie fremd sind.
Über den Gipfeln
seines Gefühls gehn sie hervor und ergießen
süß verwandelte Nacht ins verlassene
Tal seiner Arme. Es rauscht
Wind ihres Aufgangs im Laub seines Leibes. Es glänzen
seine Bäche dahin.

Aber der Mann
schweige erschütterter. Er, der
pfadlos die Nacht im Gebirg
seiner Gefühle geirrt hat:
schweige.

Wie der Seemann schweigt, der ältere,
und die bestandenen
Schrecken spielen in ihm wie in zitternden Käfigen.

# 'WE MUST DIE BECAUSE WE HAVE KNOWN THEM'

*(Papyrus Prisse. From the sayings of Ptah-hotep,
manuscript from ca. 2000 B.C.)*

'We must die because we have known them.' Die
of their smile's unsayable flower. Die
of their delicate hands. Die
of women.

Let the young man sing of them, praise
these death-bringers, when they move through his
  heart-space,
high overhead. From his blossoming breast
let him sing to them:
unattainable! Ah, how distant they are.
Over the peaks
of his feeling, they float and pour down
sweetly transfigured night into the abandoned
valley of his arms. The wind
of their rising rustles in the leaves of his body. His brooks
  run
sparkling into the distance.

But the grown man
shudders and is silent. The man who
has wandered pathless at night
in the mountain-range of his feelings:
is silent.

As the old sailor is silent,
and the terrors that he has endured
play inside him as though in quivering cages.

## AN HÖLDERLIN

Verweilung, auch am Vertrautesten nicht,
ist uns gegeben; aus den erfüllten
Bildern stürzt der Geist zu plötzlich zu füllenden; Seen
sind erst im Ewigen. Hier ist Fallen
das Tüchtigste. Aus dem gekonnten Gefühl
überfallen hinab ins geahndete, weiter.

Dir, du Herrlicher, war, dir war, du Beschwörer, ein ganzes
Leben das dringende Bild, wenn du es aussprachst,
die Zeile schloß sich wie Schicksal, ein Tod war
selbst in der lindesten, und du betratest ihn; aber
der vorgehende Gott führte dich drüben hervor.

O du wandelnder Geist, du wandelndster! Wie sie doch alle
wohnen im warmen Gedicht, häuslich, und lang
bleiben im schmalen Vergleich. Teilnehmende. Du nur
ziehst wie der Mond. Und unten hellt und verdunkelt
deine nächtliche sich, die heilig erschrockene Landschaft,
die du in Abschieden fühlst. Keiner
gab sie erhabener hin, gab sie ans Ganze
heiler zurück, unbedürftiger. So auch
spieltest du heilig durch nicht mehr gerechnete Jahre
mit dem unendlichen Glück, als wär es nicht innen, läge
keinem gehörend im sanften
Rasen der Erde umher, von göttlichen Kindern verlassen.
Ach, was die Höchsten begehren, du legtest es wunschlos
Baustein auf Baustein: es stand. Doch selber sein Umsturz
irrte dich nicht.

Was, da ein solcher, Ewiger, war, mißtraun wir
immer dem Irdischen noch? Statt am Vorläufigen ernst
die Gefühle zu lernen für welche
Neigung, künftig im Raum?

# TO HÖLDERLIN

We are not permitted to linger, even with what is most
intimate. From images that are full, the spirit
plunges on to others that suddenly must be filled;
there are no lakes till eternity. Here,
falling is best. To fall from the mastered emotion
into the guessed-at, and onward.

To you, O majestic poet, to you the compelling image,
O caster of spells, was a life, entire; when you uttered it
a line snapped shut like fate, there was a death
even in the mildest, and you walked straight into it; but
the god who preceded you led you out and beyond it.

O wandering spirit, most wandering of all! How snugly
the others live in their heated poems and stay,
content, in their narrow similes. Taking part. Only you
move like the moon. And underneath brightens and darkens
the nocturnal landscape, the holy, the terrified landscape,
which you feel in departures. No one
gave it away more sublimely, gave it back
more fully to the universe, without any need to hold on.
Thus for years that you no longer counted, holy, you played
with infinite joy, as though it were not inside you,
but lay, belonging to no one, all around
on the gentle lawns of the earth, where the godlike children
          had left it.
Ah, what the greatest have longed for: you built it, free of
          desire,
stone upon stone, till it stood. And when it collapsed,
even then you weren't bewildered.

Why, after such an eternal life, do we still
mistrust the earthly? Instead of patiently learning from
          transience
the emotions for what future
slopes of the heart, in pure space?

Ausgesetzt auf den Bergen des Herzens. Siehe, wie klein
    dort,
siehe: die letzte Ortschaft der Worte, und höher,
aber wie klein auch, noch ein letztes
Gehöft von Gefühl. Erkennst du's?
Ausgesetzt auf den Bergen des Herzens. Steingrund
unter den Händen. Hier blüht wohl
einiges auf; aus stummem Absturz
blüht ein unwissendes Kraut singend hervor.
Aber der Wissende? Ach, der zu wissen begann
und schweigt nun, augesetzt auf den Bergen des Herzens.
Da geht wohl, heilen Bewußtseins,
manches umher, manches gesicherte Bergtier,
wechselt und weilt. Und der große geborgene Vogel
kreist um der Gipfel reine Verweigerung.—Aber
ungeborgen, hier auf den Bergen des Herzens . . . .

## [Exposed on the cliffs of the heart]

Exposed on the cliffs of the heart. Look, how tiny down
    there,
look: the last village of words and, higher,
(but how tiny) still one last
farmhouse of feeling. Can you see it?
Exposed on the cliffs of the heart. Stoneground
under your hands. Even here, though,
something can bloom; on a silent cliff-edge
an unknowing plant blooms, singing, into the air.
But the one who knows? Ah, he began to know
and is quiet now, exposed on the cliffs of the heart.
While, with their full awareness,
many sure-footed mountain animals pass
or linger. And the great sheltered bird flies, slowly
circling, around the peak's pure denial.—But
without a shelter, here on the cliffs of the heart . . . .

Immer wieder, ob wir der Liebe Landschaft auch kennen
und den kleinen Kirchhof mit seinen klagenden Namen
und die furchtbar verschweigende Schlucht, in welcher die
   andern
enden: immer wieder gehn wir zu zweien hinaus
unter die alten Bäume, lagern uns immer wieder
zwischen die Blumen, gegenüber dem Himmel.

# [Again and again, however we know the landscape of love]

Again and again, however we know the landscape of love
and the little churchyard there, with its sorrowing names,
and the frighteningly silent abyss into which the others
fall: again and again the two of us walk out together
under the ancient trees, lie down again and again
among the flowers, face to face with the sky.

## DER TOD

Da steht der Tod, ein bläulicher Absud
in einer Tasse ohne Untersatz.
Ein wunderlicher Platz für eine Tasse:
steht auf dem Rücken einer Hand. Ganz gut
erkennt man noch an dem glasierten Schwung
den Bruch des Henkels. Staubig. Und: *'Hoff-nung'*
an ihrem Bug in aufgebrauchter Schrift.

Das hat der Trinker, den der Trank betrifft,
bei einem fernen Frühstück ab-gelesen.

Was sind denn das für Wesen,
die man zuletzt wegschrecken muß mit Gift?

Blieben sie sonst? Sind sie denn hier vernarrt
in dieses Essen voller Hindernis?
Man muß ihnen die harte Gegenwart
ausnehmen, wie ein künstliches Gebiß.
Dann lallen sie. Gelall, Gelall . . . .
. . . . . . . . . . . . . . . . . . . . . . . . . . .

O Sternenfall,
von einer Brücke einmal eingesehn—:
Dich nicht vergessen. Stehn!

# DEATH

There stands death, a bluish distillate
in a cup without a saucer. Such a strange
place to find a cup: standing on
the back of a hand. One recognizes clearly
the line along the glazed curve, where the handle
snapped. Covered with dust. And *HOPE* is written
across the side, in faded Gothic letters.

The man who was to drink out of that cup
read it aloud at breakfast, long ago.

What kind of beings are they then,
who finally must be scared away by poison?

Otherwise would they stay here? Would they keep
chewing so foolishly on their own frustration?
The hard present moment must be pulled
out of them, like a set of false teeth. Then
they mumble. They go on mumbling, mumbling. . . .
. . . . . . . . . . . . . . . . . . . . . . . . . . . . . . . . . . . . . . . . .

O shooting star
that fell into my eyes and through my body—:
Not to forget you. To endure.

## AN DIE MUSIK

Musik: Atem der Statuen. Vielleicht:
Stille der Bilder. Du Sprache wo Sprachen
enden. Du Zeit,
die senkrecht steht auf der Richtung vergehender Herzen.

Gefühle zu wem? O du der Gefühle
Wandlung in was?—: in hörbare Landschaft.
Du Fremde: Musik. Du uns entwachsener
Herzraum. Innigstes unser,
das, uns übersteigend, hinausdrängt,—
heiliger Abschied:
da uns das Innre umsteht
als geübteste Ferne, als andre
Seite der Luft:
rein,
riesig,
nicht mehr bewohnbar.

# TO MUSIC

Music: breathing of statues. Perhaps:
silence of paintings. You language where all language
ends. You time
standing vertically on the motion of mortal hearts.

Feelings for whom? O you the transformation
of feelings into what?—: into audible landscape.
You stranger: music. You heart-space
grown out of us. The deepest space *in* us,
which, rising above us, forces its way out,—
holy departure:
when the innermost point in us stands
outside, as the most practiced distance, as the other
side of the air:
pure,
boundless,
no longer habitable.

Du nur, einzig du *bist*.
Wir aber gehn hin, bis einmal
unsres Vergehens so viel ist,
daß du entstehst: Augenblick,
schöner, plötzlicher,
in der Liebe entstehst oder,
entzückt, in des Werkes Verkürzung.

Dein bin ich, dein; wieviel mir die Zeit auch
anhat. Von dir zu dir
bin ich befohlen. Dazwischen
hängt die Guirlande im Zufall, daß aber du sie
auf- und auf- und aufnimmst:
siehe: die Feste!

## [You, you only, exist]

You, you only, exist.
*We* pass away, till at last,
our passing is so immense
that you arise: beautiful moment,
in all your suddenness,
arising in love, or enchanted
in the contraction of work.

To you I belong, however time may
wear me away. From you to you
I go commanded. In between
the garland is hanging in chance; but if you
take it up and up and up: look:
all becomes festival!

## HAÏ-KAÏ

Kleine Motten taumeln schauernd quer aus dem Buchs;
sie sterben heute Abend und werden nie wissen,
daß es nicht Frühling war.

## HAIKU

Little moths stagger quivering out of the hedge;
they will die tonight and will never know
that it wasn't spring.

# Uncollected Poems

*1922–1926*

Wir, in den ringenden Nächten,
wir fallen von Nähe zu Nähe;
und wo die Liebende taut,
sind wir ein stürzender Stein.

## [We, in the struggling nights]

We, in the struggling nights,
keep falling from nearness to nearness;
where the woman in love is dew,
we are a plummeting stone.

## ODETTE R . . . .

Tränen, die innigsten, *steigen!*

O wenn ein Leben
völlig stieg und aus Wolken des eigenen Herzleids
niederfällt: so nennen wir Tod diesen Regen.

Aber fühlbarer wird darüber, uns Armen, das dunkle—,
köstlicher wird, uns Reichen, darüber das seltsame Erdreich.

## ODETTE R . . . .

Tears, the most fervent ones, *rise!*

Oh when a life has
wholly risen and from clouds of its own heart-grief
plunges down: we give the name death to that rain.

But more feelable because of that, becomes (to us in our
    poverty)—
more precious (to us in our wealth) becomes the strange
    dampened soil.

Wir sagen Reinheit und wir sagen Rose
und klingen an an alles, was geschieht;
dahinter aber ist das Namenlose
uns eigentlich Gebilde und Gebiet.

Mond ist uns Mann und Erde ist uns weiblich,
die Wiese scheint voll Demut, stolz der Wald;
doch über alles wandelt unbeschreiblich
die immer unentschiedene Gestalt.

Die Welt bleibt Kind; nur wir erwachsen leider.
Blume und Stern sind still, uns zuzusehn.
Und manchmal scheinen wir die Prüfung beider
und dürfen fühlen, wie sie uns bestehn.

## [We say release, and radiance, and roses]

We say release, and radiance, and roses,
and echo upon everything that's known;
and yet, behind the world our names enclose is
the nameless: our true archetype and home.

The sun seems male, and earth is like a woman,
the field is humble, and the forest proud;
but over everything we say, inhuman,
moves the forever-undetermined god.

We grow up; but the world remains a child.
Star and flower, in silence, watch us go.
And sometimes we appear to be the final
exam they must succeed on. And they do.

## IMAGINÄRER LEBENSLAUF

Erst eine Kindheit, grenzenlos und ohne
Verzicht und Ziel. O unbewußte Lust.
Auf einmal Schrecken, Schranke, Schule, Frohne
und Absturz in Versuchung und Verlust.

Trotz. Der Gebogene wird selber Bieger
und rächt an anderen, daß er erlag.
Geliebt, gefürchtet, Retter, Ringer, Sieger
und Überwinder, Schlag auf Schlag.

Und dann allein im Weiten, Leichten, Kalten.
Doch tief in der errichteten Gestalt
ein Atemholen nach dem Ersten, Alten . . .

Da stürzte Gott aus seinem Hinterhalt.

# IMAGINARY CAREER

At first a childhood, limitless and free
of any goals. Ah sweet unconsciousness.
Then sudden terror, schoolrooms, slavery,
the plunge into temptation and deep loss.

Defiance. The child bent becomes the bender,
inflicts on others what he once went through.
Loved, feared, rescuer, wrestler, victor,
he takes his vengeance, blow by blow.

And now in vast, cold, empty space, alone.
Yet hidden deep within the grown-up heart,
a longing for the first world, the ancient one . . .

Then, from His place of ambush, God leapt out.

## TRÄNENKRÜGLEIN

Andere fassen den Wein, andere fassen die Öle
in dem gehöhlten Gewölb, das ihre Wandung umschrieb.
Ich, als ein kleineres Maß, und als schlankestes, höhle
mich einem andern Bedarf, stürzenden Tränen zulieb.

Wein wird reicher, und Öl klärt sich noch weiter im Kruge.
Was mit den Tränen geschieht?—Sie machten mich schwer,
machten mich blinder und machten mich schillern am Buge,
machten mich brüchig zuletzt und machten mich leer.

## LITTLE TEAR-VASE

Other vessels hold wine, other vessels hold oil
inside the hollowed-out vault circumscribed by their clay.
I, as a smaller measure, and as the slimmest of all,
humbly hollow myself so that just a few tears can fill me.

Wine becomes richer, oil becomes clear, in its vessel.
What happens with tears?—They made me blind in my
    glass,
made me heavy and made my curve iridescent,
made me brittle, and left me empty at last.

## ZUEIGNUNG AN M . . . .

*geschrieben am 6. und 8. November 1923*
*(als Arbeits-Anfang eines neuen Winters auf Muzot)*


Schaukel des Herzens. O sichere, an welchem unsichtbaren
Aste befestigt. Wer, wer gab dir den Stoß,
daß du mit mir bis ins Laub schwangst.
Wie nahe war ich den Früchten, köstlichen. Aber nicht
	Bleiben
ist im Schwunge der Sinn. Nur das Nahesein, nur
am immer zu Hohen plötzlich das mögliche
Nahsein. Nachbarschaften und dann
von unaufhaltsam erschwungener Stelle
—wieder verlorener schon—der neue, der Ausblick.
Und jetzt: die befohlene Umkehr
zurück und hinüber hinaus in des Gleichgewichts Arme.
Unten, dazwischen, das Zögern, der irdische Zwang, der
	Durchgang
durch die Wende der Schwere—, vorbei: und es spannt sich
	die Schleuder,
von der Neugier des Herzens beschwert,
in das andere Gegenteil aufwärts.
Wieder wie anders, wie neu! Wie sie sich beide beneiden
an den Enden des Seils, diese Hälften der Lust.

Oder, wag ich es: Viertel?—Und rechne, weil er sich weigert,
jenen, den Halbkreis hinzu, der die Schaukel verstößt?
Nicht ertäusch ich mir ihn, als meiner hiesigen Schwünge
Spiegel. Errat nichts. Er sei
einmal neuer. Aber von Endpunkt zu Endpunkt
meines gewagtesten Schwungs nehm ich ihn schon in Besitz:
Überflüsse aus mir stürzen dorthin und erfülln ihn,
spannen ihn fast. Und mein eigener Abschied,
wenn die werfende Kraft an ihm abbricht,
macht ihn mir eigens vertraut.

# DEDICATION TO M . . . .

*written on the 6th and 8th of November, 1923*
*(as the beginning of a new winter's work at Muzot)*

Swing of the heart. O firmly hung, fastened on what
invisible branch. Who, who gave you the push,
that you swung with me into the leaves?
How near I was to the exquisite fruits. But not-staying
is the essence of this motion. Only the nearness, only
toward the forever-too-high, all at once the possible
nearness. Vicinities, then
from an irresistibly swung-up-to place
—already, once again, lost—the new sight, the outlook.
And now: the commanded return
back and across and into equilibrium's arms.
Below, in between, hesitation, the pull of earth, the passage
through the turning-point of the heavy—, past it: and the
    catapult stretches,
weighted with the heart's curiosity,
to the other side, opposite, upward.
Again how different, how new! How they envy each other
at the ends of the rope, these opposite halves of pleasure.

Or, shall I dare it: these quarters?—And include, since it
    withholds itself,
that other half-circle, the one whose impetus pushes the
    swing?
I'm not just imagining it, as the mirror of my here-and-now
arcs. Guess nothing. It will be
newer someday. But from endpoint to endpoint
of the arc that I have most dared, I already fully possess it:
overflowings from me plunge over to it and fill it,
stretch it apart, almost. And my own parting,
when the force that pushes me someday
stops, makes it all the more near.

## FÜR MAX PICARD

Da stehen wir mit Spiegeln:
einer dort . . . . . . , und fangen auf,
und einer da, am Ende nicht verständigt;
auffangend aber und das Bild weither
uns zuerkennend, dieses reine Bild
dem andern reichend aus dem Glanz des Spiegels.
Ballspiel für Götter. Spiegelspiel, in dem
vielleicht drei Bälle, vielleicht neun sich kreuzen,
und keiner jemals, seit sich Welt besann,
fiel je daneben. Fänger, die wir sind.
Unsichtbar kommt es durch die Luft, und dennoch,
wie ganz der Spiegel ihm begegnet, diesem
(in ihm nur völlig Ankunft) diesem Bild,
das nur so lang verweilt, bis wir ermessen,
mit wieviel Kraft es weiter will, wohin.

Nur dies. Und dafür war die lange Kindheit,
und Not und Neigung und der tiefe Abschied
war nur für dieses. Aber dieses lohnt.

## FOR MAX PICARD

Here we stand with mirrors:
someone over there. . . . , and catch,
and someone here, not truly in agreement;
catching, though, and passing on the image
we've glimpsed from far off, passing this pure image
on to the other from the mirror's gleam.
Ball-game for gods. Mirror-game, in which
perhaps three balls, or perhaps nine, will cross
and not one of them, since world began to think,
ever fell wide. Catchers that we are.
Invisible it comes through the air, and yet
how entirely the mirror meets it, this
(only within it fully realized) image,
which stays just long enough for us to judge
what force it will continue with, and where.

Just this. And for its sake was our long childhood,
and grief and inclination and deep parting
was just for this. But this is worth it, all.

## FÜR HANS CAROSSA

Auch noch Verlieren ist *unser*; und selbst das Vergessen
hat noch Gestalt in dem bleibenden Reich der Verwandlung.
Losgelassenes kreist; und sind wir auch selten die Mitte
einem der Kreise: sie ziehn um uns die heile Figur.

## FOR HANS CAROSSA

Losing too is still *ours*; and even forgetting
still has a shape in the kingdom of transformation.
When something's let go of, it circles; and though we are
    rarely the center
of the circle, it draws around us its unbroken, marvelous
    curve.

## DER MAGIER

Er ruft es an. Es schrickt zusamm und steht.
Was steht? Das Andre; alles, was nicht er ist,
wird Wesen. Und das ganze Wesen dreht
ein raschgemachtes Antlitz her, das mehr ist.

Oh Magier, halt aus, halt aus, halt aus!
Schaff Gleichgewicht. Steh ruhig auf der Waage,
damit sie einerseits dich und das Haus
und drüben jenes Angewachsne trage.

Entscheidung fällt. Die Bindung stellt sich her.
Er weiß, der Anruf überwog das Weigern.
Doch sein Gesicht, wie mit gedeckten Zeigern,
hat Mitternacht. Gebunden ist auch er.

## THE MAGICIAN

He calls it up. It shudders and begins.
What does? The Other; all that he is not
comes into being. And the whole being turns
a sudden face, far realer than he thought.

Magician, oh endure, endure, endure!
Make equilibrium. Stand upon one scale
with all you own, and let the far side bear
It, growing to decision or denial.

The spell takes hold. He knows the scales have tipped,
the call weighs heavier. Yet his face, as though
its hour-hand and minute- overlapped,
has stopped at midnight. He is spell-bound too.

Da dich das geflügelte Entzücken
über manchen frühen Abgrund trug,
baue jetzt der unerhörten Brücken
kühn berechenbaren Bug.

Wunder ist nicht nur im unerklärten
Überstehen der Gefahr;
erst in einer klaren reingewährten
Leistung wird das Wunder wunderbar.

Mitzuwirken ist nicht Überhebung
an dem unbeschreiblichen Bezug,
immer inniger wird die Verwebung,
nur Getragensein ist nicht genug.

Deine ausgeübten Kräfte spanne,
bis sie reichen, zwischen zwein
Widersprüchen . . . Denn im Manne
will der Gott beraten sein.

# [As once the wingèd energy of delight]

As once the wingèd energy of delight
carried you over childhood's dark abysses,
now beyond your own life build the great
arch of unimagined bridges.

Wonders happen if we can succeed
in passing through the harshest danger;
but only in a bright and purely granted
achievement can we realize the wonder.

To work *with* Things in the indescribable
relationship is not too hard for us;
the pattern grows more intricate and subtle,
and being swept along is not enough.

Take your practiced powers and stretch them out
until they span the chasm between two
contradictions . . . For the god
wants to know himself in you.

An der sonngewohnten Straße, in dem
hohlen halben Baumstamm, der seit lange
Trog ward, eine Oberfläche Wasser
in sich leis erneuernd, still' ich meinen
Durst: des Wassers Heiterkeit und Herkunft
in mich nehmend durch die Handgelenke.
Trinken schiene mir zu viel, zu deutlich;
aber diese wartende Gebärde
holt mir helles Wasser ins Bewußtsein.

Also, kämst du, braucht ich, mich zu stillen,
nur ein leichtes Anruhn meiner Hände,
sei's an deiner Schulter junge Rundung,
sei es an den Andrang deiner Brüste.

# [Along the sun-drenched roadside, from the great]

Along the sun-drenched roadside, from the great
hollow half-treetrunk, which for generations
has been a trough, renewing in itself
an inch or two of rain, I satisfy
my thirst: taking the water's pristine coolness
into my whole body through my wrists.
Drinking would be too powerful, too clear;
but this unhurried gesture of restraint
fills my whole consciousness with shining water.

Thus, if you came, I could be satisfied
to let my hand rest lightly, for a moment,
lightly, upon your shoulder or your breast.

Durch den sich Vögel werfen, ist nicht der
vertraute Raum, der die Gestalt dir steigert.
(Im Freien, dorten, bist du dir verweigert
und schwindest weiter ohne Wiederkehr.)

Raum greift aus uns und übersetzt die Dinge:
daß dir das Dasein eines Baums gelinge,
wirf Innenraum um ihn, aus jenem Raum,
der in dir west. Umgieb ihn mit Verhaltung.
Er grenzt sich nicht. Erst in der Eingestaltung
in dein Verzichten wird er wirklich Baum.

[What birds plunge through is not
the intimate space]

What birds plunge through is not the intimate space
in which you see all forms intensified.
(Out in the Open, you would be denied
your self, would disappear into that vastness.)

Space reaches *from* us and construes the world:
to know a tree, in its true element,
throw inner space around it, from that pure
abundance in you. Surround it with restraint.
It has no limits. Not till it is held
in your renouncing is it truly there.

## DAUER DER KINDHEIT
*(Für E.M.)*

Lange Nachmittage der Kindheit . . . ., immer noch nicht
Leben; immer noch Wachstum,
das in den Knien zieht—, wehrlose Wartezeit.
Und zwischen dem, was man sein wird, vielleicht,
und diesem randlosen Dasein—: Tode,
unzählige. Liebe umkreist, die besitzende,
das immer heimlich verratene Kind
und verspricht es der Zukunft; nicht seiner.

Nachmittage, da es allein blieb, von einem Spiegel zum
        andern
starrend; anfragend beim Rätsel des eigenen
Namens: Wer? Wer?—Aber die Andern
kehren nachhause und überwältigens.
Was ihm das Fenster, was ihm der Weg,
was ihm der dumpfe Geruch einer Lade
gestern vertraut hat: sie übertönens, vereitelns.
Wieder wird es ein Ihriges.
Ranken werfen sich so manchmal aus dichteren
Büschen heraus, wie sich sein Wunsch auswirft
aus dem Gewirr der Familie, schwankend in Klarheit.
Aber sie stumpfen ihm täglich den Blick an ihren
        gewohnteren
Wänden, jenen, den Aufblick, der den Hunden begegnet
und höhere Blumen
immer noch fast gegenüber hat.

Oh wie weit ists von diesem
überwachten Geschöpf zu allem, was einmal
sein Wunder sein wird, oder sein Untergang.
Seine unmündige
Kraft lernt List zwischen den Fallen.

Und das Gestirn seiner künftigen Liebe

# DURATION OF CHILDHOOD
*(For E.M.)*

Long afternoons of childhood . . . . , not yet really
life; still only growing-time
that drags at the knees—, time of defenseless waiting.
And between what we will perhaps become
and this edgeless existence—: deaths,
uncountable. Love, the possessive, surrounds
the child forever betrayed in secret
and promises him to the future; which is not his own.

Afternoons that he spent by himself, staring
from mirror to mirror; puzzling himself with the riddle
of his own name: Who? Who?—But the others
come home again, overwhelm him.
What the window or path
or the mouldy smell of a drawer
confided to him yesterday: they drown it out and destroy it.
Once more he belongs to them.
As tendrils sometimes fling themselves out from the thicker
bushes, his desire will fling itself out
from the tangle of family and hang there, swaying in the
    light.
But daily they blunt his glance upon their inhabited
walls—that wide innocent glance which lets dogs in
and holds the tall flowers,
still almost face to face.

Oh how far it is
from this watched-over creature to everything that will
    someday
be his wonder or his destruction.
His immature strength
learns cunning among the traps.

But the constellation

geht doch schon längst unter den Sternen,
gültig. Welches Erschrecken
wird ihm das Herz einmal reißen dorthin,
daß es abkommt vom Weg seiner Flucht
und gerät in Gehorsam und heiteren Einfluß?

of his future love has long
been moving among the stars. What terror
will tear his heart out of the track of its fleeing
to place it in perfect submission, under the calm
influence of the heavens?

Welt war in dem Antlitz der Geliebten—,
aber plötzlich ist sie ausgegossen:
Welt ist draußen, Welt ist nicht zu fassen.

Warum trank ich nicht, da ich es aufhob,
aus dem vollen, dem geliebten Antlitz
Welt, die nah war, duftend meinem Munde?

Ach, ich trank. Wie trank ich unerschöpflich.
Doch auch ich war angefüllt mit zuviel
Welt, und trinkend ging ich selber über.

## [World was in the face of the beloved]

World was in the face of the beloved—,
but suddenly it poured out and was gone:
world is outside, world can not be grasped.

Why didn't I, from the full, beloved face
as I raised it to my lips, why didn't I drink
world, so near that I could almost taste it?

Ah, I drank. Insatiably I drank.
But I was filled up also, with too much
world, and, drinking, I myself ran over.

## HANDINNERES

Innres der Hand. Sohle, die nicht mehr geht
als auf Gefühl. Die sich nach oben hält
und im Spiegel
himmlische Straßen empfängt, die selber
wandelnden.
Die gelernt hat, auf Wasser zu gehn,
wenn sie schöpft,
die auf den Brunnen geht,
aller Wege Verwandlerin.
Die auftritt in anderen Händen,
die ihresgleichen
zur Landschaft macht:
wandert und ankommt in ihnen,
sie anfüllt mit Ankunft.

## PALM

Interior of the hand. Sole that has come to walk
only on feelings. That faces upward
and in its mirror
receives heavenly roads, which travel
along themselves.
That has learned to walk upon water
when it scoops,
that walks upon wells,
transfiguring every path.
That steps into other hands,
changes those that are like it
into a landscape:
wanders and arrives within them,
fills them with arrival.

## SCHWERKRAFT

Mitte, wie du aus allen
dich ziehst, auch noch aus Fliegenden dich
wiedergewinnst, Mitte, du Stärkste.

Stehender: wie ein Trank den Durst
durchstürzt ihn die Schwerkraft.

Doch aus dem Schlafenden fällt,
wie aus lagernder Wolke,
reichlicher Regen der Schwere.

# GRAVITY

Center, how from all beings
you pull yourself, even from those that fly
winning yourself back, irresistible center.

He who stands: as a drink through thirst
gravity plunges down through him.

But from the sleeper falls
(as though from a motionless cloud)
the abundant rain of the heavy.

## MAUSOLEUM

Königsherz. Kern eines hohen
Herrscherbaums. Balsamfrucht.
Goldene Herznuß. Urnen-Mohn
mitten im Mittelbau,
(wo der Widerhall abspringt,
wie ein Splitter der Stille,
wenn du dich rührst,
weil es dir scheint,
daß deine vorige
Haltung zu laut war . . .)
Völkern entzogenes,
sterngesinnt,
im unsichtbaren Kreisen
kreisendes Königsherz.

Wo ist, wohin,
jenes der leichten
Lieblingin?
: Lächeln, von außen,
auf die zögernde Rundung
heiterer Früchte gelegt;
oder der Motte, vielleicht,
Kostbarkeit, Florflügel, Fühler . . .

Wo aber, wo, das sie sang,
das sie in Eins sang,
das Dichterherz?
: Wind,
unsichtbar,
Windinnres.

# MAUSOLEUM

King's-heart. Core of a high
ruler-tree. Balsam-fruit.
Golden heart-nut. Urn-poppy
in the center of the central shrine
(where the echo rebounds,
like a splinter of silence,
when you make a movement
because you can feel
that the way you were standing
was a little too noisy . . . ),
removed from the nations,
star-inclined,
in invisible orbits
orbiting king's-heart.

Where has it gone,
the heart of the gentle
Beloved?
: Smile, from outside
placed on the hesitant
roundness of cheerful fruits;
or, it may be, the moth's
preciousness, gauze-wing, feeler . . .

Where, though, where is the heart
that sang them both into oneness,
the poet's-heart?
: Wind,
invisible,
wind's-inside.

## Ô LACRIMOSA

*(Trilogie, zu einer künftigen Musik von Ernst Křenek)*

### I

Oh Tränenvolle, die, verhaltner Himmel,
über der Landschaft ihres Schmerzes schwer wird.
Und wenn sie weint, so weht ein weicher Schauer
schräglichen Regens an des Herzens Sandschicht.

Oh Tränenschwere. Waage aller Tränen!
Die sich nicht Himmel fühlte, da sie klar war,
und Himmel sein muß um der Wolken willen.

Wie wird es deutlich und wie nah, dein Schmerzland,
unter des strengen Himmels Einheit. Wie ein
in seinem Liegen langsam waches Antlitz,
das waagrecht denkt, Welttiefe gegenüber.

### II

Nichts als ein Atemzug ist das Leere, und jenes
grüne Gefülltsein der schönen
Bäume: ein Atemzug!
Wir, die Angeatmeten noch,
heute noch Angeatmeten, zählen
diese, der Erde, langsame Atmung,
deren Eile wir sind.

### III

Aber die Winter! Oh diese heimliche
Einkehr der Erde. Da um die Toten
in dem reinen Rückfall der Säfte
Kühnheit sich sammelt,
künftiger Frühlinge Kühnheit.
Wo das Erdenken geschieht
unter der Starre; wo das von den großen

# O LACRIMOSA

*(trilogy for future music of Ernst Křenek)*

## I

Oh tear-filled figure who, like a sky held back,
grows heavy above the landscape of her sorrow.
And when she weeps, the gentle raindrops fall,
slanting upon the sand-bed of her heart.

Oh heavy with weeping. Scale to weigh all tears.
Who felt herself not sky, since she was shining
and sky exists only for clouds to form in.

How clear it is, how close, your land of sorrow,
beneath the stern sky's oneness. Like a face
that lies there, slowly waking up and thinking
horizontally, into endless depths.

## II

It is nothing but a breath, the void.
And that green fulfillment
of blossoming trees: a breath.
We, who are still the breathed-upon,
today still the breathed-upon, count
this slow breathing of earth,
whose hurry we are.

## III

Ah, but the winters! The earth's mysterious
turning-within. Where around the dead
in the pure receding of sap,
boldness is gathered,
the boldness of future springtimes.
Where imagination occurs
beneath what is rigid; where all the green

Sommern abgetragene Grün
wieder zum neuen
Einfall wird und zum Spiegel des Vorgefühls;
wo die Farbe der Blumen
jenes Verweilen unserer Augen vergißt.

worn thin by the vast summers
again turns into a new
insight and the mirror of intuition;
where the flowers' color
wholly forgets that lingering of our eyes.

Ach, nicht getrennt sein,
nicht durch so wenig Wandung
ausgeschlossen vom Sternen-Maß.
Innres, was ists?
Wenn nicht gesteigerter Himmel,
durchworfen mit Vögeln und tief
von Winden der Heimkehr.

## [Ah, not to be cut off]

Ah, not to be cut off,
not through the slightest partition
shut out from the law of the stars.
The inner—what is it?
if not intensified sky,
hurled through with birds and deep
with the winds of homecoming.

Jetzt wär es Zeit, daß Götter träten aus
bewohnten Dingen . . .
Und daß sie jede Wand in meinem Haus
umschlügen. Neue Seite. Nur der Wind,
den solches Blatt im Wenden würfe, reichte hin,
die Luft, wie eine Scholle, umzuschaufeln:
ein neues Atemfeld. Oh Götter, Götter!
Ihr Oftgekommnen, Schläfer in den Dingen,
die heiter aufstehn, die sich an den Brunnen,
die wir vermuten, Hals und Antlitz waschen
und die ihr Ausgeruhtsein leicht hinzutun
zu dem, was voll scheint, unserm vollen Leben.
Noch einmal sei es euer Morgen, Götter.
Wir wiederholen. Ihr allein seid Ursprung.
Die Welt steht auf mit euch, und Anfang glänzt
an allen Bruchstelln unseres Mißlingens . . .

## [Now it is time that gods came walking out]

Now it is time that gods came walking out
of lived-in Things . . .
Time that they came and knocked down every wall
inside my house. New page. Only the wind
from such a turning could be strong enough
to toss the air as a shovel tosses dirt:
a fresh-turned field of breath. O gods, gods!
who used to come so often and are still
asleep in the Things around us, who serenely
rise and at wells that we can only guess at
splash icy water on your necks and faces,
and lightly add your restedness to what seems
already filled to bursting: our full lives.
Once again let it be your morning, gods.
We keep repeating. You alone are source.
With you the world arises, and your dawn
gleams on each crack and crevice of our failure . . .

Rose, oh reiner Widerspruch, Lust,
Niemandes Schlaf zu sein unter soviel
Lidern.

## [Rose, oh pure contradiction]

Rose, oh pure contradiction, joy
of being No-one's sleep under so many
lids.

## IDOL

Gott oder Göttin des Katzenschlafs,
kostende Gottheit, die in dem dunkeln
Mund reife Augen-Beeren zerdrückt,
süßgewordnen Schauns Traubensaft,
ewiges Licht in der Krypta des Gaumens.
Schlaf-Lied nicht,—Gong! Gong!
Was die anderen Götter beschwört,
entläßt diesen verlisteten Gott
an seine einwärts fallende Macht.

## IDOL

God or goddess of the sleep of cats,
savoring godhead that in the dark
vat of the mouth crushes eye-berries, ripe,
into the sweet-grown nectar of vision,
eternal light in the palate's crypt.
Not a lullaby,—Gong! Gong!
What casts a spell over other gods
lets this most cunning god escape
into his ever-receding power.

## GONG

Nicht mehr für Ohren . . . : Klang,
der, wie ein tieferes Ohr,
uns, scheinbar Hörende, hört.
Umkehr der Räume. Entwurf
innerer Welten im Frein . . . ,
Tempel vor ihrer Geburt,
Lösung, gesättigt mit schwer
löslichen Göttern . . . : Gong!

Summe des Schweigenden, das
sich zu sich selber bekennt,
brausende Einkehr in sich
dessen, das an sich verstummt,
Dauer, aus Ablauf gepreßt,
um-gegossener Stern . . . : Gong!

Du, die man niemals vergißt,
die sich gebar im Verlust,
nichtmehr begriffenes Fest,
Wein an unsichtbarem Mund,
Sturm in der Säule, die trägt,
Wanderers Sturz in den Weg,
unser, an Alles, Verrat . . . : Gong!

# GONG

No longer for ears . . . : sound
which, like a deeper ear,
hears *us,* who only seem
to be hearing. Reversal of spaces.
Projection of innermost worlds
into the Open . . . , temple
before their birth, solution
saturated with gods
that are almost insoluble . . . : Gong!

Sum of all silence, which
acknowledges itself to itself,
thunderous turning-within
of what is struck dumb in itself,
duration pressed from time passing,
star re-liquefied . . . : Gong!

You whom one never forgets,
who gave birth to herself in loss,
festival no longer grasped,
wine on invisible lips,
storm in the pillar that upholds,
wanderer's plunge on the path,
our treason, to everything . . . : Gong!

*À Monique:*
*un petit recueillement de ma gratitude*

## L'Heure du Thé

Buvant dans cette tasse sur laquelle, dans une langue inconnue, sont peut-être inscrits des signes de bénédiction et de bonheur, je la tiens dans cette main pleine de lignes à son tour que je ne saurais expliquer. Sont-elles d'accord ces deux écritures, et puisqu'elles sont seules entre elles et toujours secrètes souls la coupole de mon regard, vont-elles dialoguer à leur façon et se concilier, ces deux textes millénaires qu'un geste de buveur rapproche?

## Chapelle Rustique

Comme la maison est calme: écoute! Mais, là-haut, dans la blanche chapelle, d'où vient ce surcroît de silence?—De tous ceux qui depuis plus d'un siècle y sont entrés pour ne pas être dehors, et qui, en s'agenouillant, se sont effrayés de leur bruit? De cet argent qui, en tombant dans le tronc, a perdu sa voix et qui n'aura qu'un petit bruissement de grillon quand il sera recueilli? Ou de cette douce absence de Sainte-Anne, patronne du sanctuaire, qui n'ose pas approcher, pour ne pas abîmer cette pure distance que suppose un appel?

## "Farfallettina"

Toute agitée elle arrive vers la lampe, et son vertige lui donne un dernier répit confus avant d'être brûlée. Elle s'est abattue sur le vert tapis de la table, et sur ce fond avantageux s'étale pour un instant (pour une durée à elle que nous ne saurions mesurer) le luxe de son inconcevable splendeur. On dirait, en trop petit, une dame qui avait une panne en se rendant au Théâtre. Elle n'y arrivera point. Et d'ailleurs où est le Théâtre pour de si frêles spectateurs? . . . Ses ailes dont on aperçoit les minuscules baguettes d'or remuent comme un double éventail devant nulle figure; et, entre elles, ce corps mince, bilboquet où sont retombés deux yeux en boule d'émeraude . . .

## [FOUR SKETCHES]

*To Monique:*
*a small reflection of my gratitude*

### Teatime

Drinking from this cup inscribed with signs in an unknown language, perhaps a message of blessing and joy, I hold it in this hand full of its own indecipherable lines. Do the two messages agree? And since they are alone with each other and forever hidden beneath the dome of my gaze, will they talk to each other in their own way and be reconciled, these two ancient texts brought together by the gesture of a man drinking tea?

### Rustic Chapel

How calm the house is: listen! But up there, in the white chapel, where does that greater silence come from?—From all those who, for more than a century, have come in so as not to be out in the cold and, kneeling down, have been frightened at their own noise? From the money that lost its voice falling into the collection box and will speak in just a small cricket-chirp when it is taken out? Or from the sweet absence of Saint Anne, the sanctuary's patron, who doesn't dare to come closer, lest she damage that pure distance which a call implies?

### "Farfallettina"

Shaking all over, she arrives near the lamp, and her dizziness grants her one last vague reprieve before she goes up in flames. She has fallen onto the green tablecloth, and upon that advantageous background she stretches out for a moment (for a unit of her own time which we have no way of measuring) the profusion of her inconceivable splendor. She looks like a miniature lady who is having a heart attack on the way to the theater. She will never arrive. Besides, where is there a theater for such fragile spectators? . . . Her wings, with their tiny golden threads, are moving like a double fan in front of no face; and between them is this thin body, a bilboquet onto which two eyes like emerald balls have fallen back . . .

C'est en toi, ma belle, que Dieu s'est épuisé. Il te lance à la flamme pour regagner un peu de sa force. (Comme un enfant qui casse sa tirelire.)

## Le Mangeur de Mandarines

Oh quelle prévoyance! Ce lapin entre les fruits. Pense! trente sept petits noyaux dans un seul exemplaire prêts à tomber un peu partout et à faire progéniture. Il a fallu que nous corrigions ça. Elle eût été capable de peupler la terre cette petite Mandarine entêtée qui porte une robe si large comme si elle devait encore grandir. Mal habillée en somme; plus occupée de multiplication que de mode. Montre-lui la grenade dans son armure de cuir de Cordoue: elle éclate d'avenir, se retient, dédaigne. . . . Et laissant entrevoir sa lignée possible, elle l'étouffe dans un berceau de pourpre. La terre lui semble trop évasive pour faire avec elle un pacte d'abondance.

It is in you, my dear, that God has exhausted himself. He tosses you into the fire so that he can recover a bit of his strength. (Like a little boy breaking into his piggy bank.)

## The Tangerine-eater

Oh what foresight! This rabbit of the fruit-world! Imagine: thirty-seven little pits in a single specimen, ready to fall every-which-way and create offspring. We had to correct that. She could have populated the whole earth—this little headstrong Tangerine, wearing a dress too big for herself, as if she intended to keep on growing. In short: badly dressed; more concerned with reproduction than with style. Show her the pomegranate, in her armor of Cordova leather: *she* is bursting with future, holds herself back, condescends. . . . And, letting us catch just a glimpse of her possible progeny, she smothers them in a dark-red cradle. She thinks earth is too evasive to sign a pact of abundance.

## FÜR VERONIKA ERDMANN

Daß solcher Auftrag *unser* Auftrag werde,
wieviel Gehorsam, wieviel Frohn.
Ach, zwischen unseren Zeilen singt die Erde
und reißt uns weiter vom Geräusch zum Ton.

Oder ist es der Widerstand, der besser
in uns den gültigen Vollzug erzieht?
Der Liebendste: ein Mörder ohne Messer?
Und das Bedrohteste des Lebens: Lied?

## FOR VERONIKA ERDMANN

That such a mission may become *our* mission,
how much obedience, how much joy.
Between our lines the earth is singing with us
and sweeps us on from noise to melody.

Or is it opposition that must drive
us to create a valid Thing?
Is love: a murderer without a knife?
And is the most endangered species: song?

## ELEGIE

*an Marina Zwetajewa-Efron*

O die Verluste ins All, Marina, die stürzenden Sterne!
Wir vermehren es nicht, wohin wir uns werfen, zu welchem
Sterne hinzu! Im Ganzen ist immer schon alles gezählt.
So auch, wer fällt, vermindert die heilige Zahl nicht.
Jeder verzichtende Sturz stürzt in den Ursprung und heilt.
Wäre denn alles ein Spiel, Wechsel des Gleichen,
     Verschiebung,
nirgends ein Name und kaum irgendwo heimisch Gewinn?
Wellen, Marina, wir Meer! Tiefen, Marina, wir Himmel.
Erde, Marina, wir Erde, wir tausendmal Frühling, wie
     Lerchen,
die ein ausbrechendes Lied in die Unsichtbarkeit wirft.
Wir beginnens als Jubel, schon übertrifft es uns völlig;
plötzlich, unser Gewicht dreht zur Klage abwärts den Sang.
Aber auch so: Klage? Wäre sie nicht: jüngerer Jubel nach
     unten.
Auch die unteren Götter wollen gelobt sein, Marina.
So unschuldig sind Götter, sie warten auf Lob wie die
     Schüler.
Loben, du Liebe, laß uns verschwenden mit Lob.
Nichts gehört uns. Wir legen ein wenig die Hand um die
     Hälse
ungebrochener Blumen. Ich sah es am Nil in Kôm-Ombo.
So, Marina, die Spende, selber verzichtend, opfern die
     Könige.
Wie die Engel gehen und die Türen bezeichnen jener zu
     Rettenden,
also rühren wir dieses und dies, scheinbar Zärtliche, an.
Ach wie weit schon Entrückte, ach, wie Zerstreute, Marina,
auch noch beim innigsten Vorwand. Zeichengeber, sonst
     nichts.
Dieses leise Geschäft, wo es der Unsrigen einer
nicht mehr erträgt und sich zum Zugriff entschließt,

# ELEGY

*to Marina Tsvetayeva-Efron*

Oh the losses into the All, Marina, the stars that are falling!
We can't make it larger, wherever we fling ourselves, to
   whatever
star we may go! In the Whole, all things are already
   numbered.
So when anyone falls, the perfect sum is not lessened.
Whoever lets go in his fall, dives into the source and is
   healed.
Is all of life then a game, a meaningless fluctuation
of sameness, nowhere a name, nowhere a lasting
   achievement?
Waves, Marina, we are ocean! Depths, Marina, we are sky.
Earth, Marina, we are earth, a thousand times April, like
   larks
that a song bursting out of them flings into invisible heights.
We begin it as joy, and already it wholly exceeds us;
suddenly the force of our weight bends the song down to
   lament.
Yet isn't lament really a younger, descending joy?
Even the gods below want to be praised, Marina.
So innocent are gods, they listen for praise like children.
Praising, my dearest—let us be lavish with praise.
Nothing really belongs to us. We put our hands lightly
   around
the necks of unbroken flowers. I saw it on the Nile, in Kom
   Ombo.
Just so, Marina, the kings offer up the gifts they renounce.
As angels draw marks as a signal on the doors of those to be
   saved,
we, though we seem to be tender, stop and touch this or that.
Ah, how remote already, how inattentive, Marina,
even in our innermost pretense. Signalers: nothing more.
This silent commerce, when life is no longer willing
to endure one of our kind, when it seizes him in its grip,

rächt sich und tötet. Denn daß es tödliche Macht hat,
merkten wir alle an seiner Verhaltung und Zartheit
und an der seltsamen Kraft, die uns aus Lebenden zu
Überlebenden macht. Nicht-Sein. Weißt du's, wie oft
trug uns ein blinder Befehl durch den eisigen Vorraum
neuer Geburt. . . . Trug: *uns?* Einen Körper aus Augen
unter zahllosen Lidern sich weigernd. Trug das in uns
niedergeworfene Herz eines ganzen Geschlechts. An ein
    Zugvogelziel
trug er die Gruppe, das Bild unserer schwebenden
    Wandlung.
Liebende dürften, Marina, dürfen soviel nicht
von dem Untergang wissen. Müssen wie neu sein.
Erst ihr Grab is alt, erst ihr Grab besinnt sich, verdunkelt
unter dem schluchzenden Baum, besinnt sich auf Jeher.
Erst ihr Grab bricht ein; sie selber sind biegsam wie Ruten;
was übermäßig sie biegt, ründet sie reichlich zum Kranz.
Wie sie verwehen im Maiwind! Von der Mitte des Immer,
drin du atmest und ahnst, schließt sie der Augenblick aus.
(O wie begreif ich dich, weibliche Blüte am gleichen
unvergänglichen Strauch. Wie streu ich mich stark in die
    Nachtluft,
die dich nächstens bestreift.) Frühe erlernten die Götter
Hälften zu heucheln. Wir in das Kreisen bezogen
füllten zum Ganzen uns an wie die Scheibe des Monds.
Auch in abnehmender Frist, auch in den Wochen der
    Wendung
niemand verhülfe uns je wieder zum Vollsein, als der
einsame eigene Gang über der schlaflosen Landschaft.

avenges itself, kills. For the fact that its strength *can* kill
was plain to us all from its delicacy and restraint
and from the curious power that transforms us from living
        beings
into survivors. Non-being. Do you remember how often
a blind command would carry us through the icy
waiting-room of new birth? . . . Us?—a body of eyes
under numberless lids, refusing. Carried the down-
thrown heart in our breast, the heart of a whole generation.
To a goal as welcome as the South is for migrating birds,
it carried the soaring image and plan of our transformation.
Lovers were not, Marina, *are* not permitted to know
destruction so deeply. Must be as if they were new.
Only their grave is old, only *it* ponders and darkens
under the sobbing tree, remembering all that has been.
Only their grave collapses; *they* are supple as reeds;
what bends them too far, rounds them into rich garlands.
How they blow about in the May wind! From the midst of
        the Ever,
in which you breathe and surmise, the moment has shut
        them out.
(Oh how I understand you, female flower on the same
imperishable stalk. How wildly I scatter myself into the
        night air
that in a moment will touch you.) The gods long ago
learned to dissemble halves. We, drawn into the cycle,
filled ourselves out to the whole, like the disk of the moon.
Even in the time of waning, in the weeks of our gradual
        change,
nothing could ever again help us to fulfillment, except
our own solitary course over the sleepless landscape.

*Für Erika, zum Feste der Rühmung*

Taube, die draußen blieb, außer dem Taubenschlag,
wieder in Kreis und Haus, einig der Nacht, dem Tag,
weiß sie die Heimlichkeit, wenn sich der Einbezug
fremdester Schrecken schmiegt in den gefühlten Flug.

Unter den Tauben, die allergeschonteste,
niemals gefährdetste, kennt nicht die Zärtlichkeit;
wiedererholtes Herz ist das bewohnteste:
freier durch Widerruf freut sich die Fähigkeit.

Über dem Nirgendssein spannt sich das Überall!
Ach der geworfene, ach der gewagte Ball,
füllt er die Hände nicht anders mit Wiederkehr:
rein um sein Heimgewicht ist er mehr.

## [Dove that ventured outside]

*To Erika, for the festival of praise*

Dove that ventured outside,     flying far from the dovecote:
housed and protected again,     one with the day, the night,
knows what serenity is,     for she has felt her wings
pass through all distance and fear   in the course of her wanderings.

The doves that remained at home,     never exposed to loss,
innocent and secure,     cannot know tenderness;
only the won-back heart     can ever be satisfied: free,
through all it has given up,     to rejoice in its mastery.

Being arches itself     over the vast abyss.
Ah the ball that we dared,     that we hurled into infinite space,
doesn't it fill our hands     differently with its return:
heavier by the weight     of where it has been.

*Notes*

The German text in this book is that of the standard edition (*Sämtliche Werke* [SW], Frankfurt am Main: Insel Verlag, 1955–1966), except for two lines in the Fifth Duino Elegy, where I have followed the Thurn und Taxis manuscript and the first edition.

Letters excerpted and translated in these notes can be found in the following collections (except where otherwise indicated):

*Briefe aus den Jahren 1902–1906.* Leipzig: Insel Verlag, 1930.

*Briefe aus den Jahren 1907–1914.* Leipzig: Insel Verlag, 1933.

*Briefe aus Muzot, 1921–1926.* Leipzig: Insel Verlag, 1937.

*Briefe.* Wiesbaden: Insel Verlag, 1950.

*Rainer Maria Rilke und Marie von Thurn und Taxis: Briefwechsel.* Zürich/ Wiesbaden: Niehans & Rokitansky Verlag und Insel Verlag, 1951.

*Rainer Maria Rilke/Lou Andreas-Salomé: Briefwechsel.* Wiesbaden: Insel Verlag, 1952.

*Rainer Maria Rilke/Katharina Kippenberg: Briefwechsel.* Wiesbaden: Insel Verlag, 1954.

*Briefwechsel mit Benvenuta.* Eßlingen: Bechtle Verlag, 1954.

*Briefe an Sidonie Nádherný von Borutin.* Frankfurt am Main: Insel Verlag, 1973.

*Briefe an Nanny Wunderly-Volkart.* Frankfurt am Main: Insel Verlag, 1977.

FROM THE BOOK OF HOURS (1905)

I began with Things, which were the true confidants of my lonely childhood, and it was already a great achievement that, without any outside help, I managed to get as far as animals. But then Russia opened itself to me and granted me the brotherliness and the darkness of God, in whom alone there is community. That was what I *named* him then, the God who had broken in upon me, and for a long time I lived in the antechamber of his name, on my knees. Now, you would hardly ever hear me name him; there is an indescribable discretion between us, and where nearness and penetration once were, new distances stretch forth, as in the atom, which the new science conceives of as a universe in miniature. The comprehensible slips away, is transformed; instead of possession one learns relationship [*statt des Besitzes lernt man den Bezug*], and there arises a namelessness that must begin once more in our relations with God if we are to be complete and without evasion. The experience of feeling him recedes behind an infinite delight in everything that can be felt; all attributes are taken away from God, who is no longer sayable, and fall back into creation, into love and death. It is perhaps only this that again and again took place in certain passages in the Book of Hours, this ascent of God out of the breathing heart—so that the sky was covered with him—, and his falling to earth as rain. But saying even that is already too much.

(To Ilse Jahr, February 22, 1923)

[I live my life in widening rings] (Berlin-Schmargendorf, September 20, 1899)

[I am, O Anxious One. Don't you hear my voice] (Berlin-Schmargendorf, September 24, 1899)

[I find you, Lord, in all Things and in all] (Berlin-Schmargendorf, September 24, 1899)

FROM THE BOOK OF PICTURES (First edition, 1902; second edition, 1906)

Lament (Berlin-Schmargendorf, October 21, 1900)

Autumn Day (Paris, September 21, 1902)

Evening (Undated: 1902/1906; perhaps Sweden, autumn 1904)

The Blindman's Song (Paris, June 7, 1906)

This and the following three songs are part of a ten-poem cycle called *The Voices*.

To want to improve the situation of another human being presupposes an insight into his circumstances such as not even a poet has toward a character he himself has created. How much less insight is there in the so infinitely excluded helper, whose scatteredness becomes complete with his gift. Wanting to change or improve some-one's situation means offering him, in exchange for difficulties in which he is practiced and experienced, other difficulties that will find him perhaps even more bewildered. If at any time I was able to pour out into the mold of my heart the imaginary voices of the dwarf or the beggar, the metal of this cast was not obtained from any wish that the dwarf or the beggar might have a less difficult time. On the contrary: only through a praising of their incomparable fate could the poet, with his full attention suddenly given to them, be true and fundamental, and there is nothing that he would have to fear and refuse so much as a corrected world in which the dwarfs are stretched out and the beggars enriched. The God of completeness sees to it that these varieties do not cease, and it would be a most superficial attitude to consider the poet's joy in this suffering multiplicity as an esthetic pretense.

(To Hermann Pongs, October 21, 1924)

The Drunkard's Song (Paris, June 7/12, 1906)

The Idiot's Song (Paris, June 7, 1906)

The Dwarf's Song (Paris, June 7, 1906)

FROM NEW POEMS (First Part, 1907; Second Part, 1908)

Do the *New Poems* still seem so impersonal to you? You see, in order to speak about what happened to me, what I needed was not so much an instrument of emotion, but rather: clay. Involuntarily I undertook to make use of "lyric poetry" in order to *form* not feelings but *things I had felt;* every one of life's events had to find a place in this forming, independently of the suffering or pleasure it had at first brought me. This formation would have been worthless if it hadn't gone as far as the *trans*-formation of every accidental detail; it had to arrive at the essence.

(To "une amie," February 3, 1923)

Love Song (Capri, mid-March 1907)

The Panther (Paris, 1903, or possibly late in 1902)

In addition to the panther in the Jardin des Plantes, Rilke was probably re-membering a small Greek statue of a panther (or tiger).

In his studio in the rue de l'Université, Rodin has a tiny plaster cast of a tiger (antique) which he values very highly: C'est beau, c'est tout [It's beautiful, it's everything], he says of it. And from this little plas-ter copy I have seen what he means, what antiquity is and what links him to it. There is in this animal the same kind of aliveness in the modeling; on this little Thing (it is no higher than my hand is wide, and no longer than my hand is) there are a hundred thousand places, as if it were something really huge—a hundred thousand places that are all alive, active, and different. All this just in plaster! And the rep-resentation of the prowling stride is intensified to the highest degree, the powerful downward tread of the broad paws, and simultaneously that caution in which all strength is wrapped, that noiselessness.

(To Clara Rilke, September 27, 1902)

In Rodin's studio there is a cast of a panther, of Greek workmanship, hardly as big as a hand (the original is in the medallion collection of the Bibliothèque Nationale in Paris). If you look from the front under its body into the space formed by the four powerful soft paws, you seem to be looking into the depths of an Indian stone temple; so huge and all-inclusive does this work become.

(*Auguste Rodin,* 1902, SW 5, 173)

The Gazelle (Paris, July 17, 1907)

Yesterday I spent the whole morning in the Jardin des Plantes, look-ing at the gazelles. Gazella Dorcas, Linnaeus. There are a pair of them and also a single female. They were lying a few feet apart, chewing their cuds, resting, gazing. As women gaze out of pictures, they were gazing out of something, with a soundless, final turn of the head. And when a horse whinnied, the single one listened, and I saw the radiance from ears and horns around her slender head. . . . I saw the single one stand up, for a moment; she lay right down again; but while she was stretching and testing herself, I could see the magnificent workman-ship of those legs (they are like rifles from which leaps are fired). I just couldn't tear myself away, they were so beautiful.

(To Clara Rilke, June 13, 1907)

l. 6, *songs of love:* Possibly a reference to the Song of Songs, which, in the translation that Rilke used, frequently compares the beloved to a gazelle.

The Swan (Meudon, winter 1905/1906)

The Grown-up (Paris, July 19, 1907)

There is an insightful study of this poem in Geoffrey H. Hartman's *The Unmediated Vision* (New Haven: Yale University Press, 1954).

l. 4, *the Ark of God:* The ark of the tabernacle, Exodus 25.

Going Blind (Paris, late June 1906)

Before Summer Rain (Paris, early July 1906)

Written after a visit to the Château de Chantilly.

l. 6, *Saint Jerome* (ca. 347-ca. 420): One of the four great Doctors of the Western Church, noted for his asceticism and pugnacity. Rilke may have been thinking of the Dürer engraving, dated 1514.

The Last Evening (Paris, June 1906)

Dedication, *Frau Nonna:* Rilke's friend Julie Freifrau von Nordeck zur Rabenau, whose first husband was killed in the battle of Königgrätz, July 3, 1866, at the age of thirty-one.

l. 14, *shako:* "A military cap in the shape of a truncated cone, with a peak and either a plume or a ball or 'pompom.' " (OED)

Portrait of My Father as a Young Man (Paris, June 27, 1906)

This poem, written three months after Josef Rilke's death, describes

the fine colored daguerreotype of my father that was taken when he was seventeen, just before his departure on the [Austrian army's] Italian campaign. Those first, naive photographs could be so movingly real—this one gives you the impression that you are looking at him through his mother's eyes, seeing the beautiful young face in its solemn, barely smiling presentiment of bravery and danger. In my childhood I must have seen it once among my father's papers; later it seemed as though it was missing for years—useless to ask where it had gone. Then, after he died, I found it among the possessions he had left behind, framed like a miniature in antique red velvet, intact—and I realized how unutterably it had taken form in my heart.

(To Magda von Hattingberg, February 11, 1914)

Self-Portrait, 1906 (Probably Paris, spring 1906)

Spanish Dancer (Paris, June 1906)

Tombs of the Hetaerae (Rome, early in 1904)

*Hetaerae:* Courtesans.

Orpheus. Eurydice. Hermes (Rome, early in 1904)

According to Ovid: After Eurydice, Orpheus' wife, died of a snakebite, the poet descended to the land of shadows to retrieve her, and held the whole underworld spellbound by the beauty of his song.

Neither the dark queen
nor the lord who rules the underworld could deny
what he in his song had asked for, and they called
Eurydice. She was there among the shades
just recently arrived, and now walked toward them,
slowly, the wound still fresh upon her ankle.
Orpheus took her, with the one condition:
if he should turn to look at her before
they had passed the dismal valleys of Avernus,
the gift would be revoked.
They climbed the path
through the deep silence, wrapped in total darkness.

They had almost reached the rim of the upper world
when he, afraid that she might slip, impatient
to see her bright, beloved face, looked back:
and in an instant, she began to fade,
reaching out, struggling desperately to hold on
to him, or to be held; but her hands could grasp
nothing but thin air. She didn't blame
her appalled husband for this second death
(how could she blame such love?) and, calling out
a last *Farewell!*, which he could barely hear,
she vanished.

(Ovid, Metamorphoses X, 46 ff.)

*Hermes:* The messenger of the gods and the guide (*psychopompos*) who took the souls of the dead to the underworld.

l. 15, *in the blue cloak:* In Homer, dark blue is the color of mourning.

Alcestis (Capri, between February 7 and 10, 1907)

Several years after King Admetus' marriage, Death arrived to announce that Admetus had been condemned to die immediately, and could be saved only if someone else was willing to be taken in his stead. Only Alcestis, his wife, volunteered. Later, Hercules was so moved by Admetus' mourning that he pursued Death, snatched Alcestis away from him, and brought her back to Admetus. (This myth is the theme of the tragicomic *Alcestis* by Euripides.)

l. 1, *the messenger:* Hermes (the poem was originally entitled "Admetus. Alcestis. Hermes").

l. 72, *she:* The goddess Artemis, who was offended because Admetus had forgotten the customary prenuptial sacrifice to her.

Archaic Torso of Apollo (Paris, early summer 1908)

The inspiration for this sonnet, which is the first poem in *New Poems, Second Part,* was the early-fifth-century B.C. *Torso of a Youth from Miletus* in the Salle Archaïque of the Louvre.

The incomparable value of these rediscovered Things lies in the fact that you can look at them as if they were completely unknown. No one knows what their intention is and (at least for the unscientific) no subject matter is attached to them, no irrelevant voice interrupts the silence of their concentrated reality, and their duration is without retrospect or fear. The masters from whom they originate are nothing; no misunderstood fame colors their pure forms; no history casts a shadow over their naked clarity—: they *are*. That is all. This is how I see ancient art. The little tiger at Rodin's is like that, and the many fragments and broken pieces in the museums (which you pass by many times without paying attention, until one day one of them reveals itself to you, and shines like a first star . . . )

(To Lou Andreas-Salomé, August 15, 1903)

The companion piece, "Early Apollo," is the first poem in *New Poems* (Part One):

> . . . so ist in seinem Haupte
> nichts was verhindern könnte, daß der Glanz
>
> aller Gedichte uns fast tödlich träfe;
> denn noch kein Schatten ist in seinem Schaun,
> zu kühl für Lorbeer sind noch seine Schläfe
> und später erst wird aus den Augenbraun . . .

> . . . *so, in his head,*
> *nothing can stop the radiance of all*
>
> *poems from nearly burning us to death;*
> *for there is still no shadow in his gaze,*
> *his forehead is too cool for a laurel-wreath,*
> *and not for another century will his eyebrows*
>
> *blossom . . .*

Washing the Corpse (Paris, summer 1908)

Black Cat (Paris, summer 1908)

The Flamingos (Paris, autumn 1907, or Capri, spring 1908)

l. 1, *Fragonard:* Jean-Honoré Fragonard (pronounced Fragonár), 1732–1806, French painter.

l. 8, *Phryne* (fourth century B.C.E.): Greek courtesan, famous for her beauty.

Buddha in Glory (Paris, summer 1908)

This is the final poem in *New Poems, Second Part.*

Soon after supper I retire, and am in my little house by 8:30 at the latest. Then I have in front of me the vast blossoming starry night, and below, in front of the window, the gravel walk goes up a little hill on which, in fanatic taciturnity, a statue of the Buddha rests, distributing, with silent discretion, the unutterable self-containedness of his gesture beneath all the skies of the day and night. C'est le centre du monde [He is the center of the world], I said to Rodin.

(To Clara Rilke, September 20, 1905)

Cf. the two earlier poems called "Buddha" in the first part of *New Poems* ("As though he were listening. Silence: something far" and "From far away the awe-struck pilgrim feels").

FROM REQUIEM (1909)

Requiem for a Friend (Paris, October 31–November 2, 1908)

Written in memory of the painter Paula Modersohn-Becker (1876–1907).

The fate that I tried to tell of and to lament in the Requiem is perhaps the essential conflict of the artist: the opposition and contradiction between objective and personal enjoyment of the world. It is no less conclusively demonstrated in a man who is an artist by necessity; but in a woman who has committed herself to the infinite transpositions of the artist's existence the pain and danger of this choice become inconceivably visible. Since she is physical far into her soul and is designed for bearing children of flesh and blood, something like a complete transformation of all her organs must take place if she is to attain a true fruitfulness of soul.

The birth processes which, in a purely spiritual way, the male artist enjoys, suffers, and survives, may, in a woman who is capable of giving birth to a work of art, broaden and be exalted into something that is of the utmost spirituality. But these processes undergo just a gradual intensification, and still remain, in unlimited ramifications, within the realm of the physical. (So that, exaggerating, one could say that even what is most spiritual in woman is still body: body become sublime.) Therefore, for her, any relapse into a more primitive and narrow kind of suffering, enjoying, and bringing forth is an overfilling of her organs with the blood that has been augmented for another, greater circulation.

Long ago I had a presentiment of this fate; but I experienced it in all its intensity when it actually brushed against me: when it stood in front of me, so huge and close that I could not shut my eyes.

(To Hugo Heller, June 12, 1909; in *Berliner Tageblatt*, November 29, 1929)

l. 5, *return:*

. . . his body became indescribably touching to him and of no further use than to be purely and cautiously present in, just as a ghost [*Revenant*], already dwelling elsewhere, sadly enters the realm that was tenderly laid aside, in order to belong once again, even if inattentively, to this once so indispensable world.

("An Experience," p. 290 f.)

l. 15, *transformation:*

> Und sind nicht alle so, nur sich enthaltend,
> wenn Sich-enthalten heißt: die Welt da draußen
> und Wind und Regen und Geduld des Frühlings
> und Dunkelheit der abendlichen Erde
> bis auf der Wolken Wandel, Flucht und Anflug,
> bis auf den vagen Einfluß ferner Sterne
> in eine Hand voll Innres zu verwandeln.

> *And aren't all of them that way: self-containing?*
> *If self-containing means to take the outside*
> *world, and wind and rain and springtime's patience*
> *and guilt and restlessness and muffled fate*

*and darkness of the evening earth and sky,*
*out to the clouds' approach and change and flight,*
*out to the vaguest influence of the stars—*
*to take these outward qualities and transform them*
*into a handful of perfect innerness.*

("The Bowl of Roses," *New Poems*)

The poet's task is

hart sich in die Worte zu verwandeln,
wie sich der Steinmetz einer Kathedrale
verbissen umsetzt in des Steines Gleichmut.

*to transform himself austerely into words,*
*just as the mason of a great cathedral*
*persists in changing his whole life and passion*
*into the equanimity of stones.*

("Requiem for Count Wolf von Kalckreuth," *Requiem*)

ll. 49 f., *a country / you never saw:* Rilke was probably thinking of Egypt here. Both he and Paula Becker were deeply impressed by the Egyptian sculptures in the Louvre. (H. W. Petzet, *Das Bildnis des Dichters: Paula Modersohn-Becker und Rainer Maria Rilke,* Frankfurt am Main: Insel Verlag, 1976, p. 49 f.)

l. 80, *your naked body:* This probably refers to the wonderful *Self-Portrait on her Fifth Anniversary* (1906), where Paula Becker is wearing her amber necklace and is naked to the hips. There are two other self-portraits from 1906, half-length, in which she appears naked, wearing the amber necklace, and with pink flowers in her hands and hair. (Those interested should consult Gillian Perry, *Paula Modersohn-Becker,* New York: Harper & Row, 1979, which contains twenty-five color plates and ninety-three duotone illustrations.)

l. 83, *and didn't say: I am that; no: this is:* In one of his great letters on Cézanne, Rilke wrote:

You notice better each time you look at these paintings how necessary it was to go beyond even love. It is of course natural to love each one of these Things if you have made them. But if you show that, you make them less well; you *judge* them instead of *saying* them. You cease to be impartial; and what is best of all, the love, remains outside the work, does not enter it, is left untransformed beside it. That is how mood-painting arose (which is in no way better than realism). They painted: I love this; instead of painting: here it is. In the latter, everyone must then look carefully to see whether I have loved it. That is not shown at all, and many people would even say that there is no love in it. So utterly has it been consumed in the act of making. This consuming of love in anonymous work, out of which such pure Things arise—perhaps no one has so completely succeeded in doing that as this old man.

(To Clara Rilke, October 13, 1907)

ll. 85 f., *of such true / poverty:*

Any kind of work delighted him: he worked even during meals, he read, he drew. He drew as he walked along the street, and quite early in the morning he drew the sleepy animals in the Jardin des Plantes. And when pleasure did not tempt him to work, poverty drove him to it. Poverty, without which his life would be unthinkable. He never forgets that it included him with the animals and flowers, without possessions among all those who are without possessions, and who have only God to depend on.

(*Auguste Rodin,* 1907, SW 5, 228)

l. 117, *someone:* Otto Modersohn.

ll. 129 ff., *the objective world expanded . . . . :* Paula's pregnancy.

l. 223, *Nikē:*

I have seen such beautiful things in the Louvre. . . . The Nikē of Samothrace, the goddess of victory on the ship's hull, with the wonderful movement and the vast sea-wind in her clothes, is a miracle and seems like a whole world.

(To Clara Rilke, September 26, 1902)

l. 232, *the freedom of a love:*

For one human being to love another human being: that is perhaps the most difficult task that has been given to us, the ultimate, the final problem and proof, the work for which all other work is merely preparation. . . . Love does not at first mean merging, surrendering, and uniting with another person . . . Rather, it is a high inducement for the individual to ripen, to become something in himself, to become world, to become world in himself for another's sake. . . . We are only just now beginning to consider the relation of one individual to a second individual objectively and without prejudice, and our attempts to live such relationships have no model before them. And yet in the changes brought about by time there are already many things that can help our timid novitiate.

The girl and the woman, in their new, individual unfolding, will only in passing be imitators of male behavior and misbehavior and repeaters of male professions. After the uncertainty of such transitions, it will become obvious that women were going through the abundance and variation of those (often ridiculous) disguises just so that they could purify their own essential nature and wash out the deforming influences of the other sex. . . . This humanity of woman, carried in her womb through all her suffering and humiliation, will come to light when she has stripped off the conventions of mere femaleness in the transformations of her outward status, and those men who do not yet feel it approaching will be surprised and struck by it. Someday . . . there will be girls and women whose name will no longer mean the mere opposite of the male, but something in itself, something that makes one think not of any complement and limit, but only of life and reality: the female human being.

This advance will (at first much against the will of the outdistanced men) transform the love experience, which is now filled with error, will change it from the ground up, and reshape it into a relation of one human being to another, no longer of man to woman. And this more human love (which will fulfill itself with infinite consideration and gentleness, and kindness and clarity in binding and releasing) will resemble what we are now preparing painfully and with great struggle: the love that consists in this—that two solitudes protect and border and greet each other.

(To Franz Xaver Kappus, May 14, 1904)

l. 235, *letting each other go:* In describing his admiration for the "incomparable" Leonora Christina Ulfeldt, daughter of King Christian IV of Denmark, who, because her husband had been accused of high treason, was imprisoned in the Blue Tower in Copenhagen from 1663 until 1685, Rilke wrote:

It seems to me that you could predict her conduct in prison if you knew of a certain little scene that was enacted just before her arrest in England. At this critical moment it happened that a young officer who was sent to her misunderstood his orders and demanded that she take off all the jewelry she was wearing and hand it over to him. Although this ought to have startled her (since she was not yet aware that she was in any danger) and thrown her into the utmost alarm, nevertheless, after a moment's consideration, she takes off all her jewels—the earrings, the necklaces, the brooches, the bracelets, the rings—and puts them into the officer's hands. The young man brings these treasures to his superior, who, at first terrified, then enraged, at this imprudence, which threatens to upset the whole undertaking, orders him, curtly and in the coarsest language, to return and give everything back to the Countess, and to beg her forgiveness, in any way he can think of, for his unauthorized blunder. What happened now is unforgettable. After considering for a moment, not longer than that first moment was, Countess Ulfeldt gestures for the bewildered officer to follow her, walks over to the mirror, and there takes the magnificent necklaces and brooches and rings from his hands, as if from the hands of a servant, and puts them on, with the greatest attentiveness and serenity, one after another.

Tell me, dear friend, do you know any other story in which it is so sublimely evident how we ought to behave toward the vicissitudes of life? This went through and through me: this same repose vis-à-vis giving up and keeping, this repose that is so filled with power. This should truly be taken to heart: it is perhaps nothing more than what individual saints have done, who, because they have lost what they love or were reminded of the continual possibility of loss, threw off all possessions and condemned the very desire for possession (: for that may be an enormous, hardly surpassable achievement—.) But this is more human, more patient, more adequate. *That* gesture of renunciation is magnificent, thrilling,—but it is not without arrogance, which is again cancelled only because it, in its own way, already belongs to heaven. But this silent, composed keeping and letting go, on the contrary, is full of moderation, is still earthly, through and through, and yet is already so great as to be incomprehensible.

(To Sidonie Nádherný von Borutin, February 4, 1912)

l. 245, *fame:*

Rodin was solitary before he was famous. And fame, when it arrived, made him perhaps even more solitary. For fame is, after all, only the sum of all the misunderstandings that gather around a new name.

(*Auguste Rodin*, 1902, SW 5, 141)

ll. 264 f., *an ancient enmity / between our daily life and the great work:*

The modest domestic circumstances of Tolstoy, the lack of comfort in Rodin's rooms—it all points to the same thing: that one must make up one's mind: either this or that. Either happiness or art. On doit trouver le bonheur dans son art [one must find happiness in one's art]: that too, more or less, is what Rodin said. And it is all so clear, so clear. The great artists have all let their lives become overgrown like an old path and have borne everything in their art. Their lives have become atrophied, like an organ they no longer use.

(To Clara Rilke, September 5, 1902)

Someday people will understand what made this great artist so great: the fact that he was a worker, who desired nothing but to enter, completely and with all his powers, into the humble and austere reality of his art. In this there was a certain renunciation of life. But precisely by such patience did he win life: for the world offered itself to his art.

(*Auguste Rodin*, 1902, SW 5, 201)

## UNCOLLECTED POEMS, 1911–1920

[To Lou Andreas-Salomé] (Duino, November or December 1911)

[The Almond Trees in Blossom] (Ronda, approximately January 1, 1913)

The Spanish Trilogy (Ronda, between January 6 and 14, 1913)

ll. 41 f., *the distant call of birds / already deep inside him:*

Later, he remembered certain moments in which the power of *this* moment was already contained, as in a seed. He thought of the hour in that other southern garden (Capri) when the call of a bird did not, so to speak, break off at the edge of his body, but was simultaneously outside and in his innermost being, uniting both into one uninterrupted space in which, mysteriously protected, only one single place of purest, deepest consciousness remained. On that occasion he had closed his eyes, so that he might not be confused, in so generous an experience, by the outline of his body, and the Infinite passed into him from all sides, so intimately that he believed he could feel the stars which had in the meantime appeared, gently reposing within his breast.

("An Experience," 1913, SW 6, 1040)

l. 54, *the daily task of the shepherd:*

What I most took part in when I was in Ronda was the life of the shepherds on the great stony hillsides with the picturesque stone-oaks, each of them filling up with darkness the way a cloud's shadow moves over the fields. The morning departure, when after their night's rest the shepherds walk out carrying their long staffs on their shoulders; their quiet, lingering, contemplative outdoor presence, through which, in all its breadth, the greatness of the day pours down; and the evenings when they unrecognizably, with the twilight, climb up out of the valley in the air echoing with their flocks, and, above, on the valley's rim, again darkly gather themselves into the simplest of forms; and that they still use the long slings woven of bast, just like the one which David put his stone into, and with an exactly aimed throw, frighten back a straying animal into the mass of the flock; and that the air knows the color and weave of their thick clothing and treats it as it treats the other tempered presences of Nature; in short, that there are people there who are placed out in the overflowing fullness which we are only sometimes aware of, when we step out of the world of human relationships or when we look up from a book: how such a figure is and endures and, almost godlike, walks on, unhurried, over the hurrying events in which we spend our lives: all this could be counted among the pure experiences which could teach us the days and nights and everything that is most elemental.

(To Katharina Kippenberg, March 27, 1913)

Ariel (Ronda, early in 1913)

(*after reading Shakespeare's* Tempest): Rilke had just read the play for the first time.

l. 1, *you had set him free:* Cf. *The Tempest,* I.ii.250 ff.

l. 12, *to give up all your magic:* Cf. *The Tempest,* V.i.50 ff.

I know now that psychoanalysis would make sense for me only if I were really serious about the strange possibility of *no longer writing,* which during the completion of *Malte* I often dangled in front of my nose as a kind of relief. Then one might let one's devils be exorcised, since in daily life they are truly just disturbing and painful. And if it happened that the angels left too, one would have to understand this as a further simplification and tell oneself that in the new profession (which?), there would certainly be no use for them.

(To Lou Andreas-Salomé, January 24, 1912)

[Straining so hard against the strength of night] (Paris, late February, 1913)

[Ignorant before the heavens of my life] (Paris, spring 1913)

[Overflowing heavens of lavished stars] (Paris, April 1913)

[Startle me, Music, with rhythmical fury!] (Paris, May 1913)

[Behind the innocent trees] (Heiligendamm, first half of August 1913)

The Vast Night (Paris, January 1914)

[You who never arrived] (Paris, winter 1913/1914)

Turning-point (Paris, June 20, 1914)

Lou, dear, here is a strange poem, written this morning, which I am sending you right away because I involuntarily called it "Turning-point," because it describes *the* turning-point which no doubt must come if I am to stay alive.

(To Lou Andreas-Salomé, June 20, 1914)

Epigraph, *sacrifice:* Rilke had defined sacrifice as "the boundless resolve, no longer limitable in any direction, to achieve one's purest inner possibility." (To Magda von Hattingberg, February 17, 1914)

Epigraph, *Kassner:* Rudolf Kassner (1873–1959), Austrian writer. The Eighth Elegy is dedicated to him.

l. 1, *For a long time he attained it in looking:*

I love in-seeing. Can you imagine with me how glorious it is to in-see a dog, for example, as you pass it—by *in-see* I don't mean to look *through,* which is only a kind of human gymnastic that lets you immediately come out again on the other side of the dog, regarding it merely, so to speak, as a window upon the human world lying behind it: not that; what I mean is to let yourself precisely into the dog's center, the point from which it begins to be a dog, the place in it where God, as it were, would have sat down for a moment when the dog was finished, in order to watch it during its first embarrassments and inspirations and to nod that it was good, that nothing was lacking, that it couldn't have been better made. For a while you can endure being inside the dog; you just have to be alert and jump out in time, before its environment has completely enclosed you, since otherwise you would simply remain the dog in the dog and be lost for everything else. Though you may laugh, dear confidante, if I tell you *where* my very greatest feeling, my world-feeling, my earthly bliss was, I must confess to you: it was, again and again, here and there, in such in-seeing—in the indescribably swift, deep, timeless moments of this godlike in-seeing.

(To Magda von Hattingberg, February 17, 1914)

Lament (Paris, early July 1914)

'We Must Die Because We Have Known Them' (Paris, July 1914)

*Ptah-hotep:* A high official under the pharaoh Asosi, during the Fifth Dynasty (ca. 2600 B.C.E.).

To Hölderlin (Irschenhausen, September 1914)

*Hölderlin:* Johann Christian Friedrich Hölderlin (1770–1843), one of the greatest German poets.

> During the past few months I have been reading your edition of Hölderlin with extraordinary feeling and devotion. His influence upon me is great and generous, as only the influence of the richest and inwardly mightiest can be. . . . I cannot tell you how deeply these poems are affecting me and with what inexpressible clarity they stand before me.
>
> (To Norbert von Hellingrath, July 24, 29, 1914)

l. 20, *for years that you no longer counted:* Hölderlin went incurably insane in 1806.

[Exposed on the cliffs of the heart] (Irschenhausen, September 20, 1914)

[Again and again, however we know the landscape of love] (end of 1914)

Death (Munich, November 9, 1915)

> Rilke told me how this poem arose. He was walking, alone as always, in a Munich park. All at once he seemed to see a hand before his eyes; on its level back a cup was standing. He saw this quite distinctly, and the verses describing it formed by themselves. He didn't quite know what to make of this, and went home still hazy about the meaning of what had been begun. As in a dream he continued the poem to its conclusion—and understood. And suddenly the last three lines were there, in strongest contrast to the preceding ones. As for the shooting star, he had seen it in Toledo. One night he had been walking across the bridge and suddenly a glorious meteor had plunged across the sky, from the zenith down to the dark horizon, and vanished.—That was death, in all its wonder.
>
> (Princess Marie von Thurn und Taxis-Hohenlohe,<br>*Erinnerungen an Rainer Maria Rilke,* München-<br>Berlin-Zürich: R. Oldenbourg, 1932, p. 80 f.)

l. 1, *There stands death:*

Tolstoy's enormous experience of Nature (I know hardly anyone who had so passionately entered inside Nature) made him astonishingly able to think and write out of a sense of the whole, out of a feeling for life which was permeated by the finest particles of death, a sense that death was contained everywhere in life, like a peculiar spice in life's powerful flavor. But that was precisely why this man could be so deeply, so frantically terrified when he realized that somewhere there was pure death, the bottle full of death or the hideous cup with the handle broken off and the meaningless inscription "Faith, love, hope," out of which people were forced to drink a bitterness of undiluted death.

(To Lotte Hepner, November 8, 1915)

l. 17, *O shooting star:*

At the end of the poem "Death," the moment is evoked (I was standing at night on the wonderful bridge of Toledo) when a star, falling through cosmic space in a tensed slow arc, simultaneously (how should I say this?) fell through my inner space: the body's dividing outline was no longer there. And whereas this happened then through my eyes, once at an earlier time (in Capri) the same unity had been granted me through my hearing.

(To Adelheid von der Marwitz, January 14, 1919)

To Music (Munich, January 11–12, 1918)

Written in the guestbook of Frau Hanna Wolff, after a concert at her house.

[You, you only, exist] (Berg am Irchel, December 25, 1920)

Haiku (Berg am Irchel, December 25, 1920)

UNCOLLECTED POEMS, 1922–1926

[We, in the struggling nights] (Muzot, February 9, 1922)

Odette R . . . . (Muzot, December 21, 1922)

Written in a copy of *The Notebooks of Malte Laurids Brigge* for Margarethe Masson-Ruffy, in memory of her sister, Odette Ruffy, a painter, who had died young.

[We say release, and radiance, and roses] (Muzot, approximately May 20, 1923)

Rilke wrote these verses in a book of his poems transcribed by his old friend Marie von Thurn und Taxis for her eldest granddaughter. He added the following inscription: "Written (on Pentecost 1923, during her visit to Muzot) for Princess Marie-Thérèse von Thurn und Taxis, as a 'clasp' for the lovingly chosen sequence on the previous pages."

Imaginary Career (Schöneck, September 15, 1923)

Little Tear-Vase (Schöneck, September 16, 1923)

Second section of "Two Poems (for E.S.)," dedicated to Elisabeth Gundolf-Salomon.

Dedication to M . . . . (Muzot, November 6 and 8, 1923)

Written for Rilke's lover, the artist Baladine Klossowska (a.k.a. Merline), in a copy of the *Duino Elegies*.

For Max Picard (Muzot, November 1923)

Written in a copy of the *Duino Elegies*. Max Picard was a doctor and writer whom Rilke met in 1918.

For Hans Carossa (Muzot, February 7, 1924)

Hans Carossa was a doctor and a well-known German poet. Rilke wrote this dedication-poem in a copy of the *Duino Elegies*.

The Magician (Muzot, February 12, 1924)

This poem grew out of some verses written in a copy of the *Duino Elegies* intended for Gertrud Ouckama Knoop. It is dated "12.II.(around midnight)."

[As once the wingèd energy of delight] (Muzot, mid-February 1924)

[Along the sun-drenched roadside, from the great] (Muzot, beginning of June 1924)

[What birds plunge through is not the intimate space] (Muzot, June 16, 1924)

Duration of Childhood (Ragaz, July 4 or 5, 1924)

> Dedication, *E.M.:* Erika Mitterer. In May 1924, at the age of eighteen, she had sent Rilke two poems, initiating an extensive correspondence in verse, from which this poem and "Dove that ventured outside" are taken.

[World was in the face of the beloved] (Ragaz, mid-July 1924)

Palm (Muzot, around October 1, 1924)

Gravity (Muzot, October 5, 1924)

> This "taking life heavily" that my books are filled with . . . means nothing (don't you agree?) but a taking according to true weight, and thus according to truth: an attempt to weigh Things by the carat of the heart, instead of by suspicion, happiness, or chance.
> (To Rudolf Bodländer, March 13, 1922)

> He who is solitary . . . can remember that all beauty in animals and plants is a silent, enduring form of love and yearning, and he can see animals, as he sees plants, patiently and willingly uniting and increasing and growing, not out of physical pleasure, not out of physical pain, but bowing to necessities that are greater than pleasure and pain, and more powerful than will and withstanding. If only human beings could more humbly receive this mystery—which the world is filled with, even in its smallest Things—, could bear it, endure it, more solemnly, feel how terribly heavy it is, instead of taking it lightly. If only they could be more reverent toward their own fruitfulness, which is essentially *one,* whether it is manifested as mental or physical . . .
> (To Franz Xaver Kappus, July 16, 1903)

Women, in whom life lingers and dwells more immediately, more
fruitfully, and more confidently, must surely have become riper and
more human in their depths than light easygoing man, who is not
pulled down beneath the surface of life by the weight of any bodily
fruit . . .

(Ibid., May 14, 1904)

Mausoleum (Muzot, October 1924)

O Lacrimosa (Paris, May or June 1925)

*O Lacrimosa:* "O tearful [woman]." The epithet usually refers to Mary la-
menting for Jesus at the foot of the cross.

*Ernst Křenek* (1900–1991): Austrian composer. His setting for this poem, for
"high voice" with piano accompaniment, was published in 1926 as his opus
48.

You know that, in general, all attempts to surprise my verses with
music have been unpleasant for me, since they are unrequested addi-
tions to something already complete in itself. It has rarely happened
that I have written verses which seemed either suited for, or in need
of, stirring up the musical element, out of a mutual center. With the
little trilogy "O Lacrimosa" (which would like to pretend an imagi-
nary Italian origin, in order to be still more anonymous than it already
is—) something remarkable happened to me: this poem arose *for
music*—, and then came the wish that sometime (sooner or later) it
might be *your* music in which these impulses could find their fulfill-
ment and their permanence.

(To Ernst Křenek, November 5, 1925)

[Ah, not to be cut off] (Paris, summer 1925)

[Now it is time that gods came walking out] (Muzot, mid-October 1925)

[Rose, oh pure contradiction] (In the testament of October 27, 1925)

At Rilke's request, these lines were carved on his gravestone in the churchyard of Raron.

Idol (First line: Paris, summer 1925; completed: Muzot, November, 1925)

Gong (Muzot, November 1925)

[Four Sketches] (Muzot, December 8, 1925)

The "little notebook with four prose-pieces" was sent to Monique Briod on December 10.

p. 201, *Rustic Chapel:* The small St. Anne chapel next to Muzot.

. . . the abandoned rustic chapel which I take care of; because of its decrepitude, no mass is read in it any longer, and so it is now given back to all the gods and is always filled with open simple homage.
(To Clara Rilke, April 23, 1923)

p. 201, *"Farfallettina":* Little butterfly.

p. 201, *bilboquet:* A wooden toy, consisting of a cord with a ball on one end and a stick on the other; the object of the game is to catch the ball on the spike-end of the stick.

For Veronika Erdmann (Val-Mont, March 10, 1926)

Dedication-poem in a copy of his translation of poems by Paul Valéry.

Elegy (Muzot, June 8, 1926)

Dedication, *Marina Tsvetayeva* (1892–1941): One of the great modern Russian poets. She and Rilke never met in person, but they exchanged a number of intense letters during the spring and summer of 1926. Her long elegy, "Novogodnee" ("For the New Year"), written early in 1927, describes the impact of Rilke's death on her.

l. 18, *Kom Ombo:* Probably a stop on Rilke's trip to Egypt in 1911.

l. 20, *marks as a signal on the doors:* Cf. Exodus 12:7, 13.

[Dove that ventured outside] (Ragaz, August 24, 1926)

Written to Erika Mitterer after she had undergone a serious operation.

That a person who through the horrible obstructions of those years had felt himself split to the very depths of his soul, into a Once and an irreconcilable, dying Now: that such a person should experience the grace of perceiving how in yet more mysterious depths, beneath this torn-open split, the continuity of his work and of his spirit was being re-established—this seems to me more than just a private event. For with it, a measure is given for the inexhaustible stratification of our nature; and many people who, for one reason or another, believe that they have been torn apart, might draw special comfort from this example of continuability. (The thought occurs to me that this comfort too may somehow have entered into the achievement of the great Elegies, so that they express themselves more completely than they could have done without endangerment and rescue.)

(To Arthur Fischer-Colbrie, December 18, 1925)

# PART 2

## Selected Prose

FROM

# The Notebooks of
# Malte Laurids Brigge

*(1910)*

# [FACES]

Have I said it before? I am learning to see. Yes, I am beginning. It's still going badly. But I intend to make the most of my time.

For example, it never occurred to me before how many faces there are. There are multitudes of people, but there are many more faces, because each person has several of them. There are people who wear the same face for years; naturally it wears out, gets dirty, splits at the seams, stretches like gloves worn during a long journey. They are thrifty, uncomplicated people; they never change it, never even have it cleaned. It's good enough, they say, and who can convince them of the contrary? Of course, since they have several faces, you might wonder what they do with the other ones. They keep them in storage. Their children will wear them. But sometimes it also happens that their dogs go out wearing them. And why not? A face is a face.

Other people change faces incredibly fast, put on one after another, and wear them out. At first, they think they have an unlimited supply; but when they are barely forty years old they come to their last one. There is, to be sure, something tragic about this. They are not accustomed to taking care of faces; their last one is worn through in a week, has holes in it, is in many places as thin as paper, and then, little by little, the lining shows through, the non-face, and they walk around with that on.

But the woman, the woman: she had completely fallen into herself, forward into her hands. It was on the corner of rue Notre-Dame-des-Champs. I began to walk quietly as soon as I saw her. When poor people are thinking, they shouldn't be disturbed. Perhaps their idea will still occur to them.

The street was too empty; its emptiness had gotten bored and pulled my steps out from under my feet and clattered around in them, all over the street, as if they were wooden clogs. The woman sat up, frightened, she pulled out of herself, too quickly, too violently, so that her face was left in her two hands. I could see it lying there: its hollow form. It cost me an indescribable effort to stay with those two hands, not to look at what had been torn out of them. I shuddered to see a face from the inside, but I was much more afraid of that bare flayed head waiting there, faceless.

## [THE DEATH OF CHAMBERLAIN BRIGGE]

When I think back to my home, where there is no one left now, it always seems to me that things must have been different back then. Then, you knew (or perhaps you sensed it) that you had your death *inside* you as a fruit has its core. The children had a small one in them and the grownups a large one. The women had it in their womb and the men in their chest. You *had* it, and that gave you a strange dignity and a quiet pride.

It was obvious that my grandfather, old Chamberlain Brigge, still carried a death inside him. And what a death it was: two months long and so loud that it could be heard as far away as the manor farm.

The long, ancient manor-house was too small for this death; it seemed as if new wings would have to be added on, for the Chamberlain's body grew larger and larger, and he kept wanting to be carried from one room to another, bursting into a terrible rage if, before the day had ended, there were no more rooms that he hadn't already been brought to. Then he had to go upstairs, with the whole retinue of servants, chambermaids, and dogs which he always had around him, and, ushered in by the chief steward, they entered the room where his dear mother had died. It had been kept exactly as she had left it twenty-three years before, and since then no one had ever been allowed to set foot in it. Now the whole pack burst in. The curtains were pulled back, and the robust light of a summer afternoon examined all the shy, terrified objects and turned around clumsily in the forced-open mirrors. And the people did the same. There were maids who, in their curiosity, didn't know where their hands were loitering, young servants who gaped at everything, and older ones who walked around trying to remember all the stories they had been told about this locked room which they had now, incredibly, entered.

But it was especially the dogs who were excited by this place where everything had a smell. The tall, slender Russian wolfhounds loped busily back and forth behind the armchairs, moved across the rug swaying slightly in long dance-steps, stood up on their hind legs like the dogs on a coat-of-arms, and, leaning their slender paws on the white-and-gold windowsill, with sharp, attentive faces and wrinkled foreheads gazed right and left into the courtyard. Small, glove-yellow dachshunds sat on the large silk easychair by the window, looking as if everything were quite normal. A wire-haired, sullen-faced setter rubbed its back on the edge of a gilt-legged table, and on the painted top the Sèvres cups trembled.

Yes, it was a terrible time for these drowsy, absentminded Things. Down out of books which some careless hand had clumsily opened, rose leaves fluttered to the floor and were trampled underfoot; small, fragile objects were seized and, instantly broken, were quickly put back in place; others, dented or bent out of shape, were thrust beneath the curtains or even thrown behind the golden net of the fire-screen. And from time to time something fell, fell with a muffled sound onto the rug, fell with a clear sound onto the hard parquet floor, but breaking here and there, with a sharp crack or almost soundlessly; for these Things, pampered as they were, could not endure a fall.

And if anyone had thought of asking what had caused all this, what had called down such intense destruction upon this anxiously protected room,—there could have been only one answer: death.

The death of Chamberlain Christoph Detlev Brigge at Ulsgaard. For he lay on the floor in the middle of the room, enormously swelling out of his dark blue uniform, and did not stir. In his large, strange face, which no one could recognize now, the eyes had closed: he no longer saw what was happening. At first they had tried to lay him on the bed, but he had put up a fight, for he hated beds ever since those nights when his illness had first grown. Besides, the bed in this room had turned out to be too small, so there was nothing left but to lay him on the rug; for he refused to go downstairs.

So now he lay, and one might think that he had died. As it slowly began to grow dark, the dogs had one after another slipped out through the half-closed door. Only the stiff-haired setter with the sullen face sat beside its master, and one of its wide, shaggy forepaws lay on Christoph Detlev's large gray hand. Most of the servants were now standing outside in the white hallway, which was brighter than the room; but those who had stayed inside sometimes stole a glance at the large darkening heap in the middle of the room, and they wished that it were nothing more than a large blanket over some rotten inanimate object.

But there was something more. There was a voice, the voice that, seven weeks before, no one had known: for it wasn't the Chamberlain's voice. This voice didn't belong to Christoph Detlev, but to Christoph Detlev's death.

Christoph Detlev's death was alive now, had already been living at Ulsgaard for many, many days, talked with everyone, made demands. Demanded to be carried, demanded the blue room, demanded the small salon, demanded the great banquet-hall. Demanded the dogs, demanded that people laugh, talk, play, stop talking, and all at the same time. Demanded to see friends, women, and people who had died, and demanded to die itself: demanded. Demanded and screamed.

For, when night had come and, exhausted, those of the servants who didn't have to sit up tried to get some sleep, Christoph Detlev's death began screaming, it screamed and groaned, it howled so long and continuously that the dogs, which at first had howled along with it, fell silent and didn't dare to lie down and, standing on their long, thin, trembling legs, were afraid. And when, through the huge, silvery Danish summer night, the villagers heard it howling, they got up out of bed as if there were a thunderstorm, dressed, and stayed seated around the lamp, without a word, until it was over. And the women who would soon give birth were brought to the most remote rooms and to the most inaccessible alcoves; but they heard it, they heard it, as if it were screaming from inside their own bodies, and they begged to be allowed to get up, and came, white and heavy, and sat down among the others with their blurred faces. And the cows that were calving then were helpless and miserable, and the dead fruit had to be torn out of one of them, along with all the entrails, since it refused to come out at all. And everyone did their daily work badly and forgot to bring in the hay because they spent the day dreading the arrival of night and because they were so worn out by the sleeplessness and the terrified awakenings that they couldn't concentrate on anything. And when on Sunday they went to the white, peaceful church, they prayed that there might no longer be a master at Ulsgaard: for this one was a terrifying master. And what they were all thinking and praying, the minister said out loud up in the pulpit, for he too had no nights anymore and could no longer understand God. And the churchbell said it, having found a terrible rival which boomed out all night long and against which, even when it rang with all its metal, it could do nothing. Indeed, they all said it; and one of the young men dreamed that he had gone to the manor-house and killed the master with his pitchfork; and they were so exasperated, so overstrained, that they all listened as he told his dream and, quite unconsciously, looked at him to see if he were really brave enough to do that. This is how people felt and talked in the whole district where, just a few weeks before, the Chamberlain had been loved and pitied. But though there was all this talk, nothing changed. Christoph Detlev's death, which had moved in at Ulsgaard, refused to let itself be hurried. It had come for ten weeks, and for ten weeks it stayed. And during that time it was master, more than Christoph Detlev Brigge had ever been; it was like a king who is called the Terrible, afterward and for all time.

This was not the death of just any old man with dropsy; this was the sinister, princely death which the Chamberlain had, all his life, carried inside him and nourished with his own experiences. Every excess of pride, will, and authority that he himself had not been able to use up during his peaceful days, had passed into his death, into the death that now sat squandering these things at Ulsgaard.

How Chamberlain Brigge would have looked at anyone who asked him to die any other death than this. He was dying his own hard death.

## [FOR THE SAKE OF A SINGLE POEM]

. . . Ah, poems amount to so little when you write them too early in your life. You ought to wait and gather sense and sweetness for a whole lifetime, and a long one if possible, and then, at the very end, you might perhaps be able to write ten good lines. For poems are not, as people think, simply emotions (one has emotions early enough)— they are experiences. For the sake of a single poem, you must see many cities, many people and Things, you must understand animals, must feel how birds fly, and know the gesture which small flowers make when they open in the morning. You must be able to think back to streets in unknown neighborhoods, to unexpected encounters, and to partings you had long seen coming; to days of childhood whose mystery is still unexplained, to parents whom you had to hurt when they brought in a joy and you didn't pick it up (it was a joy meant for somebody else—); to childhood illnesses that began so strangely with so many profound and difficult transformations, to days in quiet, restrained rooms and to mornings by the sea, to the sea itself, to seas, to nights of travel that rushed along high overhead and went flying with all the stars,—and it is still not enough to be able to think of all that. You must have memories of many nights of love, each one different from all the others, memories of women screaming in labor, and of light, pale, sleeping girls who have just given birth and are closing again. But you must also have been beside the dying, must have sat beside the dead in the room with the open window and the scattered noises. And it is not yet enough to have memories. You must be able to forget them when they are many, and you must have the immense patience to wait until they return. For the memories themselves are not important. Only when they have changed into our very blood, into glance and gesture, and are nameless, no longer to be distinguished from ourselves—only then can it happen that in some very rare hour the first word of a poem arises in their midst and goes forth from them.

# [FEARS]

I am lying in my bed five flights up, and my day, which nothing interrupts, is like a clock-face without hands. As something that has been lost for a long time reappears one morning in its old place, safe and sound, almost newer than when it vanished, just as if someone had been taking care of it—: so, here and there on my blanket, lost feelings out of my childhood lie and are like new. All the lost fears are here again.

The fear that a small woolen thread sticking out of the hem of my blanket may be hard, hard and sharp as a steel needle; the fear that this little button on my night-shirt may be bigger than my head, bigger and heavier; the fear that the breadcrumb which just dropped off my bed may turn into glass, and shatter when it hits the floor, and the sickening worry that when it does, everything will be broken, for ever; the fear that the ragged edge of a letter which was torn open may be something forbidden, which no one ought to see, something indescribably precious, for which no place in the room is safe enough; the fear that if I fell asleep I might swallow the piece of coal lying in front of the stove; the fear that some number may begin to grow in my brain until there is no more room for it inside me; the fear that I may be lying on granite, on gray granite; the fear that I may start screaming, and people will come running to my door and finally force it open, the fear that I might betray myself and tell everything I dread, and the fear that I might not be able to say anything, because everything is unsayable,— and the other fears . . . the fears.

I prayed to rediscover my childhood, and it has come back, and I feel that it is just as difficult as it used to be, and that growing older has served no purpose at all.

## [THE MAN WITH ST. VITUS' DANCE]

Yesterday my fever was better, and this morning the day began like spring, like spring in paintings. I want to go out to the Bibliothèque Nationale and spend some time with my poet, whom I haven't read for many weeks, and afterward perhaps I can take a leisurely walk through the gardens. Perhaps there will be a wind over the large pond which has such real water, and children will come to sail their little red boats.

Today I really didn't expect it; I went out so bravely, as if that were the simplest and most natural thing in the world. And yet something happened again that took me up and crumpled me like a piece of paper and threw me away: something incredible.

The Boulevard Saint-Michel lay in front of me, empty and vast, and it was easy to walk along its gentle slope. Window-casements overhead opened with a clear, glassy sound, and their brilliance flew over the street like a white bird. A carriage with bright red wheels rolled past, and farther down someone was carrying something green. Horses in their glittering harnesses trotted along the dark, freshly sprinkled boulevard. The wind was brisk and mild, and everything was rising: odors, cries, bells.

I came to one of those cafés where false red gypsies perform in the evening. From the open windows, the air of the previous night crept out with a bad conscience. Sleek-haired waiters were busy sweeping in front of the door. One of them was bent over, tossing handful after handful of yellowish sand under the tables. A passerby stopped, nudged him, and pointed down the street. The waiter, who was all red in the face, looked sharply in that direction for a moment or two; then a laugh spread over his beardless cheeks, as if it had been spilled across them. He gestured to the other waiters, turned his laughing face quickly from right to left several times, to call everyone over without missing anything himself. Now they all stood there, seeing or trying to see what was happening down the street, smiling or annoyed that they hadn't yet found out what was so funny.

I felt a slight fear beginning inside me. Something was urging me to cross the street; but all I did was start to walk faster; and when I looked at the few people in front of me, I didn't notice anything unusual. I did see that one of them, an errand-boy with a blue apron and an empty basket slung over one shoulder, was staring at someone. When he had seen enough, he turned around toward the houses and gestured to a laughing clerk across the street, moving his finger in front of his forehead with that circular motion whose meaning everyone knows. Then his dark eyes flashed and he came toward me, swaggering and content.

I expected that as soon as I had a better view I would see some extraordinary and striking figure; but it turned out that there was no one in front of me except a tall, emaciated man in a dark coat, with a soft black hat on his short, faded-blond hair. I was sure there was nothing laughable about this man's clothing or behavior, and was already trying to look past him down the boulevard, when he tripped over something. Since I was walking close behind him I was on my guard, but when I came to the place, there was nothing there, absolutely nothing. We both kept walking, he and I, with the same distance between us. Now there was an intersection; the man in front of me hopped down from the sidewalk on one leg, the way children, when they are happy, will now and then hop or skip as they walk. On the other side of the street, he simply took one long step up onto the sidewalk. But almost immediately he raised one leg slightly and hopped on the other, once, quite high, and then again and again. This time too you might easily have thought the man had tripped over some small object on the corner, a peach pit, a banana peel, anything; and the strange thing was that he himself seemed to believe in the presence of an obstacle: he turned around every time and looked at the offending spot with that half-annoyed, half-reproachful expression people have at such moments. Once again some intuition warned me to cross the street, but I didn't listen to it; I continued to follow this man, concentrating all my attention on his legs. I must admit I felt very relieved when for about twenty steps the hopping didn't recur; but as I looked up, I noticed that something else had begun to annoy the man. His coat collar had somehow popped up; and as hard as he tried to fold it back in place, first with one hand, then with both at once, it refused to budge. This kind of thing can happen. It didn't upset me. But then I saw, with boundless astonishment, that in his busy hands there were two distinct movements: one a quick, secret movement that flipped up the collar, while the other one, elaborate, prolonged, exaggeratedly spelled out, was meant to fold it back down. This observation disconcerted me so greatly that two minutes passed before I recognized in the man's neck, behind his hunched-up coat and his nervously scrambling hands, the same horrible, bisyllabic hopping that had just left his legs. From this moment I was bound to him. I saw that the hopping was wandering through his body, trying to break out here or there. I understood why he was afraid of people, and I myself began to examine the passersby, cautiously, to see if they noticed anything. A cold twinge shot down my spine when his legs suddenly made a small, convulsive leap; but no one had seen it, and I decided that I would also trip slightly if anyone began to look. That would certainly be a way of making them think there had been some small, imperceptible object on the sidewalk, which both of us had happened to step on. But while I was thinking about how I could help, he himself had found a new and excellent device. I forgot to mention that he had a cane; it was an ordinary cane, made of dark wood, with a plain, curved handle. In his anxious searching, he had hit upon the idea of holding this cane against his back, at first with one hand (who knows what he might still need the other hand for), right along his spine, pressing it firmly into the small of his back and sliding the curved end under his collar, in such a way that you felt it standing behind the cervical and first dorsal vertebrae like a neck-brace. This posture didn't look strange; at most it was a bit cocky, but the unexpected spring day might excuse that. No one thought of turning around to look, and now everything was all right. Perfectly all right. True, at the next intersection two hops escaped, two small, half-suppressed hops, but they didn't amount to anything; and the one really visible leap was so skillfully timed (just at the spot where a hose was lying across the sidewalk) that there was nothing to be afraid of. Yes, everything was still all right; from time to time his other hand too seized the cane and pressed it in more firmly, and right away the danger was again overcome. But I couldn't keep my anxiety from growing. I knew that as he walked and with infinite effort tried to appear calm and detached, the terrible spasms were accumulating inside his body; I could feel the anxiety *he* felt as the spasms grew and grew, and I saw how he clutched his cane when the shaking began inside him. The expression of his hands became so severe and relentless then that I placed all my hope in his willpower, which was bound to be strong. But what could mere willpower do? The moment had to come when his strength would be exhausted; it couldn't be long now. And I, who followed him with my heart pounding, I gathered my little strength together like money and, gazing at his hands, I begged him to take it if it could be of any use.

I think he took it; is it my fault that it wasn't enough?

At the Place Saint-Michel there were many vehicles, and pedestrians hurrying here and there; several times we were caught between two carriages, and then he would take a breath and relax a bit, and there would be a bit of hopping and nodding. Perhaps that was the trick by which the imprisoned illness hoped to subdue him. His willpower had cracked in two places, and the damage had left in his possessed muscles a gentle, alluring stimulation and this compelling two-beat rhythm. But the cane was still in its place, and the hands looked annoyed and angry. As we stepped onto the bridge, it was all right. It was still all right. But now his walk became noticeably uncertain; first he ran two steps, then he stopped. Stopped. His left hand gently let go of the cane, and rose so slowly that I could see it tremble in the air. He pushed his hat back slightly and drew his hand across his brow. He turned his head slightly, and his gaze wobbled over sky, houses, and water, without grasping a thing. And then he gave in. The cane was gone, he stretched out his arms as if he were trying to fly, and some kind of elemental force exploded from him and bent him forward and dragged him back and made him keep nodding and bowing and flung a horrible dance out of him into the midst of the crowd. For he was already surrounded by people, and I could no longer see him.

What sense would there have been in going anywhere now; I was empty. Like a blank piece of paper, I drifted along past the houses, up the boulevard again.

## [THE BIRD-FEEDERS]

I don't underestimate it. I know it takes courage. But let us suppose for a moment that someone had it, this *courage de luxe* to follow them, in order to know for ever (for who could forget it again or confuse it with anything else?) where they creep off to afterward and what they do with the rest of the long day and whether they sleep at night. That especially should be ascertained: whether they sleep. But it will take more than courage. For they don't come and go like other people, whom it would be child's play to follow. They are here and then gone, put down and snatched away like toy soldiers. The places where they can be found are somewhat out-of-the-way, but by no means hidden. The bushes recede, the path curves slightly around the lawn: there they are, with a large transparent space around them, as if they were standing under a glass dome. You might think they were pausing, absorbed in their thoughts, these inconspicuous men, with such small, in every way unassuming bodies. But you are wrong. Do you see the left hand, how it is grasping for something in the slanted pocket of the old coat? how it finds it and takes it out and holds the small object in the air, awkwardly, attracting attention? In less than a minute, two or three birds appear, sparrows, which come hopping up inquisitively. And if the man succeeds in conforming to their very exact idea of immobility, there is no reason why they shouldn't come even closer. Finally one of them flies up, and flutters nervously for a while at the level of that hand, which is holding out God knows what crumbs of used-up bread in its unpretentious, explicitly renunciatory fingers. And the more people gather around him—at a suitable distance, of course—the less he has in common with them. He stands there like a candle that is almost consumed and burns with the small remnant of its wick and is all warm with it and has never moved. And all those small, foolish birds can't understand how he attracts, how he tempts them. If there were no onlookers and he were allowed to stand there long enough, I'm certain that an angel would suddenly appear and, overcoming his disgust, would eat the stale, sweetish breadcrumbs from that stunted hand. But now, as always, people keep that from happening. They make sure that only birds come; they find this quite sufficient and assert that he expects nothing else. What else could it expect, this old, weather-beaten doll, stuck into the ground at a slight angle, like a painted figurehead in an old sea-captain's garden? Does it stand like that because it too had once been placed somewhere on the forward tip of its life, at the point where motion is greatest? Is it now so washed out because it was once so bright? Will you go ask it?

Only don't ask the women anything when you see them feeding the birds. You could even follow them; they do it just in passing; it would be easy. But leave them alone. They don't know how it happens. All at once they have a whole purseful of bread, and they hold out large pieces from under their flimsy shawls, pieces that are a bit chewed and soggy. It does them good to think that their saliva is getting out into the world a little, that the small birds will fly off with the taste of it in their mouths, even though a moment later they naturally forget it again.

## [IBSEN]

There I sat before your books, obstinate man, trying to understand them as the others do, who don't leave you in one piece but chip off their little portion and go away satisfied. For I still didn't understand fame, that public demolition of someone who is in the process of becoming, whose building-site the mob breaks into, knocking down his stones.

Young man anywhere, in whom something is welling up that makes you shiver, be grateful that no one knows you. And if those who think you are worthless contradict you, and if those whom you call your friends abandon you, and if they want to destroy you because of your precious ideas: what is this obvious danger, which concentrates you inside yourself, compared with the cunning enmity of fame, later, which makes you innocuous by scattering you all around?

Don't ask anyone to speak about you, not even contemptuously. And when time passes and you notice that your name is circulating among men, don't take this more seriously than anything else you might find in their mouths. Think rather that it has become cheapened, and throw it away. Take another name, *any* other, so that God can call you in the night. And hide it from everyone.

Loneliest of men, holding aloof from them all, how quickly they have caught up with you because of your fame. A little while ago they were against you body and soul; and now they treat you as their equal. And they pull your words around with them in the cages of their presumption, and exhibit them in the streets, and tease them a little, from a safe distance. All your terrifying wild beasts.

When I first read you, these words broke loose and fell upon me in my wilderness, in all their desperation. As desperate as you yourself became in the end, you whose course is drawn incorrectly on every chart. Like a crack it crosses the heavens, this hopeless hyperbola of your path, which curves toward us only once, then recedes again in terror. What did you care if a woman stayed or left, if this man was seized by vertigo and that one by madness, if the dead were alive and the living seemed dead: what did you care? It was all so natural for you; you passed through it the way someone might walk through a vestibule, and didn't stop. But you lingered, bent over, where our life boils and precipitates and changes color: inside. Farther in than anyone has ever been; a door had sprung open before you, and now you were among the alembics in the firelight. In there, where, mistrustful, you wouldn't take anyone with you, in there you sat and discerned transitions. And there, since your blood drove you not to form or to speak, but to reveal, there you made the enormous decision to so magnify these tiny events, which you yourself first perceived only in test tubes, that they would be seen by thousands of people, immense before them all. Your theater came into being. You couldn't wait until this life almost without spatial reality, this life which had been condensed by the weight of the centuries into a few small drops, could be discovered by the other arts: until it could gradually be made visible to a few connoisseurs who, little by little, acquire insight and finally demand to see these august rumors confirmed in the parable of the scene opened in front of them. You couldn't wait for that; you were there, and everything that is barely measurable—an emotion that rises by half a degree, the angle of deflection, read off from up close, of a will burdened by an almost infinitesimal weight, the slight cloudiness in a drop of longing, and that barely perceptible color-change in an atom of confidence—all this you had to determine and record. For it is in such reactions that life existed, *our* life, which had slipped into us, had drawn back inside us so deeply that it was hardly possible even to make conjectures about it any more.

Because you were a revealer, a timelessly tragic poet, you had to transform this capillary action all at once into the most convincing gestures, into the most available forms. So you began that unprecedented act of violence in your work, which, more and more impatiently, desperately, sought equivalents in the visible world for what you had seen inside. There was a rabbit there, an attic, a room where someone was pacing back and forth; there was a clatter of glass in a nearby bedroom, a fire outside the windows; there was the sun. There was a church, and a rock-strewn valley that was like a church. But this wasn't enough: finally towers had to come in and whole mountain-ranges; and the avalanches that bury landscapes spilled onto a stage overwhelmed with what is tangible, for the sake of what cannot be grasped. Then you could do no more. The two ends, which you had bent together until they touched, sprang apart; your demented strength escaped from the flexible wand, and your work was as if it had never existed.

If this hadn't happened, who could understand why in the end you refused to go away from the window, obstinate as you always were? You wanted to see the people passing by; for the thought had occurred to you that someday you might make something out of them, if you decided to begin.

# [COSTUMES]

When I think about it now, I can't help being astonished that I always managed to completely return from the world of these fevers and was able to adjust to that social existence where everyone wanted to be reassured that they were among familiar objects and people, where they all conspired to remain in the realm of the intelligible. If you looked forward to something, it either came or didn't come, there was no third possibility. There were Things that were sad, once and for all, and there were pleasant Things, and a great number of incidental ones. And if a joy was arranged for you, it was in fact a joy, and you had to behave accordingly. All this was basically very simple, and once you got the knack of it, it took care of itself. For everything entered into these appointed boundaries: the long, monotonous school hours, when it was summer outside; the walks that afterward you had to describe in French; the visitors into whose presence you were summoned and who thought you were amusing, just when you were feeling sad, and laughed at you the way people laugh at the melancholy expression of certain birds, who don't have any other face. And of course the birthday parties, to which children were invited whom you hardly knew, embarrassed little girls who made *you* embarrassed, or rude little boys who scratched your face, and broke the presents you had just received, and then suddenly left when all the toys had been pulled out of their boxes and wrappings and were lying piled up on the floor. But when you played by yourself, as always, it could happen that you inadvertently stepped out of this agreed-upon, generally harmless world, and found yourself in circumstances that were completely different, and unimaginable.

At times Mademoiselle had her migraine, which was extremely violent, and these were the days when I was hard to find. I know that on these occasions the coachman was sent to look for me in the park when Father happened to ask for me and I wasn't there. From one of the upper guest-rooms I could see him running out and calling my name at the entrance to the long tree-lined driveway. These rooms were situated, side by side, in the gable of Ulsgaard and, since we very seldom had house-guests in those days, were almost always empty. But adjoining them was that large corner room that attracted me to it so powerfully. There was nothing in it except an old bust of Admiral Juel, I think, but all around, the walls were paneled with deep, gray wardrobes, so that the window had had to be installed in the bare, whitewashed space above them. In one of the wardrobe doors I had found a key, and it opened all the others. So in a short time I had examined everything: eighteenth-century chamberlains' coats, cold with their inwoven silver threads, and the beautiful embroidered vests that went with them; official costumes of the Order of Danneborg and the Order of the Elephant, so rich and ceremonious, with linings so soft when you touched them, that at first you thought they were women's dresses. Then real gowns which, held out by their panniers, hung stiffly like marionettes from some too-large puppet show, now so completely outmoded that their heads had been taken off and used for some other purpose. But alongside these, there were wardrobes that were dark when you opened them, dark with high-buttoned uniforms that seemed much more worn than all the others and that wished they had never been preserved.

No one will find it surprising that I pulled all these clothes out and took them into the light; that I held one of them up to my chest or wrapped another one around me; that I hastily tried on some costume that might fit me and, curious and excited, ran to the nearest guest-room, in front of the tall, narrow mirror, which was made up of irregular pieces of green glass. Ah, how I trembled to be there, and how thrilling when I was: when something approached out of the cloudy depths, more slowly than myself, for the mirror hardly believed it and, sleepy as it was, didn't want to promptly repeat what I had recited to it. But in the end it had to, of course. And now it was something very astonishing, strange, totally different from what I had expected, something sudden, independent, which I glanced over quickly, only to recognize myself a moment later, not without a certain irony, which came within a hairsbreadth of spoiling all the fun. But if I immediately began to talk, to bow, to nod at myself, if I walked away, looking around at the mirror all the while, and walked back, brisk and determined, I had imagination on my side, as long as I wanted.

It was then that I first came to know the influence that can emanate from a particular costume. Hardly had I put on one of them when I had to admit to myself that it had me in its power; that it dictated my movements, my facial expression, even my thoughts. My hand, over which the lace cuff fell and fell again, was in no way my ordinary hand; it moved like an actor; I might even say that it watched itself move, however exaggerated that sounds. These disguises, though, never went so far as to make me feel a stranger to myself; on the contrary, the more complete my transformation, the more convinced I was of my own identity. I grew bolder and bolder; flung myself higher and higher; for my skill at catching myself again was beyond all doubt. I didn't notice the temptation in this quickly growing security. My undoing came when the last wardrobe, which I hadn't been able to open before, yielded one day, furnishing me with, not specific costumes, but all kinds of random paraphernalia for masquerades, whose fantastic possibilities made my head spin. There is no way to describe everything I found there. In addition to a *bautta* that I remember, there were dominos in various colors, women's skirts which tinkled brightly with the coins that were sewn into them; there were Pierrot costumes, which I thought looked ridiculous, and pleated Turkish pants, and Persian fezzes, from which little sacks of camphor slipped out, and coronets with stupid, expressionless stones. All these I rather despised; they were so shabbily unreal, and hung there so stripped and wretched, and collapsed so helplessly when they were dragged out into the light. But what transported me into a kind of intoxication were the spacious cloaks, the scarves, the shawls, the veils, all those yielding, wide, unused fabrics that were so soft and caressing, or so smooth that I could hardly keep hold of them, or so light that they flew by me like a wind, or simply heavy with all their own weight. It was in them that I first saw possibilities that were free and infinitely varied: I could be a slave-girl who was about to be sold, or Joan of Arc or an old king or a wizard; all this was possible now, especially since there were also masks, enormous menacing or astonished faces with real beards and thick or upraised eyebrows. I had never seen any masks before, but I immediately understood that masks ought to exist. I had to laugh when it occurred to me that we had a dog who looked as if he wore one. I remembered his affectionate eyes, which always seemed to be looking out from behind two holes in his hairy face. I was still laughing as I put on the clothes, and in the process I completely forgot what I had intended to dress up as. All right, it was new and exciting not to decide until I was in front of the mirror. The face I tied on had a peculiarly hollow smell; it fitted closely over my own face, but I was able to see through it comfortably, and only after the mask was on did I choose all kinds of materials, which I wound around my head like a turban, in such a way that the edge of the mask, which extended downward into a gigantic yellow cloak, was almost completely hidden on top also and on the sides. Finally, when there was nothing more to add, I considered myself adequately disguised. To complete the costume, I picked up a large staff and walked it along beside me at arm's length, and in this way, not without difficulty but, as it seemed to me, full of dignity, I trailed into the guest-room toward the mirror.

It was really magnificent, beyond all expectation. And the mirror repeated it instantly: it was too convincing. It wouldn't have been at all necessary to move; this apparition was perfect, even though it didn't do a thing. But I wanted to find out what I actually was, so I turned around slightly and lifted both arms: large gestures, as if I were a sorcerer, were (as I saw immediately) the only appropriate ones. But just at this solemn moment I heard quite near me, muffled by my disguise, a multiple, complicated noise. Very frightened, I lost sight of the creature in the mirror and, to my great dismay, saw that I had knocked over a small round table with heaven knows what on it, probably very fragile objects. I bent down as well as I could and found my worst fears confirmed: everything seemed to be in pieces. The two useless, green-violet porcelain parrots were of course shattered, each in a different, malign way. A small bowl had spilled out its pieces of candy, which looked like insects in their silk cocoons, and had tossed its cover far away—only half of it was visible, the other half had completely disappeared. But the most annoying sight of all was a perfume bottle that had broken into a thousand tiny fragments, from which the remnant of some ancient essence had spurted out, that now formed a stain with a very repulsive physiognomy on the light rug. I quickly tried to wipe it up with some of the material that was hanging all over me, but it only got darker and more unpleasant. I was truly desperate now. I got up and looked for some object I could repair the damage with. But there was nothing. Besides, I was so hampered, in my vision and in every movement, that a violent rage flared up against my absurd situation, which I no longer understood. I began to pull at the knots of my costume, but that only made them tighter. The strings of the cloak were strangling me, and the material on my head was pressing down as if more and more were being added to it. In addition, the air had grown thick and misty with the vapor of the spilled liquid.

Hot and furious, I rushed to the mirror and with difficulty watched, through the mask, the frantic movements of my hands. But the mirror had been waiting for just this. Its moment of revenge had come. While I, with a boundlessly growing anguish, kept trying to somehow squeeze out of my disguise, it forced me, I don't know how, to look up, and dictated to me an image, no, a reality, a strange, incomprehensible, monstrous reality that permeated me against my will: for now it was the stronger one, and I was the mirror. I stared at this large, terrifying stranger in front of me, and felt appalled to be alone with him. But at the very moment I thought this, the worst thing happened: I lost all sense of myself, I simply ceased to exist. For one second, I felt an indescribable, piercing, futile longing for myself, then only *he* remained: there was nothing except him.

I began to run, but now it was he that was running. He knocked against everything, he didn't know the house, had no idea where to go; he stumbled down a flight of stairs, he tripped over someone who screamed and struggled free. A door opened, people came out: Ah, what a relief it was to recognize them. Sieversen was there, with her kind face, and the chambermaid and the butler: now everything would be decided. But they didn't rush forward to rescue me. They stood there, with infinite cruelty, and laughed; my God, they just stood there and laughed. I was crying, but the mask didn't let the tears escape, they fell inside it, onto my face, and dried immediately, and fell again and dried. And finally I kneeled in front of them, as no one had ever kneeled before; I kneeled and lifted my hands toward them and begged: "Take me out, if you still can, save me," but they didn't hear; there was no voice left in me.

To the day of her death, Sieversen used to tell how I had collapsed onto the floor and how they had kept on laughing, thinking this was part of the game. They were used to that from me. But then I had continued to lie there and hadn't answered. And the fright when they had finally discovered that I was unconscious and lay there like a piece of cloth among all those wrappings, yes, just like a piece of cloth.

## [NEIGHBORS]

There exists a creature that is perfectly harmless; when it passes before your eyes, you hardly notice it and immediately forget it again. But as soon as it somehow, invisibly, gets into your ears, it begins to develop, it hatches, and cases have been known where it has penetrated into the brain and flourished there devastatingly, like the pneumococci in dogs which gain entrance through the nose.

This creature is Your Neighbor.

Now ever since I have been drifting about on my own like this, I have had innumerable neighbors; neighbors above me and below me, neighbors on my right and on my left, sometimes all four kinds at once. I could simply write the history of my neighbors; that would take up a whole lifetime. Actually, it would be more of a history of the symptoms they have generated in me; because they share with all creatures of a similar nature the characteristic that their presence can be detected only through the disturbances they cause in certain tissues.

I have had unpredictable neighbors and others whose habits were extremely regular. I have sat for hours trying to discover the law of the former type; for I was convinced that even they were acting in accordance with some law. And when my punctual neighbors failed to come home at their usual time one evening, I have imagined the disasters that might have happened to them, and have kept my candle burning, and have been as anxious as a young wife. I have had neighbors who felt nothing but hatred, and neighbors who were involved in a passionate love affair; or I experienced the moment when one emotion abruptly turned into the other, in the middle of the night, and then, of course, sleep was unthinkable. In fact, this led me to observe that sleep is much less frequent than people generally suppose. My two neighbors in St. Petersburg, for example, attached very little importance to sleep. One of them stood and played the violin, and I'm sure that as he played he looked across into the too-awake houses that never stopped being brightly lit during those improbable August nights. As to my neighbor on the right, I know at least that he lay in bed; in my time, indeed, he no longer got up at all. He even kept his eyes closed; but you couldn't say that he slept. He lay there and recited long poems, poems by Pushkin and Nekrasov, in the singsong tone that children use when they are asked to recite a poem. And despite the music of my neighbor on the left, it was this fellow with his poems who wove a cocoon inside my head, and God knows what would have hatched out of it if the student who occasionally visited him hadn't knocked on the wrong door one day. He told me the story of his friend, and it turned out to be more or less reassuring. At any rate, it was a simple, unambiguous story, which put an end to the swarming maggots of my conjectures.

This petty bureaucrat next door had one Sunday decided to solve a strange problem. He assumed that he would live for quite a long time, say another fifty years. The generosity he thus showed toward himself put him in a radiantly good mood. But now he wanted to outdo himself. It occurred to him that these years could be changed into days, hours, minutes, even (if you could stand it) into seconds; and he multiplied and multiplied, and a grand total appeared such as he had never seen before. It made him giddy. He had to recover for a while. Time was valuable, he had always heard, and he was astonished that a man who possessed such a vast quantity of time didn't have a guard beside him at every moment. How easy it would be to rob him! But then his good, almost exuberant humor came back again; he put on his fur coat, to appear a little broader and more imposing, and gave himself the whole of this fabulous capital, addressing himself in a slightly condescending manner:

"Nikolai Kuzmitch," he said benevolently, and imagined himself also sitting without the fur coat, thin and shabby on the horsehair sofa; "I do hope, Nikolai Kuzmitch," he said, "that you won't get a swelled head from your new fortune. You must always bear in mind that wealth isn't the main thing; there are poor people who are thoroughly respectable; there are even impoverished noblemen and generals' daughters who go around peddling things on the sidewalk." And the benefactor cited a few more examples that were well known throughout the city.

The other Nikolai Kuzmitch, the one on the horsehair sofa, the recipient of this gift, didn't look the slightest bit puffed up; you might safely assume that he was going to be reasonable. In fact he didn't make any changes in his modest, regular way of life, and he now spent his Sundays putting his accounts in order. But after a few weeks it became obvious that he was spending an incredible amount. I will have to economize, he thought. He got up earlier, he washed his face less thoroughly, he drank his tea standing up, he ran to the office and arrived much too early. He saved a little time everywhere. But when Sunday came around, there was nothing left of all this saving. Then he realized that he had been duped. I should never have gotten change, he said to himself. How long a fine, unbroken year would have lasted! But these damned small coins—they keep disappearing, God knows how. And one ugly afternoon, he sat down in a corner of the sofa, waiting for the gentleman in the fur coat, from whom he meant to demand his time back. He would bolt the door and not let him out until he had forked over the whole amount. "In bills," he would say, "of ten years, if you don't mind." Four bills of ten and one of five, and the rest he could keep and go to hell with. Yes, he was prepared to give him the rest, as long as there were no difficulties. Exasperated, he sat on the horsehair sofa and waited; but the gentleman never came. And he, Nikolai Kuzmitch, who just a few weeks before had so easily seen himself sitting there, was unable, now that he really sat there, to picture the other Nikolai Kuzmitch, the one in the fur coat, the benefactor. What had become of him, only heaven knew; probably his embezzlements had been traced, and he was behind bars somewhere. Certainly there must have been many others whose lives he had ruined. Swindlers like that always work on a large scale.

It occurred to him that there had to be some public agency, a kind of Time Bank, where he could change at least some part of his miserable seconds. After all, they *were* genuine. He had never heard of an institution like this, but he would certainly be able to find something of the sort in the directory, under T, or perhaps it was called "Bank of Time"; he could easily look under B. If necessary he might also check under the letter I, for presumably it was an imperial institution; that would be in keeping with its importance.

Later, Nikolai Kuzmitch always used to give his word of honor that, although he was understandably in a very depressed mood that Sunday evening, he hadn't had a thing to drink. He was therefore perfectly sober when the following incident occurred, as far as one can tell what actually happened. Perhaps he had dozed off for a few minutes in the corner of the sofa; he might easily have done that. At first this little nap gave him the greatest relief. I have been meddling with numbers, he said to himself. All right, I don't understand the first thing about numbers. But it's obvious that they shouldn't be granted too much importance; they are, after all, just a kind of arrangement created by the government for the sake of public order. No one had ever seen them anywhere but on paper. It was impossible, for instance, to meet a Seven or a Twenty-five at a party. There simply weren't any there. And so this slight confusion had taken place, out of pure absent-mindedness: time and money, as if there were no difference between the two. Nikolai Kuzmitch almost laughed. It was really wonderful to have found the mistake, and in good time, that was the important thing, in good time. Now it would be different. Time was certainly a great embarrassment. But was he the only one this had happened to? Didn't time pass for other people, just as he had discovered, in seconds, even if they weren't aware of it?

Nikolai Kuzmitch was not entirely free from enjoying other people's misfortune. "Let it nevertheless . . . ," he was just about to think, when something bizarre happened. He suddenly felt a breath on his face; it moved past his ears; it was on his hands now. He opened his eyes wide. The window was definitely closed. And as he sat there in the dark room, with eyes wide open, he began to realize that what he was feeling now was *real* time, as it passed by. He recognized, with absolute clarity, all these tiny seconds, all equally tepid, each one exactly like the others, but fast, but fast. What else they were planning, only God knew. Why was this happening to him, of all people, who experienced every kind of draft as an insult? Now he would sit there, and the breeze would go past him like this, ceaselessly, his whole life long. He foresaw all the attacks of neuralgia that would result from this; he was beside himself with rage. He jumped up, but the surprises were not yet over. Beneath his feet too there was something moving; not just one motion, but several, which strangely shook in and against one another. He stiffened with terror: could that be the earth? Of course it was. The earth did, after all, move. He had heard about that in school; but it was passed over rather quickly, and later on was completely hushed up; it was considered not a proper subject for discussion. But now that he had become more sensitive, he was able to feel this too. Did the others feel it? Perhaps, but you couldn't really tell. Probably it didn't bother them, good sailors as they were. But it was in precisely this respect that Nikolai Kuzmitch was so delicate; he avoided even the streetcars. He staggered around in his room as if he were on the deck of a ship and had to reach out left and right for support. Unfortunately he then remembered something else, about the oblique position of the earth's axis. No, he couldn't endure all these motions. He felt sick. Lying down and keeping quiet were the best remedy, he had once read somewhere. And since that day Nikolai Kuzmitch had been lying in bed.

He lay there and kept his eyes closed. And there were times, during the less shaken days, so to speak, when it was quite bearable. And then he had devised this routine with the poems. It was unbelievable how much that helped. When you recited a poem slowly, with a regular emphasis on the rhyme words, then something more or less stable existed, which you could keep a steady gaze on, inwardly of course. It was lucky that he knew all these poems by heart. But he had always been particularly interested in literature. He didn't complain about his situation, said the student, who had known him for many years. But in the course of time an exaggerated admiration had developed in him for those who, like the student, managed to walk around and endured the motion of the earth.

I remember this story in such detail because it was extraordinarily reassuring to me. I can even say that I have never again had such a pleasant neighbor as this Nikolai Kuzmitch, who certainly would also have admired me.

# [THE TEMPTATION OF THE SAINT]

How well I understand those strange pictures in which Things meant
for limited and ordinary uses stretch out and stroke one another, lewd
and curious, quivering in the random lechery of distraction. Those
kettles that walk around steaming, those pistons that start to think,
and the indolent funnel that squeezes into a hole for its pleasure. And
already, tossed up by the jealous void, and among them, there are arms
and legs, and faces that warmly vomit onto them, and windy buttocks
that offer them satisfaction.

And the saint writhes and pulls back into himself; yet in his eyes
there was still a look which thought this was possible: he had glimpsed
it. And already his senses are precipitating out of the clear solution of
his soul. His prayer is already losing its leaves and stands up out of his
mouth like a withered shrub. His heart has fallen over and poured out
into the muck. His whip strikes him as weakly as a tail flicking away
flies. His sex is once again in one place only, and when a woman comes
toward him, upright through the huddle, with her naked bosom full of
breasts, it points at her like a finger.

There was a time when I considered these pictures obsolete. Not
that I doubted their reality. I could imagine that long ago such things
had happened to saints, those overhasty zealots, who wanted to begin
with God, right away, whatever the cost. We no longer make such de-
mands on ourselves. We suspect that he is too difficult for us, that we
must postpone him, so that we can slowly do the long work that sepa-
rates us from him. Now, however, I know that this work leads to com-
bats just as dangerous as the combats of the saint; that such difficulties
appear around everyone who is solitary for the sake of that work, as
they took form around God's solitaries in their caves and empty shel-
ters, long ago.

## [THE PRODIGAL SON]

It would be difficult to persuade me that the story of the Prodigal Son is not the legend of a man who didn't want to be loved. When he was a child, everyone in the house loved him. He grew up not knowing it could be any other way and got used to their tenderness, when he was a child.

But as a boy he tried to lay aside these habits. He wouldn't have been able to say it, but when he spent the whole day roaming around outside and didn't even want to have the dogs with him, it was because they too loved him; because in their eyes he could see observation and sympathy, expectation, concern; because in their presence too he couldn't do anything without giving pleasure or pain. But what he wanted in those days was that profound indifference of heart which sometimes, early in the morning, in the fields, seized him with such purity that he had to start running, in order to have no time or breath to be more than a weightless moment in which the morning becomes conscious of itself.

The secret of that life of his which had never yet come into being, spread out before him. Involuntarily he left the footpath and went running across the fields, with outstretched arms, as if in this wide reach he would be able to master several directions at once. And then he flung himself down behind some bush and didn't matter to anyone. He peeled himself a willow flute, threw a pebble at some small animal, he leaned over and forced a beetle to turn around: none of this became fate, and the sky passed over him as over nature. Finally afternoon came with all its inspirations; you could become a buccaneer on the isle of Tortuga, and there was no obligation to be that; you could besiege Campeche, take Vera Cruz by storm; you could be a whole army or an officer on horseback or a ship on the ocean: according to the way you felt. If you thought of kneeling, right away you were Deodatus of Gozon and had slain the dragon and understood that this heroism was pure arrogance, without an obedient heart. For you didn't spare yourself anything that belonged to the game. But no matter how many scenes arose in your imagination, in between them there was always enough time to be nothing but a bird, you didn't even know what kind. Though afterward, you had to go home.

My God, how much there was then to leave behind and forget. For you really had to forget; otherwise you would betray yourself when they insisted. No matter how much you lingered and looked around, the gable always came into sight at last. The first window up there kept its eye on you; someone might be standing there. The dogs, in whom expectation had been growing all day long, ran through the hedges and drove you together into the one they recognized. And the house did the rest. Once you walked in to its full smell, most matters were already decided. A few details might still be changed; but on the whole you were already the person they thought you were; the person for whom they had long ago fashioned a life, out of his small past and their own desires; the creature belonging to them all, who stood day and night under the influence of their love, between their hope and their mistrust, before their approval or their blame.

It is useless for such a person to walk up the front steps with infinite caution. They will all be in the living room, and as soon as the door opens they will all look his way. He remains in the dark, wants to wait for their questions. But then comes the worst. They take him by the hands, lead him over to the table, and all of them, as many as are there, gather inquisitively in front of the lamp. They have the best of it; they stay in the shadows, and on him alone falls, along with the light, all the shame of having a face.

Can he stay and conform to this lying life of approximations which they have assigned to him, and come to resemble them all in every feature of his face? Can he divide himself between the delicate truthfulness of his will and the coarse deceit which corrupts it in his own eyes? Can he give up becoming what might hurt those of his family who have nothing left but a weak heart?

No, he will go away. For example, while they are all busy setting out on his birthday table those badly guessed presents which, once again, are supposed to make up for everything. He will go away for ever. Not until long afterward would he realize how thoroughly he had decided never to love, in order not to put anyone in the terrible position of being loved. He remembered this years later and, like other good intentions, it too had proved impossible. For he had loved again and again in his solitude, each time squandering his whole nature and in unspeakable fear for the freedom of the other person. Slowly he learned to let the rays of his emotion shine through into the beloved object, instead of consuming the emotion in her. And he was pampered by the joy of recognizing, through the more and more transparent form of the beloved, the expanses that she opened to his infinite desire for possession.

Sometimes he would spend whole nights in tears, longing to be filled with such rays himself. But a woman loved, who yields, is still far from being a woman who loves. Oh nights of no consolation, which returned his flooding gifts in pieces heavy with transience. How often he thought then of the Troubadours, who feared nothing more than having their prayers answered. All the money he had acquired and increased, he gave away so as not to experience that himself. He hurt them by so grossly offering payment, more and more afraid that they might try to respond to his love. For he had lost hope of ever meeting the woman whose love could pierce him.

Even during the time when poverty terrified him every day with new hardships, when his head was the favorite toy of misery, and utterly worn ragged by it, when ulcers broke out all over his body like emergency eyes against the blackness of tribulation, when he shuddered at the filth to which he had been abandoned because he was just as foul himself: even then, when he thought about it, his greatest terror was that someone would respond to him. What were all the darknesses of that time, compared with the thick sorrow of those embraces in which everything was lost? Didn't you wake up feeling that you had no future? Didn't you walk around drained of all meaning, without the right to even the slightest danger? Didn't you have to promise, a hundred times, not to die? Perhaps it was the stubbornness of this most painful memory, which wanted to reserve a place in him to return to again and again, that allowed him, amid the dunghills, to continue living. Finally, he found his freedom again. And not until then, not until his years as a shepherd, was there any peace in his crowded past.

Who can describe what happened to him then? What poet has the eloquence to reconcile the length of those days with the brevity of life? What art is broad enough to simultaneously evoke his thin, cloaked form and the vast spaciousness of his gigantic nights?

This was the time which began with his feeling as general and anonymous as a slowly recovering convalescent. He didn't love anything, unless it could be said that he loved existing. The humble love that his sheep felt for him was no burden; like sunlight falling through clouds, it dispersed around him and softly shimmered upon the meadows. On the innocent trail of their hunger, he walked silently over the pastures of the world. Strangers saw him on the Acropolis, and perhaps for many years he was one of the shepherds in Les Baux, and saw petrified time outlast that noble family which, in spite of all their conquests under the holy numbers seven and three, could not overcome the fatal sixteen-rayed star on their own coat-of-arms. Or should I imagine him at Orange, resting against the rustic triumphal arch? Should I see him in the soul-inhabited shade of Alyscamps, where, among the tombs that lie open as the tombs of the resurrected, his glance chases a dragonfly?

It doesn't matter. I see more than him: I see his whole existence, which was then beginning its long love toward God, that silent work undertaken without thought of ever reaching its goal. For though he had wanted to hold himself back for ever, he was now once again overcome by the growing urgency of his heart. And this time he hoped to be answered. His whole being, which during his long solitude had become prescient and imperturbable, promised him that the one he was now turning to would be capable of loving with a penetrating, radiant love. But even while he longed to be loved in so masterful a way, his emotion, which had grown accustomed to great distances, realized how extremely remote God was. There were nights when he thought he would be able to fling himself into space, toward God; hours full of disclosure, when he felt strong enough to dive back to earth and pull it up with him on the tidal wave of his heart. He was like someone who hears a glorious language and feverishly decides to write poetry in it. Before long he would, to his dismay, find out how very difficult this language was; at first he was unwilling to believe that a person might spend a whole life putting together the words of the first short meaningless exercises. He threw himself into this learning like a runner into a race; but the density of what had to be mastered slowed him down. It would be hard to imagine anything more humiliating than this apprenticeship. He had found the philosopher's stone, and now he was being forced to ceaselessly transform the quickly produced gold of his happiness into the gross lead of patience. He, who had adapted himself to infinite space, had now become like a worm crawling through crooked passageways, without exit or direction. Now that he was learning to love, learning so laboriously and with so much pain, he could see how careless and trivial all the love had been which he thought he had achieved; how nothing could have come of it, because he had not begun to devote to it the work necessary to make it real.

During those years the great transformations were taking place inside him. He almost forgot God in the difficult work of approaching him, and all that he hoped to perhaps attain with him in time was "sa patience de supporter une âme." The accidents of fate, which most men cling to, had long ago fallen away from him; but now even the necessary pleasures and pains lost their spicy aftertaste and became pure and nourishing for him. From the roots of his being grew the sturdy evergreen plant of a fruitful joyousness. He became totally absorbed in mastering what constituted his inner life; he didn't want to omit anything, for he had no doubt that in all this his love existed and was growing. Indeed, his inward composure went so far that he decided to retrieve the most important of the experiences which he had been unable to accomplish before, those that had merely been waited through. Above all, he thought of his childhood, and the more calmly he recalled it, the more unfinished it seemed; all its memories had the vagueness of premonitions, and the fact that they were past made them almost arise as future. To take all this past upon himself once more, and this time really, was the reason why, from the midst of his estrangement, he returned home. We don't know whether he stayed there; we only know that he came back.

Those who have told the story try at this point to remind us of the house as it was then; there, only a short time has passed, a short period of counted time, everyone in the house knows exactly how much. The dogs have grown old, but they are still alive. It is reported that one of them let out a howl. All the daily tasks stop. Faces appear in the window, faces that have aged or grown up and touchingly resemble how they used to look. And in one old face, grown suddenly pale, recognition breaks through. Recognition? Is it really just recognition?—Forgiveness. Forgiveness of what?—Love. My God: it is love.

He, the one who was recognized, had no longer thought, preoccupied as he was, that love could still exist. It is easy to understand how, of everything that happened then, only this has been handed down to us: his gesture, the incredible gesture which had never been seen before, the gesture of supplication with which he threw himself at their feet, imploring them not to love. Dizzy with fright, they made him stand up, embraced him. They interpreted his outburst in their own way, forgiving him. It must have been an indescribable relief for him that, in spite of the desperate clarity of his posture, they all misunderstood him. He was probably able to stay. For every day he recognized more clearly that their love, of which they were so vain and to which they secretly encouraged one another, had nothing to do with him. He almost had to smile at their exertions, and it was obvious how little they could have him in mind.

How could they know who he was? He was now terribly difficult to love, and he felt that only One would be capable of it. But He was not yet willing.

# Uncollected Prose

## 1902–1922

# THE LION CAGE

She paces back and forth like the sentinels out at the edge of the fortifications, where there is nothing left. And as in the sentinels, there is homesickness in her, heavy homesickness in fragments.

As somewhere down in the ocean there must be mirrors, mirrors from the cabins of sunken ships, fragments of mirrors, which of course no longer contain anything: not the faces of the travelers, not one of their gestures; not the way they turned and looked so strangely awkward from the back; not the wall, not the corner where they slept; still less what swayingly shone in from there and outside; nothing, no. But as nevertheless a piece of seaweed perhaps, an open, sinking polyp, the sudden face of a fish, or even just the water itself, floating, parted, coming together again, evokes resemblances in those mirrors, distant, oblique, false, soon abandoned resemblances with what once existed—:

thus memories, fragments of memories, lie, broken-edged, in the dark at the bottom of her blood.

She paces back and forth around him, the lion, who is sick. Being sick doesn't concern him and doesn't diminish him; it just hems him in. The way he lies, his soft bent paws intentionless, his proud face heaped with a worn-out mane, his eyes no longer loaded, he is erected upon himself as a monument to his own sadness, just as he once (always beyond himself) was the exaggeration of his strength.

Now it still twitches here and there in his muscles, it tenses, here and there small spots of anger are forming, too distant from one another; the blood bursts angrily, with a leap, from the chambers of his heart, and certainly it still has its carefully tested turns of sudden decision when it rushes into the brain.

But he just lets things happen, because the end hasn't yet come, and he no longer exerts any energy and no longer takes part. Only far off, as though held away from himself, he paints with the soft paintbrush of his tail, again and again, a small, semicircular gesture of indescribable disdain. And this takes place so significantly that the lioness stops and looks over: troubled, aroused, expectant.

But then she begins her pacing again, the desperate, ridiculous pacing of the sentinel, which falls back into the same tracks, again and again. She paces and paces, and sometimes her distracted mask appears, round and full, crossed out by the bars.

She moves the way clocks move. And on her face, as on a clock dial which someone shines a light onto at night, a strange, briefly shown hour stands: a terrifying hour, in which someone dies.

# A MEETING

Any road outside the town. (Sole condition: that there is no chance of meeting someone on it.) The dog all at once appears, like a sudden thought. He acts doggishly, on purpose, seems to be completely occupied with his own small affairs; but as inconspicuously as he can, he directs precisely aimed, remarkably sure glances at the stranger, who continues on his way. Not one of these glances is lost. The dog is now in front of the man, now beside him, absorbed in this secret observation, which grows more and more intense. Suddenly, catching up with the stranger:

I knew it! I knew it!

He gives hurried signs of joy, by which he tries to finally stop the man. The man makes a quick, friendly, calming and at the same time dismissing gesture, and with a half step to the left passes the dog easily.

The dog, in joyous expectation:

It's still going to happen.

He groans from the overabundance of his emotions. Finally he flings himself again in front of the more rapidly striding man: Now it's coming, he thinks, and holds up his face, urgently, to show that he understands. Now it's coming.

What? says the stranger, hesitating for a moment.

The excitement in the dog's eyes changes into embarrassment, doubt, alarm. If the man doesn't know what should come, how can it come? —Both of them have to know; only then will it come.

The man again takes his half step to the left, quite mechanically this time; he looks distracted. The dog keeps in front of him and tries—now almost without any attempt at caution—to see into the stranger's eyes. At one moment he believes he has met them, but their glances don't adhere to each other.

Is it possible that this small problem . . . thinks the dog.

It's *not* a small problem, says the stranger suddenly, alert and impatient.

The dog is startled: How (he controls himself with difficulty) . . . But I feel that we . . . My instinct . . . my . . .

Don't say it, interrupts the stranger, almost angrily. They are standing opposite each other. This time their glances interpenetrate, the man's sliding into the dog's like a knife into its sheath.

The dog is the first to give way; he looks down, jumps to the side, and with an upward glance that comes sideways from the right he confesses:

I'd like to do something for you. I'd do anything for you. Anything.

The man has already started walking again. He acts as if he hasn't understood. He walks apparently without noticing the dog, but he tries to look toward him now and then. He sees him running around, clumsy and bewildered, getting ahead, staying behind. All of a sudden the dog is a couple of steps ahead, turned toward the approaching man, stretched forward from his raised hindquarters as if he were about to scratch the ground. With enormous self-control he makes a couple of childishly frisky pounces, pretending that his front paws hold something alive. And then without a word he picks up the stone, which has to play this role, in his mouth.

Now I am innocuous and can't say anything more; this is expressed in the nod he makes as he looks back. There is something almost intimate in this nod, a kind of agreement, which, however, must on no account be taken too seriously. The whole thing is just a silly game, and that's how the business with the stone should be understood.

But now that the dog has the stone in his mouth, the man can't help speaking:

Let's be reasonable, he says as he walks on, without bending down toward the dog.

That's really all we can do. What would be the use of getting to know each other? We mustn't let certain memories arise. I felt the same way as you did for a few moments, and I almost asked you who you are. You would have said "Me," since there are no names between us. But, you see, that wouldn't have helped. It would only have confused us even more. For I can confess to you now that for a few moments I was truly unsettled. Now I'm calmer. If I could only convince you how very much the same our situation is. In my nature there are, if possible, even more obstacles to another meeting. You have no idea how difficult things are for us.

When the stranger spoke in this way, the dog realized that it was useless to go on with the pretense of a superficial game. In a way he was glad, but at the same time he seemed filled with a growing fear that he might want to interrupt.

He succeeds in doing this only when the stranger, astonished and alarmed, sees the animal opposite him in a posture that he at first thinks is hostile. The next moment, though, he realizes that the dog, far from showing hatred or hostility, is uneasy, troubled; in the timid brightness of his glance and in the tilt of his head this is clearly expressed, and it occurs again in the way he is now carrying the stone, which lies between the spasmodically retracted lips in all its hardness and heaviness.

Suddenly the man understands, and he can't hold back a passing smile.

You're right, dear fellow, it should remain unexpressed between us, this word that has given rise to so many misunderstandings.

And the dog puts the stone down, carefully, like something breakable, to the side of the road, so as not to delay the stranger any longer.

And in fact the man walks on and, absorbed as he is, doesn't notice till later that the dog is accompanying him, unobtrusively, devotedly, without an opinion of his own, the way a dog follows his master. This almost hurts him.

No, he says, no; not like this. Not after this experience. We should both forget what we went through today. Daily life blunts everything, and your nature has a tendency to subordinate itself to mine. In the end a responsibility would arise, which I can't accept. You wouldn't notice how completely you had come to trust me; you would overvalue me and expect from me what I can't perform. You would watch me and approve of everything, even of what is unworthy. If I want to give you a joy: will I find one? And if one day you are sad and complain to me—will I be able to help you? —And you shouldn't think that *I* am the one who lets you die. Go away, I beg of you: go away.

And the man almost broke into a run, and it looked as if he were trying to escape from something. Only gradually did his steps slow down, until finally he was walking more slowly than before.

He thought, slowly: What else would have been spoken between us today. And how in the end we would have shaken hands—.

An indescribable longing stirs inside him. He stops and turns backward. But the stretch of road bends right behind him into the twilight which has in the meantime fallen, and there is no one to be seen.

# THE FISHMONGER'S STALL

*(Naples)*

On a slightly inclined marble tabletop, they lie in groups, some on the damp stone, with a bit of blackish moss stuck under them, others in flat splint-baskets that have grown dark from the moisture. Silver-scaled, among them one that is bent upward like a sword arm in an escutcheon, so that the silver is stretched and shimmers. Silver-scaled, they lie across one another, as if of antique silver, with a blackish patina, and on top, one which, mouth forward, seems to be returning, terrified, out of the pile in back of it. Once you have noticed its mouth, you see, here and there, one more, another one, quickly turned toward you, lamenting. (What you want to call "lamenting" probably comes about because here the place from which voice emanates, at once means muteness: an image of the poet.) And now, as a result of a thought perhaps, you look for the eyes. All these flat, laterally placed eyes, covered as if with watch crystals, toward which, as long as they looked, floating images drifted. They weren't any different then, they were just as gazelessly indifferent: for water doesn't permit active looking. Just as shallow and depthless, empty, turned inside out like carriage lanterns during the day. But carried along by the resistance and movement of that denser world, they lightly and surely cast sketch upon sketch, signal and turn, inward into a consciousness unknown to us. Silently and surely they swam along, before the smooth decision, without betraying it; silently and surely they stood, for days on end, against the current, underneath its rush, darkened by fleeting shadows. But now they have been peeled out from the long strands of their looking, laid out flat, and it is impossible for anything to enter them. The pupil as if covered with black cloth, the surrounding circle laid on like the thinnest of gold foil. With a shock, as if you had bitten onto something hard, you notice the impenetrability of these eyes—, and suddenly you have the impression that you are standing in front of nothing but stone and metal, as you look across the table. Everything bent looks hard, and the pile of steel-glistening, awl-shaped fish lies there cold and heavy like a pile of tools with which others, that look like stones, have been polished. For there beside them they lie: round smooth agates, streaked with brown, pale, and golden veins, strips of reddish-white marble, jade pieces rounded and carefully polished, partly worked topazes, rock crystals with tips of amethyst, opals of jellyfish. And a very thin sheet of water is still spread over them all and separates them from this light, in which they are alien, closed, containers, which someone has tried in vain to pry open.

## ACROBATS

In front of the Luxembourg Gardens, near the Panthéon, Père Rollin and his troupe have spread themselves out again. The same carpet is lying there, the same coats, thick winter overcoats, taken off and piled on top of a chair, leaving just enough room for the little boy, the old man's grandson, to come and sit down now and then during breaks. He still needs to, he is still just a beginner, and those headlong leaps out of high somersaults down onto the ground make his feet ache. He has a large face that can contain a great many tears, but sometimes they stand in his widened eyes almost out to the edge. Then he has to carry his head cautiously, like a too-full cup. It's not that he is sad, not at all; he wouldn't even notice it if he were; it is simply the pain that is crying, and he has to let it cry. In time it gets easier and finally it goes away. Father has long since forgotten what it was like, and Grandfather—oh it has been sixty years since he forgot, otherwise he wouldn't be so famous. But look, Père Rollin, who is so famous at all the fairs, doesn't "work" anymore. He doesn't lift the huge weights anymore, and though he was once the most eloquent of all, he says nothing now. He has been transferred to beating the drum. Touchingly patient, he stands with his too-far-gone athlete's face, its features now sagging into one another, as if a weight had been hung on each of them and had stretched it out. Dressed simply, a sky-blue knitted tie around his colossal neck, he has retired at the peak of his glory, in this coat, into this modest position upon which, so to speak, no glitter ever falls. But anyone among these young people who has ever seen him, knows that in those sleeves the famous muscles lie hidden whose slightest touch used to bring the weights leaping up into the air. The young people have clear memories of such a masterful performance, and they whisper a few words to their neighbors, show them where to look, and then the old man feels their eyes on him, and stands pensive, undefined, and respectful. That strength is still there, young people, he says to himself; it's not as available as it used to be, that's all; it has descended into the roots; it's still there somewhere, all of it. And it is really far too great for just beating a drum. He lays into it, and beats it much too often. Then his son-in-law has to whistle over to him and make a warning sign just when he is in the middle of one of his tirades. The old man stops, frightened; he tries to excuse himself with his heavy shoulders, and stands ceremoniously on his other leg. But already he has to be whistled at again. "Diable. Père! Père Rollin!" He has already hit the drum again and is hardly aware that he has done it. He could go on drumming forever, they mustn't think he will get tired. But there, his daughter is speaking to him; quick-witted and strong, and with more brains than any of the others. She is the one who holds everything together, it's a joy to see her in action. The son-in-law works well, no one can deny that, and he likes his work, it's a part of him. But she has it in her blood; you can see that. This is something she was born to. She's ready now: "Musique!" she shouts. And the old man drums away like fourteen drummers. "Père Rollin, hey, Père Rollin," calls one of the spectators, and steps right up, recognizing him. But the old man only incidentally nods in response; it is a point of honor, his drumming, and he takes it seriously.

# AN EXPERIENCE

It could have been little more than a year ago that, in the castle garden which sloped down quite steeply to the sea, something strange happened to him. Walking back and forth with a book, as was his custom, he had happened to recline into the more or less shoulder-high fork of a shrublike tree, and in this position he immediately felt himself so pleasurably supported and so deeply soothed that he remained as he was, without reading, completely absorbed into Nature, in a nearly unconscious contemplation. Little by little his attention awakened to a feeling he had never known before: it was as if almost unnoticeable pulsations were passing into him from the inside of the tree; he explained this to himself quite easily by supposing that an otherwise invisible wind, perhaps blowing down the slope close to the ground, was making itself felt in the wood, though he had to acknowledge that the trunk seemed too thick to be moved so forcibly by such a mild breeze. What concerned him, however, was not to pass any kind of judgment; rather, he was more and more surprised, indeed astonished, by the effect of this pulsation which kept ceaselessly passing over into him; it seemed to him that he had never been filled by more delicate movements; his body was being treated, so to speak, like a soul, and made capable of absorbing a degree of influence which, in the usual distinctness of physical conditions, wouldn't really have been sensed at all. Nor could he correctly determine, during the first few moments, which of his senses it was through which he was receiving so delicate and extended a communication; moreover, the condition it had created in him was so perfect and continuous, different from all others, but so impossible to describe by the intensification of anything experienced before, that for all its exquisiteness he couldn't think of calling it a pleasure. Nevertheless, concerned as he always was to account for precisely the subtlest impressions, he asked himself insistently what was happening to him, and almost immediately found an expression that satisfied him as he said it aloud: he had passed over to the other side of Nature. As happens sometimes in a dream, this phrase now gave him joy, and he considered it almost completely apt. Everywhere and more and more regularly filled with this impulse which kept recurring in strangely interior intervals, his body became indescribably touching to him and of no further use than to be purely and cautiously present in, just as a ghost, already dwelling elsewhere, sadly enters what was tenderly laid aside, in order to belong once again, even if inattentively, to this once so indispensable world. Slowly looking around himself, without otherwise shifting his position, he recognized everything, remembered it, smiled at it with a kind of distant affection, let it be, as if it were something which had once, in circumstances long since vanished, taken part in his life. A bird flew through his gaze, a shadow engrossed him, the very path, the way it continued and was lost, filled him with a contemplative insight, which seemed to him all the more pure in that he knew he was independent of it. *Where* his usual dwelling place was he couldn't have conceived, but that he was only *returning* to all this here, that he was standing in this body as if in the recess of an abandoned window, looking out:——of this he was for a few seconds so thoroughly convinced that the sudden apparition of one of his friends from the house would have shocked him in the most excruciating way; whereas he truly, deep inside himself, was prepared to see Polyxène or Raimondine or some other long-dead inhabitant of the house step forth from the path's turn. He understood the quiet superabundance of these Things; he was allowed, intimately, to see these ephemeral earthly forms used in such an absolute way that their harmony drove out of him everything else he had learned; he was sure that if he were to move in their midst he wouldn't seem strange to them. A periwinkle that stood near him and whose blue gaze he had already met a number of times, touched him now from a more spiritual distance, but with so inexhaustible a meaning that it seemed as if there were nothing more that could be concealed. Altogether, he was able to observe how all objects yielded themselves to him more distantly and, at the same time, somehow more truly; this might have been due to his own vision, which was no longer directed forward and diluted in empty space; he was looking, as if over his shoulder, *backward* at Things, and their now completed existence took on a bold, sweet aftertaste, as though everything had been spiced with a trace of the blossom of parting.——Saying to himself from time to time that this couldn't last, he nevertheless wasn't afraid that the extraordinary condition would suddenly break off, as if he could only expect from it, as from music, a conclusion that would be in infinite conformity to its own law.

All at once his position began to be uncomfortable, he could feel the trunk, the fatigue of the book in his hand, and he emerged. An obvious wind was blowing now in the leaves, it came from the sea, the bushes up the slope were tossing together.

# ON THE YOUNG POET

Still hesitating to distinguish, among cherished experiences, the more important from the lesser, I am limited to quite provisional means when I try to describe the nature of a poet: this immense and childlike nature which arose (we don't grasp how) not only in definitively great figures long ago, no, but which right here, beside us, converges in this boy perhaps, who lifts his great gaze and doesn't see us; this nature which seizes young hearts at a time when they are still incapable of the most insignificant life, in order to fill them with abilities and connections that immediately surpass all possible attainments of a whole existence: yes, who would be able to speak calmly of this nature? If it were true that it no longer occurred, that we could see it only from a great distance, completed, in its improbable manifestation: we would gradually move toward comprehending it, we would give it a name and a time, like the other things of antiquity; for what is it but antiquity that bursts out in hearts startled by such forces. Here among us, in this complex modern city, in that honestly busy house, amid the noise of vehicles and factories and while the newspaper sellers are shouting their wares—spacious sheets filled to the edge with events—suddenly, who knows, all this effort, all this fervor, all this energy are outweighed by the appearance of the Titans in the depths of a child. Nothing indicates it but the coldness of a boy's hand; nothing but an upward glance taken back with terror; nothing but the indifference of this young creature, who doesn't talk with his brothers and who, as soon as he can, gets up from the dinner table, which exposes him much too long to the judgment of his family. He hardly knows if he still belongs to his mother: so greatly have all the measures of his feeling been displaced since the irruption of the elements into his infinite heart.

O you mothers of poets. You favorite dwelling places of the gods, in whose womb the unheard-of must already have been appointed. Did you hear voices deep inside your conception, or did the divinities communicate with one another only by signs?

I don't know how one can deny the utterly miraculous quality of a world in which the increase of the calculated has never even touched the supplies of what passes beyond all limits. It is true, the gods have neglected no opportunity of exposing us: they let us uncover the great kings of Egypt in their tombs, and we were able to see them in their natural decay, how they were spared no indignity. All the utmost achievements of that architecture and art—led to nothing; behind the fumes of the balsam cake no heaven lit up, and the loaves and concubines, long turned to clay, had not apparently been used by any subterranean revelers. Anyone who considers what an abundance of the purest and most powerful ideas were here (and continually) rejected and repudiated by the inconceivable beings to whom they had been dedicated: how could he not tremble for our more exalted future? But he should also consider what the human heart would be if, outside it, anywhere in the world, certainty existed; final certainty. Suddenly it would lose all the readiness it had gathered during thousands of years; it would still be a place that was praiseworthy, but in secret people would tell of what it had been in former times. For truly, even the greatness of the gods depends upon their need: upon the fact that, whatever shrines are kept for them, they are safe nowhere but in our heart. That is the place they plunge into, out of their sleep, with their still-unsifted plans, the place where they gather to take counsel, and where their decree is irresistible.

What do all disillusionments prove, all unsatisfied tombs, all diskerneled temples, if here, beside me, in a suddenly darkened youth, God becomes conscious. His parents see no future for him, his teachers think they have the clue to his apathy, his own mind makes the world seem inexact to him, and his death already keeps trying to find the place in him where he could most easily be broken; but so great is the carelessness of the heavenly power that it pours its streams into this untrustworthy vessel. Just an hour ago the most fleeting glance of his mother was capable of surrounding this nature; now she wouldn't even be able to take its measure: even if she gathered together the resurrection and the angels' fall.

\*

But how can a new creature, who hardly knows his own hands, inexperienced in his true nature, a novice in the most ordinary turnings of his mind, adapt himself to such an unheard-of presence? How is he, who is obviously destined later on to act with the greatest precision, supposed to achieve his development between threats and pampering, which both exceed the utmost exertion of his unprepared strengths? And it is not only that eruption of greatness in his depths makes the heroic landscape of his feeling almost impassable to him: in the same proportion as his true nature takes control, he becomes aware, as he looks up, of mistrustful questions, bitter demands and curiosity in the faces loved until then in all confidence. Surely a boy in such a situation might go away and become a shepherd. He might, in long speechless days and nights, enrich his confused inner objects with marvelingly felt space; he might make the crowded images in his soul equal to the outspread constellations. Ah, if only no one urged him and no one contradicted him. Do you really want to engage *this* creature, who is measurelessly claimed, to whom, prematurely, an inexhaustible nature has given a task?

Is it possible to explain how he endures? The power that suddenly inhabits him finds contact and kinship with his childhood, which still lingers in all the corners of his heart; now, for the first time, it becomes apparent toward what immense relationships this outwardly so inadequate condition lies open. The disproportionate spirit, which has no room in the consciousness of the young man, hovers there above a developed under-world full of joys and dreads. Only by using this world, disregarding the whole outer universe, might it be able to achieve its mighty intentions. But already it is tempted to have dealings with the world that exists on the other side of the purely conducting senses. And just as, inside, it finds its contact with the most powerful hidden forces, so in the visible it is quickly and exactly served by small beckoning occasions: it would, after all, be incompatible with Nature's reticence to separate the significant from the intelligible otherwise than with discretion.

Whoever reads the early letters of Kleist will, to the extent that he grasps this figure which clarifies itself in thunderstorms, understand the importance of the passage which describes the arch of a certain gateway in Würzburg, one of the first impressions upon which, lightly touched, the already stretched genius burst outward. Any thoughtful reader of Stifter (to take another example) might suspect that the inner vocation of this poetic storyteller became inevitable at the moment when, one unforgettable day, he first tried to bring closer, by means of a telescope, some extremely distant point in the landscape, and then, in an utterly startled vision, felt a flight of spaces, of clouds, of objects, a terror of such richness that during these seconds his openly surprised spirit received World, as Danaë received the outpoured Zeus.

In the end, every determination to be a poet may have been formed this unexpectedly, by just such incidental occasions, not only when it took possession of a temperament for the first time, but again and again, at each turning of a nature which had to fulfil itself artistically.

Who can name you all, you accomplices of inspiration, you who are nothing but sounds, or bells that stop, or strangely new birdvoices in the neglected woods. Or gleam that an opening window throws out into the hovering dawn; or cascading water; or air; or glances. Accidental glances of passersby, glances, lifted for a moment, of women who sit sewing by the window, down to the unsayably anxious looking-around of squatting dogs, so close to the expression of schoolchildren. What a decision to call forth greatness goes through the most trivial everyday object. Events so insignificant that they wouldn't be able to deflect the most yielding fate by a ten-thousandth degree—, look: they beckon here, and the godlike verse steps over them out into the eternal.

Certainly the poet will, with growing insight into his boundless tasks, attach himself to what is greatest; when he finds it, it will delight or humble him, as it wishes. But the signal for the rebellion in his heart will be given willingly by a messenger that doesn't know what it is doing. It is impossible to imagine him aligning himself with greatness from the start, since he is, precisely, destined to approach it, his ever-present goal, by still indescribably personal paths. And how, truly, should it first have become known to him, since in the world that originally surrounded him it appeared perhaps only in camouflage, concealing itself or despised, like that saint who lived in the space under the stairs? But if it lay before him, openly, in its confident glory, which has no regard for us,—wouldn't he then, like Petrarch before the numberless vistas of the mountain he had climbed, have to flee back into the ravines of his soul, which, even though he will never search into their depths, are of inexpressibly closer concern to him than that alien and, if need be, explorable region.

Terrified within himself by the distant thunder of the god, bewildered from outside by an unstoppable excess of phenomena, the young man treated so violently has just enough room to stand on the strip between both worlds, until, all at once, an indifferent little happening floods his monstrous situation with innocence. This is the mo-

ment that places in the scales, on one tray of which rests his heart over-
burdened with endless responsibilities, to balance it with sublime se-
renity: the great poem.

\*

The great poem. As I say it, it becomes clear to me that until a
little while ago I have accepted it as something that certainly exists,
removing it from all suspicion of coming into being. Even if the
originator were to step out from behind it and appear before me, I
wouldn't be able to imagine the power which, with *one* burst, had bro-
ken so much silence. Just as the builders of the cathedrals, comparable
to grains of seed, immediately arose, without residue, into growth and
blossoming, in their work, which already stood there as if it had always
existed and was no longer explicable as coming from them: in the same
way the great poets of the past and the present have remained purely
ungraspable, each single one of them replaced by the tower and the
bell of his heart. Only since a younger generation, pushing upward
and at the same time into the future, has not insignificantly expressed
their own becoming in the becoming of their poems, does my glance
try to recognize, alongside the achievement, the conditions of the gen-
erative spirit. But even now, when I have to admit that poems are
formed, I am far from thinking that they are invented; it seems to me
rather as if in the soul of someone gripped by poetry a spiritual predis-
position appeared, which was already (like some undiscovered constel-
lation) spread out between us.

If we consider what fine accomplishments even now stand surety
for some of those who have recently entered their thirties, we might
almost hope that they would soon make everything that in the past
thirty years has claimed our growing admiration seem just a preface to
the perfection of their later work. The most diverse favorable circum-
stances, it is clear, have to collaborate, for such a decided success to be
possible. If we examine these circumstances, the outer ones are so nu-
merous that we finally give up trying to penetrate to the inner ones.
The excited curiosity and endless cleverness of an age freed from a
hundred restraints penetrates into every hiding place of the spirit and
effortlessly lifts up works which, in the past, their authors would have
slowly and painfully brought to birth. Too practiced in insight to stop,
this age suddenly finds itself in inner places where perhaps no age has
ever been in public without divine pretext; walking in everywhere, it

makes workplaces into exhibition halls and has no objection to having its dinners in the storerooms. It may be right, since it comes from the future. It occupies us in a way that no age has, for a long time, occupied its inhabitants; it pushes and displaces and clears away, each of us owes a lot to it. And yet, who hasn't looked at it, at least for a moment, with distrust; asked himself if it is really concerned with fruitfulness, or only with a mechanically better and more exhaustive exploitation of the soul? It bewilders us with constantly new visibilities; but how much has it already placed before us for which there was no corresponding progress inside us? Now I will assume that it offers, at the same time, to this determined younger generation the most unexpected means of giving external form to its purest inner realities, little by little, visibly, in exact equivalents; I can even believe that it possesses these means in the highest degree. But while I am now prepared to attribute to it much new artistic achievement, my admiration passes beyond it to the poems, as ungraspable now as ever.

Even if there were not one of the young poets who, for his own sense of things, wasn't happy to make good use of the dared and intensified quality of these days, I still wouldn't be afraid that I had burdened myself too heavily with describing the poetic nature and its effect on the inner self. All lightenings, however penetrating they may be, cannot reach into the place where the heavy rejoices in being heavy. What can finally change the situation of someone who, from early on, has been destined to arouse within his heart the utmost, which other people hold off and appease in theirs? And what kind of peace could be made for him, when, inside, he is undergoing the onslaught of his god.

# PRIMAL SOUND

When I was a boy in school, the invention of the phonograph must have been quite recent. At any rate, it was still at the center of public astonishment, and this may be the reason that our physics teacher, who liked to tinker at all kinds of mechanical projects, taught us to build one of these devices, out of the most ordinary materials. The only things needed were the following: a piece of light cardboard, taped into the form of a funnel, whose narrower round opening you immediately pasted over with a piece of waterproof paper, the kind used to seal jars of preserves, improvising in this way a vibrating membrane, in the center of which you next stuck, vertically, a bristle from a stiff clothesbrush. With these few items the first part of the mysterious machine was made, receiver and transmitter were ready, and now all you had to do was build a recording cylinder, which, turned by means of a small handle, could be moved up to the needle that marked the sounds. I don't remember what we made this out of; some kind of roll was found which we covered, as well as we could, with a thin layer of candle wax, which was barely cold and hard before, already—with an impatience that grew in us as we excitedly glued and fitted, shoving one another aside—we put our work to the test. It is easy to imagine how this was done. When someone spoke or sang into the funnel, the needle in the parchment transferred the sound waves onto the impressionable surface slowly turning beneath it, and then, when the zealous pointer was allowed to retrace its own path (which had been fixed in the meantime with a coat of varnish)—trembling, wavering out of the paper cone, the sound that was just a moment ago still ours, unsteady now, indescribably soft and timid and at times fading out altogether, came back to us. This always had a most powerful effect. Our class wasn't exactly disciplined, and there couldn't have been many moments when it attained such a degree of silence. The phenomenon was just as surprising, was in fact truly staggering, every time it was repeated. We children stood, as it were, opposite a new, infinitely sensitive place in reality, from which we were addressed by something that far surpassed us, yet that was, in some unsayable way, still a beginner and in need of our help. At that time, and over the years, I thought that this independent sound, taken from us and preserved outside us, was what would remain most unforgettable about the experience. That this wasn't the case is the reason I am writing now. As will be shown, what remained most present in my memory was not the sound from the funnel; it was rather those marks scratched onto the cylinder that much more distinctly remained.

Fourteen or fifteen years must have gone by before I became aware of this. It happened during my first stay in Paris, when I was attending, with a good deal of enthusiasm, the anatomy lectures at the École des Beaux-Arts, in which I was attracted not so much by the complex interweaving of the muscles and sinews or the perfect accord among the internal organs, but rather by the arid skeleton, whose restrained energy and elasticity had already at that time become visible to me in the notebooks of Leonardo. However deeply I puzzled over the structure of the whole, it was too much for me; my attention always returned to the study of the skull, which seemed to me to represent the utmost achievement, so to speak, which this chalky element was capable of, as if precisely here it had been persuaded to strain all its forces into a decisive function, so that it could take something which had been ultimately dared—something which, in a narrow enclosure, was already boundlessly active again—into its most solid protection. The enchantment which this strange container, shut off from every kind of outer space, exerted on me, finally became so intense that I procured a skull, in order to spend many night hours with it; and, as always happens to me with Things: it wasn't only the moments of deliberate attention that made this ambiguous object truly my own—, unquestionably I owe my intimacy with it, in part, to the passing glance with which we unconsciously examine and take in our customary environment, if it has even some slight relationship with us. It was this kind of glance that I suddenly stopped in its course and focussed, exactly and attentively. In the often so strangely awake and challenging light of the candle, the coronal suture had become strikingly visible, and I immediately knew what it reminded me of: one of those unforgotten grooves which had once been scratched by the point of a bristle onto a small roll of wax!

And now I don't know: is it because of some rhythmic peculiarity of my imagination that ever since then, often at intervals many years apart, again and again the impulse arises in me to leap from this abruptly perceived resemblance into a whole series of unprecedented experiments? I must admit that whenever this desire has made itself known I have treated it with the most severe mistrust,—if proof is needed, it lies in the fact that only now, more than a decade and a half later, have I made up my mind, cautiously, to communicate my idea. Nor is there anything I can add in its favor except its stubborn recurrence, which, without the slightest relation to the rest of my concerns, now here, now there, in the most diverse circumstances, has continually taken me by surprise.

*What* is it that keeps suggesting itself inside me? It is this:

The coronal suture of the skull has (this assertion would first need to be investigated, but let us assume it is true) a certain similarity to the wavy line that the needle of a phonograph engraves onto the receptive rotating cylinder of the machine. But what if you tricked the needle and, for its return path, directed it along a groove that didn't originate from the graphic translation of a sound, but already existed in nature—, all right: let's be quite explicit: along (for example) the coronal suture—: What would happen?—A sound would have to arise, a succession of sounds, a music . . .

Emotions—, which? Incredulousness, timidity, fear, awe—: yes, which one of all the emotions that might be possible here? prevents me from suggesting a name for the primal sound that would at that moment come into the world . . .

Putting this aside for now: couldn't *any* kind of lines, appearing anywhere, be put under the needle and tested? Couldn't any contour be, as it were, prolonged in this way, so that we could then feel it, transformed, approaching us in another sense-realm?

*

It wasn't until I became interested in Arabic poetry, in which the five senses seem to have a more simultaneous and equal share, that I first realized, with a shock, how unequally and isolatedly the modern European poet makes use of these informants, of which only one, sight, overburdened with world, constantly overwhelms him; how feeble, in comparison, are the reports that come to him through the inattentive ears, not to mention the apathy of the other senses, which act only off to the side and with many interruptions, in their circumscribed areas. And yet the fully achieved poem can arise only on condition that the world, acted upon simultaneously by all five levers, appear in a particular form on the supernatural level which is, in fact, the level of the poem.

A woman to whom these thoughts were proposed in a conversation exclaimed that this marvelous capacity of the senses to act together simultaneously is simply the presence and grace of love,—and in saying this she (parenthetically) testified to the sublime reality of the poem. But someone in love is in such magnificent danger precisely because he has to depend on the mutuality of his senses, which he knows can come together only in that single, dared center where, giving up all dimension, they converge, and where there is no duration.

As I express myself in this way, I have before me the diagram I used as a pleasant expedient whenever ideas of this kind forced themselves on me. If we picture the world's whole realm of experience, including all its areas that exceed us, as a complete circle, it is immediately obvious how much larger the dark sectors are, which stand for what we are incapable of experiencing, compared with the other arcs representing what is lit up by the searchlights of our senses.

Now the situation of someone in love is this: he feels himself suddenly placed in the center of the circle, that is to say, where the known and the incomprehensible presses together in one single point, becomes complete, becomes possession, though, to be sure, with a removal of all particular details. This transposition wouldn't help the poet, for him the minute particulars must remain present, he is obliged to use the sense-sectors to their full extent, and thus he must also wish to extend each one as far as possible, so that someday his tucked-up delight may leap through the five gardens in one breath.

As the lover's danger lies in the undimensionality of his standpoint, the poet's lies in his awareness of the abysses that separate one order of sense perception from the others: these are, in fact, so vast and so engulfing that they could easily tear the greater part of the world—and who knows how many worlds—away from us.

A question arises here: can scientific research significantly enlarge the extent of the sectors on the level which we have assumed? The acquisitions of the microscope, the telescope, and all the other devices that displace the senses upward or downward—don't they lie in a *different* layer, since most of the increase gained in this way can't be penetrated by the senses, and thus can't be truly "experienced." It may not be premature to conjecture that the artist, who develops this five-fingered hand of his senses (if one may call it that) to an ever more dexterous and more spiritual grasp, is working most decisively toward an expansion of the various sense-areas, although his substantiating achievement, which is ultimately impossible without the miraculous, doesn't allow him to put the areas he has personally gained on the open, general map.

But to someone who is looking for a means of establishing the ultimately urgent connection among realms so strangely separated, what could be more promising than the experiment suggested in the first pages of this memoir? If, here at the end, it is proposed again, with the previously affirmed caution, may the writer be given a certain degree of credit for resisting the temptation to arbitrarily carry the hypothesis further in the free movements of his imagination. The mission to do this, neglected for so many years and reappearing again and again, seemed to him too limited and too explicit.

—Soglio, Feast of the Assumption, 1919

# MITSOU

*Forty Drawings by Balthus*
Preface

Who knows cats?—Do you, for example, think that you do? I must admit that, for me, their existence was never more than a tolerably risked hypothesis.

Animals (don't you agree?), in order to belong to our world, must enter into it a little. They must consent, however partially, to our way of life, they must tolerate it; otherwise, whether timidly or with hostility, they will measure the distance that separates them from us, and that will be the way they relate to us.

Take dogs: their confidential and admiring nearness is such that certain of them seem to have renounced their most ancient canine traditions, in order to adore our habits, and even our errors. This is precisely what makes them tragic and sublime. Their decision to admit us forces them to live, so to speak, at the very boundaries of their nature, which they constantly pass beyond with their humanized gaze and their nostalgic muzzle.

But what is the attitude of cats?—Cats are, quite simply, cats, and their world is the world of cats from one end to the other. They look at us, you say? But has anyone ever known if they really deign to lodge for a moment, in the depths of their retina, our futile image? Perhaps, in staring at us, they are quite simply facing us with a magical refusal of their forever complete pupils?—It is true that certain persons among us allow themselves to be influenced by their charming and electric caresses. But let them remember the strange and abrupt distraction with which their favorite animal often put an end to the effusions which they thought were reciprocal. They too, these privileged persons admitted into the presence of cats, have been disowned and repudiated time and time again, and, even as they still held the mysteriously apathetic animal in their arms, they felt themselves stopped at the threshold of this world which is the world of cats and which they inhabit exclusively, surrounded by circumstances that none of us can ever guess.

Was man ever their contemporary? —I doubt it. And I assure you that sometimes, in the twilight, the neighbor's cat leaps across my body completely unaware of me, or to prove to the bewildered Things that I don't exist.

*

Tell me, am I wrong to get you involved in these considerations, when my real purpose is to lead you toward the story my small friend Balthusz is going to tell you? True, he *draws* the story, without speaking to you any further, but his images will more than satisfy your curiosity. Why should I repeat them in another form? I would rather add what he has not yet said. But first, to summarize:

Balthusz (I think he was ten years old at the time) finds a cat. This happens at the château de Nyon, which you probably know. He is allowed to keep his small, trembling discovery, and he travels home with him. Here is the boat, here is the arrival at Geneva, at Molard, here is the streetcar. He introduces his new companion to domestic life, he tames him, he pampers him, he loves him. "Mitsou" consents, joyously, to the conditions set forth for him, although occasionally he breaks the monotony of the household with some frisky and ingenious improvisation. Do you find it excessive that his master, when taking him for a walk, ties him to this annoying string? It is because he distrusts all the whims that pass through this tom-cat heart—loving, but unknown and adventurous. He is mistaken, though. Even the dangers of moving to a new house take place without a single accident, and the small, capricious animal adapts to the new surroundings with an amused docility. Then, all at once, he disappears. The whole house is in an uproar; but, thank goodness, it is not serious this time: Mitsou is found in the middle of the lawn, and Balthusz, far from scolding the deserter, installs him on the pipes of the beneficent radiator. I think you will appreciate, as I do, the calm, the plenitude that follows this anxiety. Alas, it is just a short reprieve. Christmas sometimes turns out to be much too filled with temptations. You eat cookies, without really keeping track of how many; you get sick. And to recover, you fall asleep. Mitsou, bored with your too long nap, instead of waking you up, runs away. What a shock! Fortunately, Balthusz is feeling well enough to rush off in search of the fugitive. He begins by crawling under his bed: nothing. Look how brave he is here, all alone, in the cellar, with his candle, which he then carries as an emblem of the search, everywhere, out to the garden, into the street: nothing! Look at his small, solitary form: *Who* has abandoned him? A cat? —Will he be consoled by the portrait of Mitsou that his father recently sketched? No; there was some kind of foreboding in it; and loss begins God knows when. It is definitive, it is fatal. He goes back into the house. He cries. He shows you his tears with his two hands:

Look at them carefully.

There you have the story. The artist has told it better than I can. What is left for me to say? Very little.

\*

Finding a Thing is always enjoyable; a moment before, it wasn't yet there. But finding a cat: that is unheard of! For this cat, you must agree, doesn't entirely enter into your life, as, for example, some toy would do; even though he belongs to you now, he remains a bit outside, and that always means:

life + a cat,

which, I assure you, adds up to an enormous sum.

Losing a Thing is very sad. You imagine that it is in pain, that it gets broken, that it ends up in some garbage heap. But losing a cat: No! that is not allowed. Never has anyone lost a cat. *Can* you lose a cat, a living thing, a living being, a life? But losing a life: is death!

Well then, it is death.

\*

Finding. Losing. Have you really thought about what loss is? It is not simply the negation of that generous moment which came to gratify an expectation you yourself never imagined you had. For between that moment and loss, there is always what is called—rather clumsily, I agree—possession.

Now loss, cruel though it may be, can have no effect on possession; it ends it, perhaps; it affirms it; basically it is just a second acquisition, completely inner this time, and intense in a different way.

That is what you felt, Balthusz; no longer seeing Mitsou, you began to see him even more.

Is he still alive? He survives in you, and his joy, the joy of a small carefree cat, having given you pleasure, now puts you under an obligation: you had to express it by the resources of your laborious sorrow.

Thus, a year later, I found you grown up and consoled.

For those, nevertheless, who will see you forever tearful at the end of your book, I have composed the first—somewhat whimsical—part of this preface. So that I could say at its conclusion: "Set your minds at ease: I am. Balthusz exists. Our world is quite solid.

There are no cats."

Berg-am-Irchel Castle
November 1920

# THE YOUNG WORKMAN'S LETTER

At a meeting last Thursday, some of your poems were read to us, Monsieur V.; they keep returning to me; I can't help writing down for you what is on my mind, as well as I can.

The day after that reading, I happened to attend, by chance, an event sponsored by a Christian group, and maybe this was really the impetus which caused the explosion, which unleashed such commotion and urgency that I find myself rushing toward you with all my might. It takes an enormous act of violence to begin something. I can't *begin*. I simply jump over what should be the beginning. Nothing is as strong as silence. It would never have been broken, if we hadn't each been born into the midst of talk.

Monsieur V.—I don't want to speak about the evening when we received your poetry. I want to speak about the other evening. Something is forcing me to say: Who, yes (I can't express it any other way now), *who* is this Christ who meddles with everything we do;—who has never known a thing about us, or about our work, or about our griefs, or about our joys, as we achieve them today, live them, and bring them forth—, and who nevertheless, it seems, constantly demands to be the *first* in our life? Or has that just been put into his mouth? What does he want of us? He wants to help us, supposedly. Yes, but he seems so strangely bewildered when he's near us. His situation was so completely different. Or don't the circumstances really matter; if he entered right here, into my room, or appeared over at the factory—everything would immediately be different, right? Would my heart burst open inside me and, so to speak, continue in some other realm and always in his direction? My instinct tells me that he isn't *able* to come. That it would have no sense. Our world isn't just outwardly different,—it has no access for him. He wouldn't *shine* through a department-store coat, it isn't true, he just wouldn't shine through. It's no accident that he went around in a seamless robe, and I think the kernel of light in him, the thing that made him shine so strongly, day and night, is long since dissolved, and distributed somewhere else. But if he was so great, this would, it seems to me, be the least we could demand of him—that somehow he should have vanished without any residue, yes, without any residue at all—traceless.

I can't imagine that the *cross* should have *remained,* which was, after all, just a crossroads. It shouldn't be burned onto us, all over our flesh, like a brand. It should have been dissolved in Christ himself. For isn't the truth *this:* he simply wanted to create the higher tree on which we would be better able to ripen. He, on the cross, is this new tree in God, and we were supposed to be the warm, happy fruit at the top of it.

Now we shouldn't always talk of what was *before:* the *after* should already have begun. This tree, I feel, should have become so one with us, or we with it, *on* it, that we wouldn't have to be continually concerned with it but, simply and peacefully, with God, since Christ's purpose was, after all, to more purely hold us up into God.

When I say: God, this is a great conviction in me, and not something I have been taught. The whole creation, it seems to me, says this word, without thinking, though often out of a deep meditativeness. If this Christ has helped us to say it with a clearer voice, more fully, more genuinely—so much the better; but leave him out of the question. Don't force us to always fall back into the trouble and affliction that it cost him to, as you say, "redeem" us. Let us finally enter into this redemption. —Otherwise the Old Testament is a much better resource, it is full of fingers pointing to God, wherever you open it, and whenever someone becomes heavy there, he always falls right into God's center. And once I tried to read the Koran, I didn't get very far, but I understood this much, that in it too there is a powerful finger, and God stands at the end of the path it is pointing to, grasped in his eternal rising, in an East that will never end. Christ surely wanted the same thing. To point. But the people here have been like dogs, who don't understand pointing fingers and think they are supposed to snap at the hand. Instead of taking the crossroads, where the signpost was raised high into the night of sacrifice, instead of taking this crossroads as a point of departure, Christianity has settled there, and claims that it is living there in Christ, although there was no room in him, not even for his mother, and not for Mary Magdalene: as in every guide, who is a gesture and not a dwelling-place.—And that's why they aren't living in Christ, these stubborn-hearted people, who keep bringing him back again and live from the raising of a tilted or fully blown-down cross. They have this mob on their conscience, this standing around on the overcrowded place, it's their fault that the journey doesn't continue in the direction the cross's arms point to. Out of what is Christian they have made a career, a bourgeois occupation, an alternately drained and refilled pool. Everything that they do themselves, according to their unsuppressible nature (insofar as they are still alive), is a contradiction of this remarkable tendency, and thus they muddy their own waters and have to renew them again and again. In their zeal they keep making the earthly, which ought to be a source of joy and trust, evil and worthless,—and thus, more and more, they hand over the earth to those who are ready—failed and suspect as it is, and undeserving of anything better—to wrest a temporary, quickly won profit from it. This growing exploitation of life, isn't it a result of the centuries-long devaluation of the earthly? What insanity to deflect us toward a Beyond, when right here we are surrounded by tasks and expectations and futures. What a swindle to steal the images of earthly delight and sell them to heaven, behind our backs! The impoverished earth should long ago have called in all those loans that have been drawn on its blessedness so that an afterfuture might be adorned with them. Does death really become more transparent because of these lights that have been dragged into place behind it? And, since no void can continue to exist, won't everything that has been taken away here be replaced by a fraud?—is this why the cities are filled with so much ugly noise and artificial light, because true radiance and song have been handed over to a Jerusalem that can be inhabited only later? Christ may have been right when, in a time filled with decayed and defoliated gods, he spoke unkind words about the earthly, although (I can't help thinking this) it is really an insult to God not to see that what is given to us here is thoroughly capable of making us happy, out to the edge of our senses, if only we use it well. *The proper use, that's the important thing.* To take the earthly in our hands, properly, in a truly loving way, with awe, as our temporary and unique treasure: this is also, to use an everyday expression, God's great "instructions for use," it is what Saint Francis of Assisi intended to write in his canticle to the sun, a song that on his deathbed was more glorious to him than the cross, which stood there only *to point* into the sun. But what people call the Church had in the meantime already swollen to such a chaos of voices that the hymn of the dying man, drowned out on every side, was only noticed by a few simple monks and infinitely assented to by the landscape of his graceful valley. How often must such attempts have been made, to bring about a reconciliation between that Christian refusal and the obvious friendship and cheerfulness of the earth. But in other ways too, within the Church, even in its own crown, the earthly gained its fullness and its innate profusion. Why don't people praise the Church for being vigorous enough not to crumble beneath the life-weight of certain popes, whose throne was loaded with bastard children, courtesans, and corpses. Wasn't there more Christianity in them than in the dry restorers of the Gospels—that is to say, a living, irrepressible, transformed Christianity. I mean, we don't really know *what* will come out of the great teachings, we just have to let them flow forth and go their own way and not be frightened when they suddenly burst into the fissured channels of life, and roll, deep under the earth, in imperceptible beds.

I once worked for a couple of months in Marseilles. It was a special time for me, I owe a lot to it. Chance brought me in touch with a young painter, who remained my friend till his death. He had lung disease and had just come back from Tunis. We spent a lot of time together and, because the end of my job coincided with his return to Paris, we were able to arrange a few days in Avignon. They were unforgettable. Partly because of the town itself, its buildings and the area around it, and also because my friend, during these days of uninterrupted and, somehow, heightened intimacy, opened up to me about many matters, especially about his *inner* life, with an eloquence that seems to be at times characteristic of people suffering from that disease. Everything he said had a strange prophetic power; through everything that burst out in often almost breathless talks, one saw, as it were, the bottom of the river, the stones on the bottom . . . I mean by that, more than something that is just ours: Nature itself, its oldest and hardest essence, which we nevertheless touch at so many places and which we probably depend upon at our most urgent moments, since its downward slope determines our inclination. In addition, there was an unexpected and happy love affair, his heart was in an uncommon state of exaltation, for days on end, and thus the sparkling fountain of his life shot up to a considerable height. To view an extraordinary town and a more than pleasing landscape in the company of someone who finds himself in such a situation is a rare privilege; and that is why those tender and at the same time passionate spring days seem to me, when I think back, the only holidays that I have ever known. The time was so ridiculously short, for anyone else it would barely have been enough to gather a few impressions,—to me, unaccustomed as I am to spending free days, it seemed vast. Actually, it seems almost wrong to call it *time*, since it was rather a new condition of freedom, quite feelably a *space*, a being-surrounded by the Open, not a passing. I caught up with childhood then, if one may put it that way, and with a part of early youth, all of which I had never had time to achieve in myself; I looked, I learned, I understood—, and these days also gave rise to the discovery that saying "God" is so easy, so genuine, so—as my friend would have expressed it—so unproblematically simple. How could this house, which the popes erected for themselves there, not have seemed to me powerful? I had the impression that it couldn't contain any inner space at all, that it must be built, through and through, out of solid blocks, as if the exiles' only purpose was to pile up the weight of the papacy with such abundance that it would tip history's scales. And in reality this ecclesiastical palace towers up over an antique torso of a Heracles, which was walled into the rocky foundations—"hasn't it," said Pierre, "grown up colossally as if out of this seed?"—That *this* is Christianity, in one of its transformations, would be much more understandable to me than to recognize its strength and its taste in the constantly weaker infusion of that herb tea which people say was prepared from its first, tenderest leaves.

But even the cathedrals aren't the bodies of that spirit which we are now supposed to believe is the authentically Christian one. I could imagine that beneath some of them the fallen statue of a Greek goddess is resting; so much blossoming, so much reality sprang up in them, even if, as in a fear that arose during their time, they struggled away from that hidden body up into the heavens, which the sound of their huge bells was appointed to keep continually open.

After my return from Avignon I went to church quite often, in the evening and on Sunday,—at first alone . . . and later . . .

I am in love with a woman, hardly older than a child, who works at home, so that she is often in a bad situation when there isn't much work. She is skilled, it would be easy for her to find a job in a factory, but she's afraid of the boss. Her idea of freedom is boundless. It won't surprise you that she perceives God too as a kind of boss, actually as the "head boss," as she said to me, laughing, but with such terror in her eyes. It was a long time before she decided to accompany me one evening to St. Eustache, where I liked to go because of the music of the May services. Once we went together as far as Maux and looked at the tombstones in the church there. Gradually she noticed that God leaves you alone in the churches, that he demands nothing; you might think that he wasn't there at all,—and yet, Marthe thought, the moment you're about to say that he isn't in the church, something holds you back. Perhaps only what people themselves have for so many centuries brought into this high, oddly strengthened air. And perhaps it is only that the vibration of the powerful and sweet music can never completely get outside, it must have long since penetrated into the stones, and they must be remarkably affected stones, these pillars and vaults, and even though a stone is hard and almost inaccessible, in the end it is deeply moved by continual singing and these assaults from the organ, these onslaughts, these storms of song, every Sunday, these hurricanes of the great holidays. A lull. That's what, strictly speaking, reigns in the old churches. I said it to Marthe. A lull. We listened, she understood it immediately, she has a wonderfully prepared sensibility. After that, we sometimes entered when we heard singing, and stood there, close to each other. It was the most beautiful when we had a stained-glass window in front of us, one of those old picture windows, with many partitions, each one completely filled with shapes, huge people and small towers and all kinds of events. Nothing was too strange for them, you see castles and battles and a hunt, and the beautiful white stag appears again and again in the hot red and in the burning blue. I was once given a very old wine to drink. That's what it's like for your eyes, this window, only that the wine was just dark red in my mouth,—but this is the same in blue also and in violet and in green. There is really *everything* in the old churches, no shrinking from anything, as there is in the newer ones, where only the "good" examples appear. Here you see also what is bad and evil and horrible; what is deformed and suffering, what is ugly, what is unjust—and you could say that all this is somehow loved for God's sake. Here is the angel, who doesn't exist, and the devil, who doesn't exist; and the human being, who does exist, stands between them, and (I can't help saying it) their unreality makes him more real to me. What I feel when I hear the expression "a human being," I can figure it out better in there than on the street among people who have absolutely nothing recognizable about them. But that is hard to say. And what I want to say now is even harder to express. Which is that in regard to the boss, the power, (this too became clear to me in there, very slowly, when we stood completely in the music), there is just *one* way of struggling against it: to go further than it does itself. What I mean is this: we should strive to see in every power that claims a right over us: all power, the whole of power, power universally, the power of God. We should say to ourselves, there is just *one*, and understand the weak, the false, the defective kind as if it were the kind that rightfully grips us. Wouldn't it become harmless in this way? If in every power, even in the evil and malignant, we always saw power itself, I mean that which ultimately has the right to be powerful, wouldn't we then overcome, intact so to speak, even the unrightful and arbitrary? Isn't this exactly how we stand in relation to all the unknown great forces? We don't experience any of them in their purity. We accept each with its faults, which perhaps are adapted to our own faults.—But with all scholars, discoverers, inventors, hasn't the awareness that they are dealing with great forces led them suddenly to the greatest? I am young, and there is a lot of protest in me; I can't give any assurance that I act wisely every time impatience and disgust get the better of me,—but in my depths I know that submission leads further than rebellion; it shames that which is usurpation, and it contributes indescribably to the glorification of the rightful power. The rebel pulls himself out from the attraction of one center of power, and he may perhaps succeed in escaping from its field; but beyond it he finds himself in the void and has to look around for another gravitational force to draw him in. And this one is generally even less legitimate than the first. Why not then see in the power we live in, the greatest power of all, unperturbed by its weaknesses and fluctuations? Somewhere the arbitrary will of itself collide against the law, and we save energy if we leave it to convert itself. Of course, that is one of those long and slow processes which are in such complete contradiction with the strange upheavals of our time. But alongside the quickest movements there will always be slow ones, even ones that are of such extreme slowness that we can't in the least perceive their advance. But humanity is there, isn't it, to wait for what stretches out beyond the individual.—From its point of view, the slowest is often the quickest, that is to say, it turns out that we called it slow only because it could not be measured.

Now there is, it seems to me, something absolutely immeasurable, which humans are never tired of misappropriating with their criteria, measurements, and institutions. And here, in the love which, with an unbearable mixture of contempt, desire, and curiosity, they call "sensual love," here we find the worst consequences of that devaluation which Christianity felt obliged to assign to the earthly. Here everything is distortion and repression, even though we come forth from this deepest of events and ourselves possess again in it the center of our delights. I find it, if I may say so, more and more incomprehensible that a doctrine which puts us in the wrong *there*, where all creation enjoys its most blissful right—that such a doctrine is able, if not anywhere to establish itself as true, nevertheless to hold its ground so permanently over such a wide area.

I think, here again, of the animated conversations I had with my deceased friend, that time, in the meadows of the Barthelasse Island in the spring and later. Even the night before his death (he died the following afternoon a little after five o'clock), he opened for me such pure vistas into a realm of the blindest suffering that my life seemed to begin anew in a thousand places, and when I tried to answer, I had no control over my voice. I didn't know that there are tears of joy. I cried my first ones, like a beginner, into the hands of this young man who in a few hours would be dead, and felt how the tide of life in Pierre was once again rising and overflowing, as these hot teardrops were added to it. Am I being excessive? I'm speaking of a *too-much*.

Why, I ask you, Monsieur V., when people want to help us, we who are so often helpless, why do they leave us in the lurch, there at the root of all experience? Anyone who would stand by us *there* could be confident that we would want nothing further of him. For the help he gave us would grow by itself with our life and would become greater and stronger together with it. And would never end. Why aren't we placed into our most mysterious part? Why must we sneak around it, and finally enter into like burglars and thieves, into our own beautiful sex, where we get lost and bang into things and stumble, and finally, like criminals caught in the act, rush out again into the twilight of Christianity. Why, even if, because of the inner tension of the soul, guilt or sin had to be invented, why didn't they fasten it to some other part of our body, why did they let it fall there, and wait till, as it dissolved, it poisoned and muddied our pure source? Why have they made our sex homeless, instead of transferring there the festival of our competence?

All right, I'll admit that it shouldn't belong to us, we who are incapable of assuming and administering such inexhaustible bliss. But why don't we belong to God starting from *this* place?

A priest would point out to me that there is marriage, although he would not be unaware of the state this institution is in. Nor does it help to move the will-to-propagation into the sunlight of grace—, my sex is not just turned toward the future, it is the mystery of my own life—, and it's only because, as it seems, it may not occupy the central place there that so many people have pushed it out to their edge and thereby lost their equilibrium. What good is all this? The terrible untruth and uncertainty of our time has its foundation in our not acknowledging the happiness of sex, in this strangely mistaken guiltiness, which continually increases, and cuts us off from all the rest of Nature, even from the child, although, as I learned during that unforgettable night, his, the child's, innocence doesn't at all consist in the fact that he, so to speak, doesn't know sex,—"on the contrary," said Pierre almost voicelessly, "that inconceivable happiness which, for us, awakens in *one* place deep within the fruitflesh of a closed embrace is still namelessly scattered everywhere in his whole body." To describe the peculiar situation of our sensuality, we would have to say: Once we were children *everywhere,* now we are children just in one place.—But if there were only one single person among us for whom this was certain and who was capable of showing the proof for it, why do we let it happen that one generation after the other wakes up under the rubble of Christian prejudices and moves in a trance through the darkness, in such a narrow space between mere refusals!?

Monsieur V.: I write and write. A whole night almost has gone by on this. I have to come to an end.—Have I said that I have a job in a factory? I work in the office, sometimes I'm also at a machine. Before, I was once able for a short time to take some courses. Well, I just want to say how I feel. You see, I want to be usable to God just the way I am. What I do here, my work, I want to keep doing it toward him, without having my stream interrupted, if I can express it like that, not even in Christ, who was once the water for many. The machine, for example—I can't explain it to him, he doesn't grasp it. I know you won't laugh if I say this so simply, it's the best way. God, though: I have a feeling I can bring it to *him,* my machine and its firstborn, or even my whole work, it enters him without any trouble. Just as it was easy once for the shepherds to bring the gods of their life a lamb or a vegetable-basket or the most beautiful bunch of grapes.

You see, Monsieur V., I've been able to write this long letter without using the word faith even once. For that seems to me a complicated and difficult business, and none of mine. I don't want to let myself be made bad for Christ's sake, but good for God. I don't want to be considered a priori as a sinner, perhaps I'm not. I have such pure mornings! I could talk with God, I don't need anyone to help me compose letters to him.

I know your poems only from that reading the other night, I own just a few books, which mostly have to do with my job. A few of them, it's true, are about art, and history books, just what I could get.—But your poems, you'll have to accept this, have caused this commotion in me. My friend once said, "Give us teachers who praise the earthly for us." You *are* one of these.

*Notes*

FROM THE NOTEBOOKS OF MALTE LAURIDS BRIGGE (1910; begun in Rome, February 8, 1904; written mostly during 1908/1909; finished in Leipzig, January 27, 1910)

The speaker in these passages is Malte Laurids Brigge, a twenty-eight-year-old Danish writer living in Paris.

[The Bird-feeders]

p. 257, *painted figurehead:*

The so-called galleon-figures: carved and painted statues from the bow of a ship. The sailors in Denmark sometimes set up these wooden statues, which have survived from old sailing-ships, in their gardens, where they look quite strange.

(To Witold Hulewicz, November 10, 1925)

[Ibsen]

p. 259, *and now you were among the alembics:*

where the most secret chemistry of life takes place, its transformations and precipitations.

(Ibid.)

p. 259, *You couldn't wait:*

Life, *our* present life, is hardly capable of being presented on stage, since it has wholly withdrawn into the invisible, the inner, communicating itself to us only through "august rumors." The dramatist, however, couldn't wait for it to become showable; he had to inflict violence upon it, this not yet producible life; and for that reason too his work, like a wand too strongly bent back, sprang from his hands and was as though it had never been done.

(Ibid.)

p. 260, *go away from the window:*

Ibsen spent his last days beside his window, observing with curiosity the people who passed by and in a way confusing these real people with the characters he might have created.

(Ibid.)

[Costumes]

p. 262, *Admiral Juel:* Niels Juel (1629–1697). In July 1677, having overwhelmingly defeated the Swedish fleet in the Battle of Køge Bay, one of the greatest sea victories in Danish history, he was acclaimed as a national hero and raised to the highest naval rank.

p. 263, bautta (pronounced ba-oot'-ta): Venetian mask, covering the lower part of the face.

p. 263, *dominos:* Venetian cloaks, worn chiefly at masquerades.

p. 263, *Pierrot:* Character in French pantomime.

[The Temptation of the Saint]

p. 271, *those strange pictures:* The reference is to the paintings of Pieter Bruegel the Elder or of Hieronymus Bosch.

[The Prodigal Son]

Cf. Luke 15:11–32.

p. 272, *Tortuga:* Island off northwest Haiti. In the seventeenth century it was a base for the French and English pirates who ravaged the Caribbean.

p. 272, *Campeche:* Port in southeastern Mexico, frequently raided by pirates during the seventeenth century.

p. 272, *Vera Cruz:* City in east-central Mexico; the country's chief port of entry. It was looted by pirates in 1653 and 1712.

p. 272, *Deodatus of Gozon:* A fourteenth-century member of the Order of the

Knights of St. John of Jerusalem (Knights of Malta). Because so many had lost their lives trying to kill the famous dragon of Rhodes, the Grand Master of the Order had forbidden all knights even to approach its cave. Deodatus went ahead and killed the dragon, but because of his disobedience he was stripped of his knighthood. Later he was pardoned, and in 1346 he himself became Grand Master.

p. 275, *Les Baux:*

Magnificent landscape in Provence, a land of shepherds, even today still imprinted with the remains of the castles built by the princes of Les Baux, a noble family of prodigious bravery, famous in the 14th and 15th centuries for the splendor and strength of its men and the beauty of its women. As far as the princes of Les Baux are concerned, one might well say that a petrified time outlasts this family. Its existence is, as it were, petrified in the harsh, silver-gray landscape into which the unheard-of castles have crumbled. This landscape, near Arles, is an unforgettable drama of Nature: a hill, ruins, and village, abandoned, entirely turned to rock again with all its houses and fragments of houses. Far around, pasture: hence the shepherd is evoked: here, at the theater of Orange, and on the Acropolis, moving with his herds, mild and timeless, like a cloud, across the still-excited places of a great dilapidation. Like most Provençal families, the princes of Les Baux were superstitious gentlemen. Their rise had been immense, their good fortune measureless, their wealth beyond compare. The daughters of this family walked about like goddesses and nymphs, the men were turbulent demigods. From their battles they brought back not only treasures and slaves, but the most unbelievable crowns; they called themselves, by the way, "Emperors of Jerusalem." But in their coat-of-arms sat the worm of contradiction: to those who believe in the power of the number seven, "sixteen" appears the most dangerous counter-number, and the lords of Les Baux bore in their coat-of-arms the 16-rayed star (the star that led the three kings from the East and the shepherds to the manger in Bethlehem: for they believed that the family originated from the holy king Balthazar). The "good fortune" of this family was a struggle of the holy number "7" (they possessed cities, villages, and convents always in sevens) against the "16" rays of their coat-of-arms. And the seven succumbed.

(To Witold Hulewicz, November 10, 1925)

p. 275, *Alyscamps:* The ancient cemetery near Arles, with its uncovered sarcophagi.

p. 276, *"sa patience de supporter une âme"*: "his patience in enduring a soul."

> This comes, I think, from Saint Theresa (of Avila).
>
> (To Witold Hulewicz, November 10, 1925)

## UNCOLLECTED PROSE, 1902–1922

The Lion Cage (First draft, Paris, probably November 5–6, 1902; edited and completed, Paris, summer 1907)

A Meeting (Capri, between January 5 and 7, 1907)

The Fishmonger's Stall (First draft, Naples, shortly before January 16, 1907; edited, Paris, summer 1907; completed, Muzot, end of 1925)

> How much we have seen in Naples! A table with fish was itself enormous, so enormous that I would have to tell you about it more precisely: you above all. But it wants to be made, not told; and if someday I make it well enough, you shall read it.
>
> (To Paula Modersohn-Becker, February 5, 1907)

Acrobats (Paris, July 14, 1907)

An Experience (Ronda, approximately February 1, 1913)

> I am offering you a prose piece whose contents are so important to me, and which is so complete in its manifestation, that it is not easy for me to part with it. The small, precise sketch seems adequate for publication inasmuch as not often is a more indescribable experience presented, which here, to some extent, is apprehended and described,—if I am not totally mistaken.
>
> (To Katharina Kippenberg, July 19, 1918)

> Thank you for your kind and extremely sympathetic response to my piece. I had myself wondered, as I was revising "An Experience," whether to erase the word *Duino;* so let it be left out: this way, the

most intimate connection stays contained and concealed in the names Polyxène and Raimondine, and for the reader in general the prose piece, not being linked to a specific place, is more uncircumscribed and thus more valid. / If my desk drawers were full, I would perhaps not yet have parted from this sketch; it is, after all, in a certain sense, the most intimate that I have ever written down—, on the other hand, though, one cannot possibly have a large enough conception of the shelter in which the most deeply inner remains hidden, when it once has entered in its most absolute form.

(To Katharina Kippenberg, August 10, 1918)

p. 291, *Polyxène or Raimondine:* Two sisters of Marie von Thurn und Taxis' mother; both of them died young.

On the Young Poet (Probably late summer 1913)

p. 295, *Kleist:* Heinrich von Kleist (1777–1811), German playwright, poet, and short story writer.

p. 295, *Stifter:* Adalbert Stifter (1805–1868), Austrian novelist and short story writer.

p. 295, *Danaë:* In Greek mythology, the daughter of Acrisius, king of Argos. After her father was warned by an oracle that she would bear a son who would one day kill him, he imprisoned her in a dungeon of bronze. But Zeus descended and entered her in the form of a shower of gold, and she later gave birth to Perseus.

p. 296, *Petrarch:* Francesco Petrarca (1304–1374), Italian poet, scholar, and diplomat. After he and his brother succeeded in climbing to the top of Mt. Ventoux (he describes this incident in a famous letter of 1336), he opened Augustine's *Confessions* at random:

And my eyes (I call on my brother, and God too, as witnesses) happened to fall on this passage: "And men go about marveling at the high mountains, and the mighty sea, and the wide rivers, and the vast ocean, and the revolution of the stars, but they do not consider themselves." I was ashamed, and asking my brother, who was anxious to hear more, not to disturb me, I closed the book, angry with myself that I was still admiring earthly things, while I might long ago have learned from even the pagan philosophers that nothing is wonderful but the soul.

Primal Sound (Soglio, August 15, 1919)

Mitsou (Berg am Irchel, November 26, 1920)

Subtitle, *Balthus:* The well-known painter Balthus (Balthasar Klossowski, 1908– ). He was the son of Rilke's lover, Baladine Klossowska. The drawings have been published in *Mitsou: Forty Images* by Balthus, New York: Metropolitan Museum of Art and Harry N. Abrams, 1984.

The Young Workman's Letter (Muzot, between February 12 and 15, 1922)

p. 308, *Monsieur V.:* Emile Verhaeren (1855–1916), Flemish-French poet.

p. 310, *canticle to the sun:* For a translation of the poem, see *The Enlightened Heart: An Anthology of Sacred Poetry,* ed. Stephen Mitchell, New York: Harper & Row, 1989, p. 43 f.

# PART 3

# *Duino Elegies*

## AND

# *The Sonnets to Orpheus*

# Duino Elegies

## (1923)

*The property of Princess Marie von Thurn und Taxis-Hohenlohe*
*(1912/1922)*

## DIE ERSTE ELEGIE

Wer, wenn ich schriee, hörte mich denn aus der Engel
Ordnungen? und gesetzt selbst, es nähme
einer mich plötzlich ans Herz: ich verginge von seinem
stärkeren Dasein. Denn das Schöne ist nichts
als des Schrecklichen Anfang, den wir noch grade ertragen,
und wir bewundern es so, weil es gelassen verschmäht,
uns zu zerstören. Ein jeder Engel ist schrecklich.
    Und so verhalt ich mich denn und verschlucke den
        Lockruf
dunkelen Schluchzens. Ach, wen vermögen
wir denn zu brauchen? Engel nicht, Menschen nicht,
und die findigen Tiere merken es schon,
daß wir nicht sehr verläßlich zu Haus sind
in der gedeuteten Welt. Es bleibt uns vielleicht
irgend ein Baum an dem Abhang, daß wir ihn täglich
wiedersähen; es bleibt uns die Straße von gestern
und das verzogene Treusein einer Gewohnheit,
der es bei uns gefiel, und so blieb sie und ging nicht.
    O und die Nacht, die Nacht, wenn der Wind voller
        Weltraum
uns am Angesicht zehrt—, wem bliebe sie nicht, die
        ersehnte,
sanft enttäuschende, welche dem einzelnen Herzen
mühsam bevorsteht. Ist sie den Liebenden leichter?
Ach, sie verdecken sich nur mit einander ihr Los.
    Weißt du's *noch* nicht? Wirf aus den Armen die Leere
zu den Räumen hinzu, die wir atmen; vielleicht daß die
        Vögel
die erweiterte Luft fühlen mit innigerm Flug.

Ja, die Frühlinge brauchten dich wohl. Es muteten manche
Sterne dir zu, daß du sie spürtest. Es hob
sich eine Woge heran im Vergangenen, oder
da du vorüberkamst am geöffneten Fenster,
gab eine Geige sich hin. Das alles war Auftrag.

## THE FIRST ELEGY

Who, if I cried out, would hear me among the angels'
hierarchies? and even if one of them pressed me
suddenly against his heart: I would be consumed
in that overwhelming existence. For beauty is nothing
but the beginning of terror, which we still are just able to
    endure,
and we are so awed because it serenely disdains
to annihilate us. Every angel is terrifying.
    And so I hold myself back and swallow the call-note
of my dark sobbing. Ah, whom can we ever turn to
in our need? Not angels, not humans,
and already the knowing animals are aware
that we are not really at home in
our interpreted world. Perhaps there remains for us
some tree on a hillside, which every day we can take
into our vision; there remains for us yesterday's street
and the loyalty of a habit so much at ease
when it stayed with us that it moved in and never left.
    Oh and night: there is night, when a wind full of infinite
    space
gnaws at our faces. Whom would it not remain for—that
    longed-after,
mildly disillusioning presence, which the solitary heart
so painfully meets. Is it any less difficult for lovers?
But they keep on using each other to hide their own fate.
    Don't you know *yet*? Fling the emptiness out of your arms
into the spaces we breathe; perhaps the birds
will feel the expanded air with more passionate flying.

Yes—the springtimes needed you. Often a star
was waiting for you to notice it. A wave rolled toward you
out of the distant past, or as you walked
under an open window, a violin
yielded itself to your hearing. All this was mission.

Aber bewältigtest du's? Warst du nicht immer
noch von Erwartung zerstreut, als kündigte alles
eine Geliebte dir an? (Wo willst du sie bergen,
da doch die großen fremden Gedanken bei dir
aus und ein gehn und öfters bleiben bei Nacht.)
Sehnt es dich aber, so singe die Liebenden; lange
noch nicht unsterblich genug ist ihr berühmtes Gefühl.
Jene, du neidest sie fast, Verlassenen, die du
so viel liebender fandst als die Gestillten. Beginn
immer von neuem die nie zu erreichende Preisung;
denk: es erhält sich der Held, selbst der Untergang war ihm
nur ein Vorwand, zu sein: seine letzte Geburt.
Aber die Liebenden nimmt die erschöpfte Natur
in sich zurück, als wären nicht zweimal die Kräfte,
dieses zu leisten. Hast du der Gaspara Stampa
denn genügend gedacht, daß irgend ein Mädchen,
dem der Geliebte entging, am gesteigerten Beispiel
dieser Liebenden fühlt: daß ich würde wie sie?
Sollen nicht endlich uns diese ältesten Schmerzen
fruchtbarer werden? Ist es nicht Zeit, daß wir liebend
uns vom Geliebten befrein und es bebend bestehn:
wie der Pfeil die Sehne besteht, um gesammelt im Absprung
*mehr* zu sein als er selbst. Denn Bleiben ist nirgends.

Stimmen, Stimmen. Höre, mein Herz, wie sonst nur
Heilige hörten: daß sie der riesige Ruf
aufhob vom Boden; sie aber knieten,
Unmögliche, weiter und achtetens nicht:
*So* waren sie hörend. Nicht, daß du *Gottes* ertrügest
die Stimme, bei weitem. Aber das Wehende höre,
die ununterbrochene Nachricht, die aus Stille sich bildet.
Es rauscht jetzt von jenen jungen Toten zu dir.
Wo immer du eintratst, redete nicht in Kirchen
zu Rom und Neapel ruhig ihr Schicksal dich an?

But could you accomplish it? Weren't you always
distracted by expectation, as if every event
announced a beloved? (Where can you find a place
to keep her, with all the huge strange thoughts inside you
going and coming and often staying all night.)
But when you feel longing, sing of women in love;
for their famous passion is still not immortal. Sing
of women abandoned and desolate (you envy them, almost)
who could love so much more purely than those who were
      gratified.
Begin again and again the never-attainable praising;
remember: the hero lives on; even his downfall was
merely a pretext for achieving his final birth.
But Nature, spent and exhausted, takes lovers back
into herself, as if there were not enough strength
to create them a second time. Have you imagined
Gaspara Stampa intensely enough so that any girl
deserted by her beloved might be inspired
by that fierce example of soaring, objectless love
and might say to herself, "Perhaps I can be like her"?
Shouldn't this most ancient of sufferings finally grow
more fruitful for us? Isn't it time that we lovingly
freed ourselves from the beloved and, quivering, endured:
as the arrow endures the bowstring's tension, so that
gathered in the snap of release it can be more than
itself. For there is no place where we can remain.

Voices. Voices. Listen, my heart, as only
saints have listened: until the gigantic call lifted them
off the ground; yet they kept on, impossibly,
kneeling and didn't notice at all:
so complete was their listening. Not that you could endure
God's voice—far from it. But listen to the voice of the wind
and the ceaseless message that forms itself out of silence.
It is murmuring toward you now from those who died
      young.
Didn't their fate, whenever you stepped into a church
in Naples or Rome, quietly come to address you?

Oder es trug eine Inschrift sich erhaben dir auf,
wie neulich die Tafel in Santa Maria Formosa.
Was sie mir wollen? leise soll ich des Unrechts
Anschein abtun, der ihrer Geister
reine Bewegung manchmal ein wenig behindert.

Freilich ist es seltsam, die Erde nicht mehr zu bewohnen,
kaum erlernte Gebräuche nicht mehr zu üben,
Rosen, und andern eigens versprechenden Dingen
nicht die Bedeutung menschlicher Zukunft zu geben;
das, was man war in unendlich ängstlichen Händen,
nicht mehr zu sein, und selbst den eigenen Namen
wegzulassen wie ein zerbrochenes Spielzeug.
Seltsam, die Wünsche nicht weiterzuwünschen. Seltsam,
alles, was sich bezog, so lose im Raume
flattern zu sehen. Und das Totsein ist mühsam
und voller Nachholn, daß man allmählich ein wenig
Ewigkeit spürt.—Aber Lebendige machen
alle den Fehler, daß sie zu stark unterscheiden.
Engel (sagt man) wüßten oft nicht, ob sie unter
Lebenden gehn oder Toten. Die ewige Strömung
reißt durch beide Bereiche alle Alter
immer mit sich und übertönt sie in beiden.

Schließlich brauchen sie uns nicht mehr, die Früheent-
    rückten,
man entwöhnt sich des Irdischen sanft, wie man den Brüsten
milde der Mutter entwächst. Aber wir, die so große
Geheimnisse brauchen, denen aus Trauer so oft
seliger Fortschritt entspringt—: *könnten* wir sein ohne sie?
Ist die Sage umsonst, daß einst in der Klage um Linos

Or high up, some eulogy entrusted you with a mission,
as, last year, on the plaque in Santa Maria Formosa.
What they want of me is that I gently remove the appearance
of injustice about their death—which at times
slightly hinders their souls from proceeding onward.

Of course, it is strange to inhabit the earth no longer,
to give up customs one barely had time to learn,
not to see roses and other promising Things
in terms of a human future; no longer to be
what one was in infinitely anxious hands; to leave
even one's own first name behind, forgetting it
as easily as a child abandons a broken toy.
Strange to no longer desire one's desires. Strange
to see meanings that clung together once, floating away
in every direction. And being dead is hard work
and full of retrieval before one can gradually feel
a trace of eternity.—Though the living are wrong to believe
in the too-sharp distinctions which they themselves have
    created.
Angels (they say) don't know whether it is the living
they are moving among, or the dead. The eternal torrent
whirls all ages along in it, through both realms
forever, and their voices are drowned out in its thunderous
    roar.

In the end, those who were carried off early no longer need
    us:
they are weaned from earth's sorrows and joys, as gently as
    children
outgrow the soft breasts of their mothers. But we, who do
    need
such great mysteries, we for whom grief is so often
the source of our spirit's growth—: could we exist without
    *them*?
Is the legend meaningless that tells how, in the lament for
    Linus,

wagende erste Musik dürre Erstarrung durchdrang;
daß erst im erschrockenen Raum, dem ein beinah göttlicher
   Jüngling
plötzlich für immer enttrat, das Leere in jene
Schwingung geriet, die uns jetzt hinreißt und tröstet und
   hilft.

the daring first notes of song pierced through the barren
    numbness;
and then in the startled space which a youth as lovely as a
    god
had suddenly left forever, the Void felt for the first time
that harmony which now enraptures and comforts and helps
    us.

## DIE ZWEITE ELEGIE

Jeder Engel ist schrecklich. Und dennoch, weh mir,
ansing ich euch, fast tödliche Vögel der Seele,
wissend um euch. Wohin sind die Tage Tobiae,
da der Strahlendsten einer stand an der einfachen Haustür,
zur Reise ein wenig verkleidet und schon nicht mehr
    furchtbar;
(Jüngling dem Jüngling, wie er neugierig hinaussah).
Träte der Erzengel jetzt, der gefährliche, hinter den Sternen
eines Schrittes nur nieder und herwärts: hochauf-
schlagend erschlüg uns das eigene Herz. Wer seid ihr?

Frühe Geglückte, ihr Verwöhnten der Schöpfung,
Höhenzüge, morgenrötliche Grate
aller Erschaffung,—Pollen der blühenden Gottheit,
Gelenke des Lichtes, Gänge, Treppen, Throne,
Räume aus Wesen, Schilde aus Wonne, Tumulte
stürmisch entzückten Gefühls und plötzlich, einzeln,
*Spiegel:* die die entströmte eigene Schönheit
wiederschöpfen zurück in das eigene Antlitz.

enn wir, wo wir fühlen, verflüchtigen; ach wir
atmen uns aus und dahin; von Holzglut zu Holzglut
geben wir schwächern Geruch. Da sagt uns wohl einer:
ja, du gehst mir ins Blut, dieses Zimmer, der Frühling
füllt sich mit dir . . . Was hilfts, er kann uns nicht halten,
wir schwinden in ihm und um ihn. Und jene, die schön sind,
o wer hält sie zurück? Unaufhörlich steht Anschein
auf in ihrem Gesicht und geht fort. Wie Tau von dem
    Frühgras
hebt sich das Unsre von uns, wie die Hitze von einem

## THE SECOND ELEGY

Every angel is terrifying. And yet, alas,
I invoke you, almost deadly birds of the soul,
knowing about you. Where are the days of Tobias,
when one of you, veiling his radiance, stood at the front
    door,
slightly disguised for the journey, no longer appalling;
(a young man like the one who curiously peeked through the
    window).
But if the archangel now, perilous, from behind the stars
took even one step down toward us: our own heart, beating
higher and higher, would beat us to death. Who *are* you?

Early successes, Creation's pampered favorites,
mountain-ranges, peaks growing red in the dawn
of all Beginning,—pollen of the flowering godhead,
joints of pure light, corridors, stairways, thrones,
space formed from essence, shields made of ecstasy, storms
of emotion whirled into rapture, and suddenly, alone,
*mirrors:* which scoop up the beauty that has streamed from
    their face
and gather it back, into themselves, entire.

But we, when moved by deep feeling, evaporate; we
breathe ourselves out and away; from moment to moment
our emotion grows fainter, like a perfume. Though someone
    may tell us:
"Yes, you've entered my bloodstream, the room, the whole
    springtime
is filled with you . . ."—what does it matter? he can't contain
    us,
we vanish inside him and around him. And those who are
    beautiful,
oh who can retain them? Appearance ceaselessly rises
in their face, and is gone. Like dew from the morning grass,
what is ours floats into the air, like steam from a dish

heißen Gericht. O Lächeln, wohin? O Aufschaun:
neue, warme, entgehende Welle des Herzens—;
weh mir: wir *sinds* doch. Schmeckt denn der Weltraum,
in den wir uns lösen, nach uns? Fangen die Engel
wirklich nur Ihriges auf, ihnen Entströmtes,
oder ist manchmal, wie aus Versehen, ein wenig
unseres Wesens dabei? Sind wir in ihre
Züge soviel nur gemischt wie das Vage in die Gesichter
schwangerer Frauen? Sie merken es nicht in dem Wirbel
ihrer Rückkehr zu sich. (Wie sollten sie's merken.)

Liebende könnten, verstünden sie's, in der Nachtluft
wunderlich reden. Denn es scheint, daß uns alles
verheimlicht. Siehe, die Bäume *sind;* die Häuser,
die wir bewohnen, bestehn noch. Wir nur
ziehen allem vorbei wie ein luftiger Austausch.
Und alles ist einig, uns zu verschweigen, halb als
Schande vielleicht und halb als unsägliche Hoffnung.

Liebende, euch, ihr in einander Genügten,
frag ich nach uns. Ihr greift euch. Habt ihr Beweise?
Seht, mir geschiehts, daß meine Hände einander
inne werden oder daß mein gebrauchtes
Gesicht in ihnen sich schont. Das giebt mir ein wenig
Empfindung. Doch wer wagte darum schon zu *sein?*
Ihr aber, die ihr im Entzücken des anderen
zunehmt, bis er euch überwältigt
anfleht: nicht *mehr*—; die ihr unter den Händen
euch reichlicher werdet wie Traubenjahre;
die ihr manchmal vergeht, nur weil der andre
ganz überhand nimmt: euch frag ich nach uns. Ich weiß,
ihr berührt euch so selig, weil die Liebkosung verhält,
weil die Stelle nicht schwindet, die ihr, Zärtliche,
zudeckt; weil ihr darunter das reine
Dauern verspürt. So versprecht ihr euch Ewigkeit fast

of hot food. O smile, where are you going? O upturned
    glance:
new warm receding wave on the sea of the heart . . .
alas, but that is what we *are*. Does the infinite space
we dissolve into, taste of us then? Do the angels really
reabsorb only the radiance that streamed out from
    themselves, or
sometimes, as if by an oversight, is there a trace
of our essence in it as well? Are we mixed in with their
features even as slightly as that vague look
in the faces of pregnant women? They do not notice it
(how could they notice) in their swirling return to
    themselves.

Lovers, if they knew how, might utter strange, marvelous
words in the night air. For it seems that everything
hides us. Look: trees do exist; the houses
that we live in still stand. We alone
fly past all things, as fugitive as the wind.
And all things conspire to keep silent about us, half
out of shame perhaps, half as unutterable hope.

Lovers, gratified in each other, I am asking *you*
about us. You hold each other. Where is your proof?
Look, sometimes I find that my hands have become aware
of each other, or that my time-worn face
shelters itself inside them. That gives me a slight
sensation. But who would dare to exist, just for that?
You, though, who in the other's passion
grow until, overwhelmed, he begs you:
"No *more* . . ."; you who beneath his hands
swell with abundance, like autumn grapes;
you who may disappear because the other has wholly
emerged: I am asking *you* about us. I know,
you touch so blissfully because the caress preserves,
because the place you so tenderly cover
does not vanish; because underneath it
you feel pure duration. So you promise eternity, almost,

von der Umarmung. Und doch, wenn ihr der ersten
Blicke Schrecken besteht und die Sehnsucht am Fenster,
und den ersten gemeinsamen Gang, *ein* Mal durch den
   Garten:
Liebende, *seid* ihrs dann noch? Wenn ihr einer dem andern
euch an den Mund hebt und ansetzt—: Getränk an Getränk:
o wie entgeht dann der Trinkende seltsam der Handlung.

Erstaunte euch nicht auf attischen Stelen die Vorsicht
menschlicher Geste? war nicht Liebe und Abschied
so leicht auf die Schultern gelegt, als wär es aus anderm
Stoffe gemacht als bei uns? Gedenkt euch der Hände,
wie sie drucklos beruhen, obwohl in den Torsen die Kraft
   steht.
Diese Beherrschten wußten damit: so weit sind wirs,
*dieses* ist unser, uns *so* zu berühren; stärker
stemmen die Götter uns an. Doch dies ist Sache der Götter.

Fänden auch wir ein reines, verhaltenes, schmales
Menschliches, einen unseren Streifen Fruchtlands
zwischen Strom und Gestein. Denn das eigene Herz
   übersteigt uns
noch immer wie jene. Und wir können ihm nicht mehr
nachschaun in Bilder, die es besänftigen, noch in
göttliche Körper, in denen es größer sich mäßigt.

from the embrace. And yet, when you have survived
the terror of the first glances, the longing at the window,
and the first walk together, once only, through the garden:
lovers, *are* you the same? When you lift yourselves up
to each other's mouth and your lips join, drink against drink:
oh how strangely each drinker seeps away from his action.

Weren't you astonished by the caution of human gestures
on Attic gravestones? wasn't love and departure
placed so gently on shoulders that it seemed to be made
of a different substance than in our world? Remember the
    hands,
how weightlessly they rest, though there is power in the
    torsos.
These self-mastered figures know: "We can go this far,
this is ours, to touch one another this lightly; the gods
can press down harder upon us. But that is the gods' affair."

If only we too could discover a pure, contained,
human place, our own strip of fruit-bearing soil
between river and rock. For our own heart always exceeds
    us,
as theirs did. And we can no longer follow it, gazing
into images that soothe it or into the godlike bodies
where, measured more greatly, it achieves a greater repose.

## DIE DRITTE ELEGIE

Eines ist, die Geliebte zu singen. Ein anderes, wehe,
jenen verborgenen schuldigen Fluß-Gott des Bluts.
Den sie von weitem erkennt, ihren Jüngling, was weiß er
selbst von dem Herren der Lust, der aus dem Einsamen oft,
ehe das Mädchen noch linderte, oft auch als wäre sie nicht,
ach, von welchem Unkenntlichen triefend, das Gotthaupt
aufhob, aufrufend die Nacht zu unendlichem Aufruhr.
O des Blutes Neptun, o sein furchtbarer Dreizack.
O der dunkele Wind seiner Brust aus gewundener Muschel.
Horch, wie die Nacht sich muldet und höhlt. Ihr Sterne,
stammt nicht von euch des Liebenden Lust zu dem Antlitz
seiner Geliebten? Hat er die innige Einsicht
in ihr reines Gesicht nicht aus dem reinen Gestirn?

Du nicht hast ihm, wehe, nicht seine Mutter
hat ihm die Bogen der Braun so zur Erwartung gespannt.
Nicht an dir, ihn fühlendes Mädchen, an dir nicht
bog seine Lippe sich zum fruchtbarern Ausdruck.
Meinst du wirklich, ihn hätte dein leichter Auftritt
also erschüttert, du, die wandelt wie Frühwind?
Zwar du erschrakst ihm das Herz; doch ältere Schrecken
stürzten in ihn bei dem berührenden Anstoß.
Ruf ihn . . . du rufst ihn nicht ganz aus dunkelem Umgang.
Freilich, er *will*, er entspringt; erleichtert gewöhnt er
sich in dein heimliches Herz und nimmt und beginnt sich.
Aber begann er sich je?
Mutter, *du* machtest ihn klein, du warsts, die ihn anfing;
dir war er neu, du beugtest über die neuen
Augen die freundliche Welt und wehrtest der fremden.

# THE THIRD ELEGY

It is one thing to sing the beloved. Another, alas,
to invoke that hidden, guilty river-god of the blood.
Her young lover, whom she knows from far away—what
      does *he* know of
the lord of desire who often, up from the depths of his
      solitude,
even before she could soothe him, and as though she didn't
      exist,
held up his head, ah, dripping with the unknown,
erect, and summoned the night to an endless uproar.
Oh the Neptune inside our blood, with his appalling trident.
Oh the dark wind from his breast out of that spiraled conch.
Listen to the night as it makes itself hollow. O stars,
isn't it from you that the lover's desire for the face
of his beloved arises? Doesn't his secret insight
into her pure features come from the pure constellations?

Not you, his mother: alas, you were not the one
who bent the arch of his eyebrows into such expectation.
Not for you, girl so aware of him, not for your mouth
did his lips curve themselves into a more fruitful expression.
Do you really think that your gentle steps could have shaken
      him
with such violence, you who move like the morning breeze?
Yes, you did frighten his heart; but more ancient terrors
plunged into him at the shock of that feeling. Call him . . .
but you can't quite call him away from those dark
      companions.
Of course, he *wants* to escape, and he does; relieved, he
      nestles
into your sheltering heart, takes hold, and begins himself.
But did he ever begin himself, really?
Mother, *you* made him small, it was you who started him;
in *your* sight he was new, over his new eyes you arched
the friendly world and warded off the world that was alien.

Wo, ach, hin sind die Jahre, da du ihm einfach
mit der schlanken Gestalt wallendes Chaos vertratst?
Vieles verbargst du ihm so; das nächtlich-verdächtige
    Zimmer
machtest du harmlos, aus deinem Herzen voll Zuflucht
mischtest du menschlichern Raum seinem Nacht-Raum
    hinzu.
Nicht in die Finsternis, nein, in dein näheres Dasein
hast du das Nachtlicht gestellt und es schien wie aus
    Freundschaft.
Nirgends ein Knistern, das du nicht lächelnd erklärtest,
so als wüßtest du längst, *wann* sich die Diele benimmt . . .
Und er horchte und linderte sich. So vieles vermochte
zärtlich dein Aufstehn; hinter den Schrank trat
hoch im Mantel sein Schicksal, und in die Falten des
    Vorhangs
paßte, die leicht sich verschob, seine unruhige Zukunft.

Und er selbst, wie er lag, der Erleichterte, unter
schläfernden Lidern deiner leichten Gestaltung
Süße lösend in den gekosteten Vorschlaf—:
*schien* ein Gehüteter . . . Aber *innen:* wer wehrte,
hinderte innen in ihm die Fluten der Herkunft?
Ach, da *war* keine Vorsicht im Schlafenden; schlafend,
aber träumend, aber in Fiebern: wie er sich ein-ließ.
Er, der Neue, Scheuende, wie er verstrickt war,
mit des innern Geschehns weiterschlagenden Ranken
schon zu Mustern verschlungen, zu würgendem Wachstum, zu tierhaft
jagenden Formen. Wie er sich hingab—. Liebte.
Liebte sein Inneres, seines Inneren Wildnis,
diesen Urwald in ihm, auf dessen stummem Gestürztsein
lichtgrün sein Herz stand. Liebte. Verließ es, ging die

Ah, where are the years when you shielded him just by
    placing
your slender form between him and the surging abyss?
How much you hid from him then. The room that filled
    with suspicion
at night: you made it harmless; and out of the refuge of your
    heart
you mixed a more human space in with his night-space.
And you set down the lamp, not in that darkness, but in
your own nearer presence, and it glowed at him like a friend.
There wasn't a creak that your smile could not explain,
as though you had long known just when the floor would do
    that . . .
And he listened and was soothed. So powerful was your
    presence
as you tenderly stood by the bed; his fate,
tall and cloaked, retreated behind the wardrobe, and his
    restless
future, delayed for a while, adapted to the folds of the
    curtain.

And he himself, as he lay there, relieved, with the sweetness
of the gentle world you had made for him dissolving beneath
his drowsy eyelids, into the foretaste of sleep—:
he *seemed* protected . . . But inside: who could ward off,
who could divert, the floods of origin inside him?
Ah, there *was* no trace of caution in that sleeper; sleeping,
yes but dreaming, but flushed with what fevers: how he
    threw himself in.
All at once new, trembling, how he was caught up
and entangled in the spreading tendrils of inner event
already twined into patterns, into strangling undergrowth,
    prowling
bestial shapes. How he submitted—. Loved.
Loved his interior world, his interior wilderness,
that primal forest inside him, where among decayed
    treetrunks
his heart stood, light-green. Loved. Left it, went through

eigenen Wurzeln hinaus in gewaltigen Ursprung,
wo seine kleine Geburt schon überlebt war. Liebend
stieg er hinab in das ältere Blut, in die Schluchten,
wo das Furchtbare lag, noch satt von den Vätern. Und jedes
Schreckliche kannte ihn, blinzelte, war wie verständigt.
Ja, das Entsetzliche lächelte . . . Selten
hast du so zärtlich gelächelt, Mutter. Wie sollte
er es nicht lieben, da es ihm lächelte. *Vor* dir
hat ers geliebt, denn, da du ihn trugst schon,
war es im Wasser gelöst, das den Keimenden leicht macht.

Siehe, wir lieben nicht, wie die Blumen, aus einem
einzigen Jahr; uns steigt, wo wir lieben,
unvordenklicher Saft in die Arme. O Mädchen,
*dies:* daß wir liebten *in* uns, nicht Eines, ein Künftiges,
    sondern
das zahllos Brauende; nicht ein einzelnes Kind,
sondern die Väter, die wie Trümmer Gebirgs
uns im Grunde beruhn; sondern das trockene Flußbett
einstiger Mütter—; sondern die ganze
lautlose Landschaft unter dem wolkigen oder
reinen Verhängnis—: *dies* kam dir, Mädchen, zuvor.

Und du selber, was weißt du—, du locktest
Vorzeit empor in dem Liebenden. Welche Gefühle
wühlten herauf aus entwandelten Wesen. Welche
Frauen haßten dich da. Wasfür finstere Männer
regtest du auf im Geäder des Jünglings? Tote
Kinder wollten zu dir . . . O leise, leise,
tu ein liebes vor ihm, ein verläßliches Tagwerk,—führ ihn
nah an den Garten heran, gieb ihm der Nächte
Übergewicht . . . . . .
                    Verhalt ihn . . . . . .

his own roots and out, into the powerful source
where his little birth had already been outlived. Loving,
he waded down into more ancient blood, to ravines
where Horror lay, still glutted with his fathers. And every
Terror knew him, winked at him like an accomplice.
Yes, Atrocity smiled . . . Seldom
had you smiled so tenderly, mother. How could he help
loving what smiled at him. Even before he knew you,
he had loved it, for already while you carried him inside you,
    it
was dissolved in the water that makes the embryo weightless.

No, we don't accomplish our love in a single year
as the flowers do; an immemorial sap
flows up through our arms when we love. Dear girl,
this: that we loved, inside us, not One who would someday
    appear, but
seething multitudes; not just a single child,
but also the fathers lying in our depths
like fallen mountains; also the dried-up riverbeds
of ancient mothers—; also the whole
soundless landscape under the clouded or clear
sky of its destiny—: all this, my dear, preceded you.

And you yourself, how could you know
what primordial time you stirred in your lover. What
    passions
welled up inside him from departed beings. What
women hated you there. How many dark
sinister men you aroused in his young veins. Dead
children reached out to touch you . . . Oh gently, gently,
let him see you performing, with love, some confident daily
    task,—
lead him out close to the garden, give him what outweighs
the heaviest night . . . . . .
               Restrain him . . . . . .

## DIE VIERTE ELEGIE

O Bäume Lebens, o wann winterlich?
Wir sind nicht einig. Sind nicht wie die Zug-
vögel verständigt. Überholt und spät,
so drängen wir uns plötzlich Winden auf
und fallen ein auf teilnahmslosen Teich.
Blühn und verdorrn ist uns zugleich bewußt.
Und irgendwo gehn Löwen noch und wissen,
solang sie herrlich sind, von keiner Ohnmacht.

Uns aber, wo wir Eines meinen, ganz,
ist schon des andern Aufwand fühlbar. Feindschaft
ist uns das Nächste. Treten Liebende
nicht immerfort an Ränder, eins im andern,
die sich versprachen Weite, Jagd und Heimat.
    Da wird für eines Augenblickes Zeichnung
ein Grund von Gegenteil bereitet, mühsam,
daß wir sie sähen; denn man ist sehr deutlich
mit uns. Wir kennen den Kontur
des Fühlens nicht: nur, was ihn formt von außen.
    Wer saß nicht bang vor seines Herzens Vorhang?
Der schlug sich auf: die Szenerie war Abschied.
Leicht zu verstehen. Der bekannte Garten,
und schwankte leise: dann erst kam der Tänzer.
Nicht *der.* Genug! Und wenn er auch so leicht tut,
er ist verkleidet und er wird ein Bürger
und geht durch seine Küche in die Wohnung.
    Ich will nicht diese halbgefüllten Masken,
lieber die Puppe. Die ist voll. Ich will
den Balg aushalten und den Draht und ihr
Gesicht aus Aussehn. Hier. Ich bin davor.
Wenn auch die Lampen ausgehn, wenn mir auch
gesagt wird: Nichts mehr—, wenn auch von der Bühne
das Leere herkommt mit dem grauen Luftzug,
wenn auch von meinen stillen Vorfahrn keiner
mehr mit mir dasitzt, keine Frau, sogar

# THE FOURTH ELEGY

O trees of life, when does your winter come?
We are not in harmony, our blood does not forewarn us
like migratory birds'. Late, overtaken,
we force ourselves abruptly onto the wind
and fall to earth at some iced-over lake.
Flowering and fading come to us both at once.
And somewhere lions still roam and never know,
in their majestic power, of any weakness.

But we, while we are intent upon one object,
already feel the pull of another. Conflict
is second nature to us. Aren't lovers
always arriving at each other's boundaries?—
although they promised vastness, hunting, home.
    As when for some quick sketch, a wide background
of contrast is laboriously prepared
so that we can see more clearly: we never know
the actual, vital contour of our own
emotions—just what forms them from outside.
    Who has not sat, afraid, before his heart's
curtain? It rose: the scenery of farewell.
Easy to recognize. The well-known garden,
which swayed a little. Then the dancer came.
Not *him*. Enough! However lightly he moves,
he's costumed, made up—an ordinary man
who hurries home and walks in through the kitchen.
    I won't endure these half-filled human masks;
better, the puppet. It at least is full.
I'll put up with the stuffed skin, the wire, the face
that is nothing but appearance. Here. I'm waiting.
Even if the lights go out; even if someone
tells me "That's all"; even if emptiness
floats toward me in a gray draft from the stage;
even if not one of my silent ancestors
stays seated with me, not one woman, not

der Knabe nicht mehr mit dem braunen Schielaug:
Ich bleibe dennoch. Es giebt immer Zuschaun.

Hab ich nicht recht? Du, der um mich so bitter
das Leben schmeckte, meines kostend, Vater,
den ersten trüben Aufguß meines Müssens,
da ich heranwuchs, immer wieder kostend
und, mit dem Nachgeschmack so fremder Zukunft
beschäftigt, prüftest mein beschlagnes Aufschaun,—
der du, mein Vater, seit du tot bist, oft
in meiner Hoffnung, innen in mir, Angst hast,
und Gleichmut, wie ihn Tote haben, Reiche
von Gleichmut, aufgiebst für mein bißchen Schicksal,
hab ich nicht recht? Und ihr, hab ich nicht recht,
die ihr mich liebtet für den kleinen Anfang
Liebe zu euch, von dem ich immer abkam,
weil mir der Raum in eurem Angesicht,
da ich ihn liebte, überging in Weltraum,
in dem ihr nicht mehr wart . . . . : wenn mir zumut ist,
zu warten vor der Puppenbühne, nein,
so völlig hinzuschaun, daß, um mein Schauen
am Ende aufzuwiegen, dort als Spieler
ein Engel hinmuß, der die Bälge hochreißt.
Engel und Puppe: dann ist endlich Schauspiel.
Dann kommt zusammen, was wir immerfort
entzwein, indem wir da sind. Dann entsteht
aus unsern Jahreszeiten erst der Umkreis
des ganzen Wandelns. Über uns hinüber
spielt dann der Engel. Sieh, die Sterbenden,
sollten sie nicht vermuten, wie voll Vorwand
das alles ist, was wir hier leisten. Alles
ist nicht es selbst. O Stunden in der Kindheit,
da hinter den Figuren mehr als nur
Vergangnes war und vor uns nicht die Zukunft.
Wir wuchsen freilich und wir drängten manchmal,
bald groß zu werden, denen halb zulieb,

the boy with the immovable brown eye—
I'll sit here anyway. One can always watch.

Am I not right? You, to whom life tasted
so bitter after you took a sip of mine,
the first, gritty infusion of my will,
Father—who, as I grew up, kept on tasting
and, troubled by the aftertaste of so
strange a future, searched my unfocused gaze—
you who, so often since you died, have trembled
for my well-being, within my deepest hope,
relinquishing that calmness which the dead
feel as their very essence, countless realms
of equanimity, for my scrap of life—
tell me, am I not right? And you, dear women
who must have loved me for my small beginning
of love toward you, which I always turned away from
because the space in your features grew, changed,
even while I loved it, into cosmic space,
where you no longer were—: am I not right
to feel as if I *must* stay seated, must
wait before the puppet stage, or, rather,
gaze at it so intensely that at last,
to balance my gaze, an angel has to come and
make the stuffed skins startle into life.
Angel and puppet: a real play, finally.
Then what we separate by our very presence
can come together. And only then, the whole
cycle of transformation will arise,
out of our own life-seasons. Above, beyond us,
the angel plays. If no one else, the dying
must notice how unreal, how full of pretense,
is all that we accomplish here, where nothing
is allowed to be itself. Oh hours of childhood,
when behind each shape more than the past appeared
and what streamed out before us was not the future.
We felt our bodies growing and were at times
impatient to *be* grown up, half for the sake

die andres nicht mehr hatten, als das Großsein.
Und waren doch, in unserem Alleingehn,
mit Dauerndem vergnügt und standen da
im Zwischenraume zwischen Welt und Spielzeug,
an einer Stelle, die seit Anbeginn
gegründet war für einen reinen Vorgang.

Wer zeigt ein Kind, so wie es steht? Wer stellt
es ins Gestirn und giebt das Maß des Abstands
ihm in die Hand? Wer macht den Kindertod
aus grauem Brot, das hart wird,—oder läßt
ihn drin im runden Mund, so wie den Gröps
von einem schönen Apfel? . . . . . . Mörder sind
leicht einzusehen. Aber dies: den Tod,
den ganzen Tod, noch *vor* dem Leben so
sanft zu enthalten und nicht bös zu sein,
ist unbeschreiblich.

of those with nothing left but their grownupness.
Yet were, when playing by ourselves, enchanted
with what alone endures; and we would stand there
in the infinite, blissful space between world and toy,
at a point which, from the earliest beginning,
had been established for a pure event.

Who shows a child as he really is? Who sets him
in his constellation and puts the measuring-rod
of distance in his hand? Who makes his death
out of gray bread, which hardens—or leaves it there
inside his round mouth, jagged as the core
of a sweet apple? . . . . . . Murderers are easy
to understand. But this: that one can contain
death, the whole of death, even before
life has begun, can hold it to one's heart
gently, and not refuse to go on living,
is inexpressible.

## DIE FÜNFTE ELEGIE

*Frau Hertha Koenig zugeeignet*

Wer aber *sind* sie, sag mir, die Fahrenden, diese ein wenig
Flüchtigern noch als wir selbst, die dringend von früh an
wringt ein *wem, wem* zu Liebe
niemals zufriedener Wille? Sondern er wringt sie,
biegt sie, schlingt sie und schwingt sie,
wirft sie und fängt sie zurück; wie aus geölter,
glatterer Luft kommen sie nieder
auf dem verzehrten, von ihrem ewigen
Aufsprung dünneren Teppich, diesem verlorenen
Teppich im Weltall.
Aufgelegt wie ein Pflaster, als hätte der Vorstadt-
Himmel der Erde dort wehe getan.
                            Und kaum dort,
aufrecht, da und gezeigt: des Dastehns
großer Anfangsbuchstab . . . , schon auch, die stärksten
Männer, rollt sie wieder, zum Scherz, der immer
kommende Griff, wie August der Starke bei Tisch
einen zinnenen Teller.

Ach und um diese
Mitte, die Rose des Zuschauns:
blüht und entblättert. Um diesen
Stampfer, den Stempel, den von dem eignen
blühenden Staub getroffnen, zur Scheinfrucht
wieder der Unlust befruchteten, ihrer
niemals bewußten,—glänzend mit dünnster
Oberfläche leicht scheinlächelnden Unlust.

Da: der welke, faltige Stemmer,
der alte, der nur noch trommelt,
eingegangen in seiner gewaltigen Haut, als hätte sie früher
*zwei* Männer enthalten, und einer

## THE FIFTH ELEGY
*Dedicated to Frau Hertha Koenig*

But tell me, who *are* they, these wanderers, even more
transient than we ourselves, who from their earliest days
are savagely wrung out
by a never-satisfied will (for *whose* sake)? Yet it wrings them,
bends them, twists them, swings them and flings them
and catches them again; and falling as if through oiled
slippery air, they land
on the threadbare carpet, worn constantly thinner
by their perpetual leaping, this carpet that is lost
in infinite space.
Stuck on like a bandage, as if the suburban sky
had wounded the earth.
                          And hardly has it appeared
when, standing there, upright, is: the large capital D
that begins Duration . . . , and the always-approaching grip
takes them again, as a joke, even the strongest
men, and crushes them, the way King Augustus the Strong
would crush a pewter plate.

Ah and around this
center: the rose of Onlooking
blooms and unblossoms. Around this
pestle pounding the carpet,
this pistil, fertilized by the pollen
of its own dust, and producing in turn
the specious fruit of displeasure: the unconscious
gaping faces, their thin
surfaces glossy with boredom's specious half-smile.

There: the shriveled-up, wrinkled weight-lifter,
an old man who only drums now,
shrunk in his enormous skin, which looks as if it had once
contained *two* men, and the other

läge nun schon auf dem Kirchhof, und er überlebte den
  andern,
taub und manchmal ein wenig
wirr, in der verwitweten Haut.

Aber der junge, der Mann, als wär er der Sohn eines
  Nackens
und einer Nonne: prall und strammig erfüllt
mit Muskeln und Einfalt.

Oh ihr,
die ein Leid, das noch klein war,
einst als Spielzeug bekam, in einer seiner
langen Genesungen . . . .

Du, der mit dem Aufschlag,
wie nur Früchte ihn kennen, unreif,
täglich hundertmal abfällt vom Baum der gemeinsam
erbauten Bewegung (der, rascher als Wasser, in wenig
Minuten Lenz, Sommer und Herbst hat)—
abfällt und anprallt ans Grab:
manchmal, in halber Pause, will dir ein liebes
Antlitz entstehn hinüber zu deiner selten
zärtlichen Mutter; doch an deinen Körper verliert sich,
der es flächig verbraucht, das schüchtern
kaum versuchte Gesicht . . . Und wieder
klatscht der Mann in die Hand zu dem Ansprung, und eh
  dir
jemals ein Schmerz deutlicher wird in der Nähe des immer
trabenden Herzens, kommt das Brennen der Fußsohln
ihm, seinem Ursprung, zuvor mit ein paar dir
rasch in die Augen gejagten leiblichen Tränen.
Und dennoch, blindlings,
das Lächeln . . . . .

Engel! o nimms, pflücks, das kleinblütige Heilkraut.
Schaff eine Vase, verwahrs! Stells unter jene, uns *noch* nicht
offenen Freuden; in lieblicher Urne

were already lying in the graveyard, while this one lived on
    without him,
deaf and sometimes a little
confused, in the widowed skin.

And the young one over there, the man, who might be the
    son of a neck
and a nun: firm and vigorously filled
with muscles and innocence.

Children,
whom a grief that was still quite small
once received as a toy, during one of its
long convalescences . . . .

You, little boy, who fall down
a hundred times daily, with the thud
that only unripe fruits know, from the tree of mutually
constructed motion (which more quickly than water, in a few
minutes, has its spring, summer, and autumn)—
fall down hard on the grave:
sometimes, during brief pauses, a loving look
toward your seldom affectionate mother tries to be born
in your expression; but it gets lost along the way,
your body consumes it, that timid
scarcely-attempted face . . . And again
the man is clapping his hands for your leap, and before
a pain can become more distinct near your constantly racing
heart, the stinging in your soles rushes ahead of
that other pain, chasing a pair
of physical tears quickly into your eyes.
And nevertheless, blindly,
the smile . . . . .

Oh gather it, Angel, that small-flowered herb of healing.
Create a vase and preserve it. Set it among those joys
not *yet* open to us; on that lovely urn

rühms mit blumiger schwungiger Aufschrift:
'Subrisio Saltat.'

Du dann, Liebliche,
du, von den reizendsten Freuden
stumm Übersprungne. Vielleicht sind
deine Fransen glücklich für dich—,
oder über den jungen
prallen Brüsten die grüne metallene Seide
fühlt sich unendlich verwöhnt und entbehrt nichts.
Du,
immerfort anders auf alle des Gleichgewichts schwankende
        Waagen
hingelegte Marktfrucht des Gleichmuts,
öffentlich unter den Schultern.

Wo, o *wo* ist der Ort—ich trag ihn im Herzen—,
wo sie noch lange nicht *konnten,* noch von einander
abfieln, wie sich bespringende, nicht recht
paarige Tiere;—
wo die Gewichte noch schwer sind;
wo noch von ihren vergeblich
wirbelnden Stäben die Teller
torkeln . . . . .

Und plötzlich in diesem mühsamen Nirgends, plötzlich
die unsägliche Stelle, wo sich das reine Zuwenig
unbegreiflich verwandelt—, umspringt
in jenes leere Zuviel.
Wo die vielstellige Rechnung
zahlenlos aufgeht.

Plätze, o Platz in Paris, unendlicher Schauplatz,
wo die Modistin, Madame Lamort,
die ruhlosen Wege der Erde, endlose Bänder,
schlingt und windet und neue aus ihnen
Schleifen erfindet, Rüschen, Blumen, Kokarden, künstliche
        Früchte—, alle
unwahr gefärbt,—für die billigen

praise it with the ornately flowing inscription:
                              "Subrisio Saltat."

    And you then, my lovely darling,
you whom the most tempting joys
have mutely leapt over. Perhaps
your fringes are happy *for* you—,
or perhaps the green
metallic silk stretched over your firm young breasts
feels itself endlessly indulged and in need of nothing.
You
display-fruit of equanimity,
set out in front of the public, in continual variations
on all the swaying scales of equipoise,
lifted among the shoulders.

Oh *where* is the place—I carry it in my heart—,
where they still were far from mastery, still fell apart
from each other, like mating cattle that someone
has badly paired;—
where the weights are still heavy; where
from their vainly twirling sticks
the plates still wobble
and drop . . . . .

And suddenly in this laborious nowhere, suddenly
the unsayable spot where the pure Too-little is transformed
incomprehensibly—, leaps around and changes
into that empty Too-much;
where the difficult calculation
becomes numberless and resolved.

Squares, oh square in Paris, infinite showplace
where the milliner Madame Lamort
twists and winds the restless paths of the earth,
those endless ribbons, and, from them, designs
new bows, frills, flowers, ruffles, artificial fruits—, all
falsely colored,—for the cheap

Winterhüte des Schicksals.
. . . . . . . . . . . . . . . . . . .

Engel!: Es wäre ein Platz, den wir nicht wissen, und dorten,
auf unsäglichem Teppich, zeigten die Liebenden, die's hier
bis zum Können nie bringen, ihre kühnen
hohen Figuren des Herzschwungs,
ihre Türme aus Lust, ihre
längst, wo Boden nie war, nur an einander
lehnenden Leitern, bebend,—und *könntens,*
vor den Zuschauern rings, unzähligen lautlosen Toten:
    Würfen die dann ihre letzten, immer ersparten,
immer verborgenen, die wir nicht kennen, ewig
gültigen Münzen des Glücks vor das endlich
wahrhaft lächelnde Paar auf gestilltem
Teppich?

winter bonnets of Fate.
. . . . . . . . . . . . . . . . . .

Angel!: If there were a place that we didn't know of, and
        there,
on some unsayable carpet, lovers displayed
what they never could bring to mastery here—the bold
exploits of their high-flying hearts,
their towers of pleasure, their ladders
that have long since been standing where there was no
        ground, leaning
just on each other, trembling,—and could *master* all this,
before the surrounding spectators, the innumerable
        soundless dead:
    Would these, then, throw down their final, forever
        saved-up,
forever hidden, unknown to us, eternally valid
coins of happiness before the at last
genuinely smiling pair on the gratified
carpet?

## DIE SECHSTE ELEGIE

Feigenbaum, seit wie lange schon ists mir bedeutend,
wie du die Blüte beinah ganz überschlägst
und hinein in die zeitig entschlossene Frucht,
ungerühmt, drängst dein reines Geheimnis.
Wie der Fontäne Rohr treibt dein gebognes Gezweig
abwärts den Saft und hinan: und er springt aus dem Schlaf,
fast nicht erwachend, ins Glück seiner süßesten Leistung.
Sieh: wie der Gott in den Schwan.
                    . . . . . . Wir aber verweilen,
ach, uns rühmt es zu blühn, und ins verspätete Innre
unserer endlichen Frucht gehn wir verraten hinein.
Wenigen steigt so stark der Andrang des Handelns,
daß sie schon anstehn und glühn in der Fülle des Herzens,
wenn die Verführung zum Blühn wie gelinderte Nachtluft
ihnen die Jugend des Munds, ihnen die Lider berührt:
Helden vielleicht und den frühe Hinüberbestimmten,
denen der gärtnernde Tod anders die Adern verbiegt.
Diese stürzen dahin: dem eigenen Lächeln
sind sie voran, wie das Rossegespann in den milden
muldigen Bildern von Karnak dem siegenden König.

Wunderlich nah ist der Held doch den jugendlich Toten.
    Dauern
ficht ihn nicht an. Sein Aufgang ist Dasein; beständig
nimmt er sich fort und tritt ins veränderte Sternbild
seiner steten Gefahr. Dort fänden ihn wenige. Aber,
das uns finster verschweigt, das plötzlich begeisterte
    Schicksal
singt ihn hinein in den Sturm seiner aufrauschenden Welt.
Hör ich doch keinen wie *ihn.* Auf einmal durchgeht mich
mit der strömenden Luft sein verdunkelter Ton.

Dann, wie verbärg ich mich gern vor der Sehnsucht: O wär
    ich,

# THE SIXTH ELEGY

Fig-tree, for such a long time I have found meaning
in the way you almost completely omit your blossoms
and urge your pure mystery, unproclaimed,
into the early ripening fruit.
Like the curved pipe of a fountain, your arching boughs
     drive the sap
downward and up again: and almost without awakening
it bursts out of sleep, into its sweetest achievement.
Like the god stepping into the swan.
                  . . . . . . But *we* still linger, alas,
we, whose pride is in blossoming; we enter the overdue
interior of our final fruit and are already betrayed.
In only a few does the urge to action rise up
so powerfully that they stop, glowing in their heart's
     abundance,
while, like the soft night air, the temptation to blossom
touches their tender mouths, touches their eyelids, softly:
heroes perhaps, and those chosen to disappear early,
whose veins Death the gardener twists into a different
     pattern.
These plunge on ahead: in advance of their own smile
like the team of galloping horses before the triumphant
pharaoh in the mildly hollowed reliefs at Karnak.

The hero is strangely close to those who died young.
     Permanence
does not concern him. He lives in continual ascent,
moving on into the ever-changed constellation
of perpetual danger. Few could find him there. But
Fate, which is silent about us, suddenly grows inspired
and sings him into the storm of his onrushing world.
I hear no one like *him*. All at once I am pierced
by his darkened voice, carried on the streaming air.

Then how gladly I would hide from the longing to be once
     again

wär ich ein Knabe und dürft es noch werden und säße
in die künftigen Arme gestützt und läse von Simson,
wie seine Mutter erst nichts und dann alles gebar.

War er nicht Held schon in dir, o Mutter, begann nicht
dort schon, in dir, seine herrische Auswahl?
Tausende brauten im Schooß und wollten *er* sein,
aber sieh: er ergriff und ließ aus—, wählte und konnte.
Und wenn er Säulen zerstieß, so wars, da er ausbrach
aus der Welt deines Leibs in die engere Welt, wo er weiter
wählte und konnte. O Mütter der Helden, o Ursprung
reißender Ströme! Ihr Schluchten, in die sich
hoch von dem Herzrand, klagend,
schon die Mädchen gestürzt, künftig die Opfer dem Sohn.

Denn hinstürmte der Held durch Aufenthalte der Liebe,
jeder hob ihn hinaus, jeder ihn meinende Herzschlag,
abgewendet schon, stand er am Ende der Lächeln,—anders.

oh a boy once again, with my life before me, to sit
leaning on future arms and reading of Samson,
how from his mother first nothing, then everything, was
    born.

Wasn't he a hero inside you, mother? didn't
his imperious choosing already begin there, in you?
Thousands seethed in your womb, wanting to be *him,*
but look: he grasped and excluded—, chose and prevailed.
And if he demolished pillars, it was when he burst
from the world of your body into the narrower world, where
    again
he chose and prevailed. O mothers of heroes, O sources
of ravaging floods! You ravines into which
virgins have plunged, lamenting,
from the highest rim of the heart, sacrifices to the son.

For whenever the hero stormed through the stations of love,
each heartbeat intended for him lifted him up, beyond it;
and, turning away, he stood there, at the end of all
    smiles,—transfigured.

## DIE SIEBENTE ELEGIE

Werbung nicht mehr, nicht Werbung, entwachsene Stimme,
sei deines Schreies Natur; zwar schrieest du rein wie der
    Vogel,
wenn ihn die Jahreszeit aufhebt, die steigende, beinah
    vergessend,
daß er ein kümmerndes Tier und nicht nur ein einzelnes
    Herz sei,
das sie ins Heitere wirft, in die innigen Himmel. Wie er, so
würbest du wohl, nicht minder—, daß, noch unsichtbar,
dich die Freundin erführ, die stille, in der eine Antwort
langsam erwacht und über dem Hören sich anwärmt,—
deinem erkühnten Gefühl die erglühte Gefühlin.

O und der Frühling begriffe—, da ist keine Stelle,
die nicht trüge den Ton der Verkündigung. Erst jenen
    kleinen
fragenden Auflaut, den, mit steigernder Stille,
weithin umschweigt ein reiner bejahender Tag.
Dann die Stufen hinan, Ruf-Stufen hinan, zum geträumten
Tempel der Zukunft—; dann den Triller, Fontäne,
die zu dem drängenden Strahl schon das Fallen zuvornimmt
im versprechlichen Spiel . . . . Und vor sich, den Sommer.

Nicht nur die Morgen alle des Sommers—, nicht nur
wie sie sich wandeln in Tag und strahlen vor Anfang.
Nicht nur die Tage, die zart sind um Blumen, und oben,
um die gestalteten Bäume, stark und gewaltig.
Nicht nur die Andacht dieser entfalteten Kräfte,
nicht nur die Wege, nicht nur die Wiesen im Abend,
nicht nur, nach spätem Gewitter, das atmende Klarsein,
nicht nur der nahende Schlaf und ein Ahnen, abends . . .

## THE SEVENTH ELEGY

Not wooing, no longer shall wooing, voice that has outgrown
     it,
be the nature of your cry; but instead, you would cry out as
     purely as a bird
when the quickly ascending season lifts him up, nearly
     forgetting
that he is a suffering creature and not just a single heart
being flung into brightness, into the intimate skies. Just like
     him
you would be wooing, not any less purely—, so that, still
unseen, she would sense you, the silent lover in whom a
     reply
slowly awakens and, as she hears you, grows warm,—
the ardent companion to your own most daring emotion.

Oh and springtime would hold it—, everywhere it would
     echo
the song of annunciation. First the small
questioning notes intensified all around
by the sheltering silence of a pure, affirmative day.
Then up the stairs, up the stairway of calls, to the
     dreamed-of
temple of the future—; and then the trill, like a fountain
which, in its rising jet, already anticipates its fall
in a game of promises . . . . And still ahead: summer.

Not only all the dawns of summer—, not only
how they change themselves into day and shine with
     beginning.
Not only the days, so tender around flowers and, above,
around the patterned treetops, so strong, so intense.
Not only the reverence of all these unfolded powers,
not only the pathways, not only the meadows at sunset,
not only, after a late storm, the deep-breathing freshness,
not only approaching sleep, and a premonition . . .

sondern die Nächte! Sondern die hohen, des Sommers,
Nächte, sondern die Sterne, die Sterne der Erde.
O einst tot sein und sie wissen unendlich,
alle die Sterne: denn wie, wie, wie sie vergessen!

Siehe, da rief ich die Liebende. Aber nicht *sie* nur
käme . . . Es kämen aus schwächlichen Gräbern
Mädchen und ständen . . . Denn, wie beschränk ich,
wie, den gerufenen Ruf? Die Versunkenen suchen
immer noch Erde.—Ihr Kinder, ein hiesig
einmal ergriffenes Ding gälte für viele.
Glaubt nicht, Schicksal sei mehr, als das Dichte der
      Kindheit;
wie überholtet ihr oft den Geliebten, atmend,
atmend nach seligem Lauf, auf nichts zu, ins Freie.

Hiersein ist herrlich. Ihr wußtet es, Mädchen, *ihr* auch,
die ihr scheinbar entbehrtet, versankt—, ihr, in den ärgsten
Gassen der Städte, Schwärende, oder dem Abfall
Offene. Denn eine Stunde war jeder, vielleicht nicht
ganz eine Stunde, ein mit den Maßen der Zeit kaum
Meßliches zwischen zwei Weilen—, da sie ein Dasein
hatte. Alles. Die Adern voll Dasein.
Nur, wir vergessen so leicht, was der lachende Nachbar
uns nicht bestätigt oder beneidet. Sichtbar
wollen wirs heben, wo doch das sichtbarste Glück uns
erst zu erkennen sich giebt, wenn wir es innen verwandeln.

Nirgends, Geliebte, wird Welt sein, als innen. Unser
Leben geht hin mit Verwandlung. Und immer geringer
schwindet das Außen. Wo einmal ein dauerndes Haus war,
schlägt sich erdachtes Gebild vor, quer, zu Erdenklichem
völlig gehörig, als ständ es noch ganz im Gehirne.
Weite Speicher der Kraft schafft sich der Zeitgeist, gestaltlos
wie der spannende Drang, den er aus allem gewinnt.

but also the nights! But also the lofty summer
nights, and the stars as well, the stars of the earth.
Oh to be dead at last and know them endlessly,
all the stars: for how, how could we ever forget them!

Look, I was calling for my lover. But not just *she*
would come . . . Out of their fragile graves
girls would arise and gather . . . For how could I limit
the call, once I called it? These unripe spirits keep seeking
the earth.—Children, one earthly Thing
truly experienced, even once, is enough for a lifetime.
Don't think that fate is more than the density of childhood;
how often you outdistanced the man you loved, breathing,
      breathing
after the blissful chase, and passed on into freedom.

*Truly* being here is glorious. Even *you* knew it,
you girls who seemed to be lost, to go under—, in the
      filthiest
streets of the city, festering there, or wide open
for garbage. For each of you had an hour, or perhaps
not even an hour, a barely measurable time
between two moments—, when you were granted a sense
of being. Everything. Your veins flowed with being.
But we can so easily forget what our laughing neighbor
neither confirms nor envies. We want to display it,
to make it visible, though even the most visible happiness
can't reveal itself to us until we transform it, within.

Nowhere, Beloved, will world be but within us. Our life
passes in transformation. And the external
shrinks into less and less. Where once an enduring house
      was,
now a cerebral structure crosses our path, completely
belonging to the realm of concepts, as though it still stood in
      the brain.
Our age has built itself vast reservoirs of power,
formless as the straining energy that it wrests from the earth.

Tempel kennt er nicht mehr. Diese, des Herzens,
   Verschwendung
sparen wir heimlicher ein. Ja, wo noch eins übersteht,
ein einst gebetetes Ding, ein gedientes, geknietes—,
hält es sich, so wie es ist, schon ins Unsichtbare hin.
Viele gewahrens nicht mehr, doch ohne den Vorteil,
daß sie's nun *innerlich* baun, mit Pfeilern und Statuen,
   größer!

Jede dumpfe Umkehr der Welt hat solche Enterbte,
denen das Frühere nicht und noch nicht das Nächste gehört.
Denn auch das Nächste ist weit für die Menschen. *Uns* soll
dies nicht verwirren; es stärke in uns die Bewahrung
der noch erkannten Gestalt.—Dies *stand* einmal unter
   Menschen,
mitten im Schicksal stands, im vernichtenden, mitten
im Nichtwissen-Wohin stand es, wie seiend, und bog
Sterne zu sich aus gesicherten Himmeln. Engel,
*dir* noch zeig ich es, *da!* in deinem Anschaun
steh es gerettet zuletzt, nun endlich aufrecht.
Säulen, Pylone, der Sphinx, das strebende Stemmen,
grau aus vergehender Stadt oder aus fremder, des Doms.

War es nicht Wunder? O staune, Engel, denn *wir* sinds,
wir, o du Großer, erzähls, daß wir solches vermochten, mein
   Atem
reicht für die Rühmung nicht aus. So haben wir dennoch
nicht die Räume versäumt, diese gewährenden, diese
*unseren* Räume. (Was müssen sie fürchterlich groß sein,
da sie Jahrtausende nicht unseres Fühlns überfülln.)
Aber ein Turm war groß, nicht wahr? O Engel, er war es,—
groß, auch noch neben dir? Chartres war groß—, und Musik

Temples are no longer known. It is we who secretly save up
these extravagances of the heart. Where one of them still
    survives,
a Thing that was formerly prayed to, worshipped, knelt
    before—
just as it is, it passes into the invisible world.
Many no longer perceive it, yet miss the chance
to build it *inside* themselves now, with pillars and statues:
    greater.

Each torpid turn of the world has such disinherited ones,
to whom neither the past belongs, nor yet what has nearly
    arrived.
For even the nearest moment is far from mankind. Though
    *we*
should not be confused by this, but strengthened in our task
    of preserving
the still-recognizable form.—This once *stood* among
    mankind,
in the midst of Fate the annihilator, in the midst
of Not-Knowing-Whither, it stood as if enduring, and bent
stars down to it from their safeguarded heavens. Angel,
to *you* I will show it, *there!* in your endless vision
it shall stand, now finally upright, rescued at last.
Pillars, pylons, the Sphinx, the striving thrust
of the cathedral, gray, from a fading or alien city.

Wasn't all this a miracle? Be astonished, Angel, for we
*are* this, O Great One; proclaim that we could achieve this,
    my breath
is too short for such praise. So, after all, we have not
failed to make use of these generous spaces, these
spaces of *ours*. (How frighteningly great they must be,
since thousands of years have not made them overflow with
    our feelings.)
But a tower was great, wasn't it? Oh Angel, it was—
even when placed beside you? Chartres was great—, and
    music

reichte noch weiter hinan und überstieg uns. Doch selbst nur
eine Liebende—, oh, allein am nächtlichen Fenster. . . .
reichte sie dir nicht ans Knie—?
                                    Glaub *nicht*, daß ich werbe.
Engel, und würb ich dich auch! Du kommst nicht. Denn
    mein
Anruf ist immer voll Hinweg; wider so starke
Strömung kannst du nicht schreiten. Wie ein gestreckter
Arm ist mein Rufen. Und seine zum Greifen
oben offene Hand bleibt vor dir
offen, wie Abwehr und Warnung,
Unfaßlicher, weitauf.

reached still higher and passed far beyond us. But even
a woman in love—, oh alone at night by her window. . . .
didn't she reach your knee—?
                              Don't think that I'm wooing.
Angel, and even if I were, you would not come. For my call
is always filled with departure; against such a powerful
current you cannot move. Like an outstretched arm
is my call. And its hand, held open and reaching up
to seize, remains in front of you, open
as if in defense and warning,
Ungraspable One, far above.

## DIE ACHTE ELEGIE
*Rudolf Kassner zugeeignet*

Mit allen Augen sieht die Kreatur
das Offene. Nur unsre Augen sind
wie umgekehrt und ganz um sie gestellt
als Fallen, rings um ihren freien Ausgang.
Was draußen *ist,* wir wissens aus des Tiers
Antlitz allein; denn schon das frühe Kind
wenden wir um und zwingens, daß es rückwärts
Gestaltung sehe, nicht das Offne, das
im Tiergesicht so tief ist. Frei von Tod.
*Ihn* sehen wir allein; das freie Tier
hat seinen Untergang stets hinter sich
und vor sich Gott, und wenn es geht, so gehts
in Ewigkeit, so wie die Brunnen gehen.
    *Wir* haben nie, nicht einen einzigen Tag,
den reinen Raum vor uns, in den die Blumen
unendlich aufgehn. Immer ist es Welt
und niemals Nirgends ohne Nicht: das Reine,
Unüberwachte, das man atmet und
unendlich *weiß* und nicht begehrt. Als Kind
verliert sich eins im Stilln an dies und wird
gerüttelt. Oder jener stirbt und *ists.*
Denn nah am Tod sieht man den Tod nicht mehr
und starrt *hinaus,* vielleicht mit großem Tierblick.
Liebende, wäre nicht der andre, der
die Sicht verstellt, sind nah daran und staunen . . .
Wie aus Versehn ist ihnen aufgetan
hinter dem andern . . . Aber über ihn
kommt keiner fort, und wieder wird ihm Welt.
Der Schöpfung immer zugewendet, sehn
wir nur auf ihr die Spiegelung des Frein,
von uns verdunkelt. Oder daß ein Tier,
ein stummes, aufschaut, ruhig durch uns durch.

# THE EIGHTH ELEGY
*Dedicated to Rudolf Kassner*

With all its eyes the natural world looks out
into the Open. Only *our* eyes are turned
backward, and surround plant, animal, child
like traps, as they emerge into their freedom.
We know what is really out there only from
the animal's gaze; for we take the very young
child and force it around, so that it sees
objects—not the Open, which is so
deep in animals' faces. Free from death.
We, only, can see death; the free animal
has its decline in back of it, forever,
and God in front, and when it moves, it moves
already in eternity, like a fountain.
    Never, not for a single day, do *we* have
before us that pure space into which flowers
endlessly open. Always there is World
and never Nowhere without the No: that pure
unseparated element which one breathes
without desire and endlessly *knows*. A child
may wander there for hours, through the timeless
stillness, may get lost in it and be
shaken back. Or someone dies and *is* it.
For, nearing death, one doesn't see death; but stares
beyond, perhaps with an animal's vast gaze.
Lovers, if the beloved were not there
blocking the view, are close to it, and marvel . . .
As if by some mistake, it opens for them
behind each other . . . But neither can move past
the other, and it changes back to World.
Forever turned toward objects, we see in them
the mere reflection of the realm of freedom,
which we have dimmed. Or when some animal
mutely, serenely, looks us through and through.

Dieses heißt Schicksal: gegenüber sein
und nichts als das und immer gegenüber.

Wäre Bewußtheit unsrer Art in dem
sicheren Tier, das uns entgegenzieht
in anderer Richtung—, riß es uns herum
mit seinem Wandel. Doch sein Sein ist ihm
unendlich, ungefaßt und ohne Blick
auf seinen Zustand, rein, so wie sein Ausblick.
Und wo wir Zukunft sehn, dort sieht es Alles
und sich in Allem und geheilt für immer.

Und doch ist in dem wachsam warmen Tier
Gewicht und Sorge einer großen Schwermut.
Denn ihm auch haftet immer an, was uns
oft überwältigt,—die Erinnerung,
als sei schon einmal das, wonach man drängt,
näher gewesen, treuer und sein Anschluß
unendlich zärtlich. Hier ist alles Abstand,
und dort wars Atem. Nach der ersten Heimat
ist ihm die zweite zwitterig und windig.
    O Seligkeit der *kleinen* Kreatur,
die immer *bleibt* im Schooße, der sie austrug;
o Glück der Mücke, die noch *innen* hüpft,
selbst wenn sie Hochzeit hat: denn Schooß ist Alles.
Und sieh die halbe Sicherheit des Vogels,
der beinah beides weiß aus seinem Ursprung,
als wär er eine Seele der Etrusker,
aus einem Toten, den ein Raum empfing,
doch mit der ruhenden Figur als Deckel.
Und wie bestürzt ist eins, das fliegen muß
und stammt aus einem Schooß. Wie vor sich selbst
erschreckt, durchzuckts die Luft, wie wenn ein Sprung
durch eine Tasse geht. So reißt die Spur
der Fledermaus durchs Porzellan des Abends.

Und wir: Zuschauer, immer, überall,
dem allen zugewandt und nie hinaus!

That is what fate means: to be opposite,
to be opposite and nothing else, forever.

If the animal moving toward us so securely
in a different direction had our kind of
consciousness—, it would wrench us around and drag us
along its path. But it feels its life as boundless,
unfathomable, and without regard
to its own condition: pure, like its outward gaze.
And where we see the future, it sees all time
and itself within all time, forever healed.

Yet in the alert, warm animal there lies
the pain and burden of an enormous sadness.
For it too feels the presence of what often
overwhelms us: a memory, as if
the element we keep pressing toward was once
more intimate, more true, and our communion
infinitely tender. Here all is distance;
there it was breath. After that first home,
the second seems ambiguous and drafty.
　　Oh bliss of the *tiny* creature which remains
forever inside the womb that was its shelter;
joy of the gnat which, still *within,* leaps up
even at its marriage: for everything is womb.
And look at the half-assurance of the bird,
which knows both inner and outer, from its source,
as if it were the soul of an Etruscan,
flown out of a dead man received inside a space,
but with his reclining image as the lid.
And how bewildered is any womb-born creature
that has to fly. As if terrified and fleeing
from itself, it zigzags through the air, the way
a crack runs through a teacup. So the bat
quivers across the porcelain of evening.

And we: spectators, always, everywhere,
turned toward the world of objects, never outward.

Uns überfüllts. Wir ordnens. Es zerfällt.
Wir ordnens wieder und zerfallen selbst.

Wer hat uns also umgedreht, daß wir,
was wir auch tun, in jener Haltung sind
von einem, welcher fortgeht? Wie er auf
dem letzten Hügel, der ihm ganz sein Tal
noch einmal zeigt, sich wendet, anhält, weilt—,
so leben wir und nehmen immer Abschied.

It fills us. We arrange it. It breaks down.
We rearrange it, then break down ourselves.

Who has twisted us around like this, so that
no matter what we do, we are in the posture
of someone going away? Just as, upon
the farthest hill, which shows him his whole valley
one last time, he turns, stops, lingers—,
so we live here, forever taking leave.

## DIE NEUNTE ELEGIE

Warum, wenn es angeht, also die Frist des Daseins
hinzubringen, als Lorbeer, ein wenig dunkler als alle
andere Grün, mit kleinen Wellen an jedem
Blattrand (wie eines Windes Lächeln)—: warum dann
Menschliches müssen—und, Schicksal vermeidend,
sich sehnen nach Schicksal? . . .

                              Oh, *nicht*, weil Glück *ist*,
dieser voreilige Vorteil eines nahen Verlusts.
Nicht aus Neugier, oder zur Übung des Herzens,
das auch im Lorbeer *wäre* . . . . .

Aber weil Hiersein viel ist, und weil uns scheinbar
alles das Hiesige braucht, dieses Schwindende, das
seltsam uns angeht. Uns, die Schwindendsten. *Ein* Mal
jedes, nur *ein* Mal. *Ein* Mal und nichtmehr. Und wir auch
*ein* Mal. Nie wieder. Aber dieses
*ein* Mal gewesen zu sein, wenn auch nur *ein* Mal:
*irdisch* gewesen zu sein, scheint nicht widerrufbar.

Und so drängen wir uns und wollen es leisten,
wollens enthalten in unsern einfachen Händen,
im überfüllteren Blick und im sprachlosen Herzen.
Wollen es werden.—Wem es geben? Am liebsten
alles behalten für immer . . . Ach, in den andern Bezug,
wehe, was nimmt man hinüber? Nicht das Anschaun, das
    hier
langsam erlernte, und kein hier Ereignetes. Keins.
Also die Schmerzen. Also vor allem das Schwersein,
also der Liebe lange Erfahrung,—also
lauter Unsägliches. Aber später,
unter den Sternen, was solls: *die* sind *besser* unsäglich.
Bringt doch der Wanderer auch vom Hange des Bergrands

## THE NINTH ELEGY

Why, if this interval of being can be spent serenely
in the form of a laurel, slightly darker than all
other green, with tiny waves on the edges
of every leaf (like the smile of a breeze)—: why then
have to be human—and, escaping from fate,
keep longing for fate? . . .

                    Oh *not* because happiness *exists,*
that too-hasty profit snatched from approaching loss.
Not out of curiosity, not as practice for the heart, which
would exist in the laurel too . . . . .

But because *truly* being here is so much; because everything
    here
apparently needs us, this fleeting world, which in some
    strange way
keeps calling to us. Us, the most fleeting of all.
*Once* for each thing. Just once; no more. And we too,
just once. And never again. But to have been
this once, completely, even if only once:
to have been at one with the earth, seems beyond undoing.

And so we keep pressing on, trying to achieve it,
trying to hold it firmly in our simple hands,
in our overcrowded gaze, in our speechless heart.
Trying to become it.—Whom can we give it to? We would
hold on to it all, forever . . . Ah, but what can we take along
into that other realm? Not the art of looking,
which is learned so slowly, and nothing that happened here.
    Nothing.
The sufferings, then. And, above all, the heaviness,
and the long experience of love,—just what is wholly
unsayable. But later, among the stars,
what good is it—*they* are *better* as they are: unsayable.
For when the traveler returns from the mountain-slopes into
    the valley,

nicht eine Hand voll Erde ins Tal, die Allen unsägliche,
  sondern
ein erworbenes Wort, reines, den gelben und blaun
Enzian. Sind wir vielleicht *hier,* um zu sagen: Haus,
Brücke, Brunnen, Tor, Krug, Obstbaum, Fenster,—
höchstens: Säule, Turm. . . . aber zu *sagen,* verstehs,
oh zu sagen *so,* wie selber die Dinge niemals
innig meinten zu sein. Ist nicht die heimliche List
dieser verschwiegenen Erde, wenn sie die Liebenden drängt,
daß sich in ihrem Gefühl jedes und jedes entzückt?
Schwelle: was ists für zwei
Liebende, daß sie die eigne ältere Schwelle der Tür
ein wenig verbrauchen, auch sie, nach den vielen vorher
und vor den Künftigen . . . . , leicht.

*Hier* ist des *Säglichen* Zeit, *hier* seine Heimat.
Sprich und bekenn. Mehr als je
fallen die Dinge dahin, die erlebbaren, denn,
was sie verdrängend ersetzt, ist ein Tun ohne Bild.
Tun unter Krusten, die willig zerspringen, sobald
innen das Handeln entwächst und sich anders begrenzt.
Zwischen den Hämmern besteht
unser Herz, wie die Zunge
zwischen den Zähnen, die doch,
dennoch, die preisende bleibt.

Preise dem Engel die Welt, nicht die unsägliche, *ihm*
kannst du nicht großtun mit herrlich Erfühltem; im Weltall,
wo er fühlender fühlt, bist du ein Neuling. Drum zeig
ihm das Einfache, das, von Geschlecht zu Geschlechtern
  gestaltet,
als ein Unsriges lebt, neben der Hand und im Blick.
Sag ihm die Dinge. Er wird staunender stehn; wie du
  standest
bei dem Seiler in Rom, oder beim Töpfer am Nil.

he brings, not a handful of earth, unsayable to others, but
    instead
some word he has gained, some pure word, the yellow and
    blue
gentian. Perhaps we are *here* in order to say: house,
bridge, fountain, gate, pitcher, fruit-tree, window—
at most: column, tower. . . . But to *say* them, you must
    understand,
oh to say them *more* intensely than the Things themselves
ever dreamed of existing. Isn't the secret intent
of this taciturn earth, when it forces lovers together,
that inside their boundless emotion all things may shudder
    with joy?
Threshold: what it means for two lovers
to be wearing down, imperceptibly, the ancient threshold of
    their door—
they too, after the many who came before them
and before those to come . . . . , lightly.

*Here* is the time for the *sayable, here* is its homeland.
Speak and bear witness. More than ever
the Things that we might experience are vanishing, for
what crowds them out and replaces them is an imageless act.
An act under a shell, which easily cracks open as soon as
the business inside outgrows it and seeks new limits.
Between the hammers our heart
endures, just as the tongue does
between the teeth and, despite that,
still is able to praise.

Praise this world to the angel, not the unsayable one,
you can't impress *him* with glorious emotion; in the universe
where he feels more powerfully, you are a novice. So show
    him
something simple which, formed over generations,
lives as our own, near our hand and within our gaze.
Tell him of Things. He will stand astonished; as *you* stood
by the rope-maker in Rome or the potter along the Nile.

Zeig ihm, wie glücklich ein Ding sein kann, wie schuldlos
    und unser,
wie selbst das klagende Leid rein zur Gestalt sich
    entschließt,
dient als ein Ding, oder stirbt in ein Ding—, und jenseits
selig der Geige entgeht.—Und diese, von Hingang
lebenden Dinge verstehn, daß du sie rühmst; vergänglich,
traun sie ein Rettendes uns, den Vergänglichsten, zu.
Wollen, wir sollen sie ganz im unsichtbarn Herzen
    verwandeln
in—o unendlich—in uns! Wer wir am Ende auch seien.

Erde, ist es nicht dies, was du willst: *unsichtbar*
in uns erstehn?—Ist es dein Traum nicht,
einmal unsichtbar zu sein?—Erde! unsichtbar!
Was, wenn Verwandlung nicht, ist dein drängender
    Auftrag?
Erde, du liebe, ich will. Oh glaub, es bedürfte
nicht deiner Frühlinge mehr, mich dir zu gewinnen—, *einer*,
ach, ein einziger ist schon dem Blute zu viel.
Namenlos bin ich zu dir entschlossen, von weit her.
Immer warst du im Recht, und dein heiliger Einfall
ist der vertrauliche Tod.

Siehe, ich lebe. Woraus? Weder Kindheit noch Zukunft
werden weniger . . . . . Überzähliges Dasein
entspringt mir im Herzen.

Show him how happy a Thing can be, how innocent and
    ours,
how even lamenting grief purely decides to take form,
serves as a Thing, or dies into a Thing—, and blissfully
escapes far beyond the violin.—And these Things,
which live by perishing, know you are praising them;
    transient,
they look to us for deliverance: us, the most transient of all.
They want us to change them, utterly, in our invisible heart,
within—oh endlessly—within us! Whoever we may be at
    last.

Earth, isn't this what you want: to arise within us,
*invisible?* Isn't it your dream
to be wholly invisible someday?—O Earth: invisible!
What, if not transformation, is your urgent command?
Earth, my dearest, I will. Oh believe me, you no longer
need your springtimes to win me over—one of them,
ah, even one, is already too much for my blood.
Unspeakably I have belonged to you, from the first.
You were always right, and your holiest inspiration
is our intimate companion, Death.

Look, I am living. On what? Neither childhood nor future
grows any smaller . . . . . Superabundant being
wells up in my heart.

## DIE ZEHNTE ELEGIE

Daß ich dereinst, an dem Ausgang der grimmigen Einsicht,
Jubel und Ruhm aufsinge zustimmenden Engeln.
Daß von den klar geschlagenen Hämmern des Herzens
keiner versage an weichen, zweifelnden oder
reißenden Saiten. Daß mich mein strömendes Antlitz
glänzender mache; daß das unscheinbare Weinen
blühe. O wie werdet ihr dann, Nächte, mir lieb sein,
gehärmte. Daß ich euch knieender nicht, untröstliche
        Schwestern,
hinnahm, nicht in euer gelöstes
Haar mich gelöster ergab. Wir, Vergeuder der Schmerzen.
Wie wir sie absehn voraus, in die traurige Dauer,
ob sie nicht enden vielleicht. Sie aber sind ja
unser winterwähriges Laub, unser dunkeles Sinngrün,
*eine* der Zeiten des heimlichen Jahres—, nicht nur
Zeit—, sind Stelle, Siedelung, Lager, Boden, Wohnort.

Freilich, wehe, wie fremd sind die Gassen der Leid-Stadt,
wo in der falschen, aus Übertönung gemachten
Stille, stark, aus der Gußform des Leeren der Ausguß
prahlt: der vergoldete Lärm, das platzende Denkmal.
O, wie spurlos zerträte ein Engel ihnen den Trostmarkt,
den die Kirche begrenzt, ihre fertig gekaufte:
reinlich und zu und enttäuscht wie ein Postamt am Sonntag.
Draußen aber kräuseln sich immer die Ränder von
        Jahrmarkt.
Schaukeln der Freiheit! Taucher und Gaukler des Eifers!
Und des behübschten Glücks figürliche Schießstatt,
wo es zappelt von Ziel und sich blechern benimmt,
wenn ein Geschickterer trifft. Von Beifall zu Zufall
taumelt er weiter; denn Buden jeglicher Neugier
werben, trommeln und plärrn. Für Erwachsene aber
ist noch besonders zu sehn, wie das Geld sich vermehrt,
        anatomisch,

# THE TENTH ELEGY

Someday, emerging at last from the violent insight,
let me sing out jubilation and praise to assenting angels.
Let not even one of the clearly-struck hammers of my heart
fail to sound because of a slack, a doubtful,
or a broken string. Let my joyfully streaming face
make me more radiant; let my hidden weeping arise
and blossom. How dear you will be to me then, you nights
of anguish. Why didn't I kneel more deeply to accept you,
inconsolable sisters, and, surrendering, lose myself
in your loosened hair. How we squander our hours of pain.
How we gaze beyond them into the bitter duration
to see if they have an end. Though they are really
our winter-enduring foliage, our dark evergreen,
*one* season in our inner year—, not only a season
in time—, but are place and settlement, foundation and soil
    and home.

But how alien, alas, are the streets of the city of grief,
where, in the false silence formed of continual uproar,
the figure cast from the mold of emptiness stoutly
swaggers: the gilded noise, the bursting memorial.
Oh how completely an angel would stamp out their market
    of solace,
bounded by the church with its ready-made consolations:
clean and disenchanted and shut as a post-office on Sunday.
Farther out, though, the city's edges are curling with
    carnival.
Swings of freedom! Divers and jugglers of zeal!
And the shooting-gallery's targets of prettified happiness,
which jump and kick back with a tinny sound
when hit by some better marksman. From cheers to chance
he goes staggering on, as booths with all sorts of attractions
are wooing, drumming, and bawling. For adults only
there is something special to see: how money multiplies,
    naked,

nicht zur Belustigung nur: der Geschlechtsteil des Gelds,
alles, das Ganze, der Vorgang—, das unterrichtet und macht
fruchtbar . . . . . . . .
. . . . Oh aber gleich darüber hinaus,
hinter der letzten Planke, beklebt mit Plakaten des 'Todlos',
jenes bitteren Biers, das den Trinkenden süß scheint,
wenn sie immer dazu frische Zerstreuungen kaun . . . ,
gleich im Rücken der Planke, gleich dahinter, ists *wirklich.*
Kinder spielen, und Liebende halten einander,—abseits,
ernst, im ärmlichen Gras, und Hunde haben Natur.
Weiter noch zieht es den Jüngling; vielleicht, daß er eine
  junge
Klage liebt . . . . . Hinter ihr her kommt er in Wiesen. Sie
  sagt:
—Weit. Wir wohnen dort draußen . . . .
                              Wo? Und der Jüngling
folgt. Ihn rührt ihre Haltung. Die Schulter, der Hals—,
  vielleicht
ist sie von herrlicher Herkunft. Aber er läßt sie, kehrt um,
wendet sich, winkt . . . Was solls? Sie ist eine Klage.

Nur die jungen Toten, im ersten Zustand
zeitlosen Gleichmuts, dem der Entwöhnung,
folgen ihr liebend. Mädchen
wartet sie ab und befreundet sie. Zeigt ihnen leise,
was sie an sich hat. Perlen des Leids und die feinen
Schleier der Duldung.—Mit Jünglingen geht sie
schweigend.

Aber dort, wo sie wohnen, im Tal, der Älteren eine, der
  Klagen,
nimmt sich des Jünglinges an, wenn er fragt:—Wir waren,
sagt sie, ein Großes Geschlecht, einmal, wir Klagen. Die
  Väter

right there on stage, money's genitals, nothing concealed,
the whole action—, educational, and guaranteed
to increase your potency . . . . . . . .
. . . . Oh, but a little farther,
beyond the last of the billboards, plastered with signs for
    "Deathless,"
that bitter beer which seems so sweet to its drinkers
as long as they chew fresh distractions in between sips . . . ,
just in back of the billboard, just behind, the view becomes
    *real.*
Children are playing, and lovers are holding hands, to the
    side,
solemnly in the meager grass, and dogs are doing what is
    natural.
The young man is drawn on, farther; perhaps he is in love
    with a young
Lament . . . . . He comes out behind her, into the meadows.
    She says:
—It's a long walk. We live way out there . . . .
                        Where? And the youth
follows. He is touched by her manner. Her shoulders, her
    neck—, perhaps
she is of noble descent. But he leaves her, turns around,
looks back, waves . . . What's the use? She is a Lament.

Only those who died young, in their first condition
of timeless equanimity, while they are being weaned,
follow her lovingly. She waits
for girls and befriends them. Shows them, gently,
what she is wearing. Pearls of grief and the fine-spun
veils of patience.—With young men she walks
in silence.

But there, in the valley, where they live, one of the elder
    Laments
answers the youth when he questions her:—Long ago,
she says, we Laments were a powerful race. Our forefathers
    worked

trieben den Bergbau dort in dem großen Gebirg; bei
    Menschen
findest du manchmal ein Stück geschliffenes Ur-Leid
oder, aus altem Vulkan, schlackig versteinerten Zorn.
Ja, das stammte von dort. Einst waren wir reich.—

Und sie leitet ihn leicht durch die weite Landschaft der
    Klagen,
zeigt ihm die Säulen der Tempel oder die Trümmer
jener Burgen, von wo Klage-Fürsten das Land
einstens weise beherrscht. Zeigt ihm die hohen
Tränenbäume und Felder blühender Wehmut,
(Lebendige kennen sie nur als sanftes Blattwerk);
zeigt ihm die Tiere der Trauer, weidend,—und manchmal
schreckt ein Vogel und zieht, flach ihnen fliegend durchs
    Aufschaun,
weithin das schriftliche Bild seines vereinsamten Schreis.—
Abends führt sie ihn hin zu den Gräbern der Alten
aus dem Klage-Geschlecht, den Sibyllen und Warn-Herrn.
Naht aber Nacht, so wandeln sie leiser, und bald
mondets empor, das über Alles
wachende Grab-Mal. Brüderlich jenem am Nil,
der erhabene Sphinx—: der verschwiegenen Kammer
Antlitz.
Und sie staunen dem krönlichen Haupt, das für immer,
schweigend, der Menschen Gesicht
auf die Waage der Sterne gelegt.

Nicht erfaßt es sein Blick, im Frühtod
schwindelnd. Aber ihr Schaun,
hinter dem Pschent-Rand hervor, scheucht es die Eule. Und
    sie,
streifend im langsamen Abstrich die Wange entlang,
jene der reifesten Rundung,
zeichnet weich in das neue
Totengehör, über ein doppelt
aufgeschlagenes Blatt, den unbeschreiblichen Umriß.

        *

the mines, up there in the mountain-range; sometimes even
among men you can find a polished nugget of primal grief
or a chunk of petrified rage from the slag of an ancient
    volcano.
Yes, that came from up there. We used to be rich.—

And gently she guides him through the vast landscape of
    Lament,
shows him the pillars of the temples, and the ruined walls
of those castles from which, long ago, the princes of Lament
wisely ruled the land. Shows him the tall
trees of tears and the fields of blossoming grief
(the living know it just as a mild green shrub);
shows him the herds of sorrow, grazing,—and sometimes
a startled bird, flying low through their upward gaze,
far away traces the image of its solitary cry.—
In the twilight she leads him out to the graves of the elders
who gave warning to the race of Laments, the sibyls and
    prophets.
But as night approaches, they move more softly, and soon
the sepulchre rises up
like a moon, watching over everything. Brother to the one on
    the Nile,
the lofty Sphinx—: the taciturn chamber's
countenance.
And they look in wonder at the regal head that has silently
lifted the human face
to the scale of the stars, forever.

Still dizzy from recent death, his sight
cannot grasp it. But her gaze
frightens an owl from behind the rim of the crown. And the
    bird,
with slow downstrokes, brushes along the cheek,
the one with the fuller curve,
and faintly, in the dead youth's new
sense of hearing, as upon a double
unfolded page, it sketches the indescribable outline.

                   *

Und höher, die Sterne. Neue. Die Sterne des Leidlands.
Langsam nennt sie die Klage:—Hier,
siehe: den *Reiter,* den *Stab,* und das vollere Sternbild
nennen sie: *Fruchtkranz.* Dann, weiter, dem Pol zu:
*Wiege; Weg; Das Brennende Buch; Puppe; Fenster.*
Aber im südlichen Himmel, rein wie im Innern
einer gesegneten Hand, das klar erglänzende *M,*
das die Mütter bedeutet . . . . . . —

Doch der Tote muß fort, und schweigend bringt ihn die
    ältere
Klage bis an die Talschlucht,
wo es schimmert im Mondschein:
die Quelle der Freude. In Ehrfurcht
nennt sie sie, sagt:—Bei den Menschen
ist sie ein tragender Strom.—

Stehn am Fuß des Gebirgs.
Und da umarmt sie ihn, weinend.

Einsam steigt er dahin, in die Berge des Ur-Leids.
Und nicht einmal sein Schritt klingt aus dem tonlosen Los.

\*

Aber erweckten sie uns, die unendlich Toten, ein Gleichnis,
siehe, sie zeigten vielleicht auf die Kätzchen der leeren
Hasel, die hängenden, oder
meinten den Regen, der fällt auf dunkles Erdreich im
    Frühjahr.—

Und wir, die an *steigendes* Glück
denken, empfänden die Rührung,
die uns beinah bestürzt,
wenn ein Glückliches *fällt.*

And higher, the stars. The new stars of the land of grief.
Slowly the Lament names them:—Look, there:
the *Rider,* the *Staff,* and the larger constellation
called *Garland of Fruit.* Then, farther up toward the Pole:
*Cradle; Path; The Burning Book; Puppet; Window.*
But there, in the southern sky, pure as the lines
on the palm of a blessed hand, the clear sparkling *M*
that stands for Mothers . . . . . . —

But the dead youth must go on by himself, and silently the
    elder Lament
takes him as far as the ravine,
where shimmering in the moonlight
is the fountainhead of joy. With reverence
she names it and says: —Among men
it is a mighty stream.—

They stand at the foot of the mountain-range.
And she embraces him, weeping.

Alone, he climbs on, up the mountains of primal grief.
And not once do his footsteps echo from the soundless path.

*

But if the endlessly dead awakened a symbol in us,
perhaps they would point to the catkins hanging from the
    bare
branches of the hazel-trees, or
would evoke the raindrops that fall onto the dark earth in
    springtime.—

And we, who have always thought
of happiness as *rising,* would feel
the emotion that almost overwhelms us
whenever a happy thing *falls.*

# *Appendix to Duino Elegies*

## [FRAGMENT EINER ELEGIE]

Soll ich die Städte rühmen, die überlebenden
(die ich anstaunte) großen Sternbilder der Erde.
Denn nur zum Rühmen noch steht mir das Herz, so gewaltig
weiß ich die Welt. Und selbst meine Klage
wird mir zur Preisung dicht vor dem stöhnenden Herzen.
Sage mir keiner, daß ich die Gegenwart nicht
liebe; ich schwinge in ihr; sie trägt mich, sie giebt mir
diesen geräumigen Tag, den uralten Werktag
daß ich ihn brauche, und wirft in gewährender Großmut
über mein Dasein niegewesene Nächte.
Ihre Hand ist stark über mir und wenn sie im Schicksal
unten mich hielte, vertaucht, ich müßte versuchen
unten zu atmen. Auch bei dem leisesten Auftrag
säng ich sie gerne. Doch vermut ich, sie will nur,
daß ich vibriere wie sie. Einst tönte der Dichter
über die Feldschlacht hinaus; was will eine Stimme
neben dem neuen Gedröhn der metallenen Handlung
drin diese Zeit sich verringt mit anstürmender Zukunft.
Auch bedarf sie des Anrufes kaum, ihr eigener Schlachtlärm
übertönt sich zum Lied. So laßt mich solange
vor Vergehendem stehn; anklagend nicht, aber
noch einmal bewundernd. Und wo mich eines
das mir vor Augen versinkt, etwa zur Klage bewegt
sei es kein Vorwurf für euch. Was sollen jüngere Völker
nicht fortstürmen von dem was der morschen oft
ruhmloser Abbruch begrub. Sehet, es wäre
arg um das Große bestellt, wenn es irgend der Schonung
bedürfte. Wem die Paläste oder der Gärten
Kühnheit nicht mehr, wem Aufstieg und Rückfall
alter Fontänen nicht mehr, wem das Verhaltene
in den Bildern oder der Statuen ewiges Dastehn
nicht mehr die Seele erschreckt und verwandelt, der gehe
diesem hinaus und tue sein Tagwerk; wo anders
lauert das Große auf ihn und wird ihn wo anders
anfalln, daß er sich wehrt.

# [FRAGMENT OF AN ELEGY]

Now shall I praise the cities, those long-surviving
(I watched them in awe) great constellations of earth.
For only in praising is my heart still mine, so violently
do I know the world. And even my lament
turns into a paean before my disconsolate heart.
Let no one say that I don't love life, the eternal
presence: I pulsate in her; she bears me, she gives me
the spaciousness of this day, the primeval workday
for me to make use of, and over my existence flings,
in her magnanimity, nights that have never been.
Her strong hand is above me, and if she should hold me
        under,
submerged in fate, I would have to learn how to breathe
down there. Even her most lightly-entrusted mission
would fill me with songs of her; although I suspect
that all she wants is for me to be vibrant as she is.
Once poets resounded over the battlefield; what voice
can outshout the rattle of this metallic age
that is struggling on toward its careening future?
And indeed it hardly requires the call, its own battle-din
roars into song. So let me stand for a while
in front of the transient: not accusing, but once again
admiring, marveling. And if perhaps something founders
before my eyes and stirs me into lament,
it is not a reproach. Why shouldn't more youthful nations
rush past the graveyard of cultures long ago rotten?
How pitiful it would be if greatness needed the slightest
indulgence. Let him whose soul is no longer startled
and transformed by palaces, by gardens' boldness, by the
        rising
and falling of ancient fountains, by everything held back
in paintings or by the infinite thereness of statues—
let such a person go out to his daily work, where
greatness is lying in ambush and someday, at some turn,
will leap upon him and force him to fight for his life.

## [URSPRÜNGLICHE FASSUNG DER ZEHNTEN ELEGIE]
*[Fragmentarisch]*

Daß ich dereinst, an dem Ausgang der grimmigen Einsicht
Jubel und Ruhm aufsinge zustimmenden Engeln.
Daß von den klar geschlagenen Hämmern des Herzens
keiner versage an weichen, zweifelnden oder
jähzornigen Saiten. Daß mich mein strömendes Antlitz
glänzender mache; daß das unscheinbare Weinen
blühe. O wie werdet ihr dann, Nächte, mir lieb sein,
gehärmte. Daß ich euch knieender nicht, untröstliche
        Schwestern,
hinnahm, nicht in euer gelöstes
Haar mich gelöster ergab. Wir Vergeuder der Schmerzen.
Wie wir sie absehn voraus in die traurige Dauer,
ob sie nicht enden vielleicht. Sie aber sind ja
Zeiten von uns, unser winter-
währiges Laubwerk, Wiesen, Teiche, angeborene
        Landschaft,
von Geschöpfen im Schilf und von Vögeln bewohnt.

Oben, der hohen, steht nicht die Hälfte der Himmel
über der Wehmut in uns, der bemühten Natur?
Denk, du beträtest nicht mehr dein verwildertes Leidtum,
sähest die Sterne nicht mehr durch das herbere Blättern
schwärzlichen Schmerzlaubs, und die Trümmer von
        Schicksal
böte dir höher nicht mehr der vergrößernde Mondschein,
daß du an ihnen dich fühlst wie ein einstiges Volk?
Lächeln auch wäre nicht mehr, das zehrende derer,
die du hinüberverlorest—, so wenig gewaltsam,
eben an dir nur vorbei, traten sie rein in dein Leid.
(Fast wie das Mädchen, das grade dem Freier sich zusprach,
der sie seit Wochen bedrängt, und sie bringt ihn erschrocken
an das Gitter des Gartens, den Mann, der frohlockt und
        ungern
fortgeht: da stört sie ein Schritt in dem neueren Abschied,

# [ORIGINAL VERSION OF THE TENTH ELEGY]

*[Fragmentary]*

Someday, emerging at last from the violent insight,
let me sing out jubilation and praise to assenting angels.
Let not even one of the clearly-struck hammers of my heart
fail to sound because of a slack, a doubtful,
or an ill-tempered string. Let my joyfully streaming face
make me more radiant; let my hidden weeping arise
and blossom. How dear you will be to me then, you nights
of anguish. Why didn't I kneel more deeply to accept you,
inconsolable sisters, and, surrendering, lose myself
in your loosened hair. How we squander our hours of pain.
How we gaze beyond them into the bitter duration
to see if they have an end. Though they are really
seasons of us, our winter-
enduring foliage, ponds, meadows, our inborn landscape,
where birds and reed-dwelling creatures are at home.

High overhead, isn't half of the night sky standing
above the sorrow in us, the disquieted garden?
Imagine that you no longer walked through your grief grown
        wild,
no longer looked at the stars through the jagged leaves
of the dark tree of pain, and the enlarging moonlight
no longer exalted fate's ruins so high
that among them you felt like the last of some ancient race.
Nor would smiles any longer exist, the consuming smiles
of those you lost over there—with so little violence,
once they were past, did they purely enter your grief.
(Almost like the girl who has just said yes to the lover
who begged her, so many weeks, and she brings him
        astonished
to the garden gate and, reluctant, he walks away,
giddy with joy; and then, amid this new parting,

und sie wartet und steht und da trifft ihr vollzähliges
    Aufschaun
ganz in das Aufschaun des Fremden, das Aufschaun der
    Jungfrau,
die ihn unendlich begreift, den draußen, der ihr bestimmt
    war,
draußen den wandernden Andern, der ihr ewig bestimmt
    war.
Hallend geht er vorbei.) So immer verlorst du;
als ein Besitzender nicht: wie sterbend einer,
vorgebeugt in die feucht herwehende Märznacht,
ach, den Frühling verliert in die Kehlen der Vögel.

Viel zu weit gehörst du in's Leiden. Vergäßest
du die geringste der maßlos erschmerzten Gestalten,
riefst du, schrieest, hoffend auf frühere Neugier,
einen der Engel herbei, der mühsam verdunkelten
    Ausdrucks
leidunmächtig, immer wieder versuchend,
dir dein Schluchzen damals, um jene, beschriebe.
Engel wie wars? Und er ahmte dir nach und verstünde
nicht daß es Schmerz sei, wie man dem rufenden Vogel
nachformt, die ihn erfüllt, die schuldlose Stimme.

a step disturbs her; she waits; and her glance in its fullness
sinks totally into a stranger's: her virgin glance
that endlessly comprehends him, the outsider, who was
     meant for her;
the wandering other, who eternally was meant for her.
Echoing, he walks by.) That is how, always, you lost:
never as one who possesses, but like someone dying
who, bending into the moist breeze of an evening in March,
loses the springtime, alas, in the throats of the birds.

Far too much you belong to grief. If you could forget her—
even the least of these figures so infinitely pained—
you would call down, shout down, hoping they might still be
     curious,
one of the angels (those beings unmighty in grief)
who, as his face darkened, would try again and again
to describe the way you kept sobbing, long ago, for her.
Angel, what was it like? And he would imitate you and never
understand that it was pain, as after a calling bird
one tries to repeat the innocent voice it is filled with.

## GEGEN-STROPHEN

Oh, daß ihr hier, Frauen, einhergeht,
hier unter uns, leidvoll,
nicht geschonter als wir und dennoch imstande,
selig zu machen wie Selige.

Woher,
wenn der Geliebte erscheint,
nehmt ihr die Zukunft?
Mehr, als je sein wird.
Wer die Entfernungen weiß
bis zum äußersten Fixstern,
staunt, wenn er diesen gewahrt,
euern herrlichen Herzraum.
Wie, im Gedräng, spart ihr ihn aus?
Ihr, voll Quellen und Nacht.

Seid ihr wirklich die gleichen,
die, da ihr Kind wart,
unwirsch im Schulgang
anstieß der ältere Bruder?
Ihr Heilen.

Wo wir als Kinder uns schon
häßlich für immer verzerrn,
wart ihr wie Brot vor der Wandlung.

Abbruch der Kindheit
war euch nicht Schaden. Auf einmal
standet ihr da, wie im Gott
plötzlich zum Wunder ergänzt.

Wir, wie gebrochen vom Berg,
oft schon als Knaben scharf
an den Rändern, vielleicht

## ANTISTROPHES

Ah, Women, that you should be moving
here, among us, grief-filled,
no more protected than we, and nevertheless
able to bless like the blessed.

From what realm,
when your beloved appears,
do you take the future?
More than will ever be.
One who knows distances
out to the outermost star
is astonished when he discovers
the magnificent space in your hearts.
How, in the crowd, can you spare it?
You, full of sources and night.

Are you really the same
as those children who
on the way to school were rudely
shoved by an older brother?
Unharmed by it.

    While we, even as children,
    disfigured ourselves forever,
    you were like bread on the altar
    before it is changed.

The breaking away of childhood
left you intact. In a moment,
you stood there, as if completed
in a miracle, all at once.

    We, as if broken from crags,
    even as boys, too sharp
    at the edges, although perhaps

manchmal glücklich behaun;
wir, wie Stücke Gesteins,
über Blumen gestürzt.

Blumen des tieferen Erdreichs,
von allen Wurzeln geliebte,
ihr, der Eurydike Schwestern,
immer voll heiliger Umkehr
hinter dem steigenden Mann.

Wir, von uns selber gekränkt,
Kränkende gern und gern
Wiedergekränkte aus Not.
Wir, wie Waffen, dem Zorn
neben den Schlaf gelegt.

Ihr, die ihr beinah Schutz seid, wo niemand
schützt. Wie ein schattiger Schlafbaum
ist der Gedanke an euch
für die Schwärme des Einsamen.

sometimes skillfully cut;
we, like pieces of rock
that have fallen on flowers.

Flowers of the deeper soil,
loved by all roots,
you, Eurydice's sisters,
full of holy return
behind the ascending man.

We, afflicted by ourselves,
gladly afflicting, gladly
needing to be afflicted.
We, who sleep with our anger
laid beside us like a knife.

You, who are almost protection
where no one protects. The thought of you
is a shade-giving tree of sleep for the restless
creatures of a solitary man.

# The Sonnets to Orpheus

## (1923)

*Written as a grave-monument
for Vera Ouckama Knoop*

*Château de Muzot, February 1922*

## ERSTER TEIL

---

### I

Da stieg ein Baum. O reine Übersteigung!
O Orpheus singt! O hoher Baum im Ohr!
Und alles schwieg. Doch selbst in der Verschweigung
ging neuer Anfang, Wink und Wandlung vor.

Tiere aus Stille drangen aus dem klaren
gelösten Wald von Lager und Genist;
und da ergab sich, daß sie nicht aus List
und nicht aus Angst in sich so leise waren,

sondern aus Hören. Brüllen, Schrei, Geröhr
schien klein in ihren Herzen. Und wo eben
kaum eine Hütte war, dies zu empfangen,

ein Unterschlupf aus dunkelstem Verlangen
mit einem Zugang, dessen Pfosten beben,—
da schufst du ihnen Tempel im Gehör.

## FIRST PART

---

## I

A tree ascended there. Oh pure transcendence!
Oh Orpheus sings! Oh tall tree in the ear!
And all things hushed. Yet even in that silence
a new beginning, beckoning, change appeared.

Creatures of stillness crowded from the bright
unbound forest, out of their lairs and nests;
and it was not from any dullness, not
from fear, that they were so quiet in themselves,

but from just listening. Bellow, roar, shriek
seemed small inside their hearts. And where there had been
at most a makeshift hut to receive the music,

a shelter nailed up out of their darkest longing,
with an entryway that shuddered in the wind—
you built a temple deep inside their hearing.

## II

Und fast ein Mädchen wars und ging hervor
aus diesem einigen Glück von Sang und Leier
und glänzte klar durch ihre Frühlingsschleier
und machte sich ein Bett in meinem Ohr.

Und schlief in mir. Und alles war ihr Schlaf.
Die Bäume, die ich je bewundert, diese
fühlbare Ferne, die gefühlte Wiese
und jedes Staunen, das mich selbst betraf.

Sie schlief die Welt. Singender Gott, wie hast
du sie vollendet, daß sie nicht begehrte,
erst wach zu sein? Sieh, sie erstand und schlief.

Wo ist ihr Tod? O, wirst du dies Motiv
erfinden noch, eh sich dein Lied verzehrte?—
Wo sinkt sie hin aus mir? . . . Ein Mädchen fast . . . .

# II

And it was almost a girl and came to be
out of this single joy of song and lyre
and through her green veils shone forth radiantly
and made herself a bed inside my ear.

And slept there. And her sleep was everything:
the awesome trees, the distances I had felt
so deeply that I could touch them, meadows in spring:
all wonders that had ever seized my heart.

She slept the world. Singing god, how was that first
sleep so perfect that she had no desire
ever to wake? See: she arose and slept.

Where is her death now? Ah, will you discover
this theme before your song consumes itself?—
Where is she vanishing? . . . A girl almost . . . .

## III

Ein Gott vermags. Wie aber, sag mir, soll
ein Mann ihm folgen durch die schmale Leier?
Sein Sinn ist Zwiespalt. An der Kreuzung zweier
Herzwege steht kein Tempel für Apoll.

Gesang, wie du ihn lehrst, ist nicht Begehr,
nicht Werbung um ein endlich noch Erreichtes;
Gesang ist Dasein. Für den Gott ein Leichtes.
Wann aber *sind* wir? Und wann wendet *er*

an unser Sein die Erde und die Sterne?
Dies *ists* nicht, Jüngling, daß du liebst, wenn auch
die Stimme dann den Mund dir aufstößt,—lerne

vergessen, daß du aufsangst. Das verrinnt.
In Wahrheit singen, ist ein andrer Hauch.
Ein Hauch um nichts. Ein Wehn im Gott. Ein Wind.

# III

A god can do it. But will you tell me how
a man can enter through the lyre's strings?
Our mind is split. And at the shadowed crossing
of heart-roads, there is no temple for Apollo.

Song, as you have taught it, is not desire,
not wooing any grace that can be achieved;
song is reality. Simple, for a god.
But when can *we* be real? When does he pour

the earth, the stars, into us? Young man,
it is not your loving, even if your mouth
was forced wide open by your own voice—learn

to forget that passionate music. It will end.
True singing is a different breath, about
nothing. A gust inside the god. A wind.

## IV

O ihr Zärtlichen, tretet zuweilen
in den Atem, der euch nicht meint,
laßt ihn an eueren Wangen sich teilen,
hinter euch zittert er, wieder vereint.

O ihr Seligen, o ihr Heilen,
die ihr der Anfang der Herzen scheint.
Bogen der Pfeile und Ziele von Pfeilen,
ewiger glänzt euer Lächeln verweint.

Fürchtet euch nicht zu leiden, die Schwere,
gebt sie zurück an der Erde Gewicht;
schwer sind die Berge, schwer sind die Meere.

Selbst die als Kinder ihr pflanztet, die Bäume,
wurden zu schwer längst; ihr trüget sie nicht.
Aber die Lüfte . . . aber die Räume . . . .

# IV

O you tender ones, walk now and then
into the breath that blows coldly past.
Upon your cheeks let it tremble and part;
behind you it will tremble together again.

O you blessèd ones, you who are whole,
you who seem the beginning of hearts,
bows for the arrows and arrows' targets—
tear-bright, your lips more eternally smile.

Don't be afraid to suffer; return
that heaviness to the earth's own weight;
heavy are the mountains, heavy the seas.

Even the small trees you planted as children
have long since become too heavy; you could not
carry them now. But the winds . . . But the spaces . . . .

## V

Errichtet keinen Denkstein. Laßt die Rose
nur jedes Jahr zu seinen Gunsten blühn.
Denn Orpheus ists. Seine Metamorphose
in dem und dem. Wir sollen uns nicht mühn

um andre Namen. Ein für alle Male
ists Orpheus, wenn es singt. Er kommt und geht.
Ists nicht schon viel, wenn er die Rosenschale
um ein paar Tage manchmal übersteht?

O wie er schwinden muß, daß ihrs begrifft!
Und wenn ihm selbst auch bangte, daß er schwände.
Indem sein Wort das Hiersein übertrifft,

ist er schon dort, wohin ihrs nicht begleitet.
Der Leier Gitter zwängt ihm nicht die Hände.
Und er gehorcht, indem er überschreitet.

# V

Erect no gravestone for him. Only this:
let the rose blossom each year for his sake.
For it *is* the god. His metamorphosis
in this and that. We do not need to look

for other names. It is Orpheus once for all
whenever there is song. He comes and goes.
Isn't it enough if sometimes he can dwell
with us a few days longer than a rose?

Though he himself is afraid to disappear,
he *has* to vanish: don't you understand?
The moment his word moves out beyond our life here,

he has gone where you will never find his trace.
The lyre's strings do not constrict his hands.
And it is in overstepping that he obeys.

## VI

Ist er ein Hiesiger? Nein, aus beiden
Reichen erwuchs seine weite Natur.
Kundiger böge die Zweige der Weiden,
wer die Wurzeln der Weiden erfuhr.

Geht ihr zu Bette, so laßt auf dem Tische
Brot nicht und Milch nicht; die Toten ziehts—.
Aber er, der Beschwörende, mische
unter der Milde des Augenlids

ihre Erscheinung in alles Geschaute;
und der Zauber von Erdrauch und Raute
sei ihm so wahr wie der klarste Bezug.

Nichts kann das gültige Bild ihm verschlimmern;
sei es aus Gräbern, sei es aus Zimmern,
rühme er Fingerring, Spange und Krug.

# VI

Is he someone who dwells in this *single* world? No:
both realms are the source of his earthly power.
He alone who has known the roots of the willow
can bend the willow-branch into a lyre.

Overnight leave no bread on the table
and leave no milk: they draw back the dead—.
But he, the conjuror, may he settle
under the calm of the eye's lowered lid

to mix death into everything seen;
and may the magic of earthsmoke and rue
be as real to him as the clearest connection.

Nothing can trouble the dominance of
the true image. Whether from graves or from rooms,
let him praise finger-ring, bracelet, and jug.

## VII

Rühmen, das ists! Ein zum Rühmen Bestellter,
ging er hervor wie das Erz aus des Steins
Schweigen. Sein Herz, o vergängliche Kelter
eines den Menschen unendlichen Weins.

Nie versagt ihm die Stimme am Staube,
wenn ihn das göttliche Beispiel ergreift.
Alles wird Weinberg, alles wird Traube,
in seinem fühlenden Süden gereift.

Nicht in den Grüften der Könige Moder
straft ihm die Rühmung lügen, oder
daß von den Göttern ein Schatten fällt.

Er ist einer der bleibenden Boten,
der noch weit in die Türen der Toten
Schalen mit rühmlichen Früchten hält.

# VII

Praising is what matters! He was summoned for that,
and came to us like the ore from a stone's
silence. His mortal heart presses out
a deathless, inexhaustible wine.

Whenever he feels the god's paradigm grip
his throat, the voice does not die in his mouth.
All becomes vineyard, all becomes grape,
ripened on the hills of his sensuous South.

Neither decay in the sepulcher of kings
nor any shadow fallen from the gods
can ever detract from his glorious praising.

For he is a herald who is with us always,
holding far into the doors of the dead
a bowl with ripe fruit worthy of praise.

## VIII

Nur im Raum der Rühmung darf die Klage
gehn, die Nymphe des geweinten Quells,
wachend über unserm Niederschlage,
daß er klar sei an demselben Fels,

der die Tore trägt und die Altäre.—
Sieh, um ihre stillen Schultern früht
das Gefühl, daß sie die jüngste wäre
unter den Geschwistern im Gemüt.

Jubel *weiß*, und Sehnsucht ist geständig,—
nur die Klage lernt noch; mädchenhändig
zählt sie nächtelang das alte Schlimme.

Aber plötzlich, schräg und ungeübt,
hält sie doch ein Sternbild unsrer Stimme
in den Himmel, den ihr Hauch nicht trübt.

# VIII

Only in the realm of Praising should Lament
walk, the naiad of the wept-for fountain,
watching over the stream of our complaint,
to keep it clear upon the very stone

that bears the arch of triumph and the altar.—
Look: around her shoulders dawns the bright
sense that she may be the youngest sister
among the deities hidden in our heart.

Joy *knows,* and Longing has accepted—
only Lament still learns; upon her beads,
night after night, she counts the ancient curse.

Yet awkward as she is, she suddenly
lifts a constellation of our voice,
glittering, into the pure nocturnal sky.

## IX

Nur wer die Leier schon hob
auch unter Schatten,
darf das unendliche Lob
ahnend erstatten.

Nur wer mit Toten vom Mohn
aß, von dem ihren,
wird nicht den leisesten Ton
wieder verlieren.

Mag auch die Spieglung im Teich
oft uns verschwimmen:
*Wisse das Bild.*

Erst in dem Doppelbereich
werden die Stimmen
ewig und mild.

## IX

Only he whose bright lyre
has sounded in shadows
may, looking onward, restore
his infinite praise.

Only he who has eaten
poppies with the dead
will not lose ever again
the gentlest chord.

Though the image upon the pool
often grows dim:
*Know and be still.*

Inside the Double World
all voices become
eternally mild.

# X

Euch, die ihr nie mein Gefühl verließt,
grüß ich, antikische Sarkophage,
die das fröhliche Wasser römischer Tage
als ein wandelndes Lied durchfließt.

Oder jene so offenen, wie das Aug
eines frohen erwachenden Hirten,
—innen voll Stille und Bienensaug—
denen entzückte Falter entschwirrten;

alle, die man dem Zweifel entreißt,
grüß ich, die wiedergeöffneten Munde,
die schon wußten, was schweigen heißt.

Wissen wirs, Freunde, wissen wirs nicht?
Beides bildet die zögernde Stunde
in dem menschlichen Angesicht.

## X

You who are close to my heart always,
I welcome you, ancient coffins of stone,
which the cheerful water of Roman days
still flows through, like a wandering song.

Or those other ones that are open wide
like the eyes of a happily waking shepherd
—with silence and bee-suck nettle inside,
from which ecstatic butterflies flittered;

everything that has been wrestled from doubt
I welcome—the mouths that burst open after
long knowledge of what it is to be mute.

Do we know this, my friends, or don't we know this?
Both are formed by the hesitant hour
in the deep calm of the human face.

## XI

Sieh den Himmel. Heißt kein Sternbild 'Reiter'?
Denn dies ist uns seltsam eingeprägt:
dieser Stolz aus Erde. Und ein Zweiter,
der ihn treibt und hält und den er trägt.

Ist nicht so, gejagt und dann gebändigt,
diese sehnige Natur des Seins?
Weg und Wendung. Doch ein Druck verständigt.
Neue Weite. Und die zwei sind eins.

Aber *sind* sie's? Oder meinen beide
nicht den Weg, den sie zusammen tun?
Namenlos schon trennt sie Tisch und Weide.

Auch die sternische Verbindung trügt.
Doch uns freue eine Weile nun
der Figur zu glauben. Das genügt.

# XI

Look at the sky. Are no two stars called "Rider"?
For this is printed strangely on us here:
this pride of earth. And look, the second figure
who drives and halts it: whom it has to bear.

Aren't we, in our sinewy quintessence,
controlled like this, now raced and now reined in?
Path and turningpoint. Just a touch possesses.
New expanses. And the two are one.

Or *are* they really? Don't both signify
the path they ride together now? But table
and pasture keep them separate, utterly.

Even the starry union is a fraud.
Yet gladly let us trust the valid symbol
for a moment. It is all we need.

## XII

Heil dem Geist, der uns verbinden mag;
denn wir leben wahrhaft in Figuren.
Und mit kleinen Schritten gehn die Uhren
neben unserm eigentlichen Tag.

Ohne unsern wahren Platz zu kennen,
handeln wir aus wirklichem Bezug.
Die Antennen fühlen die Antennen,
und die leere Ferne trug . . .

Reine Spannung. O Musik der Kräfte!
Ist nicht durch die läßlichen Geschäfte
jede Störung von dir abgelenkt?

Selbst wenn sich der Bauer sorgt und handelt,
wo die Saat in Sommer sich verwandelt,
reicht er niemals hin. Die Erde *schenkt.*

# XII

Hail to the god who joins us; for through him
arise the symbols where we truly live.
And, with tiny footsteps, the clocks move
separately from our authentic time.

Though we are unaware of our true status,
our actions stem from pure relationship.
Far away, antennas hear antennas
and the empty distances transmit . . .

Pure readiness. Oh unheard starry music!
Isn't your sound protected from all static
by the ordinary business of our days?

In spite of all the farmer's work and worry,
he can't reach down to where the seed is slowly
transmuted into summer. The earth *bestows.*

## XIII

Voller Apfel, Birne und Banane,
Stachelbeere . . . Alles dieses spricht
Tod und Leben in den Mund . . . Ich ahne . . .
Lest es einem Kind vom Angesicht,

wenn es sie erschmeckt. Dies kommt von weit.
Wird euch langsam namenlos im Munde?
Wo sonst Worte waren, fließen Funde,
aus dem Fruchtfleisch überrascht befreit.

Wagt zu sagen, was ihr Apfel nennt.
Diese Süße, die sich erst verdichtet,
um, im Schmecken leise aufgerichtet,

klar zu werden, wach und transparent,
doppeldeutig, sonnig, erdig, hiesig—:
O Erfahrung, Fühlung, Freude—, riesig!

## XIII

Plump apple, smooth banana, melon, peach,
gooseberry . . . How all this affluence
speaks death and life into the mouth . . . I sense . . .
Observe it from a child's transparent features

while he tastes. This comes from far away.
What miracle is happening in your mouth?
Instead of words, discoveries flow out
from the ripe flesh, astonished to be free.

Dare to say what "apple" truly is.
This sweetness that feels thick, dark, dense at first;
then, exquisitely lifted in your taste,

grows clarified, awake and luminous,
double-meaninged, sunny, earthy, real—:
Oh knowledge, pleasure—inexhaustible.

## XIV

Wir gehen um mit Blume, Weinblatt, Frucht.
Sie sprechen nicht die Sprache nur des Jahres.
Aus Dunkel steigt ein buntes Offenbares
und hat vielleicht den Glanz der Eifersucht

der Toten an sich, die die Erde stärken.
Was wissen wir von ihrem Teil an dem?
Es ist seit lange ihre Art, den Lehm
mit ihrem freien Marke zu durchmärken.

Nun fragt sich nur: tun sie es gern? . . .
Drängt diese Frucht, ein Werk von schweren Sklaven,
geballt zu uns empor, zu ihren Herrn?

Sind *sie* die Herrn, die bei den Wurzeln schlafen,
und gönnen uns aus ihren Überflüssen
dies Zwischending aus stummer Kraft und Küssen?

## XIV

We are involved with flower, leaf, and fruit.
They speak not just the language of one year.
From darkness a bright phenomenon appears
and still reflects, perhaps, the jealous glint

of the dead, who fill the earth. How can we know
what part they play within the ancient cycle?
Long since, it has been their job to make the soil
vigorous with the force of their free marrow.

But have they done it willingly? we ask . . .
Does this fruit, formed by heavy slaves, push up
like a clenched fist, to threaten us, their masters?

Or in fact are *they* the masters, as they sleep
beside the roots and grant us, from their riches,
this hybrid Thing of speechless strength and kisses?

## XV

Wartet . . . , das schmeckt . . . Schon ists auf der Flucht.
. . . . Wenig Musik nur, ein Stampfen, ein Summen—:
Mädchen, ihr warmen, Mädchen, ihr stummen,
tanzt den Geschmack der erfahrenen Frucht!

Tanzt die Orange. Wer kann sie vergessen,
wie sie, ertrinkend in sich, sich wehrt
wider ihr Süßsein. Ihr habt sie besessen.
Sie hat sich köstlich zu euch bekehrt.

Tanzt die Orange. Die wärmere Landschaft,
werft sie aus euch, daß die reife erstrahle
in Lüften der Heimat! Erglühte, enthüllt

Düfte um Düfte. Schafft die Verwandtschaft
mit der reinen, sich weigernden Schale,
mit dem Saft, der die Glückliche füllt!

## XV

Wait . . . , that tastes good . . . But already it's gone.
. . . . A few notes of music, a tapping, a faint
hum—: you girls, so warm and so silent,
dance the taste of the fruit you have known!

Dance the orange. Who can forget it,
drowning in itself, how it struggles through
against its own sweetness. You have possessed it.
Deliciously it has converted to you.

Dance the orange. The sunnier landscape—
fling it *from* you, allow it to shine
in the breeze of its homeland! Aglow, peel away

scent after scent. Create your own kinship
with the supple, gently reluctant rind
and the juice that fills it with succulent joy.

## XVI

Du, mein Freund, bist einsam, weil . . . .
*Wir* machen mit Worten und Fingerzeigen
uns allmählich die Welt zu eigen,
vielleicht ihren schwächsten, gefährlichsten Teil.

Wer zeigt mit Fingern auf einen Geruch?—
Doch von den Kräften, die uns bedrohten,
fühlst du viele . . . Du kennst die Toten,
und du erschrickst vor dem Zauberspruch.

Sieh, nun heißt es zusammen ertragen
Stückwerk und Teile, als sei es das Ganze.
Dir helfen, wird schwer sein. Vor allem: pflanze

mich nicht in dein Herz. Ich wüchse zu schnell.
Doch *meines* Herrn Hand will ich führen und sagen:
Hier. Das ist Esau in seinem Fell.

## XVI

You are lonely, my friend, because you are . . . .
*We,* with a word or a finger-sign,
gradually make the world our own,
though perhaps its weakest, most precarious part.

How can fingers point out a smell?—
Yet of the dark forces that lurk at our side
you feel many . . . You know the dead,
and you shrink away from the magic spell.

Look, we two together must bear
piecework and parts, as if they were
the whole. But be careful. Above all, don't plant

me inside your heart. I'd outgrow you. But I
will guide *my* master's hand and will say:
Here. This is Esau beneath his pelt.

## XVII

Zu unterst der Alte, verworrn,
all der Erbauten
Wurzel, verborgener Born,
den sie nie schauten.

Sturmhelm und Jägerhorn,
Spruch von Ergrauten,
Männer im Bruderzorn,
Frauen wie Lauten . . .

Drängender Zweig an Zweig,
nirgends ein freier . . . .
Einer! O steig . . . o steig . . .

Aber sie brechen noch.
Dieser erst oben doch
biegt sich zur Leier.

# XVII

At bottom the Ancient One, gnarled
root hidden deep,
origin unbeheld
by those who branched up.

Helmet and horn of hunters,
grandfathers' truths,
men who betrayed their brothers,
women like lutes . . .

Branch upon branch crowds close,
none of them free . . . .
Keep climbing higher . . . higher . . .

Still, though, they break. Yet this
top one bends finally
into a lyre.

## XVIII

Hörst du das Neue, Herr,
dröhnen und beben?
Kommen Verkündiger,
die es erheben.

Zwar ist kein Hören heil
in dem Durchtobtsein,
doch der Maschinenteil
will jetzt gelobt sein.

Sieh, die Maschine:
wie sie sich wälzt und rächt
und uns entstellt und schwächt.

Hat sie aus uns auch Kraft,
sie, ohne Leidenschaft,
treibe und diene.

## XVIII

Master, do you hear the New
quiver and rumble?
Harbingers step forth who
blare their approval.

Surely no ear is whole
amid this noise,
yet the machine-part still
asks for our praise.

Look, the machine:
rears up and takes revenge,
brings us to crawl and cringe.

Since all its strength is from us,
let it, desireless,
serve and remain.

## XIX

Wandelt sich rasch auch die Welt
wie Wolkengestalten,
alles Vollendete fällt
heim zum Uralten.

Über dem Wandel und Gang,
weiter und freier,
währt noch dein Vor-Gesang,
Gott mit der Leier.

Nicht sind die Leiden erkannt,
nicht ist die Liebe gelernt,
und was im Tod uns entfernt,

ist nicht entschleiert.
Einzig das Lied überm Land
heiligt und feiert.

# XIX

Though the world keeps changing its form
as fast as a cloud, still
what is accomplished falls home
to the Primeval.

Over the change and the passing,
larger and freer,
soars your eternal song,
god with the lyre.

Never has grief been possessed,
never has love been learned,
and what removes us in death

is not revealed.
Only the song through the land
hallows and heals.

## XX

Dir aber, Herr, o was weih ich dir, sag,
der das Ohr den Geschöpfen gelehrt?—
Mein Erinnern an einen Frühlingstag,
seinen Abend, in Rußland—, ein Pferd . . .

Herüber vom Dorf kam der Schimmel allein,
an der vorderen Fessel den Pflock,
um die Nacht auf den Wiesen allein zu sein;
wie schlug seiner Mähne Gelock

an den Hals im Takte des Übermuts,
bei dem grob gehemmten Galopp.
Wie sprangen die Quellen des Rossebluts!

Der fühlte die Weiten, und ob!
Der sang und der hörte—, dein Sagenkreis
war *in* ihm geschlossen.
　　　　　　　Sein Bild: ich weih's.

## XX

But Master, what gift shall I dedicate to you,
who taught all creatures their ears?
—My thoughts of an evening long ago,
it was springtime, in Russia—a horse . . .

He came bounding from the village, alone, white,
with a hobble attached to one leg,
to stay alone in the fields all night;
how the mane beat against his neck

to the rhythm of his perfect joy, in that hindered
gallop across the meadow.
What leaping went on in his stallion-blood!

He felt the expanses, and oh!
He sang and he heard—your cycle of myths
was completed *in* him.
                    His image: my gift.

## XXI

Frühling ist wiedergekommen. Die Erde
ist wie ein Kind, das Gedichte weiß;
viele, o viele . . . . Für die Beschwerde
langen Lernens bekommt sie den Preis.

Streng war ihr Lehrer. Wir mochten das Weiße
an dem Barte des alten Manns.
Nun, wie das Grüne, das Blaue heiße,
dürfen wir fragen: sie kanns, sie kanns!

Erde, die frei hat, du glückliche, spiele
nun mit den Kindern. Wir wollen dich fangen,
fröhliche Erde. Dem Frohsten gelingts.

O, was der Lehrer sie lehrte, das Viele,
und was gedruckt steht in Wurzeln und langen
schwierigen Stämmen: sie singts, sie singts!

# XXI

Spring has returned. The earth resembles
a little girl who has memorized
many poems . . . . For all the trouble
of her long learning, she wins the prize.

Her teacher was strict. We loved the white
in the old man's beard and shaggy eyebrows.
Now, whatever we ask about
the blue and the green, she knows, she knows!

Earth, overjoyed to be out on vacation,
play with the children. We long to catch up,
jubilant Earth. The happiest will win.

What her teacher taught her, the numberless Things,
and what lies hidden in stem and in deep
difficult root, she sings, she sings!

## XXII

Wir sind die Treibenden.
Aber den Schritt der Zeit,
nehmt ihn als Kleinigkeit
im immer Bleibenden.

Alles das Eilende
wird schon vorüber sein;
denn das Verweilende
erst weiht uns ein.

Knaben, o werft den Mut
nicht in die Schnelligkeit,
nicht in den Flugversuch.

Alles ist ausgeruht:
Dunkel und Helligkeit,
Blume und Buch.

## XXII

We are the driving ones.
Ah, but the step of time:
think of it as a dream
in what forever remains.

All that is hurrying
soon will be over with;
only what lasts can bring
us to the truth.

Young men, don't put your trust
into the trials of flight,
into the hot and quick.

All things already rest:
darkness and morning light,
flower and book.

## XXIII

O erst *dann,* wenn der Flug
nicht mehr um seinetwillen
wird in die Himmelstillen
steigen, sich selber genug,

um in lichten Profilen,
als das Gerät, das gelang,
Liebling der Winde zu spielen,
sicher, schwenkend und schlank,—

erst, wenn ein reines Wohin
wachsender Apparate
Knabenstolz überwiegt,

wird, überstürzt von Gewinn,
jener den Fernen Genahte
*sein,* was er einsam erfliegt.

## XXIII

Not till the day when flight
no longer for its own sake ascends
into the silent heavens
propelled by its self-conceit,

so that, in luminous outlines,
as the tool that has come to power,
it can float, caressed by the winds,
streamlined, agile, and sure—

not till a pure destination
outweighs the boyish boast
of how much machines can do

will, overwhelmed with gain,
one to whom distance is close
*be* what alone he flew.

## XXIV

Sollen wir unsere uralte Freundschaft, die großen
niemals werbenden Götter, weil sie der harte
Stahl, den wir streng erzogen, nicht kennt, verstoßen
oder sie plötzlich suchen auf einer Karte?

Diese gewaltigen Freunde, die uns die Toten
nehmen, rühren nirgends an unsere Räder.
Unsere Gastmähler haben wir weit—, unsere Bäder,
fortgerückt, und ihre uns lang schon zu langsamen Boten

überholen wir immer. Einsamer nun auf einander
ganz angewiesen, ohne einander zu kennen,
führen wir nicht mehr die Pfade als schöne Mäander,

sondern als Grade. Nur noch in Dampfkesseln brennen
die einstigen Feuer und heben die Hämmer, die immer
größern. Wir aber nehmen an Kraft ab, wie Schwimmer.

# XXIV

Shall we reject our primordial friendship, the sublime
unwooing gods, because the steel that we keep
harshly bringing to hardness has never known them—
or shall we suddenly look for them on a map?

All these powerful friends, who withdraw the dead
from the reach of the senses, touch nowhere against our
    wheels.
We have moved our banquets, our baths and our festivals,
far away. And their messengers, long since outstripped by
    our speed,

have vanished. Lonelier now, dependent on one another
utterly, though not knowing one another at all,
we no longer lay out each path as a lovely meander,

but straight ahead. Only in factories do the once-consecrate
    flames still
burn and lift up the always heavier hammers.
We, though, keep losing what small strength we have, like
    swimmers.

## XXV

*Dich* aber will ich nun, *Dich,* die ich kannte
wie eine Blume, von der ich den Namen nicht weiß,
noch *ein* Mal erinnern und ihnen zeigen, Entwandte,
schöne Gespielin des unüberwindlichen Schrei's.

Tänzerin erst, die plötzlich, den Körper voll Zögern,
anhielt, als göß man ihr Jungsein in Erz;
trauernd und lauschend—. Da, von den hohen Vermögern
fiel ihr Musik in das veränderte Herz.

Nah war die Krankheit. Schon von den Schatten bemächtigt,
drängte verdunkelt das Blut, doch, wie flüchtig verdächtigt,
trieb es in seinen natürlichen Frühling hervor.

Wieder und wieder, von Dunkel und Sturz unterbrochen,
glänzte es irdisch. Bis es nach schrecklichem Pochen
trat in das trostlos offene Tor.

# XXV

But you now, dear girl, whom I loved like a flower whose
    name
I didn't know, you who so early were taken away:
I will once more call up your image and show it to them,
beautiful companion of the unsubduable cry.

Dancer whose body filled with your hesitant fate,
pausing, as though your young flesh had been cast in bronze;
grieving and listening——. Then, from the high dominions,
unearthly music fell into your altered heart.

Already possessed by shadows, with illness near,
your blood flowed darkly; yet, though for a moment
    suspicious,
it burst out into the natural pulses of spring.

Again and again interrupted by downfall and darkness,
earthly, it gleamed. Till, after a terrible pounding,
it entered the inconsolably open door.

## XXVI

Du aber, Göttlicher, du, bis zuletzt noch Ertöner,
da ihn der Schwarm der verschmähten Mänaden befiel,
hast ihr Geschrei übertönt mit Ordnung, du Schöner,
aus den Zerstörenden stieg dein erbauendes Spiel.

Keine war da, daß sie Haupt dir und Leier zerstör.
Wie sie auch rangen und rasten, und alle die scharfen
Steine, die sie nach deinem Herzen warfen,
wurden zu Sanftem an dir und begabt mit Gehör.

Schließlich zerschlugen sie dich, von der Rache gehetzt,
während dein Klang noch in Löwen und Felsen verweilte
und in den Bäumen und Vögeln. Dort singst du noch jetzt.

O du verlorener Gott! Du unendliche Spur!
Nur weil dich reißend zuletzt die Feindschaft verteilte,
sind wir die Hörenden jetzt und ein Mund der Natur.

# XXVI

But you, divine poet, you who sang on till the end
as the swarm of rejected maenads attacked you, shrieking,
you overpowered their noise with harmony, and
from pure destruction arose your transfigured song.

Their hatred could not destroy your head or your lyre,
however they wrestled and raged; and each one of the sharp
stones that they hurled, vengeance-crazed, at your heart
softened while it was in mid-flight, enchanted to hear.

At last they killed you and broke you in pieces while
your sound kept lingering on in lions and boulders,
in trees and in birds. There you are singing still.

Oh you lost god! You inexhaustible trace!
Only because you were torn and scattered through Nature
have *we* become hearers now and a rescuing voice.

## ZWEITER TEIL

---

### I

Atmen, du unsichtbares Gedicht!
Immerfort um das eigne
Sein rein eingetauschter Weltraum. Gegengewicht,
in dem ich mich rhythmisch ereigne.

Einzige Welle, deren
allmähliches Meer ich bin;
sparsamstes du von allen möglichen Meeren,—
Raumgewinn.

Wieviele von diesen Stellen der Räume waren schon
innen in mir. Manche Winde
sind wie mein Sohn.

Erkennst du mich, Luft, du, voll noch einst meiniger Orte?
Du, einmal glatte Rinde,
Rundung und Blatt meiner Worte.

## SECOND PART

I

Breathing: you invisible poem! Complete
interchange of our own
essence with world-space. You counterweight
in which I rhythmically happen.

Single wave-motion whose
gradual sea I am;
you, most inclusive of all our possible seas—
space grown warm.

How many regions in space have already been
inside me. There are winds that seem like
my wandering son.

Do you recognize me, air, full of places I once absorbed?
You who were the smooth bark,
roundness, and leaf of my words.

## II

So wie dem Meister manchmal das eilig
nähere Blatt den *wirklichen* Strich
abnimmt: so nehmen oft Spiegel das heilig
einzige Lächeln der Mädchen in sich,

wenn sie den Morgen erproben, allein,—
oder im Glanze der dienenden Lichter.
Und in das Atmen der echten Gesichter,
später, fällt nur ein Widerschein.

*Was* haben Augen einst ins umrußte
lange Verglühn der Kamine geschaut:
Blicke des Lebens, für immer verlorne.

Ach, der Erde, wer kennt die Verluste?
Nur, wer mit dennoch preisendem Laut
sänge das Herz, das ins Ganze geborne.

## II

Just as the master's *genuine* brushstroke
is sometimes caught by a hurried page
that happens to be there: so mirrors will take
into themselves the pure smiling image

of girls as they test the morning, alone—
or under the gleam of devoted candles.
And into their faces, one by one,
later, just a reflection falls.

*How much* was once gazed into the charred
slow-dying glow of a fireplace:
glances of life, irretrievable.

Who knows what losses the earth has suffered?
One who, with sounds that nonetheless praise,
can sing the heart born into the whole.

## III

Spiegel: noch nie hat man wissend beschrieben,
was ihr in euerem Wesen seid.
Ihr, wie mit lauter Löchern von Sieben
erfüllten Zwischenräume der Zeit.

Ihr, noch des leeren Saales Verschwender—,
wenn es dämmert, wie Wälder weit . . .
Und der Lüster geht wie ein Sechzehn-Ender
durch eure Unbetretbarkeit.

Manchmal seid ihr voll Malerei.
Einige scheinen *in* euch gegangen—,
andere schicktet ihr scheu vorbei.

Aber die Schönste wird bleiben—, bis
drüben in ihre enthaltenen Wangen
eindrang der klare gelöste Narziß.

## III

Mirrors: no one has ever known how
to describe what you are in your inmost realm.
As if filled with nothing but sieve-holes, you
fathomless in-between spaces of time.

You prodigals of the empty chamber—
vast as forests, at the close of day . . .
And the chandelier strides like a sixteen-pointer
through your unenterability.

Sometimes you are full of painting. A few
seem to have walked straight into your depths—
others, shyly, you sent on past you.

But the loveliest will stay—until, beyond,
into her all-absorbed cheeks she lets
Narcissus penetrate, bright and unbound.

## IV

O dieses ist das Tier, das es nicht giebt.
Sie wußtens nicht und habens jeden Falls
—sein Wandeln, seine Haltung, seinen Hals,
bis in des stillen Blickes Licht—geliebt.

Zwar *war* es nicht. Doch weil sie's liebten, ward
ein reines Tier. Sie ließen immer Raum.
Und in dem Raume, klar und ausgespart,
erhob es leicht sein Haupt und brauchte kaum

zu sein. Sie nährten es mit keinem Korn,
nur immer mit der Möglichkeit, es sei.
Und die gab solche Stärke an das Tier,

daß es aus sich ein Stirnhorn trieb. Ein Horn.
Zu einer Jungfrau kam es weiß herbei—
und war im Silber-Spiegel und in ihr.

## IV

Oh this beast is the one that never was.
They didn't know that; unconcerned, they had
loved its grace, its walk, and how it stood
looking at them calmly, with clear eyes.

It hadn't *been*. But from their love, a pure
beast arose. They always left it room.
And in that heart-space, radiant and bare,
it raised its head and hardly needed to

exist. They fed it, not with any grain,
but always just with the thought that it might be.
And this assurance gave the beast so much power,

it grew a horn upon its brow. One horn.
Afterward it approached a virgin, whitely—
and was, inside the mirror and in her.

## V

Blumenmuskel, der der Anemone
Wiesenmorgen nach und nach erschließt,
bis in ihren Schooß das polyphone
Licht der lauten Himmel sich ergießt,

in den stillen Blütenstern gespannter
Muskel des unendlichen Empfangs,
manchmal *so* von Fülle übermannter,
daß der Ruhewink des Untergangs

kaum vermag die weitzurückgeschnellten
Blätterränder dir zurückzugeben:
du, Entschluß und Kraft von *wie*viel Welten!

Wir, Gewaltsamen, wir währen länger.
Aber *wann,* in welchem aller Leben,
sind wir endlich offen und Empfänger?

V

Flower-muscle that slowly opens back
the anemone to another meadow-dawn,
until her womb can feel the polyphonic
light of the sonorous heavens pouring down;

muscle of an infinite acceptance,
stretched within the silent blossom-star,
at times *so* overpowered with abundance
that sunset's signal for repose is bare-

ly able to return your too far hurled-
back petals for the darkness to revive:
you, strength and purpose of how many worlds!

We violent ones remain a little longer.
Ah but *when,* in which of all our lives,
shall we at last be open and receivers?

## VI

Rose, du thronende, denen im Altertume
warst du ein Kelch mit einfachem Rand.
*Uns* aber bist du die volle zahllose Blume,
der unerschöpfliche Gegenstand.

In deinem Reichtum scheinst du wie Kleidung um Kleidung
um einen Leib aus nichts als Glanz;
aber dein einzelnes Blatt ist zugleich die Vermeidung
und die Verleugnung jedes Gewands.

Seit Jahrhunderten ruft uns dein Duft
seine süßesten Namen herüber;
plötzlich liegt er wie Ruhm in der Luft.

Dennoch, wir wissen ihn nicht zu nennen, wir raten . . .
Und Erinnerung geht zu ihm über,
die wir von rufbaren Stunden erbaten.

# VI

Rose, you majesty—once, to the ancients, you were
just a calyx with the simplest of rims.
But for us, you are the full, the numberless flower,
the inexhaustible countenance.

In your wealth you seem to be wearing gown upon gown
upon a body of nothing but light;
yet each separate petal is at the same time the negation
of all clothing and the refusal of it.

Your fragrance has been calling its sweetest names
in our direction, for hundreds of years;
suddenly it hangs in the air like fame.

Even so, we have never known what to call it; we guess . . .
And memory is filled with it unawares
which we prayed for from hours that belong to us.

## VII

Blumen, ihr schließlich den ordnenden Händen verwandte,
(Händen der Mädchen von einst und jetzt),
die auf dem Gartentisch oft von Kante zu Kante
lagen, ermattet und sanft verletzt,

wartend des Wassers, das sie noch einmal erhole
aus dem begonnenen Tod—, und nun
wieder erhobene zwischen die strömenden Pole
fühlender Finger, die wohlzutun

mehr noch vermögen, als ihr ahntet, ihr leichten,
wenn ihr euch wiederfandet im Krug,
langsam erkühlend und Warmes der Mädchen, wie
Beichten,

von euch gebend, wie trübe ermüdende Sünden,
die das Gepflücktsein beging, als Bezug
wieder zu ihnen, die sich euch blühend verbünden.

# VII

Flowers, you who are kin to the hands that arrange
(gentle girls' hands of present and past),
who often lay on the garden table, from edge
to edge, exhausted and slightly bruised,

waiting for the water once more to bring you back whole
from the death that had just begun—and now
lifted again between the fast-streaming poles
of sensitive fingers that are able to do

even more good than you guessed, as you lightly uncurled,
coming to yourselves again in the pitcher,
slowly cooling, and exhaling the warmth of girls

like long confessions, like dreary wearying sins
committed by being plucked, which once more
relate you to those who in blossoming are your cousins.

# VIII

Wenige ihr, der einstigen Kindheit Gespielen
in den zerstreuten Gärten der Stadt:
wie wir uns fanden und uns zögernd gefielen
und, wie das Lamm mit dem redenden Blatt,

sprachen als Schweigende. Wenn wir uns einmal freuten,
keinem gehörte es. Wessen wars?
Und wie zergings unter allen den gehenden Leuten
und im Bangen des langen Jahrs.

Wagen umrollten uns fremd, vorübergezogen,
Häuser umstanden uns stark, aber unwahr,—und keines
kannte uns je. Was war wirklich im All?

Nichts. Nur die Bälle. Ihre herrlichen Bogen.
Auch nicht die Kinder . . . Aber manchmal trat eines,
ach ein vergehendes, unter den fallenden Ball.

*(In memoriam Egon von Rilke)*

# VIII

You playmates of mine in the scattered parks of the city,
small friends from a childhood of long ago:
how we found and liked one another, hesitantly,
and, like the lamb with the talking scroll,

spoke with our silence. When we were filled with joy,
it belonged to no one: it was simply there.
And how it dissolved among all the adults who passed by
and in the fears of the endless year.

Wheels rolled past us, we stood and stared at the carriages;
houses surrounded us, solid but untrue—and none
of them ever knew us. *What* in that world was real?

Nothing. Only the balls. Their magnificent arches.
Not even the children . . . But sometimes one,
oh a vanishing one, stepped under the plummeting ball.

*(In memoriam Egon von Rilke)*

## IX

Rühmt euch, ihr Richtenden, nicht der entbehrlichen Folter
und daß das Eisen nicht länger an Hälsen sperrt.
Keins ist gesteigert, kein Herz—, weil ein gewollter
Krampf der Milde euch zarter verzerrt.

Was es durch Zeiten bekam, das schenkt das Schafott
wieder zurück, wie Kinder ihr Spielzeug vom vorig
alten Geburtstag. Ins reine, ins hohe, ins thorig
offene Herz träte er anders, der Gott

wirklicher Milde. Er käme gewaltig und griffe
strahlender um sich, wie Göttliche sind.
*Mehr* als ein Wind für die großen gesicherten Schiffe.

Weniger nicht, als die heimliche leise Gewahrung,
die uns im Innern schweigend gewinnt
wie ein still spielendes Kind aus unendlicher Paarung.

## IX

Don't boast, you judges, that you have dispensed with
    torture
and that convicts are no longer shackled by the neck or heel.
No heart is enhanced, not one is—because a tender
spasm of mercy twists your mouths into a smile.

What the scaffold received through the ages, it has given
    back
again, as children give back their battered old
birthday toys. Into the pure and lofty and gatelike
open heart he would differently enter, the god

of true mercy. Sudden, huge, he would stride through and
    grip
us dazzled with radiance all around.
*More* than a wind for the massive confident ships.

And not any less transforming than the deep intuition
that wins us over without a sound
like a quietly playing child of an infinite union.

## X

Alles Erworbne bedroht die Maschine, solange
sie sich erdreistet, im Geist, statt im Gehorchen, zu sein.
Daß nicht der herrlichen Hand schöneres Zögern mehr
   prange,
zu dem entschlossenern Bau schneidet sie steifer den Stein.

Nirgends bleibt sie zurück, daß wir ihr *ein* Mal entrönnen
und sie in stiller Fabrik ölend sich selber gehört.
Sie ist das Leben,—sie meint es am besten zu können,
die mit dem gleichen Entschluß ordnet und schafft und
   zerstört.

Aber noch ist uns das Dasein verzaubert; an hundert
Stellen ist es noch Ursprung. Ein Spielen von reinen
Kräften, die keiner berührt, der nicht kniet und bewundert.

Worte gehen noch zart am Unsäglichen aus . . .
Und die Musik, immer neu, aus den bebendsten Steinen,
baut im unbrauchbaren Raum ihr vergöttlichtes Haus.

# X

All we have gained the machine threatens, as long
as it dares to exist in the mind and not in obedience.
To dim the masterful hand's more glorious lingering,
for the determined structure it more rigidly cuts the stones.

Nowhere does it stay behind; we cannot escape it at last
as it rules, self-guided, self-oiled, from its silent factory.
It thinks it is life: thinks it does everything best,
though with equal determination it can create or destroy.

But still, existence for us is a miracle; in a hundred
places it is still the source. A playing of absolute
forces that no one can touch who has not knelt down in
        wonder.

Still there are words that can calmly approach the unsayable . . .
And from the most tremulous stones music, forever new,
builds in unusable space her deified temple.

## XI

Manche, des Todes, entstand ruhig geordnete Regel,
weiterbezwingender Mensch, seit du im Jagen beharrst;
mehr doch als Falle und Netz, weiß ich dich, Streifen von
    Segel,
den man hinuntergehängt in den höhligen Karst.

Leise ließ man dich ein, als wärst du ein Zeichen,
Frieden zu feiern. Doch dann: rang dich am Rande der
    Knecht,
—und, aus den Höhlen, die Nacht warf eine Handvoll von
    bleichen
taumelnden Tauben ins Licht . . .
                  Aber auch *das* ist im Recht.

Fern von dem Schauenden sei jeglicher Hauch des
    Bedauerns,
nicht nur vom Jäger allein, der, was sich zeitig erweist,
wachsam und handelnd vollzieht.

*Töten ist eine Gestalt unseres wandernden Trauerns* . . .
Rein ist im heiteren Geist,
was an uns selber geschieht.

## XI

Many calmly established rules of death have arisen,
ever-conquering man, since you acquired a taste
for hunting; yet more than all traps, I know you, sailcloths of
     linen
that used to be hung down into the caverns of Karst.

Gently they lowered you in as if you were a signal
to celebrate peace. But then: the boy began shaking your
     side,
—and suddenly, from the caves, the darkness would fling
     out a handful
of pale doves into the day . . .

                              But even that is all right.

Let every last twinge of pity be far from those who look on—
far not just from the conscience of the vigilant, steadfast
     hunter
who fulfills what time has allowed.

*Killing too is a form of our ancient wandering affliction . . .*
When the mind stays serene, whatever
happens to us is good.

## XII

Wolle die Wandlung. O sei für die Flamme begeistert,
drin sich ein Ding dir entzieht, das mit Verwandlungen
    prunkt;
jener entwerfende Geist, welcher das Irdische meistert,
liebt in dem Schwung der Figur nichts wie den wendenden
    Punkt.

Was sich ins Bleiben verschließt, schon *ists* das Erstarrte;
wähnt es sich sicher im Schutz des unscheinbaren Grau's?
Warte, ein Härtestes warnt aus der Ferne das Harte.
Wehe—: abwesender Hammer holt aus!

Wer sich als Quelle ergießt, den erkennt die Erkennung;
und sie führt ihn entzückt durch das heiter Geschaffne,
das mit Anfang oft schließt und mit Ende beginnt.

Jeder glückliche Raum ist Kind oder Enkel von Trennung,
den sie staunend durchgehn. Und die verwandelte Daphne
will, seit sie lorbeern fühlt, daß du dich wandelst in Wind.

# XII

*Will* transformation. Oh be inspired for the flame
in which a Thing disappears and bursts into something else;
the spirit of re-creation which masters this earthly form
loves most the pivoting point where you are no longer
    yourself.

What tightens into survival is already inert;
how safe is it really in its inconspicuous gray?
From far off a far greater hardness warns what is hard,
and the absent hammer is lifted high!

He who pours himself out like a stream is acknowledged at
    last by Knowledge;
and she leads him enchanted through the harmonious
    country
that finishes often with starting, and with ending begins.

Every fortunate space that the two of them pass through,
    astonished,
is a child or grandchild of parting. And the transfigured
    Daphne,
as she feels herself become laurel, wants you to change into
    wind.

## XIII

Sei allem Abschied voran, als wäre er hinter
dir, wie der Winter, der eben geht.
Denn unter Wintern ist einer so endlos Winter,
daß, überwinternd, dein Herz überhaupt übersteht.

Sei immer tot in Eurydike—, singender steige,
preisender steige zurück in den reinen Bezug.
Hier, unter Schwindenden, sei, im Reiche der Neige,
sei ein klingendes Glas, das sich im Klang schon zerschlug.

Sei—und wisse zugleich des Nicht-Seins Bedingung,
den unendlichen Grund deiner innigen Schwingung,
daß du sie völlig vollziehst dieses einzige Mal.

Zu dem gebrauchten sowohl, wie zum dumpfen und
         stummen
Vorrat der vollen Natur, den unsäglichen Summen,
zähle dich jubelnd hinzu und vernichte die Zahl.

## XIII

Be ahead of all parting, as though it already were
behind you, like the winter that has just gone by.
For among these winters there is one so endlessly winter
that only by wintering through it will your heart survive.

Be forever dead in Eurydice—more gladly arise
into the seamless life proclaimed in your song.
Here, in the realm of decline, among momentary days,
be the crystal cup that shattered even as it rang.

Be—and yet know the great void where all things begin,
the infinite source of your own most intense vibration,
so that, this once, you may give it your perfect assent.

To all that is used-up, and to all the muffled and dumb
creatures in the world's full reserve, the unsayable sums,
joyfully add your*self,* and cancel the count.

## XIV

Siehe die Blumen, diese dem Irdischen treuen,
denen wir Schicksal vom Rande des Schicksals leihn,—
aber wer weiß es! Wenn sie ihr Welken bereuen,
ist es an uns, ihre Reue zu sein.

Alles will schweben. Da gehn wir umher wie Beschwerer,
legen auf alles uns selbst, vom Gewichte entzückt;
o was sind wir den Dingen für zehrende Lehrer,
weil ihnen ewige Kindheit glückt.

Nähme sie einer ins innige Schlafen und schliefe
tief mit den Dingen—: o wie käme er leicht,
anders zum anderen Tag, aus der gemeinsamen Tiefe.

Oder er bliebe vielleicht; und sie blühten und priesen
ihn, den Bekehrten, der nun den Ihrigen gleicht,
allen den stillen Geschwistern im Winde der Wiesen.

# XIV

Look at the flowers, so faithful to what is earthly,
to whom we lend fate from the very border of fate.
And if they are sad about how they must wither and die,
perhaps it is our vocation to be their regret.

All Things want to fly. Only *we* are weighed down by desire,
caught in ourselves and enthralled with our heaviness.
Oh what consuming, negative teachers we are
for them, while eternal childhood fills them with grace.

If someone were to fall into intimate slumber, and slept
deeply with Things—: how easily he would come
to a different day, out of the mutual depth.

Or perhaps he would stay there; and they would blossom
and praise
their newest convert, who now is like one of them,
all those silent companions in the wind of the meadows.

## XV

O Brunnen-Mund, du gebender, du Mund,
der unerschöpflich Eines, Reines, spricht,—
du, vor des Wassers fließendem Gesicht,
marmorne Maske. Und im Hintergrund

der Aquädukte Herkunft. Weither an
Gräbern vorbei, vom Hang des Apennins
tragen sie dir dein Sagen zu, das dann
am schwarzen Altern deines Kinns

vorüberfallt in das Gefäß davor.
Dies ist das schlafend hingelegte Ohr,
das Marmorohr, in das du immer sprichst.

Ein Ohr der Erde. Nur mit sich allein
redet sie also. Schiebt ein Krug sich ein,
so scheint es ihr, daß du sie unterbrichst.

## XV

O fountain-mouth, you generous, always-filled
mouth that speaks pure oneness, constantly—
you marble mask before the water's still
flowing face. And in the background, the

slow descent of aqueducts. From far
graves, and from the sloping Apennines,
they bring you all your syllables, which pour
down from your blackened, aging chin

into the basin lying underneath.
This is the intimate and sleeping ear,
the marble ear, in which you always speak.

An ear of Earth. Just with herself alone
does she talk this way. And if a jug slips in,
she feels that you are interrupting her.

## XVI

Immer wieder von uns aufgerissen,
ist der Gott die Stelle, welche heilt.
Wir sind Scharfe, denn wir wollen wissen,
aber er ist heiter und verteilt.

Selbst die reine, die geweihte Spende
nimmt er anders nicht in seine Welt,
als indem er sich dem freien Ende
unbewegt entgegenstellt.

Nur der Tote trinkt
aus der hier vons uns *gehörten* Quelle,
wenn der Gott ihm schweigend winkt, dem Toten.

*Uns* wird nur das Lärmen angeboten.
Und das Lamm erbittet seine Schelle
aus dem stilleren Instinkt.

## XVI

Over and over by us torn in two,
the god is the hidden place that heals again.
We are sharp-edged, because we want to know,
but he is always scattered and serene.

Even the pure, the consecrated gift
he takes into his world no other way
than by positioning himself, unmoved,
to face the one end that is free.

Only the dead may drink
from the source that we just hear, the unseen pool,
when the god, mute, allows them with a gesture.

Here, to us, only the noise is offered.
And the lamb keeps begging for its bell
because of a more quiet instinct.

## XVII

Wo, in welchen immer selig bewässerten Gärten, an welchen
Bäumen, aus welchen zärtlich entblätterten Blüten-Kelchen
reifen die fremdartigen Früchte der Tröstung? Diese
köstlichen, deren du eine vielleicht in der zertretenen Wiese

deiner Armut findest. Von einem zum anderen Male
wunderst du dich über die Größe der Frucht,
über ihr Heilsein, über die Sanftheit der Schale,
und daß sie der Leichtsinn des Vogels dir nicht vorwegnahm
und nicht die Eifersucht

unten des Wurms. Giebt es denn Bäume, von Engeln
beflogen,
und von verborgenen langsamen Gärtnern so seltsam
gezogen,
daß sie uns tragen, ohne uns zu gehören?

Haben wir niemals vermocht, wir Schatten und Schemen,
durch unser voreilig reifes und wieder welkes Benehmen
jener gelassenen Sommer Gleichmut zu stören?

## XVII

Where, inside what forever blissfully watered gardens, upon
     what trees,
out of what deep and tenderly unpetaled flower-cups,
do the exotic fruits of consolation hang ripening? Those
rare delicacies, of which you find one perhaps

in the trampled meadows of your poverty. Time and again
you have stood there marveling over the sheer size of the
     fruit,
over its wholeness, its smooth and unmottled skin,
and that the lightheaded bird or the jealous worm under the
     ground had not

snatched it away from your hands. *Are* there such trees,
     flown through
by angels and so strangely cared for by gardeners hidden and
     slow
that they bear their fruit to nourish us, without being ours?

Is it true we have never been able (we who are only
shadows and shades), through our ripening and wilting so
     early,
to disturb the enormous calm of those patient summers?

## XVIII

Tänzerin: o du Verlegung
alles Vergehens in Gang: wie brachtest du's dar.
Und der Wirbel am Schluß, dieser Baum aus Bewegung,
nahm er nicht ganz in Besitz das erschwungene Jahr?

Blühte nicht, daß ihn dein Schwingen von vorhin
umschwärme,
plötzlich sein Wipfel von Stille? Und über ihr,
war sie nicht Sonne, war sie nicht Sommer, die Wärme,
diese unzählige Wärme aus dir?

Aber er trug auch, er trug, dein Baum der Ekstase.
Sind sie nicht seine ruhigen Früchte: der Krug,
reifend gestreift, und die gereiftere Vase?

Und in den Bildern: ist nicht die Zeichnung geblieben,
die deiner Braue dunkler Zug
rasch an die Wandung der eigenen Wendung geschrieben?

# XVIII

Dancing girl: transformation
of all transience into steps: how you offered it there.
And the arm-raised whirl at the end, that tree made of
      motion,
didn't it fully possess the pivoted year?

Didn't it, so that your previous swirling might swarm
in the midst of it, suddenly blossom with stillness? And
      above,
wasn't it sunshine, wasn't it summer, the warmth,
the pure, immeasurable warmth that you gave?

But it bore fruit also, it bore fruit, your tree of bliss.
Aren't they here in their tranquil season: the jug,
whirling to ripeness, and the even more ripened vase?

And in the pictures: can't we still see the drawing
which your eyebrow's dark evanescent stroke
quickly inscribed on the surface of its own turning?

## XIX

Irgendwo wohnt das Gold in der verwöhnenden Bank
und mit Tausenden tut es vertraulich. Doch jener
Blinde, der Bettler, ist selbst dem kupfernen Zehner
wie ein verlorener Ort, wie das staubige Eck unterm
Schrank.

In den Geschäften entlang ist das Geld wie zuhause
und verkleidet sich scheinbar in Seide, Nelken und Pelz.
Er, der Schweigende, steht in der Atempause
alles des wach oder schlafend atmenden Gelds.

O wie mag sie sich schließen bei Nacht, diese immer offene
Hand.
Morgen holt sie das Schicksal wieder, und täglich
hält es sie hin: hell, elend, unendlich zerstörbar.

Daß doch einer, ein Schauender, endlich ihren langen
Bestand
staunend begriffe und rühmte. Nur dem Aufsingenden
säglich.
Nur dem Göttlichen hörbar.

## XIX

Somewhere gold lives, luxurious, inside the pampering bank,
on intimate terms with thousands. Meanwhile, the wretched
blindman begging here seems, even to a penny, just like
some always-forgotten corner or the dustpile beneath a bed.

In all the most elegant shops money is at ease
and steps out in shiny costumes of furs, carnations, and silks.
He, the silent one, stands in the narrow breath-pause
made by money breathing as it slumbers or wakes.

Oh how can it close at night, that hand which is always
    open?
Tomorrow and each day Fate will arrive and hold it out:
    clear,
squalid, at any moment likely to be destroyed.

If only someone who could *see*, astonished at its long
    duration,
would understand it and praise it. Sayable only for the
    singer.
Audible only to the god.

## XX

Zwischen den Sternen, wie weit; und doch, um wievieles
  noch weiter,
was man am Hiesigen lernt.
Einer, zum Beispiel, ein Kind . . . und ein Nächster, ein
  Zweiter—,
o wie unfaßlich entfernt.

Schicksal, es mißt uns vielleicht mit des Seienden Spanne,
daß es uns fremd erscheint;
denk, wieviel Spannen allein vom Mädchen zum Manne,
wenn es ihn meidet und meint.

Alles ist weit—, und nirgends schließt sich der Kreis.
Sieh in der Schüssel, auf heiter bereitetem Tische,
seltsam der Fische Gesicht.

Fische sind stumm . . . , meinte man einmal. Wer weiß?
Aber ist nicht am Ende ein Ort, wo man das, was der Fische
Sprache wäre, *ohne* sie spricht?

## XX

In between stars, what distances; and yet, how much vaster
    the distance
that we learn from what is right *here.*
Someone, for example a child . . . and beside him, his brother
    or sister—
oh how incomprehensibly far.

Fate measures us perhaps according to what is real,
so it seems to us not our own;
think of how vast a distance there is from the girl
to the loved and avoided man.

All things are far—and nowhere does the circle close.
Look at the fish, served up on the gaily set table:
how peculiar its face on the dish.

All fish are mute . . . , one used to think. But who knows?
Isn't there at last a place where, *without* them, we would be
    able
to speak in the language of fish?

## XXI

Singe die Gärten, mein Herz, die du nicht kennst; wie in
    Glas
eingegossene Gärten, klar, unerreichbar.
Wasser und Rosen von Ispahan oder Schiras,
singe sie selig, preise sie, keinem vergleichbar.

Zeige, mein Herz, daß du sie niemals entbehrst.
Daß sie dich meinen, ihre reifenden Feigen.
Daß du mit ihren, zwischen den blühenden Zweigen
wie zum Gesicht gesteigerten Lüften verkehrst.

Meide den Irrtum, daß es Entbehrungen gebe
für den geschehnen Entschluß, diesen: zu sein!
Seidener Faden, kamst du hinein ins Gewebe.

Welchem der Bilder du auch im Innern geeint bist
(sei es selbst ein Moment aus dem Leben der Pein),
fühl, daß der ganze, der rühmliche Teppich gemeint ist.

## XXI

Sing of the gardens, my heart, that you never saw; as if glass
domes had been placed upon them, unreached forever.
Fountains and roses of Ispahan or Shiraz—
sing of their happiness, praise them: unlike all others.

Show that you always feel them, forever close.
That when their figs ripen, it is you they are ripening for.
That you know every breeze which, among the blossoms
    they bear,
is intensified till it almost becomes a face.

Avoid the illusion that there can be any lack
for someone who wishes, then fully decides: to be!
Silken thread, you were woven into the fabric.

Whatever the design with which you are inwardly joined
(even for only one moment amid years of grief),
feel that the whole, the marvelous carpet is meant.

## XXII

O trotz Schicksal: die herrlichen Überflüsse
unseres Daseins, in Parken übergeschäumt,—
oder als steinerne Männer neben die Schlüsse
hoher Portale, unter Balkone gebäumt!

O die eherne Glocke, die ihre Keule
täglich wider den stumpfen Alltag hebt.
Oder die *eine*, in Karnak, die Säule, die Säule,
die fast ewige Tempel überlebt.

Heute stürzen die Überschüsse, dieselben,
nur noch als Eile vorbei, aus dem waagrechten gelben
Tag in die blendend mit Licht übertriebene Nacht.

Aber das Rasen zergeht und läßt keine Spuren.
Kurven des Flugs durch die Luft und die, die sie fuhren,
keine vielleicht ist umsonst. Doch nur wie gedacht.

## XXII

Oh in spite of fate: the glorious overflowings
of our existence, spouted upward in parks—
or as stone-carved men who bear upon shoulders and backs
the weight overhead, braced on the sheer edge of buildings.

Oh the bronze bell that, day after day, can lift
its club to shatter our dull quotidian hum.
Or the *only* presence, in Karnak, the column, the column
in which temples that were almost eternal have been
        outlived.

For us these abundances plunge past, no longer central
but only appearing as haste, out of the horizontal
yellow day and into the overwhelmed, dazzled night.

But this frenzy too will subside, leaving no traces.
Arcs of airplanes and those who drove them through space,
none perhaps is in vain. Yet only as thought.

## XXIII

Rufe mich zu jener deiner Stunden,
die dir unaufhörlich widersteht:
flehend nah wie das Gesicht von Hunden,
aber immer wieder weggedreht,

wenn du meinst, sie endlich zu erfassen.
So Entzognes ist am meisten dein.
Wir sind frei. Wir wurden dort entlassen,
wo wir meinten, erst begrüßt zu sein.

Bang verlangen wir nach einem Halte,
wir zu Jungen manchmal für das Alte
und zu alt für das, was niemals war.

Wir, gerecht nur, wo wir dennoch preisen,
weil wir, ach, der Ast sind und das Eisen
und das Süße reifender Gefahr.

# XXIII

Call me to the one among your moments
that stands against you, ineluctably:
intimate as a dog's imploring glance
but, again, forever, turned away

when you think you've captured it at last.
What seems so far from you is most your own.
We are already free, and were dismissed
where we thought we soon would be at home.

Anxious, we keep longing for a foothold—
we, at times too young for what is old
and too old for what has never been;

doing justice only where we praise,
because we are the branch, the iron blade,
and sweet danger, ripening from within.

## XXIV

O diese Lust, immer neu, aus gelockertem Lehm!
Niemand beinah hat den frühesten Wagern geholfen.
Städte entstanden trotzdem an beseligten Golfen,
Wasser und Öl füllten die Krüge trotzdem.

Götter, wir planen sie erst in erkühnten Entwürfen,
die uns das mürrische Schicksal wieder zerstört.
Aber sie sind die Unsterblichen. Sehet, wir dürfen
jenen erhorchen, der uns am Ende erhört.

Wir, ein Geschlecht durch Jahrtausende: Mütter und Väter,
immer erfüllter von dem künftigen Kind,
daß es uns einst, übersteigend, erschüttere, später.

Wir, wir unendlich Gewagten, was haben wir Zeit!
Und nur der schweigsame Tod, der weiß, was wir sind
und was er immer gewinnt, wenn er uns leiht.

## XXIV

Oh the delight, ever new, out of loosened soil!
The ones who first dared were almost without any help.
Nonetheless, at fortunate harbors, cities sprang up,
and pitchers were nonetheless filled with water and oil.

Gods: we project them first in the boldest of sketches,
which sullen Fate keeps crumpling and tossing away.
But for all that, the gods are immortal. Surely we may
hear out the one who, in the end, will hear *us*.

We, one generation through thousands of lifetimes: women
and men, who are more and more filled with the child we
    will bear,
so that through it we may be shattered and overtaken.

We, the endlessly dared—how far we have come!
And only taciturn Death can know what we are
and how he must always profit when he lends us time.

## XXV

Schon, horch, hörst du der ersten Harken
Arbeit; wieder den menschlichen Takt
in der verhaltenen Stille der starken
Vorfrühlingserde. Unabgeschmackt

scheint dir das Kommende. Jenes so oft
dir schon Gekommene scheint dir zu kommen
wieder wie Neues. Immer erhofft,
nahmst du es niemals. Es hat dich genommen.

Selbst die Blätter durchwinterter Eichen
scheinen im Abend ein künftiges Braun.
Manchmal geben sich Lüfte ein Zeichen.

Schwarz sind die Sträucher. Doch Haufen von Dünger
lagern als satteres Schwarz in den Aun.
Jede Stunde, die hingeht, wird jünger.

## XXV

Already (listen!) you can hear the first
harrows; once more the rhythm of men
through the held-back silence of the resolute earth
in early spring. What has so often

come to you is coming once more,
vivid as if for the first time. Now,
slowly, you await what you always hoped for
but never took. It always took *you.*

Even the leaves of wintered-through oaks
seem in the twilight a future brown.
Breezes signal, then signal back.

Black are the bushes. Yet heaps of dung
lie more intensely black on the ground.
Every hour that goes by grows younger.

## XXVI

Wie ergreift uns der Vogelschrei . . .
Irgend ein einmal erschaffenes Schreien.
Aber die Kinder schon, spielend im Freien,
schreien an wirklichen Schreien vorbei.

Schreien den Zufall. In Zwischenräume
dieses, des Weltraums, (in welchen der heile
Vogelschrei eingeht, wie Menschen in Träume—)
treiben sie ihre, des Kreischens, Keile.

Wehe, wo sind wir? Immer noch freier,
wie die losgerissenen Drachen
jagen wir halbhoch, mit Rändern von Lachen,

windig zerfetzten.—Ordne die Schreier,
singender Gott! daß sie rauschend erwachen,
tragend als Strömung das Haupt und die Leier.

## XXVI

How deeply the cry of a bird can move us . . .
*Any* cry that is cried out whole.
But children, playing in their open space—
already their cries have become unreal.

They cry out chance. And into the silent
seamless world, into which birds' cries
fully (as men into dream-space) blend,
they hammer the hard-edged wedge of their noise.

Alas, where are we? Freer and freer,
like colored kites torn loose from their strings,
we toss half-high-up, framed by cold laughter,

slashed by the wind.—Oh compose the criers,
harmonious god! let them wake resounding,
let their clear stream carry the head and the lyre.

## XXVII

Giebt es wirklich die Zeit, die zerstörende?
Wann, auf dem ruhenden Berg, zerbricht sie die Burg?
Dieses Herz, das unendlich den Göttern gehörende,
wann vergewaltigts der Demiurg?

Sind wir wirklich so ängstlich Zerbrechliche,
wie das Schicksal uns wahr machen will?
Ist die Kindheit, die tiefe, versprechliche,
in den Wurzeln—später—still?

Ach, das Gespenst des Vergänglichen,
durch den arglos Empfänglichen
geht es, als wär es ein Rauch.

Als die, die wir sind, als die Treibenden,
gelten wir doch bei bleibenden
Kräften als göttlicher Brauch.

## XXVII

Does it really exist, Time, the Destroyer?
When will it crush the fortress on the peaceful height?
This heart, which belongs to the infinite gods forever,
when will the Demiurge violate *it*?

Are we really as fate keeps trying to convince us,
weak and brittle in an alien world?
And childhood, with all its divining voices,
is it later, down to its first root, stilled?

Ah, the ghost of the transient
moves through the open, innocent
heart like a summer cloud.

As who we are, desperate, driving,
we still matter among the abiding
powers as a use of the gods.

## XXVIII

O komm und geh. Du, fast noch Kind, ergänze
für einen Augenblick die Tanzfigur
zum reinen Sternbild einer jener Tänze,
darin wir die dumpf ordnende Natur

vergänglich übertreffen. Denn sie regte
sich völlig hörend nur, da Orpheus sang.
Du warst noch die von damals her Bewegte
und leicht befremdet, wenn ein Baum sich lang

besann, mit dir nach dem Gehör zu gehn.
Du wußtest noch die Stelle, wo die Leier
sich tönend hob—; die unerhörte Mitte.

Für sie versuchtest du die schönen Schritte
und hofftest, einmal zu der heilen Feier
des Freundes Gang und Antlitz hinzudrehn.

## XXVIII

Oh come and go. You, almost still a child—
for just a moment fill out the dance-figure
into the constellation of those bold
dances in which dull, obsessive Nature

is fleetingly surpassed. For she was stirred
to total hearing just when Orpheus sang.
You were still moved by those primeval words
and a bit surprised if any tree took long

to step with you into the listening ear.
You knew the place where once the lyre arose
resounding: the unheard, unheard-of center.

For *its* sake you tried out your lovely motion
and hoped that you would one day turn your friend's
body toward the perfect celebration.

## XXIX

Stiller Freund der vielen Fernen, fühle,
wie dein Atem noch den Raum vermehrt.
Im Gebälk der finstern Glockenstühle
laß dich läuten. Das, was an dir zehrt,

wird ein Starkes über dieser Nahrung.
Geh in der Verwandlung aus und ein.
Was ist deine leidendste Erfahrung?
Ist dir Trinken bitter, werde Wein.

Sei in dieser Nacht aus Übermaß
Zauberkraft am Kreuzweg deiner Sinne,
ihrer seltsamen Begegnung Sinn.

Und wenn dich das Irdische vergaß,
zu der stillen Erde sag: Ich rinne.
Zu dem raschen Wasser sprich: Ich bin.

# XXIX

Silent friend of many distances, feel
how your breath enlarges all of space.
Let your presence ring out like a bell
into the night. What feeds upon your face

grows mighty from the nourishment thus offered.
Move through transformation, out and in.
What is the deepest loss that you have suffered?
If drinking is bitter, change yourself to wine.

In this immeasurable darkness, be the power
that rounds your senses in their magic ring,
the sense of their mysterious encounter.

And if the earthly no longer knows your name,
whisper to the silent earth: I'm flowing.
To the flashing water say: I am.

# Appendix to the Sonnets
to Orpheus

## [I]

Rühmen, das ists! Ein zum Rühmen Bestellter,
ging er hervor wie das Erz aus des Steins
Schweigen. Sein Herz, o vergängliche Kelter
eines den Menschen unendlichen Weins!

Euch kanns beirren, wenn man in Grüften
Könige aufdeckt, verfault und verwürmt,—
ihn hat der Hinfall der Häupter und Hüften
zwar mit zehrendem Weh bestürmt,

aber der Zweifel war ihm verächtlich.
Er zerrang den Gestank und pries
Tägiges täglich und Nächtiges nächtlich,

denn wer erkennt die verwandelten Gnaden?
Knieend aus dem Markte der Maden
hob er das heile Goldene Vließ.

## [I]

Praising is what matters! He was summoned for that,
and came to us like the ore from a stone's
silence. His mortal heart presses out
a deathless, inexhaustible wine!

Don't be confused if kings are discovered
rotting in their sepulchers, gnawed by the worm—
for a while the decay of body and head
assailed him too with intense alarm;

he, however, despising all doubt,
throttled the stench and with praise affirmed
the daily by day and the nightly at night,

for who knows what is transformed by the graces?
Kneeling from the maggots' marketplace,
he lifted the Golden Fleece, unharmed.

## [II]

O das Neue, Freunde, ist nicht dies,
daß Maschinen uns die Hand verdrängen.
Laßt euch nicht beirrn von Übergängen,
bald wird schweigen, wer das 'Neue' pries.

Denn das Ganze ist unendlich neuer,
als ein Kabel und ein hohes Haus.
Seht, die Sterne sind ein altes Feuer,
und die neuern Feuer löschen aus.

Glaubt nicht, daß die längsten Transmissionen
schon des Künftigen Räder drehn.
Denn Aeonen reden mit Aeonen.

Mehr, als wir erfuhren, ist geschehn.
Und die Zukunft faßt das Allerfernste
rein in eins mit unserm innern Ernste.

## [II]

The New, my friends, is not a matter of
letting machines force out our handiwork.
Don't be confused by change; soon those who have
praised the "New" will realize their mistake.

For look, the Whole is infinitely newer
than a cable or a high apartment house.
The stars keep blazing with an ancient fire,
and all more recent fires will fade out.

Not even the longest, strongest of transmissions
can turn the wheels of what will be.
Across the moment, aeons speak with aeons.

*More* than we experienced has gone by.
And the future holds the most remote event
in union with what we most deeply want.

## [III]

Brau uns den Zauber, in dem die Grenzen sich lösen,
immer zum Feuer gebeugter Geist!
Diese, vor allem, heimliche Grenze des Bösen,
die auch den Ruhenden, der sich nicht rührte, umkreist.

Löse mit einigen Tropfen das Engende jener
Grenze der Zeiten, die uns belügt;
denn wie tief ist in uns noch der Tag der Athener
und der ägyptische Gott oder Vogel gefügt.

Ruhe nicht eher, bis auch der Rand der Geschlechter,
der sich sinnlos verringenden, schmolz.
Öffne die Kindheit und die Schooße gerechter

gebender Mütter, daß sie, Beschämer der Leere,
unbeirrt durch das hindernde Holz
künftige Ströme gebären, Vermehrer der Meere.

# [III]

Brew us the magic in which all limits dissolve,
spirit forever bent to the fire!
That fathomless limit of evil, first, which revolves
also around those who are resting and do not stir.

Dissolve with a few drops whatever excludes in the limit
of the ages, which makes our past wisdom a fraud;
for how deeply we have absorbed the Athenian sunlight
and the mystery of the Egyptian falcon or god.

Don't rest until the boundary that keeps the sexes
in meaningless conflict has disappeared.
Open up childhood and the wombs of more truly expectant

generous mothers so that, shaming all that is empty,
and not confused by the hindering wood,
they may give birth to future rivers, augmenting the sea.

## [IV]

Mehr nicht sollst du wissen als die Stele
und im reinen Stein das milde Bild:
beinah heiter, nur so leicht als fehle
ihr die Mühe, die auf Erden gilt.

Mehr nicht sollst du fühlen als die reine
Richtung im unendlichen Entzug—
ach, vielleicht das Kaltsein jener Steine,
die sie manchmal abends trug.

Aber sonst sei dir die Tröstung teuer,
die du im Gewohntesten erkennst.
Wind ist Trost, und Tröstung ist das Feuer.

Hier- und Dortsein, dich ergreife beides
seltsam ohne Unterschied. Du trennst
sonst das Weißsein von dem Weiß des Kleides.

## [IV]

Seek no more than what the stela knows,
and the mild image sculpted in the stone:
almost cheerfully, with a lightness, as
though they were exempt from earthly pain.

Experience no further than the pure
direction in the world's withdrawing stream—
ah, perhaps the icy jewels she wore
in that dimly lighted room.

Be all the more consoled by what you see in
the elements that are most truly yours.
Wind consoles, and fire is consolation.

Here and There: you must be gripped by both,
strangely without a difference. Otherwise
you drain the whiteness from the whitest cloth.

# [V]

Denk: Sie hätten vielleicht aneinander erfahren,
welches die teilbaren Wunder sind—.
Doch da er sich langsam verrang an den alternden Jahren,
war sie die Künftige erst, ein kommendes Kind.

*Sie*, vielleicht—, *sie*, die da ging und mit Freundinnen
spielte,
hat er im knabigen schon, im Erahnen, ersehnt,
wissend das schließende Herz, das ihn völlig enthielte,
und nun trennt sie ein Nichts, ein verfünftes Jahrzehnt.

Oh du ratloser Gott, du betrogener Hymen,
wie du die Fackel nach abwärts kehrst,
weil sie ihm Asche warf an die grauende Schläfe.

Soll er klagend vergehn und die Beginnende rühmen?
Oder sein stillster Verzicht, wird er sie erst
machen zu jener Gestalt, die ihn ganz überträfe?

# [V]

Imagine: they might have experienced through each other
which of our miracles can be shared—.
But while he gradually wrestled with growing older,
she was as yet unborn, a still-future child.

*She*, perhaps—still playing with her friends, it was *she*
whom he had foreseen with boyish longing and love,
knowing the heart that would one day hold him completely;
and now a mere nothing parts them: a decade times five.

Oh you bewildered god, you defrauded Hymen,
how sadly you extinguish the wedding-torch now
because it flung ashes onto that graying head.

Must he die in laments, and praise the beginning woman?
Or through his most silent yielding will he make her into
that unmoving form by which he is wholly exceeded?

## [VI]

Aber, ihr Freunde, zum Fest, laßt uns gedenken der Feste,
wenn uns ein eigenes nicht, mitten im Umzug, gelingt.
Seht, sie meinen auch uns, alle der Villa d'Este
spielende Brunnen, wenn auch nicht mehr ein jeglicher
    springt.

Wir sind die Erben, trotzdem, dieser gesungenen Gärten;
Freunde, o faßt sie im Ernst, diese besitzende Pflicht.
Was uns als Letzten vielleicht glückliche Götter gewährten,
hat keinen ehrlichen Platz im zerstreuten Verzicht.

Keiner der Götter vergeh. Wir brauchen sie alle und jeden,
jedes gelte uns noch, jedes gestaltete Bild.
Laßt euch, was ruhig geruht, nicht in den Herzen zerreden.

Sind wir auch anders, als die, denen noch Feste gelangen,
dieser leistende Strahl, der uns als Stärke entquillt,
ist über große, zu uns, Aquädukte gegangen.

## [VI]

When everything we create is far in spirit from the festive,
in the midst of our turbulent days let us think of what
    festivals *were*.
Look, they still play for us also, all of the Villa d'Este's
glittering fountains, though some are no longer towering
    there.

Still, we are heirs to those gardens that poets once praised in
    their songs;
let us grasp our most urgent duty: to make them fully our
    own.
We perhaps are the last to be given such god-favored,
    fortunate Things,
their final chance to find an enduring home.

Let not one god pass away. We all need each of them now,
let each be valid for us, each image formed in the depths.
Don't speak with the slightest disdain of whatever the heart
    can know.

Though we are no longer the ones for whom great festivals
    thrived,
this accomplishing fountain-jet that surges to us as strength
has traveled through aqueducts—in order, for our sake, to
    arrive.

## [VII]

Welche Stille um einen Gott! Wie hörst du in ihr
jeden Wechsel im Auffall des Brunnenstrahls
am weilenden Wasser des Marmorovals.
Und am Lorbeer vorüber ein Fühlen: drei oder vier

Blätter, die ein Falter gestreift hat. An dir
taumelt er hin, im tragenden Atem des Tals.
Und du gedenkst eines anderen Mals,
da sie dir schon so vollkommen schien, hier,

diese Stille um einen Gott. Ward sie nicht *mehr*?
Nimmt sie nicht zu? Nimmt sie nicht überhand?
Drängt sie nicht fast wie ein Widerstand

an dein tönendes Herz? Irgendwo bricht sich sein Schlag
an einer lautlosen Pause im Tag . . .
Dort ist Er.

## [VII]

What silence around a god! How, inside it, you hear
every change in the sparkling fountain-spray
on the marble pool, as it leaps up and falls back entirely.
And over the laurel a feeling: three, perhaps four

leaves that a butterfly touched. With a whir
it goes tumbling past, on the buoyant breath of the valley.
And now you remember another day
when you felt it, already so perfect, here,

the silence around a god. But was it like this?
Isn't it spreading? Isn't it immense?
Isn't it pressing almost like a resistance

upon your resounding heart? Somewhere its beat is broken
on a soundless lull in the afternoon . . .
There, He is.

## [VIII]

Wir hören seit lange die Brunnen mit.
Sie klingen uns beinah wie Zeit.
Aber sie halten viel eher Schritt
mit der wandelnden Ewigkeit.

Das Wasser ist fremd und das Wasser ist dein,
von hier und *doch* nicht von hier.
Eine Weile bist du der Brunnenstein,
und es spiegelt die Dinge in dir.

Wie ist das alles entfernt und verwandt
und lange enträtselt und unerkannt,
sinnlos und wieder voll Sinn.

Dein ist, zu lieben, was du nicht weißt.
Es nimmt dein geschenktes Gefühl und reißt
es mit sich hinüber. Wohin?

## [VIII]

We have overheard fountains all our days.
They sound to us almost like time.
But much more closely do they keep pace
with eternity's subtle rhythm.

The water is strange and the water is yours,
from here and from far below.
You are the fountain-stone, unawares,
and all Things are mirrored in you.

How distant this is, yet deeply akin,
long unriddled and never known,
senseless, then perfectly clear.

Your task is to love what you don't understand.
It grips your most secret emotion, and
rushes away with it. Where?

## [IX]

Wann war ein Mensch je so wach
wie der Morgen von heut?
Nicht nur Blume und Bach,
auch das Dach ist erfreut.

Selbst sein alternder Rand,
von den Himmeln erhellt,—
wird fühlend: ist Land,
ist Antwort, ist Welt.

Alles atmet und dankt.
O ihr Nöte der Nacht,
wie ihr spurlos versankt.

Aus Scharen von Licht
war ihr Dunkel gemacht,
das sich rein widerspricht.

## [IX]

When was a *man* as awake
as this morning is?
Not just flower and brook:
the roof too rejoices.

Even its weathered rim,
lit by the sky—
finds it can feel: is home,
is answer, is day.

Everything breathes in accord.
How tracelessly you have gone
away, you cares of the night.

Its darkness was formed,
in pure contradiction,
from legions of light.

# [BRUCHSTÜCKE]

## [i]

So wie angehaltner Atem steht
steht die Nymphe in dem vollen Baume

## [ii]

Sieh hinauf. Heut ist der Nachtraum heiter.

## [iii]

Hoher Gott der fernen Vorgesänge
überall erfahr ich dich zutiefst
in der freien Ordnung mancher Hänge
stehn die Sträucher noch wie du sie riefst

## [iv]

Spiegel, du Doppelgänger des Raums! O Spiegel, in dich fort
stürzt die Hälfte der Lächeln / vielleicht die süßesten; denn
        wie
oft dem Meister der Strich, der probende, auf dem
vorläufigen Blatt blumiger aufschwingt, als später
auf dem bereiteten Grund der geführtere Umriß:
So, oh, lächelst du hin, Unsägliche, deiner
Morgen Herkunft und Freiheit in die immer
nehmenden Spiegel

## [v]

Immer, o Nymphe, seit je / hab ich dich staunend
        bewundert
ob du auch nie aus dem Baum mir dem verschlossenen
        tratst—.
Ich bin die Zeit die vergeht—, du bist ein junges
        Jahrhundert,
alles ist immer noch neu, was du von Göttern erbatst.

## [FRAGMENTS]

### [i]

Like held-in breath, serene and motionless
stands the nymph inside the ripening tree

### [ii]

Look up. How calm the heavens are tonight.

### [iii]

Lofty god of distant harmonies
I sense you everywhere deep in every Thing
upon the gently patterned slope the trees
stand silent as when first they heard you sing

### [iv]

Mirror, you doppelgänger of space! O mirror, into you go
plunging the halves of smiles / perhaps the sweetest; for how
often the master's preliminary brushstroke, upon the
provisional page more fruitfully leaps up than, later,
the more controlled outline does on the ready background:
So do you, O unsayable presence, smile forth
your morning's descent and freedom into the ever-
accepting mirrors

### [v]

Forever, O nymph, how long / I have marveled at you,
    amazed,
though you never stepped into my sight from out of the
    closed-in tree—.
I am the time that is passing—you are the youngest age,
all that you asked from the gods has remained here, forever
    new.

Dein ist die Wiese, sie schwankt noch jetzt von dem
    Sprunge,
jenem mit dem du zuletzt in die Ulme verschwandst.
Einst in der christlichen Früh. Und ist nicht, du junge,
*Dir* unser erstes Gefühl in den Frühling gepflanzt.

Eh uns ein Mädchen noch rührt, bist du die gemeinte

[vi]

. . . . . . . . . Braun's

. . . . . . . . an den sonoren
trockenen Boden des Walds
           trommelt das Flüchten des Fauns

[vii]

Dies ist das schweigende Steigen der Phallen

[viii]

Von meiner Antwort weiß ich noch nicht
wann ich sie sagen werde.
Aber, horch eine Harke, die schon schafft.
Oben allein im Weinberg spricht
schon ein Mann mit der Erde.

[ix]

Hast du des Epheus wechselnde Blättergestalten

[x]

Wahre dich besser
        wahre dich Wandrer
mit dem selber auch gehenden Weg

Yours is the meadow, even now it sways from the leap
with which you finally vanished into the elm.
Once, in the christian dawn. And our earliest hope:
for *your* sake isn't it planted into the springtime?

Before we are moved by a girl, it is you that we think
        of

[vi]

. . . . . . . . . . of the brown

. . . . . . . . . . on the sonorous
dried-up earth of the forest
                drums the flight of the faun

[vii]

This is the silent rising of the phalli

[viii]

About my answer: I still don't know
when I will bring it forth.
But listen, a harrow that already creates.
Up there in the vineyard someone, alone,
already speaks with the earth.

[ix]

Have you [?ever observed] the changing leaf-forms of
        the ivy

[x]

Protect yourself better
                protect yourself wanderer
with the road that is walking too

[xi]

Laß uns Legenden der Liebe hören.
Zeig uns ihr kühnes köstliches Leid.
Wo sie im Recht war, war alles Beschwören,
hier ist das meiste verleugneter Eid.

[xi]

Gather us now to hear love's legends.
Tell us of its daring, exquisite throes.
Where it was right, all things could be summoned;
here there are mostly abandoned vows.

*Notes*

## DUINO ELEGIES (1923)

The Elegies take their name from Duino Castle, on the Adriatic Sea, where Rilke spent the winter of 1911/1912 as a guest of his friend Princess Marie von Thurn und Taxis-Hohenlohe (1855–1934); they are dedicated to her in gratitude, as having belonged to her from the beginning.

Rilke later told me how these Elegies arose. He had felt no premonition of what was being prepared deep inside him; though there may be a hint of it in a letter he wrote: "The nightingale is approaching—" Had he perhaps felt what was to come? But once again it fell silent. A great sadness came over him; he began to think that this winter too would be without result.

Then, one morning, he received a troublesome business letter. He wanted to take care of it quickly, and had to deal with numbers and other such tedious matters. Outside, a violent north wind was blowing, but the sun shone and the water gleamed as if covered with silver. Rilke climbed down to the bastions which, jutting out to the east and west, were connected to the foot of the castle by a narrow path along the cliffs, which abruptly drop off, for about two hundred feet, into the sea. Rilke walked back and forth, completely absorbed in the problem of how to answer the letter. Then, all at once, in the midst of his thoughts, he stopped; it seemed that from the raging storm a voice had called to him: "Who, if I cried out, would hear me among the angels' hierarchies?"

He stood still, listening. "What is that?" he whispered. "What is coming?"

Taking out the notebook that he always carried with him, he wrote down these words, together with a few lines that formed by themselves without his intervention. He knew that the god had spoken.

Very calmly he climbed back up to his room, set his notebook aside, and answered the difficult letter.

By the evening the whole First Elegy had been written.

(Princess Marie von Thurn und Taxis-Hohenlohe,
*Erinnerungen an Rainer Maria Rilke*, p. 40 f.)

The Second Elegy was written shortly afterward, along with a number of fragments, the Third and most of the Sixth a year later, and the Fourth in 1915.

Then, after years of excruciating patience, the other Elegies came through during a few days in February 1922.

> My dear friend,
> late, and though I can barely manage to hold the pen, after several days of huge obedience in the spirit—, you must be told, today, right now, before I try to sleep:
>                                        I have climbed the mountain!
> At last! The Elegies are here, they exist. . . .
>                        So.
> Dear friend, now I can breathe again and, calmly, go on to something manageable. For this was larger than life—during these days and nights I have howled as I did that time in Duino—but, even after that struggle there, I didn't know that *such* a storm out of mind and heart could come over a person! That one has endured it! that one has endured.
>         Enough. They are here.
>         I went out into the cold moonlight and stroked the little tower of Muzot as if it were a large animal—the ancient walls that granted this to me.
>                          (To Anton Kippenberg, February 9, 1922)

A year before his death, Rilke wrote to his Polish translator:

> Affirmation of *life-AND-death* turns out to be one in the Elegies. . . . We of the here-and-now are not for a moment satisfied in the world of time, nor are we bound in it; we are continually overflowing toward those who preceded us, toward our origin, and toward those who seemingly come after us. In that vast "open" world, all beings *are*—one cannot say "contemporaneous," for the very fact that time has ceased determines that they all *are*. Everywhere transience is plunging into the depths of Being. . . . It is our task to imprint this temporary, perishable earth into ourselves so deeply, so painfully and passionately, that its essence can rise again, "invisibly," inside us. We are the bees of the invisible. We wildly collect the honey of the visible, to store it in the great golden hive of the invisible. The Elegies show us at this work, the work of the continual conversion of the beloved visible and tangible world into the invisible vibrations and agitation of our own nature . . . Elegies and Sonnets support each other con-

stantly—, and I consider it an infinite grace that, with the same breath, I was permitted to fill both these sails: the little rust-colored sail of the Sonnets and the Elegies' gigantic white canvas.

(To Witold Hulewicz, November 13, 1925)

The First Elegy (Duino, between January 12 and 16, 1912)

ll. 1 f., *among the angels'/hierarchies:*

The angel of the Elegies is that creature in whom the transformation of the visible into the invisible, which we are accomplishing, already appears in its completion . . . ; that being who guarantees the recognition of a higher level of reality in the invisible.—Therefore "terrifying" for us, because we, its lovers and transformers, still cling to the visible.

(To Witold Hulewicz, November 13, 1925)

"There is really *everything* in the old churches, no shrinking from anything, as there is in the newer ones, where only the 'good' examples appear. Here you see also what is bad and evil and horrible; what is deformed and suffering, what is ugly, what is unjust—and you could say that all this is somehow loved for God's sake. Here is the angel, who doesn't exist, and the devil, who doesn't exist; and the human being, who does exist, stands between them, and (I can't help saying it) their unreality makes him more real to me."

("The Young Workman's Letter," p. 313)

l. 5, *the beginning of terror:*

More and more in my life and in my work I am guided by the effort to correct our old repressions, which have removed and gradually estranged from us the mysteries out of whose abundance our lives might become truly infinite. It is true that these mysteries are dreadful, and people have always drawn away from them. But where can we find anything sweet and glorious that would never wear *this* mask, the mask of the dreadful? Life—and we know nothing else—, isn't life itself dreadful? But as soon as we acknowledge its dreadfulness (not as opponents: what kind of match could we be for it?), but somehow with a confidence that this very dreadfulness may be something completely *ours,* though something that is just now too great, too vast, too incomprehensible for our learning hearts—: as soon as we accept life's most terrifying dreadfulness, at the risk of perishing from it (i.e., from our own Too-much!)—: then an intuition of blessedness will open up for us and, at this cost, will be ours. Whoever does not, sometime or other, give his full consent, his full and *joyous* consent, to the dreadfulness of life, can never take possession of the unutterable abundance and power of our existence; can only walk on its edge, and one day, when the judgment is given, will have been neither alive nor dead. To show the *identity* of dreadfulness and bliss, these two faces on the same divine head, indeed this one *single* face, which just presents itself this way or that, according to our distance from it or the state of mind in which we perceive it—: this is the true significance and purpose of the Elegies and the Sonnets to Orpheus.

(To Countess Margot Sizzo-Noris-Crouy, April 12, 1923)

l. 13, *our interpreted world:*

> We, *with a word or finger-sign,*
> *gradually make the world our own,*
> *though perhaps its weakest, most precarious part.*

(Sonnets to Orpheus XVI, First Part)

l. 36, *women in love:*

Certainly I have no window on human beings. They yield themselves to me only insofar as they take on words within me, and during these last few years they have been communicating with me almost entirely through two forms, upon which I base my inferences about human beings in general. What speaks to me of humanity—immensely, with a calm authority that fills my hearing with space—is the phenomenon of those who have died young and, even more absolutely, purely, inexhaustibly: *the woman in love.* In these two figures humanity gets mixed into my heart whether I want it to or not. They step forward on my stage with the clarity of the marionette (which is an exterior entrusted with conviction) and, at the same time, as completed types, which nothing can go beyond, so that the definitive natural-history of their souls could now be written.

As for the woman in love (I am not thinking of Saint Theresa or such magnificence of that sort): she yields herself to my observation much more distinctly, purely, i.e., undilutedly and (so to speak) unappliedly in the situation of Gaspara Stampa, Louize Labé, certain Venetian courtesans, and, above all, Marianna Alcoforado, that incomparable creature, in whose eight heavy letters woman's love is for the first time charted from point to point, without display, without exaggeration or mitigation, drawn as if by the hand of a sibyl. And there—my God—there it becomes evident that, as a result of the irresistible logic of woman's heart, this line was finished, perfected, not to be continued any further in the earthly realm, and could be prolonged only toward the divine, into infinity.

(To Annette Kolb, January 23, 1912)

l. 46, *Gaspara Stampa* (1523–1554): An Italian noblewoman who wrote of her unhappy love for Count Collaltino di Collalto in a series of some two hundred sonnets.

l. 36, *those who died young:*

In Padua, where one sees the tombstones of many young men who died there (while they were students at the famous university), in Bologna, in Venice, in Rome, everywhere, I stood as a pupil of death: stood before death's boundless knowledge and let myself be educated. You must also remember how they lie resting in the churches of Genoa and Verona, those youthful forms, not envious of our coming and going, fulfilled within themselves, as if in their death-spasms they had for the first time bitten into the fruit of life, and were now, forever, savoring its unfathomable sweetness.

(To Magda von Hattingberg, February 16, 1914)

l. 67, *Santa Maria Formosa:* A church in Venice, which Rilke had visited in 1911. The reference is to one of the commemorative tablets, inscribed with Latin verses, on the church walls—probably the one that reads (in translation): "I lived for others while life lasted; now, after death, / I have not perished, but in cold marble I live for myself. / I was Willem Hellemans. Flanders mourns me, / Adria sighs for me, poverty calls me. / Died October 16, 1593."

l. 86, *through both realms:*

Death is the *side of life* that is turned away from us and not il-
luminated. We must try to achieve the greatest possible conscious-
ness of our existence, which is at home in *both these unlimited realms,*
and *inexhaustibly nourished by both.* The true form of life extends
through *both* regions, the blood of the mightiest circulation pulses
through *both:* there *is neither a this-world nor an other-world, but only
the great unity,* in which the "angels," those beings who surpass us,
are at home.

(To Witold Hulewicz, November 13, 1925)

l. 93, *the lament for Linus:* This ritual lament is mentioned in the *Iliad,* as part
of a scene that Hephaestus fashioned on the shield of Achilles:

Girls and young men, with carefree hearts and innocent laughter,
were carrying the honey-sweet grapes, piled up in wicker baskets;
in their midst, a boy performed the ancient music of yearning,
plucking his clear-toned lyre and singing the lament for Linus
with his lovely voice, while the others moved to the powerful rhythm,
their feet pounding in the dance, leaping and shouting for joy.

(*Iliad* 18, 567 ff.)

According to one myth, Linus was a poet who died young and was mourned
by Apollo, his father. Other versions state that he was the greatest poet of all
time and was killed by Apollo in a jealous rage; or that he invented music and
was the teacher of Orpheus.

The Second Elegy (Duino, late January–early February, 1912)

l. 3, *Tobias:* A young man in the apocryphal Book of Tobit. The story por-
trays, in passing, the easy, casual contact between a human being and an angel:
"And when he went to look for a man to accompany him to Rages, he found
Raphael, who was an angel. But Tobias did not know that. . . . And when
Tobias had prepared everything necessary for the journey, his father Tobit
said, 'Go with this man, and may God prosper your journey, and may the
angel of God go with you.' So they both departed, and the young man's dog
went along with them."

Tobit 5:4, 16 (in the Codex Vaticanus)

l. 12, *pollen of the flowering godhead:*

What is shown so beautifully in the world of plants—how they make no secret of their secret, as if they knew that it would always be safe—is exactly what I experienced in front of the sculptures in Egypt and what I have always experienced, ever since, in front of Egyptian Things: this exposure of a secret that is so thoroughly secret, through and through, in every place, that there is no need to hide it. And perhaps everything phallic (as I *fore*-thought in the temple of Karnak, for I couldn't yet think it) is just a setting-forth of the human hidden secret in the sense of the open secret of Nature. I can't remember the smile of the Egyptian gods without thinking of the word "pollen."

(To Lou Andreas-Salomé, February 20, 1914)

ll. 16 f., mirrors: *which scoop up the beauty . . . :*

The case of the Portuguese nun is so wonderfully pure because she doesn't fling the streams of her emotion on into the imaginary, but rather, with infinite strength, conducts this magnificent feeling back into herself: enduring *it,* and nothing else. She grows old in the convent, very old; she doesn't become a saint, or even a good nun. It is repugnant to her exquisite tact to apply to God what, from the very beginning, had never been intended for him, and what the Comte de Chamilly could disdain. And yet it was almost impossible to stop the heroic onrush of this love before its final leap: almost impossible, with such a powerful emotion pulsing in her innermost being, not to become a saint. If she—that measurelessly glorious creature—had yielded for even a moment, she would have plunged into God like a stone into the sea. And if it had pleased God to attempt with her what he continually does with the angels, casting all their radiance back into them—: I am certain that, immediately, just as she was, in that sad convent, she would have become an angel, in her deepest self.

(To Annette Kolb, January 23, 1912)

l. 20, *like a perfume:* The reference in the original text is to ambergris or incense burning on a hot coal. (Ernst Zinn, editor's note, SW 1, 792)

ll. 56–59, *you touch so blissfully because . . . / you feel pure duration:* In a letter to Princess Marie about her translation of this Elegy into Italian, Rilke wrote, "I am concerned about this passage, which is so dear to me," and after quoting it, he continued:

> This is meant quite literally: that the place where the lover puts his hand is thereby withheld from passing away, from aging, from all the near-disintegration that is always occurring in our integral nature— that simply beneath his hand, this place *lasts, is.* It must be possible, just as literally, to make this clear in Italian; in any paraphrase it is simply lost. Don't you agree? And I think of these lines with a special joy in having been able to write them.
>
> (To Princess Marie von Thurn und
> Taxis-Hohenlohe, December 16, 1913)

l. 66, *Weren't you astonished:* This is said to the lovers.

ll. 66 f., *the caution of human gestures / on Attic gravestones:*

> Once, in Naples I think, in front of some ancient gravestone, it flashed through me that I should never touch people with stronger gestures than the ones depicted there. And I really think that sometimes I get so far as to express the whole impulse of my heart, without loss or destiny, by gently placing my hand on someone's shoulder. Wouldn't that, Lou, wouldn't that be the only progress conceivable within the "restraint" that you ask me to remember?
>
> (To Lou Andreas-Salomé, January 10, 1912)

> One of his most definite emotions was to marvel at Greek gravestones of the earliest period: how, upon them, the mutual touching, the resting of hand in hand, the coming of hand to shoulder, was so completely unpossessive. Indeed, it seemed as if in these lingering gestures (which no longer operated in the realm of fate) there was no trace of sadness about a future parting, since the hands were not troubled by any fear of ending or any presentiment of change, since nothing approached them but the long, pure solitude in which they were conscious of themselves as the images of two distant Things that gently come together in the unprovable inner depths of a mirror.
>
> (Notebook entry, early November 1910; quoted in
> F.W. Wodtke, *Rilke und Klopstock,* Kiel diss., 1948, p. 28)

The Third Elegy (The beginning—probably the whole first section—: Duino, January/February 1912; continued and completed in Paris, late autumn 1913)

ll. 26 ff., *Mother, you made him small . . . :*

O night without objects. Dim, outward-facing window; doors that were carefully shut; arrangements from long ago, transmitted, believed in, never quite understood. Silence on the staircase, silence from adjoining rooms, silence high up on the ceiling. O mother: you who are without an equal, who stood before all this silence, long ago in childhood. Who took it upon yourself to say: Don't be afraid; I'm here. Who in the night had the courage to *be* this silence for the child who was frightened, who was dying of fear. You strike a match, and already the noise is you. And you hold the lamp in front of you and say: I'm here; don't be afraid. And you put it down, slowly, and there is no doubt: you are there, you are the light around the familiar, intimate Things, which are there without afterthought, good and simple and sure. And when something moves restlessly in the wall, or creaks on the floor: you just smile, smile transparently against a bright background into the terrified face that looks at you, searching, as if you knew the secret of every half-sound, and everything were agreed and understood between you. Does any power equal your power among the lords of the earth? Look: kings lie and stare, and the teller of tales cannot distract them. Though they lie in the blissful arms of their favorite mistress, horror creeps over them and makes them palsied and impotent. But you come and keep the monstrosity behind you and are entirely in front of it; not like a curtain it can lift up here or there. No: as if you had caught up with it as soon as the child cried out for you. As if you had arrived far ahead of anything that might still happen, and had behind you only your hurrying-in, your eternal path, the flight of your love.

> (*The Notebooks of Malte Laurids Brigge,* New York:
> Random House, 1983, p. 75 f.)

l. 82, *some confident daily task:*

In the long, complicated solitude in which *Malte* was written, I felt perfectly certain that the strength with which I paid for him originated to a great extent from certain evenings on Capri when nothing happened except that I sat near two elderly women and a girl and watched their needlework, and sometimes at the end was given an apple that one of them had peeled.

(To Lou Andreas-Salomé, January 10, 1912)

## The Fourth Elegy (Munich, November 22–23, 1915)

l. 27, *It at least is full:* This passage was influenced by Heinrich von Kleist's short essay-dialogue "On the Marionette Theater" (1810), which Rilke called "a masterpiece that again and again fills me with astonishment" (To Princess Marie, December 13, 1913). Kleist's character Herr C., in comparing the marionette and the human dancer, says that the marionette has two advantages:

First of all, a negative one: that it would never behave affectedly. . . . In addition, these puppets have the advantage that they are antigravitational. They know nothing of the inertia of matter, that quality which is most resistant to the dance: because the force that lifts them into the air is greater than the force that binds them to the earth. . . . Puppets need the ground only in order to touch it lightly, like elves, and reanimate the swing of their limbs through this momentary stop. We humans need it to rest on so that we can recover from the exertion of the dance. This moment of rest is clearly no dance in itself; the best we can do with it is to make it as inconspicuous as possible.

l. 35, *the boy with the immovable brown eye:* Rilke's cousin, who died at the age of seven. See note to Sonnets to Orpheus VIII, Second Part, p. 589.

Beside this lady sat the small son of a female cousin, a boy about as old as I, but smaller and more delicate. His pale, slender neck rose out of a pleated ruff and disappeared beneath a long chin. His lips were thin and closed tightly, his nostrils trembled a bit, and only one of his beautiful dark-brown eyes was movable. It sometimes glanced peacefully and sadly in my direction, while the other eye remained pointed toward the same corner, as if it had been sold and was no longer being taken into account.

(*The Notebooks of Malte Laurids Brigge,* p. 28)

l. 44, *within my deepest hope:*

As for myself, what has died for me has died, so to speak, into my own heart: when I looked for him, the person who vanished has collected himself strangely and so surprisingly *in* me, and it was so moving to feel he was now *only* there that my enthusiasm for serving his new existence, for deepening and glorifying it, took the upper hand almost at the very moment when pain would otherwise have invaded and devastated the whole landscape of my spirit. When I remember how I—often with the utmost difficulty in understanding and accepting each other—loved my father! Often, in childhood, my mind became confused and my heart grew numb at the mere thought that someday he might no longer be; my existence seemed to me so wholly conditioned through him (my existence, which from the start was pointed in such a different direction!) that his departure was to my innermost self synonymous with my own destruction . . . , but *so* deeply is death rooted in the essence of love that (if only we are cognizant of death without letting ourselves be misled by the uglinesses and suspicions that have been attached to it) it nowhere contradicts love: *where,* after all, can it drive out someone whom we have carried unsayably in our heart except into this very heart, where would the "idea" of this loved being exist, and his unceasing influence (: for *how* could *that* cease which even while he lived with us was more and more independent of his tangible presence) . . . where would this always secret influence be more secure than *in* us?! Where can we come closer to it, where more purely celebrate it, when obey it better, than when it appears combined with our own voices, as if our heart had learned a new language, a new song, a new strength!

(To Countess Margot Sizzo-Noris-Crouy, January 6, 1923)

l. 59, *Angel and puppet:* In Kleist's essay the narrator goes on to say that

no matter how cleverly he might present his paradoxes, he would never make me believe that a mechanical marionette could contain more grace than there is in the structure of the human body.

Herr C. replied that, in fact, it is impossible for a human being to be anywhere near as graceful as a marionette. Only a god can equal inanimate matter in this respect. Here is the point where the two ends of the circular world meet.

I was more and more astonished, and didn't know what I should say to such extraordinary assertions.

It seemed, he said, as he took a pinch of snuff, that I hadn't read the third chapter of the Book of Genesis with sufficient attention; and if a man wasn't familiar with that first period of all human develop-ment, one could hardly expect to converse with him about later peri-ods, and certainly not about the final ones.

I told him that I was well aware what disorders consciousness pro-duces in the natural grace of a human being. [Here follow two anec-dotes: the first about a young man who by becoming aware of his physical beauty loses it; the second about a pet bear who can easily parry the thrusts of the most accomplished swordsman.]

"Now, my dear fellow," said Herr C., "you are in possession of everything you need in order to understand the point I am making. We see that in the world of Nature, the dimmer and weaker intellect grows, the more radiantly and imperiously grace emerges. But just as a section drawn through two lines, considered from one given point, after passing through infinity, suddenly arrives on the other side of that point; or as the image in a concave mirror, after vanishing into infinity, suddenly reappears right in front of us: so grace too returns when knowledge has, as it were, gone through an infinity. Grace ap-pears most purely in that human form in which consciousness is ei-ther nonexistent or infinite, i.e., in the marionette or in the god."

"Does that mean," I said, a bit bewildered, "that we must eat again of the Tree of Knowledge in order to fall back into the state of innocence?"

"Certainly," he answered. "That is the last chapter in the history of the world."

There is a complete translation of the essay in TLS, October 20, 1978.

l. 77, *a pure event:*

Extensive as the "external" world is, with all its sidereal distances it hardly bears comparison with the dimensions, the *depth-dimensions,* of our inner being, which does not even need the spaciousness of the universe to be, in itself, almost unlimited. . . . It seems to me more and more as though our ordinary consciousness inhabited the apex of a pyramid whose base in us (and, as it were, beneath us) broadens out to such an extent that the farther we are able to let ourselves down into it, the more completely do we appear to be included in the realities of earthly and, in the widest sense, *worldly,* existence, which are not de-pendent on time and space. From my earliest youth I have felt the intuition (and have also, as far as I could, lived by it) that at some deeper cross-section of this pyramid of consciousness, mere *being* could become an event, the inviolable presence and simultaneity of everything that we, on the upper, "normal," apex of self-consciousness, are permitted to experience only as entropy.

(To Nora Purtscher-Wydenbruck, August 11, 1924)

The Fifth Elegy (Muzot, February 14, 1922)

This Elegy, the last one to be written, replaced "Antistrophes."

I had intended to make a copy of the other three Elegies for you today, since it is already Sunday again. But now—imagine!—in a radiant afterstorm, another Elegy has been added, the "Saltimbanques" ["Acrobats"]. It is the most wonderful completion; only now does the circle of the Elegies seem to me truly closed. It is not added on as the Eleventh, but will be inserted (as the Fifth) before the "Hero-Elegy." Besides, the piece that previously stood there seemed to me, because of its different kind of structure, to be unjustified in that place, though beautiful as a poem. The new Elegy will replace it (and how!), and the supplanted poem will appear in the section of "Fragmentary Pieces" which, as a second part of the book of Elegies, will contain everything that is contemporaneous with them, all the poems that time, so to speak, destroyed before they could be born, or cut off in their development to such an extent that the broken edges show.— And so now the "Saltimbanques" too exist, who even from my very first year in Paris affected me so absolutely and have haunted me ever since.

(To Lou Andreas-Salomé, February 19, 1922)

Dedication, *Frau Hertha Koenig:* The owner of Picasso's large (84" × 90 $\frac{3}{8}$") 1905 painting *La Famille des Saltimbanques,* which she had bought in December 1914. The painting made such a deep impression on Rilke that he wrote to Frau Koenig asking if he could stay in her Munich home while she was away for the summer of 1915, so that he could live beneath the great work, "which gives me the courage for this request." The request was granted, and Rilke spent four months with the "glorious Picasso."

The other source for the Fifth Elegy is Rilke's experience, over a number of years, with a troupe of Parisian circus people. See "Acrobats," p. 288.

l. 14, *the large capital D:* The five standing figures in Picasso's painting seem to be arranged in the shape of a D.

l. 17, *King Augustus the Strong* (1670–1733): King of Poland and elector of Saxony. To entertain his guests at the dinner table, he would, with one hand, crush together a thick pewter plate.

l. 64, *"Subrisio Saltat.":* "Acrobats' Smile." During the printing of the Elegies, Rilke explained this in a note on the proof sheets:

> As if it were the label on a druggist's urn; abbreviation of *Subrisio Saltat(orum).* The labels on these receptacles almost always appear in abbreviated form.
> (Ernst Zinn, "Mitteilungen zu R. M. Rilkes Ausgewählten
> Werken," in *Dichtung und Volkstum* 40, p. 132)

l. 92, *Madame Lamort:* Madame Death.

The Sixth Elegy (Begun at Duino, February/March 1912; lines 1–31: Ronda, January/February 1913; lines 42–44: Paris, late autumn 1913; lines 32–41: Muzot, February 9, 1922)

l. 8, *Like the god stepping into the swan:* Cf. "Leda" (*New Poems*).

l. 20, *Karnak:* Rilke spent two months in Egypt early in 1911 and was deeply moved by

> the incomprehensible temple-world of Karnak, which I saw the very first evening, and again yesterday, under a moon just beginning to wane: saw, saw, saw—my God, you pull yourself together and with all your might you try to believe your two focused eyes—and yet it begins above them, reaches out everywhere above and beyond them (only a god can cultivate such a field of vision) . . .
> (To Clara Rilke, January 18, 1911)

In *the team of galloping horses* (l. 19) Rilke is referring to the battle scenes carved on the huge pillars in the Temple of Amun, which depict the pharaoh-generals in their conquering chariots.

l. 31, *Samson:* Judges 13:2, 24; 16:25 ff.

The Seventh Elegy (Muzot, February 7, 1922; lines 87–end: February 26, 1922)

ll. 2 ff., *you would cry out as purely as a bird:*

The bird is a creature that has a very special feeling of trust in the external world, as if she knew that she is one with its deepest mystery. That is why she sings in it as if she were singing within her own depths; that is why we so easily receive a birdcall into our own depths; we seem to be translating it without residue into our own emotion; indeed, it can for a moment turn the whole world into inner space, because we feel that the bird does not distinguish between her heart and the world's.

(To Lou Andreas-Salomé, February 20, 1914)

l. 7, *the silent lover:*

> Learn, inner man, to look on your inner woman,
> the one attained from a thousand
> natures . . .

("Turning-point," p. 129)

ll. 34 f., *one earthly Thing / truly experienced:*

These Things, whose essential life you want to express, first ask you, "Are you free? Are you prepared to devote all your love to me, to lie with me as St. Julian the Hospitaller lay beside the leper, giving him the supreme embrace which no simple, fleeting love of one's neighbor could accomplish, because its motive is love, the whole of love, all the love that exists on earth." And if the Thing sees that you are otherwise occupied, with even a particle of your interest, it shuts itself off; it may perhaps give you some slight sign of friendship, a word or a nod, but it will never give you its heart, entrust you with its patient being, its sweet sidereal constancy, which makes it so like the constellations in the sky. In order for a Thing to speak to you, you must regard it for a certain time as *the only one that exists*, as the one and only phenomenon, which through your laborious and exclusive love is now placed at the center of the universe, and which, in that incomparable place, is on that day attended by angels.

(To Baladine Klossowska, December 16, 1920)

l. 36, *Don't think that fate is more than the density of childhood:*

What we call fate does not come to us from outside: it goes forth from within us.

(To Franz Xaver Kappus, August 12, 1904)

l. 37, *how often you outdistanced the man you loved:*

Woman has something of her very own, something suffered, accomplished, perfected. Man, who always had the excuse of being busy with more important matters, and who (let us say it frankly) was not at all adequately prepared for love, has not since antiquity (except for the saints) truly entered into love. The Troubadours knew very well how little they could risk, and Dante, in whom the need became great, only skirted around love with the huge arc of his gigantically evasive poem. Everything else is, in this sense, derivative and second-rate. . . . You see, after this very salutary interval I am expecting man, the man of the "new heartbeat," who for the time being is getting nowhere, to take upon himself, for the next few thousand years, his own development into the lover—a long, difficult, and, for him, completely new development. As for the woman—withdrawn into the beautiful contour she has made for herself, she will probably find the composure to wait for this slow lover of hers, without getting bored and without too much irony, and, when he arrives, to welcome him.

(To Annette Kolb, January 23, 1912)

l. 71, *in your endless vision:*

For the angel of the Elegies, all the towers and palaces of the past are existent *because* they have long been invisible, and the still-standing towers and bridges of our reality are *already* invisible, although still (for us) physically lasting. . . . All the worlds in the universe are plunging into the invisible as into their next-deeper reality; *a few stars intensify immediately and pass away in the infinite consciousness of the angels—, others are entrusted to beings who slowly and laboriously transform them, in whose terrors and delights they attain their next invisible realization. We,* let it be emphasized once more, *we, in the sense of the Elegies, are these transformers of the earth; our entire existence, the flights and plunges of our love, everything, qualifies us for this task* (beside which there is, essentially, no other).

(To Witold Hulewicz, November 13, 1925)

l. 73, *Pillars:*

. . . a calyx column stands there, alone, a survivor, and you can't encompass it, so far out beyond your life does it reach; only together with the night can you somehow take it in, perceiving it with the stars, as a whole, and then for a second it becomes human—a human experience.

(To Clara Rilke, January 18, 1911)

l. 73, *pylons:* "The monumental gateway to an Egyptian temple, usually formed by two truncated pyramidal towers connected by a lower architectural member containing the gate." (OED)

l. 73, *the Sphinx:* See note to the Tenth Elegy, ll. 73 ff., pp. 572 ff.

l. 84, *a woman in love—, oh alone at night by her window:* Cf. "Woman in Love" (*New Poems*).

l. 87, *filled with departure:*

I sometimes wonder whether longing can't radiate out from someone so powerfully, like a storm, that nothing can come to him from the opposite direction. Perhaps William Blake has somewhere drawn that—?

(To Princess Marie von Thurn und
Taxis-Hohenlohe, May 14, 1912)

The Eighth Elegy (Muzot, February 7/8, 1922)

Dedication, *Rudolf Kassner:* See note to "Turning-point," p. 232.

l. 2, *into the Open:*

> You must understand the concept of the "Open," which I have tried
> to propose in this Elegy, as follows: The animal's degree of conscious-
> ness is such that it comes into the world without at every moment
> setting the world over against itself (as we do). The animal is *in* the
> world; we stand *in front of* the world because of the peculiar turn and
> heightening which our consciousness has taken. So by the "Open" it
> is not sky or air or space that is meant; they, too, for the human being
> who observes and judges, are "objects" and thus "opaque" and
> closed. The animal or the flower presumably *is* all that, without ac-
> counting for itself, and therefore has before itself and above itself that
> indescribably open freedom which has its (extremely fleeting) equiva-
> lents for us perhaps only in the first moments of love, when we see our
> own vastness in the person we love, and in the ecstatic surrender to
> God.
>
> > (To Lev P. Struve, February 25, 1926, in Maurice Betz,
> > *Rilke in Frankreich: Erinnerungen—Briefe—Dokumente,*
> > Wien / Leipzig / Zürich: Herbert Reichner Verlag, 1937)

ll. 2 f., *Only* our *eyes are turned / backward:* In describing his experience of
"reaching the other side of Nature," Rilke uses the mirror image of this meta-
phor:

> Altogether, he was able to observe how all objects yielded themselves
> to him more distantly and, at the same time, somehow more truly;
> this might have been due to his own vision, which was no longer di-
> rected forward and diluted in empty space; he was looking, as if over
> his shoulder, *backward* at Things, and their now completed existence
> took on a bold, sweet aftertaste, as though everything had been spiced
> with a trace of the blossom of parting.
>
> > ("An Experience," p. 291)

l. 9, *Free from death:*

Nearby there was one of the darker birdcalls, a more mature one, already sung inwardly, which was to the others as a poem is to a few words—how it shone toward God, already, already, how devout it was, how filled with itself, a song-bud still in the calyx of its sound, but already aware of its own irrepressible fullness, pre-blissful and pre-afraid. Or rather, the fear was entirely there, the indivisible pain common to all creatures, which is as simple as the blissfulness over there, on the other side, where all has been surmounted.

(To Nanny Wunderly-Volkart, February 24, 1920)

l. 13, *fountain:* Here, as well as in the Ninth Elegy, l. 33, and Sonnets to Orpheus VIII, First Part, this is meant in its older sense of "a spring or source of water issuing from the earth and collecting in a basin, natural or artificial; also, the head-spring or source of a stream or river." (OED)

l. 53 ff., *Oh bliss of the tiny creature . . . :*

That a multitude of creatures which come from externally exposed seeds have *that* as their maternal body, that vast sensitive freedom—how much at home they must feel in it all their lives; in fact they do nothing but leap for joy in their mother's womb, like little John the Baptist; for this same space has both conceived them and brought them forth, and they never leave its security.

Until in the bird everything becomes a little more uneasy and cautious. The nest that Nature has given him is already a small maternal womb, which he only covers instead of wholly containing it. And suddenly, as if it were no longer safe enough outside, the wonderful maturing flees wholly into the darkness of the creature and emerges into the world only at a later turning-point, experiencing it as a second world and never entirely weaned from the conditions of the earlier, more intimate one.

(Rivalry between mother and world—)

(Notebook entry, February 20, 1914; SW 6, 1074 f.)

The Ninth Elegy (Lines 1–6a and 77–79: Duino, March 1912; the rest: Muzot, February 9, 1922)

l. 7, *happiness*:

> The reality of any joy in the world is indescribable; only in joy does
> creation take place (happiness, on the contrary, is only a promising,
> intelligible constellation of things already there); joy is a marvelous
> increasing of what exists, a pure addition out of nothingness. How
> superficially must happiness engage us, after all, if it can leave us time
> to think and worry about how long it will last. Joy is a moment, un-
> obligated, timeless from the beginning, not to be held but also not to
> be truly lost again, since under its impact our being is changed chemi-
> cally, so to speak, and does not only, as may be the case with happi-
> ness, savor and enjoy itself in a new mixture.
>
> (To Ilse Erdmann, January 31, 1914)

ll. 9 f., *the heart, which / would exist in the laurel too:*

> Hardly had she cried her breathless prayer
> when a numbness seized her body; her soft breasts
> were sealed in bark, her hair turned into leaves,
> her arms into branches; her feet, which had been so quick,
> plunged into earth and rooted her to the spot.
> Only her shining grace was left. Apollo
> still loved her; he reached out his hand to touch
> the laurel trunk, and under the rough bark
> could feel her heart still throbbing . . .
>
> (Ovid, Metamorphoses I, 548 ff.)

ll. 32 ff., *house, / bridge* . . . :

> Even for our grandparents a "house," a "well," a familiar tower, their
> very clothes, their coat, was infinitely more, infinitely more intimate;
> almost everything was a vessel in which they found what is human
> and added to the supply of what is human.
>
> (To Witold Hulewicz, November 13, 1925)

l. 59, *the rope-maker in Rome or the potter along the Nile:*

> I often wonder whether things unemphasized in themselves haven't
> exerted the most profound influence on my development and my
> work: the encounter with a dog; the hours I spent in Rome watching a

rope-maker, who in his craft repeated one of the oldest gestures in the world—as did the potter in a little village on the Nile; standing beside his wheel was indescribably and in a most mysterious sense fruitful for me. . . .

*(To Alfred Schaer, February 26, 1924)*

ll. 68 f., *to arise within us,* / *invisible:*

The Spanish landscape (the last one that I experienced absolutely), Toledo, pushed this attitude of mine to its extreme limit: because there the external Thing itself—tower, mountain, bridge—already possessed the extraordinary, unsurpassable intensity of those inner equivalents through which one might have wished to represent it. Everywhere appearance and vision merged, as it were, in the object; in each one of them a whole inner world was revealed, as though an angel who encompassed all space were blind and gazing into himself. This, a world seen no longer from the human point of view, but inside the angel, is perhaps my real task—one, at any rate, in which all my previous attempts would converge.

*(To Ellen Delp, October 27, 1915)*

l. 77, *our intimate companion, Death:*

We should not be afraid that our strength is insufficient to endure any experience of death, even the closest and most terrifying. Death is not *beyond* our strength; it is the measuring-line at the vessel's brim: we are *full* whenever we reach it—and being full means (for us) being heavy.—I am not saying that we should *love* death; but we should love life so generously, so without calculation and selection, that we involuntarily come to include, and to love, death too (life's averted half); this is in fact what always happens in the great turmoils of love, which cannot be held back or defined. Only because we exclude death, when it suddenly enters our thoughts, has it become more and more of a stranger to us; and because we have kept it a stranger, it has become our enemy. It is conceivable that it is infinitely closer to us than life itself—. What do we know of it?!

Prejudiced as we are against death, we do not manage to release it from all its distorted images. It is a *friend,* our deepest friend, perhaps the only one who can never be misled by our attitudes and vacillations—and this, you must understand, *not* in the sentimental-romantic sense of life's opposite, a denial of life: but our friend precisely when we most passionately, most vehemently, assent to being here, to living and working on earth, to Nature, to love. Life simultaneously says Yes and No. Death (I implore you to believe this!) is the true Yes-sayer. It says *only* Yes. In the presence of eternity.

(To Countess Margot Sizzo-Noris-Crouy, January 6, 1923)

The Tenth Elegy (Lines 1–12: Duino, January/February 1912; continued in Paris, late autumn 1913; new conclusion, lines 13–end: Muzot, February 11, 1922)

Lou, dear Lou, finally:
At this moment, Saturday, the eleventh of February, at 6 o'clock, I am putting down my pen after completing the last Elegy, the Tenth. The one (even then it was intended as the last one) whose first lines were already written in Duino: "Someday, emerging at last from the violent insight, / let me sing out jubilation and praise to assenting angels. . . ." What there was of it I once read to you; but only the first twelve lines have remained, all the rest is new and: yes, very, very glorious!—Imagine! I have been allowed to survive until this. Through everything. Miracle. Grace.

(To Lou Andreas-Salomé, February 11, 1922)

l. 20, *market of solace:*

Consolation is one of the many diversions we are subject to, a distraction, hence something essentially frivolous and unfruitful.—Even time doesn't "console," as people superficially say, at most it arranges, it sets in order—, and only because we later pay so little attention to the order toward which it so quietly collaborates that instead of marveling at what is now established and assuaged, reconciled in the great whole, we think it is some forgetfulness of our own, some weakness of heart, just because it no longer hurts us so much. Ah, how little the heart really forgets it,—and how strong it would be if we didn't withdraw its tasks from it before they are fully and truly accomplished!—Our instinct shouldn't be to want to console ourselves for such a loss, rather it should become our deep and painful curiosity to wholly explore it, the particularity, the uniqueness of precisely *this* loss, to discover its effect within our life, indeed we should summon up the noble avarice of enriching our inner world by precisely *it,* by its meaning and heaviness . . . The more deeply such a loss touches us and the more intensely it affects us, the more it becomes a *task,* of newly, differently, and finally taking into our possession what now, in its being lost, is accented with hopelessness: *this* then is unending accomplishment which immediately overcomes all negative qualities that cling to pain, all laziness and indulgence that always constitute a part of pain, this is active, inward-working pain, the only kind that makes sense and is worthy of us. I don't like the Christian ideas of a Beyond, I am getting farther and farther away from them, naturally without any thought of attacking them—; they may have a right to their existence beside so many other hypotheses about the divine periphery,—but for me they contain above all the danger not only of making those who have vanished more indistinct to us and above all more inaccessible—; but also we ourselves, because we allow our longing to pull us *away* from here, thereby become less definite, less earthly: which nevertheless, for the present, as long as we are *here* and related to tree, flower, and soil, we in a purest sense have to remain, even still have to become! . . . I reproach all modern religions for having provided their believers with consolations and glossings-over of death, instead of giving them the means of coming to an understanding with it. With it and with its full, unmasked cruelty: this cruelty is so immense that it is precisely with *it* that the circle closes: it leads back into a mildness which is greater, purer, and more perfectly clear (all consolation is muddy!) than we have ever, even on the sweetest spring day, imagined mildness to be. But toward the experiencing of this deepest mildness, which, if even a few of us were to feel it with conviction, could perhaps little by little penetrate and make transparent all the relations of life: toward the experiencing of *this* most rich and complete mildness mankind has never taken even the first steps,—unless in its most ancient, most innocent ages, whose secret is all but lost to us. The content of the "initiations" was, I am sure, nothing but the communicating of a "key" that allowed people to read the word "death" *without* negation; like the moon, surely life has a side permanently turned away from us which is *not* its opposite but its counterpart toward completion, toward wholeness, toward the actual perfect and full sphere and globe of *being.*

(To Countess Margot Sizzo-Noris-Crouy, January 6, 1923)

l. 21, *the church:*

The Christian experience enters less and less into consideration; the primordial God outweighs it infinitely. The idea that we are sinful and need to be redeemed as a prerequisite for God is more and more repugnant to a heart that has comprehended the earth. Sin is the most wonderfully roundabout path to God—but why should *they* go wandering who have never left him? The strong, inwardly quivering bridge of the Mediator has meaning only where the abyss between God and us is admitted—; but this very abyss is full of the darkness of God; and where someone experiences it, let him climb down and howl away inside it (that is more necessary than crossing it). Not until we can make even the abyss our dwelling-place will the paradise that we have sent on ahead of us turn around and will everything deeply and fervently of the here-and-now, which the Church embezzled for the Beyond, come back to us; then all the angels will decide, singing praises, in favor of the earth!

(To Ilse Jahr, February 22, 1923)

l. 62, *the vast landscape of Lament:*

The land of Lament, through which the elder Lament guides the dead youth, is *not* to be *identified* with Egypt, but is only, as it were, a reflection of the Nile-land in the desert clarity of the consciousness of the dead.

(To Witold Hulewicz, November 13, 1925)

ll. 73–88, *But as night approaches . . . / . . . the indescribable outline:*

Go look at the Head of Amenophis the Fourth in the Egyptian Museum in Berlin; feel, in this face, what it means to be opposite the infinite world and, within such a limited surface, through the intensified arrangement of a few features, to form a weight that can balance the whole universe. Couldn't one turn away from a starry night to find the same law blossoming in this face, the same grandeur, depth, inconceivableness? By looking at such Things I learned to see; and when, later, in Egypt, many of them stood before me, in their extreme individuality, insight into them poured over me in such waves that I lay for almost a whole night beneath the great Sphinx, as though I had been vomited out in front of it by my whole life.

You must realize that it is difficult to be alone there; it has become a public square; the most irrelevant foreigners are dragged in *en masse*. But I had skipped dinner; even the Arabs were sitting at a distance, around their fire; one of them noticed me, but I got away by buying two oranges from him; and then the darkness hid me. I had waited for nightfall out in the desert, then I came in slowly, the Sphinx at my back, figuring that the moon must already be rising (for there was a full moon) behind the nearest pyramid, which was glowing intensely in the sunset. And when at last I had come around it, not only was the moon already far up in the sky, but it was pouring out such a stream of brightness over the endless landscape that I had to dim its light with my hand, in order to find my way among the heaps of rubble and the excavations. I found a place to sit down on a slope near the Sphinx, opposite that gigantic form, and I lay there, wrapped in my coat, frightened, unspeakably taking part. I don't know whether my existence ever emerged so completely into consciousness as during those night hours when it lost all value: for what was it in comparison with all that? The dimension in which it moved had passed into darkness; everything that is world and existence was happening on a higher plane, where a star and a god lingered in silent confrontation. You too can undoubtedly remember experiencing how the view of a landscape, of the sea, of the great star-flooded night inspires us with the sense of connections and agreements beyond our understanding. It was precisely this that I experienced, to the highest degree; here there arose an image built on the pattern of the heavens; upon which thousands of years had had no effect aside from a little contemptible decay; and most incredible of all was that this Thing had human features (the fervently recognizable features of a human face) and that, in such an exalted position, these features were enough. Ah, my dear—I said to myself, "This, this, which we alternately thrust into fate and hold in our own hands: it must be capable of some great significance if even in such surroundings its form can persist." This face had taken on the customs of the universe; single parts of its gaze and smile were damaged, but the rising and setting of the heavens had mirrored into it emotions that had endured. From time to time I closed my eyes and, though my heart was pounding, I reproached myself for not ex- periencing this deeply enough; wasn't it necessary to reach places in my astonishment where I had never been before? I said to myself, "Imagine, you could have been carried here blindfolded and been set down on a slope in the deep, barely-stirring coolness—you wouldn't have known where you were and you would have opened your eyes—" And when I really did open them, dear God: it took quite a long time for them to endure it, to take in this immense being, to achieve the mouth, the cheek, the forehead, upon which moonlight and moonshadows passed from expression to expression. How many times already had my eyes attempted this full cheek; it rounded itself out so slowly that there seemed to be room up there for *more* places than in our world. And then, as I gazed at it, I was suddenly, unex- pectedly, taken into its confidence, I received a knowledge of that cheek, experienced it in the perfect emotion of its curve. For a few moments I didn't grasp what had happened. Imagine: this: Behind the great projecting crown on the Sphinx's head, an owl had flown up and had slowly, indescribably *audibly* in the pure depths of the night, brushed the face with her faint flight: and now, upon my hearing, which had grown very acute in the hours-long nocturnal silence, the outline of that cheek was (as though by a miracle) inscribed.

(To Magda von Hattingberg, February 1, 1914)

l. 108, *hazel-trees:* Rilke had originally written "willows"; this was corrected on the advice of a friend, who sent him a small handbook of trees and shrubs.

What a kind thought it was of yours to introduce me so clearly and thoroughly to the elements of "catkinology" with your book and the explanatory letter; after this there is no need for further or more exact information: I am convinced! So (remarkably enough) there are no "hanging" willow catkins; and even if there were some rare, tropical exception, I still would not be able to use it. The place in the poem that I wanted to check for factual accuracy stands or falls according to whether the reader can understand, with his *first* intuition, precisely this *falling* of the catkins; otherwise, the image loses all meaning. So the absolutely *typical* appearance of this inflorescence must be evoked—and I immediately realized from the very instructive illustrations in your little book that the shrub which, years ago, supplied me with the impression I have now used in my work must have been a hazelnut tree; whose branches are furnished most densely, *before* the leaves come out, with long, perpendicularly hanging catkins. So I know what I needed to know and have changed the text from "willow" to "hazel."

(To Elisabeth Aman-Volkart, June 1922)

## APPENDIX TO DUINO ELEGIES

[Fragment of an Elegy] (Duino, late January 1912)

Written between the First and Second Elegies.

[Original Version of the Tenth Elegy] (Lines 1–15: Duino, January / February 1912; continued in Paris, late in 1913)

Antistrophes (Lines 1–4: Venice, summer 1912; the rest: Muzot, February 9, 1922)

See note to the Fifth Elegy, p. 561.

*Antistrophe:* "The returning movement, from left to right, in Greek choruses and dances, answering to the previous movement of the strophe from right to left; hence, the lines of choral song recited during this movement." (OED)

## THE SONNETS TO ORPHEUS (1923)

These strange Sonnets were no intended or expected work; they appeared, often *many* in one day (the first part of the book was written in about three days), completely unexpectedly, in February of last year, when I was, moreover, about to gather myself for the continuation of those other poems—the great Duino Elegies. I could do nothing but submit, purely and obediently, to the dictation of this inner impulse; and I understood only little by little the relation of these verses to the figure of Vera Knoop, who died at the age of eighteen or nineteen, whom I hardly knew and saw only a few times in her life, when she was still a child, though with extraordinary attention and emotion. Without my arranging it this way (except for a few poems at the beginning of the second part, all the Sonnets kept the chronological order of their appearance), it happened that only the next-to-last poems of both parts explicitly refer to Vera, address her, or evoke her figure.

This beautiful child, who had just begun to dance and attracted the attention of everyone who saw her, by the art of movement and transformation which was innate in her body and spirit—unexpectedly declared to her mother that she no longer could or would dance (this happened just at the end of childhood). Her body changed, grew strangely heavy and massive, without losing its beautiful Slavic features; this was already the beginning of the mysterious glandular disease that later was to bring death so quickly. During the time that remained to her, Vera devoted herself to music; finally she only drew—as if the denied dance came forth from her ever more quietly, ever more discreetly.

(To Countess Margot Sizzo-Noris-Crouy, April 12, 1923)

Even to me, in the way they arose and imposed themselves on me, they are perhaps the most mysterious, most enigmatic dictation I have ever endured and achieved; the whole first part was written down in a single breathless obedience.

(To Xaver von Moos, April 20, 1923)

I myself have only now, little by little, comprehended them and found a way to pass them on;—with brief comments that I insert when I read them aloud, I am able to make the whole more intelligible; interconnections are established everywhere, and where a darkness remains, it is the kind of darkness that requires not clarification but surrender.

(To Clara Rilke, April 23, 1923)

. . . *we, in the sense of the Elegies, are these transformers of the earth; our entire existence, the flights and plunges of our love, everything, qualifies us for this task* (beside which there is, essentially, no other). (The Sonnets show particular examples of this activity, which appears in them, placed under the name and protection of a dead girl, whose incompletion and innocence holds open the grave-door so that, having passed on, she belongs to those powers which keep the one half of life fresh, and open toward the other, wound-open half.)

(To Witold Hulewicz, November 13, 1925)

I say "sonnets." Though they are the freest, most (as it were) conjugated poems that have ever been included under this usually so motionless and stable form. But precisely this—to conjugate the sonnet, to intensify it, to give it the greatest possible scope without destroying it—was for me a strange experiment: which, in any case, I made no conscious decision to undertake. So strongly was it imposed, so fully did it contain its solution in itself.

(To Katharina Kippenberg, February 23, 1922)

Today just one favor more, which I have been wanting to ask of you for a long time: could you eventually have printed for me one copy of the "Sonnets to Orpheus," and perhaps also one copy of the "Elegies," interleaved with blank pages, using paper that can absorb good ink without making it "bleed"? I would like to append brief commentaries here and there to the more difficult poems, for my own use and for the benefit of a few friends; it would be a curious work, in which I would strangely have to account for the place of this verse within my own inner proportions. Whether or not that happens, I would in any case be glad to have both books, especially the "Sonnets," prepared in this way, so that I can make notes in it whenever I feel the inclination. (There is no hurry, of course!)

(To Anton Kippenberg, March 11, 1926)

## FIRST PART

I (Muzot, February 2/5, 1922)

II (Muzot, February 2/5, 1922)

l. 1, *almost a girl:*

Siehe, innerer Mann, dein inneres Mädchen

*Look, inner man, at your inner girl*

("Turning-point," p. 129)

The deepest experience of the creative artist is feminine, for it is an experience of conceiving and giving birth. The poet Obstfelder once wrote, speaking of the face of a stranger: "When he began to speak, it was as though a *woman* had taken a seat within him." It seems to me that every poet has had that experience in beginning to speak.

(To a young woman, November 20, 1904)

III (Muzot, February 2/5, 1922)

ll. 3f., *crossing / of heart-roads:* "The sanctuaries that stood at crossroads in classical antiquity were dedicated to sinister deities like Hecate, not to Apollo, the bright god of song." (Hermann Mörchen, *Rilkes Sonette an Orpheus*, Stuttgart: W. Kohlhammer Verlag, 1958, p. 66)

l. 13, *True singing:*

It is not only the *hearable* in music that is important (something can be pleasant to hear without being *true*). What is decisive for me, in all the arts, is not their outward appearance, not what is called the "beautiful"; but rather their deepest, most inner origin, the buried reality that calls forth their appearance.

(To Princess Marie von Thurn und Taxis-Hohenlohe, November 17, 1912)

l. 14, *A gust inside the god. A wind.:*

All in a few days, it was a nameless storm, a hurricane in the spirit (like that time at Duino), everything that was fiber and fabric in me cracked.

(Ibid., February 11, 1922, just after the completion of the Elegies)

Never have I gone through such tremendous gales of being-taken-hold-of: I was an element, Liliane, and could do everything elements can do.

(To Claire Studer-Goll, April 11, 1923)

IV (Muzot, February 2/5,1922)

V (Muzot, February 2/5, 1922)

l. 5, *It is Orpheus once for all:*

> Ultimately there is only *one* poet, that infinite one who makes himself
> felt, here and there through the ages, in a mind that can surrender to
> him.
>
> (To Nanny Wunderly-Volkart, July 29, 1920)

> True art can issue only from a purely anonymous center.
>
> (To R. S., November 22, 1920)

VI (Muzot, February 2/5, 1922)

l. 2, *both realms:*

> Angels (they say) don't know whether it is the living
> they are moving among, or the dead. The eternal torrent
> whirls all ages along in it, through both realms
> forever, and their voices are drowned out in its thunderous roar.
>
> (The First Elegy, ll. 92 ff.)

l. 4, *willow-branch:* From Psalm 137, to Desdemona's song, to modern poetry,
the willow has been a symbol of grief. Its association with the dead goes back at
least as far as Homer:

> But when the North Wind has breathed you across the River of Ocean,
> you will come to a wooded coast and the Grove of Persephone,
> dense with shadowy poplars and willows that shed their seeds.
> Beach your boat on that shore as the ocean-tide foams behind you;
> then walk ahead by yourself, into the Land of Decay.
>
> (Odyssey X, 508 ff.)

l. 10, *earthsmoke and rue:* Herbs used in summoning the dead.

> But slowly growing beside it is patience, that delicate "earthsmoke."
>
> (To Gudi Nölke, October 5, 1919)

l. 11, *connection:*

The comprehensible slips away, is transformed; instead of possession one learns connection.

(To Ilse Jahr, February 22, 1923)

VII (Muzot, February 2/5, 1922)

l. 9, *decay in the sepulcher of kings:*

It is true, the gods have neglected no opportunity of exposing us: they let us uncover the great kings of Egypt in their tombs, and we were able to see them in their natural decay, how they were spared no indignity.

("On the Young Poet," p. 293 f.)

VIII (Muzot, February 2/5, 1922)

IX (Muzot, February 2/5, 1922)

X (Muzot, February 2/5, 1922)

l. 2, *coffins of stone:* Used as troughs or basins in the fountains of Italian towns.

> Da wurde von den alten Aquädukten
> ewiges Wasser in sie eingelenkt . . .

> *Then, eternal water from the ancient*
> *aqueducts was channeled into them . . .*
> ("Roman Sarcophagi," *New Poems*)

l. 5, *those other ones:*

(what is being referred to, after the Roman ones, are those other, uncovered sarcophagi in the famous cemetery of Aliscamps, out of which flowers bloom)

—Rilke's note

l. 6, *shepherd:* See "The Spanish Trilogy," pp. 103 f.

l. 7, *bee-suck nettle: Lamium album,* white dead-nettle.

XI (Muzot, February 2/5, 1922)

    l. 1, *"Rider":*

>           —Look, there:
> the *Rider,* the *Staff,* and the larger constellation
> called *Garland of Fruit.*
>             (The Tenth Elegy, p. 395.)

XII (Muzot, February 2/5, 1922)

    l. 7, *antennas:*

> Oh how she [Vera] loved, how she reached out with the antennas of
> her heart beyond everything that is comprehensible and embraceable
> here— . . .
>         (To Gertrud Ouckama Knoop, January 1922)

XIII (Muzot, February 2/5, 1922)

>     Comme le fruit se fond en jouissance,
>     Comme en délice il change son absence
>     Dans une bouche où sa forme se meurt, . . .
>         (Valéry, "Le Cimetière Marin")

> *So wie die Frucht sich auflöst im Genusse,*
> *Abwesenheit Entzücken wird zum Schlusse*
> *in einem Mund, drin ihre Form verschwand,* . . .
>     (Rilke's translation, March 14 and 16, 1921)

l. 9, *"apple":*

> At various times I have had the experience of feeling apples, more
> than anything else—barely consumed, and often while I was still eat-
> ing them—being transposed into spirit. Thus perhaps the Fall. (If
> there *was* one.)
>         (To Princess Marie von Thurn und
>         Taxis-Hohenlohe, January 16, 1912)

XIV (Muzot, February 2/5, 1922)

XV (Muzot, February 2/5, 1922)

XVI (Muzot, February 2/5, 1922)

> One has to know—or guess—that Sonnet XVI is addressed to a dog; I didn't want to add a note to this effect, precisely because I wanted to take him completely into the whole. Any hint would just have isolated him again, singled him out. (This way he takes part down below, belonging and warned, like the dog and the child in Rembrandt's Night Watch.)
>
> (To Clara Rilke, April 23, 1923)

> Now it is my turn to thank you, not for Pierrot, for God's sake *no:* it would be his ruin, Pierrot's ruin, the saddest story in the world. How could you even think I might adopt him, what kind of match could I be for his boundless homesickness? Furthermore, apart from the torment of helplessly looking on, I would have the additional torment of sacrificing myself for his sake, which I find especially painful where dogs are involved: they touch me so deeply, these beings who are entirely dependent on us, whom we have helped up to a soul for which there is no heaven. Even though I need all of my heart, it is probable that this would end, end tragically, by my breaking off little pieces from the edge of it at first, then bigger and bigger pieces toward the middle (like dog biscuits) for this Pierrot as he cried for you and no longer understood life; I would, after hesitating for a little while, give up my writing and live entirely for his consolation.
>
> (To N. N., February 8, 1912)

l. 7, *You know the dead:*

> "And I was about to (I feel quite cold, Malte, when I think of it), but, God help me, I was just about to say, 'Where is . . .'—when Cavalier shot out from under the table, as he always did, and ran to meet her. I saw it, Malte; I saw it. He ran toward her, although she wasn't coming; for him she *was* coming."
>
> (*The Notebooks of Malte Laurids Brigge,* p. 89)

ll. 11f., *don't plant / me inside your heart:*

"In the end a responsibility would arise, which I can't accept. You wouldn't notice how completely you had come to trust me; you would overvalue me and expect from me what I can't perform. You would watch me and approve of everything, even of what is unworthy. If I want to give you a joy: will I find one? And if one day you are sad and complain to me—will I be able to help you? —And you shouldn't think that *I* am the one who lets you die. Go away, I beg of you: go away."

("A Meeting," p. 285)

l. 13, my *master's hand:*

In the poem *to the dog,* by "my master's hand" the hand of the god is meant; here, of "Orpheus." The poet wants to guide this hand so that it too may, for the sake of his [the dog's] infinite sympathy and devotion, bless the dog, who, almost like Esau, has put on his pelt only so that he could share, in his heart, an inheritance that would never come to him: could participate, with sorrow and joy, in all of human existence.

(To Countess Margot Sizzo-Noris-Crouy, June 1, 1923)

XVII (Muzot, February 2/5, 1922)

XVIII (Muzot, February 2/5, 1922)

XIX (Muzot, February 2/5, 1922)

XX (Muzot, February 2/5, 1922)

And imagine, one thing *more,* in another connection (in the "Sonnets to Orpheus," twenty-five sonnets, written, suddenly, in the prestorm, as a monument for Vera Knoop), I wrote, *made,* the *horse,* you know, the free happy white horse with the hobble on his foot, who once, as evening fell, on a Volga meadow, came bounding toward us at a gallop—:

*how*

I made him, as an "ex-voto" for Orpheus!—What is time?—*When* is

Now? Across so many years he bounded, with his absolute happiness, into my wide-open feeling.

(To Lou Andreas-Salomé, February 11, 1922)

There is also an account of the incident in Lou Andreas-Salomé's travel diary:

As we were standing by the Volga, a neigh resounded through the silent evening, and a frisky little horse, having finished its day of work, came quickly trotting toward the herd, which was spending the night somewhere, far away, in the meadow-steppes. In the distance one could now and then see the shepherds' fire blazing in the clear night. After a while a second little horse, from somewhere else, followed, more laboriously: they had tied a wooden hobble to one of his legs, in order to stop him from wildly leaping into the wheatfield.

(*Briefwechsel*, p. 611)

l. 13, *cycle of myths:*

It is done, *done! /* The blood- and myth-cycle of ten (ten!) strange years has been completed.—It was (now for the first time I feel it entirely) like a mutilation of my heart, that this did not exist. And now it is here.

(To Nanny Wunderly-Volkart, February 10, 1922)

XXI (Muzot, February 9, 1922; inserted here as a replacement for the original sonnet; see p. 525)

The little spring-song seems to me, as it were, an "interpretation" of a remarkable, dancing music that I once heard sung by the convent children at a morning Mass in the little church at Ronda (in southern Spain). The children, who kept leaping to a dance rhythm, sang a text I didn't know, to the accompaniment of triangle and tambourine.

—Rilke's note*

---

*This and the note to Sonnet XI, Second Part are the only two notes Rilke himself ever published. The others marked "Rilke's note" were handwritten in a copy of the Sonnets which he sent to Herr and Frau Leopold von Schlözer on May 30, 1923.

If the Sonnets to Orpheus were allowed to reach publication, probably two or three of them, which, I now see, just served as conduits for the stream (e.g., the XXIst) and after its passage-through remained empty, would have to be replaced by others.

(To Gertrud Ouckama Knoop, February 7, 1922)

It makes me uncomfortable to think of that XXIst poem, the "empty" one in which the "transmissions" appear ("The New, my friends, is not a matter of") . . . , please paste it over, right now, with this child's-spring-song, written today, which, I think, enriches the sound of the whole cycle and stands fairly well, as a pendant, opposite the white horse.

This little song, which had risen into my consciousness when I woke up this morning, fully formed up to the eighth line, and the rest of it immediately afterward, appears to me like an interpretation of a "Mass"—a real *Mass,* gaily accompanied as if with hanging garlands of sound: the convent children sang it to I don't know what text, but in this dance-step, in the little nuns'-church at Ronda (in southern Spain—); sang it, one can hear, to tambourine and triangle!—It fits, doesn't it, into these interrelationships of the Sonnets to Orpheus: as the brightest spring-tone in them? (I think it does.)

(Does the paper more-or-less match? I hope it is the same.)

Only this—and only because that XXIst is like a blot on my conscience.

(To Gertrud Ouckama Knoop, February 9, 1922)

XXII (Muzot, February 2/5, 1922)

XXIII (Muzot, February 13, 1922)

This Sonnet I have—at least temporarily—inserted as the XXIII, so that what has become the *first* part of the Sonnets now contains twenty-six poems.

(To Gertrud Ouckama Knoop, March 18, 1922)

XXIV (Muzot, February 2/5, 1922)

XXV (Muzot, February 2/5, 1922)

(to Vera)

—Rilke's note

XXVI (Muzot, February 2/5, 1922)

l. 2, *rejected:*

> Three years went by, but Orpheus still refused
> to love another woman: so intense
> his grief was, for his lost Eurydice;
> or else because he had vowed to stay alone.
> But many women desired him, and raged
> at his abrupt rejection.
>
> (Ovid, Metamorphoses X, 78 ff.)

l. 2, *attacked:*

> From a nearby hill the frenzied women, bristling
> in skins of savage beasts, at last caught sight
> of Orpheus, as he sat absorbed in music,
> accompanied by the sweet lyre. One of them,
> her long hair streaming in the wind, cried out:
> "Look! there he is, that man who shows us such
> contempt." And, with a yell, she hurled her spear
> straight at the singing mouth . . .
>
> (Ibid. XI, 3 ff.)

l. 5, *could not destroy your head or your lyre:*

> His limbs lay scattered; but the river Hebrus
> took the head and lyre, and as they floated
> down its stream, the lyre began to play
> a mournful tune, and the lifeless tongue sang out
> mournfully, and both the river-banks
> answered, with their own, faint, mournful echo.
>
> (Ibid. XI, 50 ff.)

l. 7, *stones:*

> Another threw a stone; but in mid-flight,
> overwhelmed by the beauty of the song,
> it fell at his feet, as though to beg forgiveness
> for its violent intention.
>
> (Ibid. XI, 10 ff.)

l. 9, *At last they killed you:*

> Such music would have moved to softness all
> these stones and spears; except that the wild shrieking,
> shrill flutes, the blare of trumpets, drumbeats, howls
> of the enraged bacchantes had completely
> drowned out the lyre's voice. Until at last
> the unhearing stones reddened with poet's blood.
>
> (Ibid. XI, 15 ff.)

## SECOND PART

I (Muzot, approximately February 23, 1922; the last of the Sonnets to be written)

II (Muzot, February 15/17, 1922)

III (Muzot, February 15/17, 1922)

l. 7, *sixteen-pointer:* A large stag, with sixteen points or branches to its antlers.

IV (Muzot, February 15/17, 1922)

Any "allusion," I am convinced, would contradict the indescribable *presence* of the poem. So in the unicorn no parallel with Christ is intended; rather, all love of the non-proven, the non-graspable, all belief in the value and reality of whatever our heart has through the centuries created and lifted up out of itself: that is what is praised in this creature. . . . The unicorn has ancient associations with virginity, which were continually honored during the Middle Ages. Therefore this Sonnet states that, though it is nonexistent for the profane, it comes into being as soon as it appears in the "mirror" which the virgin holds up in front of it (see the tapestries of the 15th century) and "in her," as in a second mirror that is just as pure, just as mysterious.

(To Countess Margot Sizzo-Noris-Crouy, June 1, 1923)

V (Muzot, February 15, 1922; chronologically the first poem of the Second Part)

l. 7, so *overpowered with abundance:*

I am like the little anemone I once saw in the garden in Rome: it had opened so wide during the day that it could no longer close at night. It was terrifying to see it in the dark meadow, wide open, still taking everything in, into its calyx, which seemed as if it had been furiously torn back, with the much too vast night above it. And alongside, all its prudent sisters, each one closed around its small measure of profusion.

(To Lou Andreas-Salomé, June 26, 1914)

VI (Muzot, February 15, 1922)

the rose of antiquity was a simple "eglantine," red and yellow, in the colors that appear in flame. It blooms here, in the Valais, in certain gardens.

—Rilke's note

Every day, as I contemplate these admirable white roses, I wonder whether they aren't the most perfect image of that unity—I would even say, that identity—of absence and presence which perhaps constitutes the fundamental equation of our life.

(To Madame M.-R., January 4, 1923)

VII (Muzot, February 15/17, 1922)

By the brook I picked marsh-marigolds, almost green, a bit of quite fresh yellow painted into the calyx at the last moment. Inside, around the stamens, an oil-soaked circle, as if they had eaten butter. Green smell from the tubelike stems. Then to find it left behind on my hand, closely related through it. Girl friends, long ago in childhood, with their hot hands: was it this that so moved me?

(Spanish Notebook, 1913; quoted in *Rilke und Benvenuta,* Wien: W. Andermann, 1943, p. 157)

VIII (Muzot, February 15/17, 1922)

l. 4, *the lamb with the talking scroll:*

The lamb (in medieval paintings) which speaks only by means of a scroll with an inscription on it.

—Rilke's note

Dedication, *Egon von Rilke* (1873–1880): Youngest child of Rilke's father's brother. He also appears in the Fourth Elegy, p. 353.

I think of him often and keep returning to his image, which has remained indescribably moving to me. So much "childhood"—the sad and helpless side of childhood—is embodied for me in his form, in the ruff he wore, his little neck, his chin, his beautiful disfigured eyes. So I evoked him once more in connection with that eighth sonnet, which expresses transience, after he had already served, in the Notebooks of Malte Laurids Brigge, as the model for little Erik Brahe, who died in childhood.

(To Phia Rilke, January 24, 1924; in Carl Sieber, *René Rilke: Die Jugend Rainer Maria Rilkes,* Leipzig: Insel Verlag, 1932, pp. 59 f.)

IX (Muzot, February 15/17, 1922)

X (Muzot, February 15/17, 1922)

XI (Muzot, February 15/17, 1922)

Refers to the way in which, according to an ancient hunting-custom in certain regions of Karst, the strangely pale grotto-doves are caught. Hunters carefully lower large pieces of cloth into the caverns and then suddenly shake them. The doves, frightened out, are shot during their terrified escape.

—Rilke's note

Meanwhile I went along on a dove-hunting expedition to one of the Karst grottos, quietly eating juniper berries while the hunters forgot me in their concentration on the beautiful wild doves flying with loud wingbeats out of the caves.

(To Katharina Kippenberg, October 31, 1911)

l. 4, *Karst:* A region along the Dalmatian coast (north of Trieste and not far from Duino Castle) known for its limestone caverns.

XII (Muzot, February 15/17, 1922)

l. 13, *Daphne:* A nymph pursued by Apollo and transformed into a laurel. See Ovid, Metamorphoses I, 452 ff.

XIII (Muzot, February 15/17, 1922)

In a letter telling Vera's mother about the unexpected appearance of the second part of the Sonnets, Rilke wrote:

> Today I am sending you only *one* of these sonnets, because, of the entire cycle, it is the one that is closest to me and ultimately the one that is the most valid.
>
> (To Gertrud Ouckama Knoop, March 18, 1922)

> The thirteenth sonnet of the second part is for me the most valid of all. It includes all the others, and it expresses *that* which—though it still far exceeds me—my purest, most final achievement would some-day, in the midst of life, have to be.
>
> (To Katharina Kippenberg, April 2, 1922)

l. 14, *cancel the count:*

> Renunciation of love or fulfillment in love: *both* are wonderful and beyond compare only where the entire love-experience, with *all* its barely differentiable ecstasies, is allowed to occupy a central position: there (in the rapture of a few lovers or saints of *all* times and *all* religions) renunciation and completion are identical. Where the infinite *wholly* enters (whether as minus or plus), the ah so human number drops away, as the road that has now been completely traveled—and what remains is the having arrived, *the being!*
>
> (To Rudolf Bodländer, March 23, 1922)

XIV (Muzot, February 15/17, 1922)

XV (Muzot, February 17, 1922)

XVI (Muzot, February 17/19, 1922)

XVII (Muzot, February 17/19, 1922)

XVIII (Muzot, February 17/19, 1922)

XIX (Muzot, February 17/23, 1922)

XX (Muzot, February 17/23, 1922)

l. 5, *Fate:*

> What we call fate does not come into us from the outside, but emerges *from* us.
>
> (To Franz Xaver Kappus, August 12, 1904)

l. 10, *fish:*

> . . . I sank, weighted down with a millstone's torpor, to the bottom of silence, below the fish, who only at times pucker their mouths into a discreet Oh, which is inaudible.
>
> (To Princess Marie von Thurn und Taxis-Hohenlohe, January 14, 1913)

l. 13, *a place:*

Jacobsen once wrote how annoyed he was that his remarkable short novel had to be called "Two Worlds"; again and again he had felt compelled to say: "Two World." In the same way, it often happens that one is at odds with the outward behavior of language and wants something inside it, an innermost language, a language of word-kernels, a language which is not plucked from stems, up above, but gathered as language-seeds—wouldn't the perfect hymn to the sun be composed in this language, and isn't the pure silence of love like heart-soil around such language-kernels? Ah, how often one wishes to speak a few levels deeper; my prose in "Proposal for an Experiment" ["Primal Sound"] lies deeper, gets a bit farther into the essential, than the prose of the *Malte,* but one penetrates such a very little way down, one remains with just an intuition of what kind of speech is possible in the place where silence is.

(To Nanny Wunderly-Volkart, February 4, 1920)

XXI (Muzot, February 17/23, 1922)

l. 3, *Ispahan* (mod., Isfahan) *or Shiraz:* Persian cities famous for their magnificent gardens. Shiraz also contains the tombs of the poets Hafiz and Sa'di.

XXII (Muzot, February 17/23, 1922)

l. 5, *bell:*

For me it was Easter just once; that was during the long, excited, extraordinary night when, with the whole populace crowding around, the bells of Ivan Veliky crashed into me in the darkness, one after another. That was my Easter, and I think it is huge enough for a whole lifetime. . . .

(To Lou Andreas-Salomé, March 31, 1904)

l. 7, *Karnak:* See note on p. 562.

XXIII (Muzot, February 17/23, 1922)

(to the reader)

—Rilke's note

l. 3, *a dog's imploring glance:*

Alas, I have not completely gotten over expecting the "nouvelle opération" to come from some human intervention; and yet, what's the use, since it is my lot to pass the human by, as it were, and arrive at the extreme limit, the edge of the earth, as recently in Cordova, when an ugly little bitch, in the last stage of pregnancy, came up to me. She was not a remarkable animal, was full of accidental puppies over whom no great fuss would be made; but since we were all alone, she came over to me, hard as it was for her, and raised her eyes enlarged by trouble and inwardness and sought my glance—and in her own way was truly everything that goes beyond the individual, to I don't know where, into the future or into the incomprehensible. The situation ended in her getting a lump of sugar from my coffee, but incidentally, oh so incidentally, we read Mass together, so to speak; in itself, the action was nothing but giving and receiving, yet the sense and the seriousness and our whole silent understanding was beyond all bounds.

(To Princess Marie von Thurn und<br>Taxis-Hohenlohe, December 17, 1912)

XXIV (Muzot, February 19/23, 1922)

l. 5, *Gods:*

Does it confuse you that I say God and gods and, for the sake of completeness, haunt you with these dogmatic words (as with a ghost), thinking that they will have some kind of meaning for you also? But grant, for a moment, that there is a realm beyond the senses. Let us agree that from his earliest beginnings man has created gods in whom just the deadly and menacing and destructive and terrifying elements in life were contained—its violence, its fury, its impersonal bewilderment—all tied together into one thick knot of malevolence: something alien to us, if you wish, but something which let us admit that we were aware of it, endured it, even acknowledged it for the sake of a sure, mysterious relationship and inclusion in it. For *we were this too;* only we didn't know what to do with this side of our experience; it was too large, too dangerous, too many-sided, it grew above and beyond us, into an excess of meaning; we found it impossible (what with the many demands of a life adapted to habit and achievement) to deal with these unwieldly and ungraspable forces; and so we agreed to place them outside us.—But since they were an overflow of our own being, its most powerful element, indeed were *too* powerful, were huge, violent, incomprehensible, often monstrous—: how could they not, concentrated in one place, exert an influence and ascendancy over us? And, remember, from the outside now. Couldn't the history of God be treated as an almost never-explored area of the human soul, one that has always been postponed, saved, and finally neglected . . . ?

And then, you see, the same thing happened with death. Experienced, yet not to be fully experienced by us in its reality, continually overshadowing us yet never truly acknowledged, forever violating and surpassing the meaning of life—it too was banished and expelled, so that it might not constantly interrupt us in the search for this meaning. Death, which is probably so close to us that the distance between it and the life-center inside us cannot be measured, now became something external, held farther away from us every day, a presence that lurked somewhere in the void, ready to pounce upon this person or that in its evil choice. More and more, the suspicion grew up against death that it was the contradiction, the adversary, the invisible opposite in the air, the force that makes all our joys wither, the perilous glass of our happiness, out of which we may be spilled at any moment. . . .

All this might still have made a kind of sense if we had been able to keep God and death at a distance, as mere ideas in the realm of the mind—: but Nature knew nothing of this banishment that we had somehow accomplished—when a tree blossoms, death as well as life blossoms in it, and the field is full of death, which from its reclining face sends forth a rich expression of life, and the animals move patiently from one to the other—and everywhere around us, death is at home, and it watches us out of the cracks in Things, and a rusty nail that sticks out of a plank somewhere, does nothing day and night except rejoice over death.

(To Lotte Hepner, November 8, 1915)

XXV (Muzot, February 19/23, 1922)

(Companion-piece to the first spring-song of the children in the First Part of the Sonnets)

—Rilke's note

XXVI (Muzot, February 19/23, 1922)

XXVII (Muzot, February 19/23, 1922)

1. 4, *Demiurge:* In the Gnostic tradition, a lower deity who created the world of time.

XXVIII (Muzot, February 19/23, 1922)

(to Vera)

—Rilke's note

XXIX (Muzot, February 19/23, 1922)

(to a friend of Vera's)

—Rilke's note

l. 3, *like a bell:*

> With this bell tower the little island, in all its fervor, is attached to the
> past; the tower fixes the dates and dissolves them again, because ever
> since it was built it has been ringing out time and destiny over the
> lake, as though it included in itself the visibility of all the lives that
> have been surrendered here; as though again and again it were send-
> ing their transitoriness into space, invisibly, in the sonorous transfor-
> mations of its notes.
>
> (To Countess Aline Dietrichstein, June 26, 1917)

l. 4, *What feeds upon your face:*

Oh and the night, the night, when the wind full of cosmic space / feeds upon
our face—

(The First Elegy, ll. 18 f.)

Breathe-in the darkness of earth and again
look up! Again. Airy and faceless,
from above, the depths bend toward you. The face that is dissolved
and contained in the night will give more space to your own.

"Overflowing heavens of lavished stars," p. 117)

l. 10, *in their magic ring:*

> [The poet's] is a naïve, aeolian soul, which is not ashamed to dwell
> where the senses intersect [*sich kreuzen*], and which lacks nothing, be-
> cause these unfolded senses form a ring in which there are no gaps.
>
> ("The Books of a Woman in Love," SW 6, 1018)

## APPENDIX TO THE SONNETS TO ORPHEUS

My dear, hardly had Strohl sent me back the little book with the 25 Orpheus Sonnets when this thread proceeded further, into a new fabric—a quantity of additional Sonnets have arisen these past few days, perhaps fifteen or more, but I won't keep them all—I am now so rich that I can afford to *choose*! What a world of grace we live in, after all! What powers are waiting to fill us, constantly shaken vessels that we are. We think we are under one kind of "guidance"—but they are already at work *inside* us. The only thing that belongs to us, as completely ours, is patience; but what immense capital that is—and what interest it bears in its time!—Consolation enough for eighthundredthirtyseven lives of average length.

(To Nanny Wunderly-Volkart, February 18, 1922)

[I] (Muzot, approximately February 3, 1922; first version of Sonnet VII, First Part)

And I would appreciate it if you could *replace* the VIIth Sonnet with the enclosed variant (just the first stanza of the previous version remains—the rest always embarrassed me by its exaggerated pathos, and I have long since crossed it out).

(To Gertrud Ouckama Knoop, March 18, 1922)

l. 14, *Golden Fleece:* In some versions of the myth, Orpheus accompanied Jason and the Argonauts on their voyage.

[II] (Muzot, February 2/5, 1922; originally Sonnet XXI, First Part)

[III] (Muzot, February 15/17, 1922)

[IV] (Muzot, February 15/17, 1922)

l. 1, *stela:* cf. the Second Elegy, ll. 66 ff., and the notes on p. 556.

[V] (Muzot, February 16/17, 1922)

This Sonnet probably refers to Goethe, who at the age of seventy-four fell in love with the nineteen-year-old Ulrike von Levetzow.

l. 9, *Hymen:* Greek god of marriage, usually depicted as a handsome young man crowned with a wreath and holding a wedding-torch.

l. 12, *laments:* Goethe commemorated his love in a poem known as the Marienbad Elegy.

[VI] (Muzot, February 16/17, 1922)

l. 3, *Villa d'Este:* Italian Renaissance palace near Tivoli, famous for its fountains and terraced gardens.

[VII] (Muzot, February 16/17, 1922)

[VIII] (Muzot, February 17/19, 1922)

[IX] (Muzot, approximately February 23, 1922)

FRAGMENTS

[i] (Muzot, approximately February 3; written between Sonnets VIII and IX, First Part)

[ii] (Muzot, approximately February 3, 1922; related to Sonnet XI, First Part)

[iii] (Muzot, approximately February 4, 1922; written between Sonnets XVII and XVIII, First Part)

[iv] (Muzot, February 12 or 13, 1922; draft of Sonnet II, Second Part)

[v] (Muzot, February 16/17, 1922)

[vi] (Muzot, February 16/17, 1922)

[vii] (Muzot, February 17/19, 1922)

[viii] (Muzot, February 19/23, 1922; draft of Sonnet XXV, Second Part)

[ix] (Muzot, February 19/23, 1922)

[x] (Muzot, approximately February 23, 1922)

[xi] (Muzot, approximately February 23, 1922)

# *Acknowledgments*

I would like once again to thank Michael André Bernstein, Chana Bloch, Jonathan Galassi (my editor at Random House), John Herman (my editor at Simon & Schuster), W. S. Merwin, Robert Pinsky, and Alan Williamson for their many helpful suggestions. A letter from Ralph Freedman persuaded me to include the two sections of early poems. I had help with the German of several of the uncollected poems from Jutta Hahne, with two German prose-poems from Brother David Steindl-Rast, and with the French prose-poems from my brother, to whom I dedicated *The Selected Poetry of Rainer Maria Rilke*.

I owe a great deal to Robert Hass for his brilliant essay "Looking for Rilke," which was the introduction to *The Selected Poetry* and was later included in his *Twentieth Century Pleasures*.

During the months when I was studying the Elegies, I lived in close daily contact with Jacob Steiner's great line-by-line commentary, *Rilkes Duineser Elegien* (Bern/München: Franke Verlag, 1962), and found it an almost never-failing source of illumination.

Finally, I must acknowledge my debt to the work of J. B. Leishman, M. D. Herter Norton, and C. F. MacIntyre, and to the Young, Boney, Guerne, and Gaspar version of the *Elegies*, the Poulin *Elegies and Sonnets*, the Betz *Cahiers de M. L. Brigge*, and miscellaneous translations by Randall Jarrell, Robert Lowell, Robert Bly, W. D. Snodgrass, and Rika Lesser.

And my greatest debt (unpayable, and paid): to Vicki.

# Index of Titles and First Lines

*(German)*

Abend   16
Aber, ihr Freunde, zum Fest, laßt uns gedenken der Feste . . .   532
Ach, nicht getrennt sein . . .   190
Achte Elegie, Die   376
Alkestis   60
Alles Erworbne bedroht die Maschine, solange . . .   480
An der sonngewohnten Straße, in dem . . .   170
An die Musik   142
An Hölderlin   134
[An Lou Andreas-Salomé]   96
Andere fassen den Wein, andere fassen die Öle . . .   158
Archaïscher Torso Apollos   66
Atmen, du unsichtbares Gedicht! . . .   462
Auch noch Verlieren is *unser*; und selbst das Vergessen . . .   164
Auf einmal ist aus allem Grün im Park . . .   40
Aus dieser Wolke, siehe: die den Stern . . .   102
Ausgesetzt auf den Bergen des Herzens. Siehe, wie klein dort . . .   136
Bestürz mich, Musik, mit rhythmischen Zürnen! . . .   118
Blumen, ihr schließlich den ordnenden Händen verwandte . . .   474
Blumenmuskel, der der Anemone . . .   470
Brau uns den Zauber, in dem die Grenzen sich lösen . . .   526
Buddha in der Glorie   74
Da dich das geflügelte Entzücken . . .   168
Da plötzlich war der Bote unter ihnen . . .   60
Da stehen wir mit Spiegeln: . . .   162
Da steht der Tod, ein bläulicher Absud . . .   140
Da stieg ein Baum. O reine Übersteigung! . . .   410
Das alles stand auf ihr und war die Welt . . .   36
Das war der Seelen wunderliches Bergwerk . . .   54
Daß ich dereinst, an dem Ausgang der grimmigen Einsicht . . .   388

Daß ich dereinst, an dem Ausgang der grimmigen Einsicht . . .   400
Daß solcher Auftrag *unser* Auftrag werde . . .   204
Dauer der Kindheit   174
Denk: Sie hätten vielleicht aneinander erfahren . . .   530
Der Abend wechselt langsam die Gewänder . . .   16
Des alten lange adligen Geschlechtes . . .   46
*Dich* aber will ich nun, *Dich,* die ich kannte . . .   458
Diese Mühsal, durch noch Ungetanes . . .   34
Dir aber, Herr, o was weih ich dir, sag . . .   448
Dritte Elegie, Die   344
Du aber, Göttlicher, du, bis zuletzt noch Ertöner . . .   460
Du im Voraus . . .   124
Du, mein Freund, bist einsam, weil . . .   440
Du nur, einzig du *bist* . . .   144
Durch den sich Vögel werfen, ist nicht der . . .   172
Ein Gespenst ist noch wie eine Stelle . . .   70
Ein Gott vermags. Wie aber, sag mir, soll . . .   414
Eines ist, die Geliebte zu singen. Ein anderes, wehe . . .   344
Elegie   206
Er ruft es an. Es schrickt zusamm und steht . . .   166
Erblindende, Die   38
Errichtet keinen Denkstein. Laßt die Rose . . .   418
Erst eine Kindheit, grenzenlos und ohne . . .   156
Erste Elegie, Die   330
Erwachsene, Die   36
Es war nicht in mir. Es ging aus und ein . . .   20
Euch, die ihr nie mein Gefühl verließt . . .   428
Feigenbaum, seit wie lange schon ists mir bedeutend . . .   364
Flamingos, Die   72
[Fragment einer Elegie]   398
Frühling ist wiedergekommen. Die Erde . . .   450
Fünfte Elegie, Die   356
Für Hans Carossa   164
Für Max Picard   162
Für Veronika Erdmann   204
Gazelle, Die   32
Gegen-Strophen   404

Geist Ariel, Der    108
Giebt es wirklich die Zeit, die zerstörende? . . .    514
Gong    198
Gott oder Göttin des Katzenschlafs . . .    196
Große Nacht, Die    122
Haï-kaï    146
Handinneres    180
Heil dem Geist, der uns verbinden mag . . .    432
Herbsttag    14
Herr: es ist Zeit. Der Sommer war sehr groß . . .    14
Hetären-Gräber    50
Hinter den schuld-losen Bäumen . . .    120
Hörst du das Neue, Herr . . .    444
Ich bin blind, ihr draußen, das ist ein Fluch . . .    18
Ich bin, du Ängstlicher. Hörst du mich nicht . . .    6
Ich finde dich in allen diesen Dingen . . .    8
Ich habe Tote, und ich ließ sie hin . . .    78
Ich hielt mich überoffen, ich vergaß . . .    96
Ich lebe mein Leben in wachsenden Ringen . . .    4
Idol    196
Im Auge Traum. Die Stirn wie in Berührung . . .    44
Imaginärer Lebenslauf    156
Immer wieder, ob wir der Liebe Landschaft auch kennen . . .    138
Immer wieder von uns aufgerissen . . .    492
In ihren langen Haaren liegen sie . . .    50
In Spiegelbildern wie von Fragonard . . .    72
Innres der Hand. Sohle, die nicht mehr geht . . .    180
Irgendwo wohnt das Gold in der verwöhnenden Bank . . .    498
Ist er ein Hiesiger? Nein, aus beiden . . .    420
Jeder Engel ist schrecklich. Und dennoch, weh mir . . .    338
Jetzt wär es Zeit, daß Götter träten aus . . .    192
Jugend-Bildnis meines Vaters    44
Klage (O wie ist alles fern . . .)    12
Klage (Wem willst du klagen, Herz? Immer gemiedener . . .)    130
Kleine Motten taumeln schauernd quer aus dem Buchs . . .    146
Königsherz. Kern eines hohen . . .    184
Lange errang ers im Anschaun . . .    126

Lange Nachmittage der Kindheit . . . ., immer noch nicht . . .   174
Leichen-Wäsche   68
Letzter Abend   42
Liebes-Lied   28
Lied des Blinden, Das   18
Lied des Idioten, Das   22
Lied des Trinkers, Das   20
Lied des Zwerges, Das   24
Magier, Der   166
Man hat ihn einmal irgendwo befreit . . .   108
'Man muß sterben weil man sie kennt.' Sterben   132
Manche, des Todes, entstand ruhig geordnete Regel . . .   482
Mausoleum   184
Mehr nicht sollst du wissen als die Stele . . .   528
Meine Seele ist vielleicht grad und gut . . .   24
Mit allen Augen sieht die Kreatur . . .   376
Mitte aller Mitten, Kern der Kerne . . .   74
Mitte, wie du aus allen . . .   182
Musik: Atem der Statuen. Vielleicht . . .   142
Neunte Elegie, Die   382
Nicht mehr für Ohren . . . : Klang . . .   198
Nur im Raum der Rühmung darf die Klage . . .   424
Nur wer die Leier schon hob . . .   426
O Bäume Lebens, o wann winterlich? . . .   350
O Brunnen-Mund, du gebender, du Mund . . .   490
O das Neue, Freunde, ist nicht dies . . .   524
O die Verluste ins All, Marina, die stürzenden Sterne! . . .   206
O diese Lust, immer neu, aus gelockertem Lehm! . . .   508
O dieses ist das Tier, das es nicht giebt . . .   468
O erst *dann*, wenn der Flug . . .   454
O ihr Zärtlichen, tretet zuweilen . . .   416
O komm und geh. Du, fast noch Kind, ergänze . . .   516
Ô Lacrimosa   186
O trotz Schicksal: die herrlichen Überflüsse . . .   504
O wie ist alles fern . . .   12
Odette R . . . .   152
Oft anstaunt ich dich, stand an gestern begonnenem Fenster . . .   122

Oh, daß ihr hier, Frauen, einhergeht . . .    404
Oh Tränenvolle, die, verhaltner Himmel . . .    186
Orpheus. Eurydike. Hermes    54
Panther, Der    30
Requiem für eine Freundin    78
Rose, du thronende, denen im Altertume . . .    472
Rose, oh reiner Widerspruch, Lust . . .    194
Rufe mich zu jener deiner Stunden . . .    506
Rühmen, das ists! Ein zum Rühmen Bestellter . . .    422
Rühmen, das ists! Ein zum Rühmen Bestellter . . .    522
Rühmt euch, ihr Richtenden, nicht der entbehrlichen Folter . . .    478
Schaukel des Herzens. O sichere, an welchem unsichtbaren . . .    160
Schon, horch, hörst du der ersten Harken . . .    510
Schwan, Der    34
Schwarze Katze    70
Schwerkraft    182
Sechste Elegie, Die    364
Sei allem Abschied voran, als wäre er hinter . . .    486
Sein Blick ist vom Vorübergehn der Stäbe . . .    30
Selbstbildnis aus dem Jahre 1906    46
Sie hatten sich an ihm gewöhnt. Doch als . . .    68
Sie hindern mich nicht. Sie lassen mich gehn . . .    22
Sie saß so wie die anderen beim Tee . . .    38
Siebente Elegie, Die    368
Sieh den Himmel. Heißt kein Sternbild 'Reiter'?    430
Siehe die Blumen, diese dem Irdischen treuen . . .    488
Singe die Gärten, mein Herz, die du nicht kennst; wie in Glas . . .    502
So angestrengt wider die starke Nacht . . .    112
So wie dem Meister manchmal das eilig . . .    464
Soll ich die Städte rühmen, die überlebenden . . .    398
Sollen wir unsere uralte Freundschaft, die großen . . .    456
Sonette an Orpheus, Die    410
Spanische Tänzerin    48
Spanische Trilogie, Die    102
Spiegel: noch nie hat man wissend beschrieben . . .    466
Stiller Freund der vielen Fernen, fühle . . .    518
Tänzerin: o du Verlegung . . .    496

Taube, die draußen blieb, außer dem Taubenschlag . . .   210
Tod, Der   140
Tränen, die innigsten, *steigen*! . . .   152
Tränenkrüglein   158
Überfließende Himmel verschwendeter Sterne . . .   116
Und fast ein Mädchen wars und ging hervor . . .   412
Und Nacht und fernes Fahren; denn der Train . . .   42
Unendlich staun ich euch an, ihr Seligen, euer Benehmen . . .   100
Unwissend vor dem Himmel meines Lebens . . .   114
[Ursprüngliche Fassung der Zehnten Elegie]   400
Verweilung, auch am Vertrautesten nicht . . .   134
Verzauberte: wie kann der Einklang zweier . . .   32
Vierte Elegie, Die   350
Voller Apfel, Birne und Banane . . .   434
Vor dem Sommerregen   40
Wandelt sich rasch auch die Welt . . .   446
Wann war ein Mensch je so wach . . .   538
Wartet . . . , das schmeckt . . . Schon ists auf der Flucht . . .   438
Warum, wenn es angeht, also die Frist des Daseins . . .   382
Welche Stille um einen Gott! Wie hörst du in ihr . . .   534
Welt war in dem Antlitz der Geliebten . . .   178
Wem willst du klagen, Herz? Immer gemiedener . . .   130
Wendung   126
Wenige ihr, der einstigen Kindheit Gespielen . . .   476
Wer aber *sind* sie, sag mir, die Fahrenden, diese ein wenig . . .   356
Wer, wenn ich schriee, hörte mich denn aus der Engel . . .   330
Werbung nicht mehr, nicht Werbung, entwachsene Stimme . . .   368
Wie ergrieft uns der Vogelschrei . . .   512
Wie in der Hand ein Schwefelzündholz, weiß . . .   48
Wie soll ich meine Seele halten, daß . . .   28
Wir gehen um mit Blume, Weinblatt, Frucht . . .   436
Wir hören seit lange die Brunnen mit . . .   536
Wir, in den ringenden Nächten . . .   150
Wir kannten nicht sein unerhörtes Haupt . . .   66
Wir sagen Reinheit und wir sagen Rose . . .   154
Wir sind die Treibenden . . .   452
Wo, in welchen immer selig bewässerten Gärten, an welchen . . .   494
Wolle die Wandlung. O sei für die Flamme begeistert . . .   484

Zehnte Elegie, Die    388
Zu unterst der Alte, verworrn . . .    442
Zueignung an M . . . .    160
Zweite Elegie, Die    338
Zwischen den Sternen, wie weit; und doch, um wievieles noch
    weiter . . .    500

# Index of Titles and First Lines

*(English)*

A ghost, though invisible, still is like a place . . .   71
A god can do it. But will you tell me how . . .   415
A tree ascended there. Oh pure transcendence! . . .   411
Acrobats   288
Again and again, however we know the landscape of love . . .   139
Ah, not to be cut off . . .   191
Ah, Women, that you should be moving . . .   405
Alcestis   61
All this stood upon her and was the world . . .   37
All we have gained the machine threatens, as long . . .   481
[Almond Trees in Blossom, The]   101
Along the sun-drenched roadside, from the great . . .   171
Already (listen!) you can hear the first . . .   511
And it was almost a girl and came to be . . .   413
And night and distant rumbling; now the army's . . .   43
Antistrophes   405
Archaic Torso of Apollo   67
Ariel   109
As on all its sides a kitchen-match darts white . . .   49
As once the wingèd energy of delight . . .   169
At bottom the Ancient One, gnarled . . .   443
At first a childhood, limitless and free . . .   157
Autumn Day   15
Be ahead of all parting, as though it already were . . .   487
Before Summer Rain   41
Behind the innocent trees . . .   121
[Bird-feeders, The]   256
Black Cat   71
Blindman's Song, The   19
Breathing: you invisible poem! Complete . . .   463

Brew us the magic in which all limits dissolve . . .    527
Buddha in Glory    75
But Master, what gift shall I dedicate to you . . .    449
But tell me, who *are* they, these wanderers, even more . . .    357
But you, divine poet, you who sang on till the end . . .    461
But you now, dear girl, whom I loved like a flower whose name . . .    459
Call me to the one among your moments . . .    507
Center, how from all beings . . .    183
Center of all centers, core of cores . . .    75
[Costumes]    261
Dancing girl: transformation . . .    497
Death    141
[Death of Chamberlain Brigge, The]    246
Dedication to M . . . .    161
Does it really exist, Time, the Destroyer? . . .    515
Don't boast, you judges, that you have dispensed with torture . . .    479
Dove that ventured outside, flying far from the dovecote: . . .    211
Drunkard's Song, The    21
Duration of Childhood    175
Dwarf's Song, The    25
Eighth Elegy, The    377
Elegy    207
Enchanted thing: how can two chosen words . . .    33
Endlessly I gaze at you in wonder, blessed ones, at your composure . . .    101
Erect no gravestone for him. Only this:    419
Evening    17
Every angel is terrifying. And yet, alas . . .    339
Everything is far . . .    13
Experience, An    290
Exposed on the cliffs of the heart. Look, how tiny down there . . .    137
[Faces]    245
[Fears]    251
Fifth Elegy, The    357
Fig-tree, for such a long time I have found meaning . . .    365
First Elegy, The    331
Fishmonger's Stall, The    286
Flamingos, The    73
Flower-muscle that slowly opens back . . .    471

Flowers, you who are kin to the hands that arrange . . .     475
For a long time he attained it in looking . . .     127
For Hans Carossa     165
For Max Picard     163
[For the Sake of a Single Poem]     250
For Veronika Erdmann     205
[Four Sketches]     201
Fourth Elegy, The     351
[Fragment of an Elegy]     399
From this cloud, look!, which has so wildly covered . . .     103
Gazelle, The     33
God or goddess of the sleep of cats . . .     197
Going Blind     39
Gong     199
Gravity     183
Grown-up, The     37
Haiku     147
Hail to the god who joins us; for through him . . .     433
He calls it up. It shudders and begins . . .     167
Here we stand with mirrors: . . .     163
His vision, from the constantly passing bars . . .     31
How can I keep my soul in me, so that . . .     29
How deeply the cry of a bird can move us . . .     513
I am blind, you outsiders. It is a curse . . .     19
I am, O Anxious One. Don't you hear my voice . . .     7
I find you, Lord, in all Things and in all . . .     9
I have my dead, and I have let them go . . .     79
I kept myself too open, I forgot . . .     97
I live my life in widening rings . . .     5
[Ibsen]     258
Idiot's Song, The     23
Idol     197
Ignorant before the heavens of my life . . .     115
Imaginary Career     157
Imagine: they might have experienced through each other . . .     531
In between stars, what distances; and yet, how much vaster the
     distance . . .     501
In the eyes: dream. The brow as if it could feel . . .     45

Interior of the hand. Sole that has come to walk . . .     181
Is he someone who dwells in this *single* world? No: . . .     421
It is one thing to sing the beloved. Another, alas . . .     345
It wasn't in me. It went out and in . . .     21
Just as the master's *genuine* brushstroke . . .     465
King's-heart. Core of a high . . .     185
Lament (Everything is far . . .)     13
Lament (Whom will you cry to, heart? More and more lonely . . .)     131
Last Evening, The     43
Lion Cage, The     281
Little moths stagger quivering out of the hedge . . .     147
Little Tear-Vase     159
Long afternoons of childhood . . . . , not yet really . . .     175
Look at the flowers, so faithful to what is earthly . . .     489
Look at the sky. Are no two stars called "Rider"? . . .     431
Lord: it is time. The huge summer has gone by . . .     15
Losing too is still *ours*; and even forgetting . . .     165
Love Song     29
Magician, The     167
[Man with St. Vitus' Dance, The]     252
Many calmly established rules of death have arisen . . .     483
Master, do you hear the New . . .     445
Mausoleum     185
Meeting, A     283
Mirrors: no one has ever known how . . .     467
Mitsou     304
Music: breathing of statues. Perhaps . . .     143
My soul itself may be straight and good . . .     25
[Neighbors]     266
Ninth Elegy, The     383
No longer for ears . . . : sound . . .     199
Not till the day when flight . . .     455
Not wooing, no longer shall wooing, voice that has outgrown it . . .     369
Now it is time that gods came walking out . . .     193
Now shall I praise the cities, those long-surviving . . .     399
O fountain-mouth, you generous, always-filled . . .     491
O Lacrimosa     187
O trees of life, when does your winter come? . . .     351

O you tender ones, walk now and then . . .   417
Odette R . . . .   153
Often I gazed at you in wonder: stood at the window begun . . .   123
Oh come and go. You, almost still a child . . .   517
Oh in spite of fate: the glorious overflowings . . .   505
Oh tear-filled figure who, like a sky held back . . .   187
Oh the delight, ever new, out of loosened soil! . . .   509
Oh the losses into the All, Marina, the stars that are falling! . . .   207
Oh this beast is the one that never was . . .   469
Once, somewhere, somehow, you had set him free . . .   109
Only he whose bright lyre . . .   427
Only in the realm of Praising should Lament . . .   425
On the Young Poet   293
[Original Version of the Tenth Elegy]   401
Orpheus. Eurydice. Hermes   55
Other vessels hold wine, other vessels hold oil . . .   159
Over and over by us torn in two . . .   493
Overflowing heavens of lavished stars . . .   117
Palm   181
Panther, The   31
Plump apple, smooth banana, melon, peach . . .   435
Portrait of My Father as a Young Man   45
Praising is what matters! He was summoned for that . . .   423
Praising is what matters! He was summoned for that . . .   523
Primal Sound   299
[Prodigal Son, The]   272
Requiem for a Friend   79
Rose, oh pure contradiction, joy . . .   195
Rose, you majesty—once, to the ancients, you were . . .   473
Second Elegy, The   339
Seek no more than what the stela knows . . .   529
Self-Portrait, 1906   47
Seventh Elegy, The   369
Shall we reject our primordial friendship, the sublime . . .   457
She sat just like the others at the table . . .   39
Silent friend of many distances, feel . . .   519
Sing of the gardens, my heart, that you never saw; as if glass . . .   503
Sixth Elegy, The   365

Someday, emerging at last from the violent insight . . .    389
Someday, emerging at last from the violent insight . . .    401
Somewhere gold lives, luxurious, inside the pampering bank . . .    499
Sonnets to Orpheus, The    411
Spanish Dancer    49
Spanish Trilogy, The    103
Spring has returned. The earth resembles . . .    451
Startle me, Music, with rhythmical fury! . . .    119
Straining so hard against the strength of night . . .    113
Suddenly, from all the green around you . . .    41
Swan, The    35
Swing of the heart. O firmly hung, fastened on what . . .    161
Tears, the most fervent ones, *rise*! . . .    153
[Temptation of the Saint, The]    271
Tenth Elegy, The    389
That such a mission may become *our* mission . . .    205
That was the deep uncanny mine of souls . . .    55
The New, my friends, is not a matter of . . .    525
The sky puts on the darkening blue coat . . .    17
The stamina of an old, long-noble race . . .    47
Then all at once the messenger was there. . . .    61
There stands death, a bluish distillate . . .    141
They had, for a while, grown used to him. But after . . .    69
They lie in their long hair, and the brown faces . . .    51
They're not in my way. They let me be . . .    23
Third Elegy, The    345
This laboring through what is still undone . . .    35
Though the world keeps changing its form . . .    447
To Hölderlin    135
[To Lou Andreas-Salomé]    97
To Music    143
Tombs of the Hetaerae    51
Turning-point    127
Vast Night, The    123
Wait . . . , that tastes good . . . But already it's gone . . .    439
Washing the Corpse    69
We are involved with flower, leaf, and fruit . . .    437
We are not permitted to linger, even with what is most . . .    135

We are the driving ones . . .     453
We cannot know his legendary head . . .     67
We have overheard fountains all our days . . .     537
We, in the struggling nights . . .     151
'We Must Die Because We Have Known Them.' Die     133
We say release, and radiance, and roses . . .     155
What birds plunge through is not the intimate space . . .     173
What silence around a god! How, inside it, you hear . . .     535
When everything we create is far in spirit from the festive . . .     533
When was a *man* as awake . . .     539
Where, inside what forever blissfully watered gardens, upon what trees . . .     495
Who, if I cried out, would hear me among the angels' . . .     331
Whom will you cry to, heart? More and more lonely . . .     131
Why, if this interval of being can be spent serenely . . .     383
*Will* transformation. Oh be inspired for the flame . . .     485
With all its eyes the natural world looks out . . .     377
With all the subtle paints of Fragonard . . .     73
World was in the face of the beloved . . .     179
You are lonely, my friend, because you are . . .     441
You playmates of mine in the scattered parks of the city . . .     477
You who are close to my heart always . . .     429
You who never arrived . . .     125
You, you only, exist . . .     145
Young Workman's Letter, The     308

## A Note on the Type

The principal text of this Modern Library edition
was composed in a digitized version of
Horley Old Style, a typeface issued by
the English type foundry Monotype in 1925.
It has such distinctive features
as lightly cupped serifs and an oblique horizontal bar
on the lowercase "e."